Passing Off Law and Practice

SEVEN DAY LOAN

This book is to be returned on
or before the date stamped below

UNIVERSITY OF PLYMOUTH

PLYMOUTH LIBRARY

Tel: (0752) 232323
This book is subject to recall if required by another reader
Books may be renewed by phone
CHARGES WILL BE MADE FOR OVERDUE BOOKS

Passing Off Law and Practice

Second edition

John Drysdale   MA MSc (Oxon)
of Gray's Inn, London
and
King's Inn, Dublin

Michael Silverleaf   BSc (London)
of Gray's Inn, London
Barrister at Law

Butterworths
London, Dublin, Edinburgh
1995

United Kingdom	Butterworth & Co (Publishers) Ltd, Halsbury House, 35 Chancery Lane, LONDON WC2A 1EL and 4 Hill Street, EDINBURGH EH2 3JZ
Australia	Butterworths, SYDNEY, MELBOURNE, BRISBANE, ADELAIDE, PERTH, CANBERRA and HOBART
Canada	Butterworths Canada Ltd, TORONTO and VANCOUVER
Ireland	Butterworth (Ireland) Ltd, DUBLIN
Malaysia	Malayan Law Journal Sdn Bhd, KUALA LUMPUR
New Zealand	Butterworths of New Zealand Ltd, WELLINGTON and AUCKLAND
Puerto Rico	Butterworth of Puerto Rico, Inc, SAN JUAN
Singapore	Butterworths Asia, SINGAPORE
South Africa	Butterworth Publishers (Pty) Ltd, DURBAN
USA	Butterworth Legal Publishers, CARLSBAD, California and SALEM, New Hampshire

A CIP Catalogue record for this book is available from the British Library.

ISBN 0 406 00488 9

Typeset by Grahame & Grahame Editorial, Brighton, East Sussex
Printed by Clays Ltd, St Ives plc

Preface

Since the first edition of this book was published in 1986 there have been many developments both in the law of passing off and in other closely related areas. Perhaps the most potentially exciting is the wholesale revision of the law of registered trade marks by the enactment of the Trade Marks Act 1994 bringing into effect in UK law the EC Directive on the Harmonisation of Trade Mark Laws. This promises to import many of the concepts of passing off into a claim for registered trade mark infringement and it may well be that the importance of passing off as a remedy for unfair competition will gradually diminish with time. There has also been the replacement of artistic copyright with unregistered design right as the primary protection for industrial designs apart from registered rights. Even though the unregistered design right has now been in force for five years, its real impact has yet to be assessed. For the time being, therefore, the action for passing off remains one of the most important tools in the armoury of a trader who wishes to protect himself against his competitors.

In the law of passing off itself our refusal in the first edition to accept the *Advocaat* decision in departing from the traditional analysis of the tort into the three constituent elements of reputation, confusion and damage has now been endorsed by the House of Lords in *Jif*, subsequently followed by the Court of Appeal in *Parma Ham*. We have also received many helpful comments from readers and colleagues on the contents of the first edition and as a result have made numerous changes going beyond simply bringing the law up to date. As we said in the preface to the first edition, the task we have set ourselves is to write a book to assist the practitioner to recognise where there is unfair competition, whether it is actionable as passing off and whether any other remedy is available. In all the changes we have sought to improve the clarity and accessibility of this guidance. Thus, chapter 3 has been rewritten to provide a more coherent structure to the analysis of reputation. Chapter 7 has also been rewritten both to improve its clarity and to reflect the many detailed procedural changes which have taken place. Damage in a passing off action is always difficult to treat analytically and chapter 5, which deals with this, has been restructured to improve its organisation. Chapters 1, 2, 4, 6 and 8 have been substantially updated and revised whilst retaining the core from the first edition. The chapters on related actions fell between two stools: they were neither brief enough to provide a simple summary nor detailed enough to provide a full analysis. They have been condensed into a single chapter,

9, covering registered trade marks (under the new 1994 Act), registered and unregistered designs and copyright and extracts from the relevant statutes have been omitted. Readers should turn to texts dedicated to these subjects for the source materials. However, we have retained the appendix containing the different forms of injunction. Finally, the approach of the European Court to parallel trading has changed almost beyond recognition in the last five years. We have therefore wholly rewritten the chapter on this subject. We hope that our readers will agree with us that the result is a substantial improvement and look forward to receiving further comments.

We would like to acknowledge our considerable thanks to the staff at Butterworths who have chided and guided us through the production of this second edition, bearing with remarkable patience and fortitude our delays and revisions to the text. Our colleagues have again been the source of much insight and assistance, the result of which have found their way into what follows. We also owe a considerable debt to Joanne Welch who proof-read the entire text, pointed out mistakes and made many helpful suggestions for improvements. We have endeavoured to make the final text as accurate as possible. The responsibility for any errors which might remain is entirely ours.

The law is stated as at 31 October 1994.

John Drysdale
Michael Silverleaf

11 South Square,
Gray's Inn,
London, WC1R 5EU

Contents

Contents

Table of statutes

Table of European legislation

List of cases

C

E

F

G

I

N

Decisions of the European Court of Justice are listed below numerically. These decisions
are also included in the preceding alphabetical Table.

CHAPTER 1

Introduction

Competition

1.01 In countries with a free market system the proper functioning of the economy depends upon competition between rival trading enterprises. It is the mechanism of competition which controls the price, quality and availability of goods and services to the public. It is of the essence of such economic systems that the existence of competition promotes the consumers' as well as the producers' interests. It is the presence in the market-place of better or cheaper goods from my rival which has the dual effect of forcing me to improve my efficiency so as to be able to match what he offers and thus in consequence to provide the consumer with the best products at the lowest prices. Left to themselves business rivals would not allow the free market to operate untrammelled. On the one hand, free competition considerably restricts their ability to profit from their endeavours and it is therefore to their advantage to run their businesses in such a way as to exert control over the operation of the market. This can be achieved in many ways of which the most common are probably the formation of cartels and monopolies and the control of subsequent selling prices for goods after they have passed out of the originator's hands. On the other hand, it is often to the advantage of an individual trader to seek to obtain a benefit from work done by other traders in establishing a market for a particular type or style of goods or services by, for example, copying the style and content of a successful advertising campaign. For these reasons the extent and nature of permitted competition is nearly always controlled by law. The nature of the control takes different forms in different countries. In countries with common law systems, some controls (though not always the same ones) have developed as part of the common law while many others have been imposed by statute. In the English legal system controls have developed piecemeal. It is nonetheless possible to distinguish two different types of control, both intended to enhance the operation of the free market economy. The first aspect of control is designed to increase competition between enterprises so as to ensure that the benefits of the free market are made available to the consumer. The second is designed to prevent competition which seeks to make unfair use of another trader's efforts.

Promotion of competition

1.02 The first aspect of the control referred to above operates by preventing traders from combining to impose restrictions on competition between them. To the extent that this is a development of the common law a number of doctrines have arisen. For example, contracts in restraint of trade are unenforceable unless the restrictions imposed are reasonably necessary for the protection of the traders' business.[1] The law of conspiracy operates to prevent enterprises uniting in such a way as to oppress others.[2] More recently, it has been recognised by the legislature that further controls are required on the freedom of traders to combine, or to dictate how the market-place operates without combining, in order to protect other members of society who do not have the power to prevent their exploitation by such activities. The legislation thus introduced commenced with the passing of the Monopolies and Mergers Acts 1948 and 1965, followed by the Restrictive Trade Practices Acts 1956 and 1968 and the Resale Prices Act 1964.[3] More recently still, when the UK joined the European Community, the provisions of the Treaty of Rome concerned to prevent the restriction or distortion of trade between member states became part of our law.[4]

---

1 See Cheshire and Fifoot *Law of Contract* (12th edn, 1991) ch 5.
2 See Street *On Torts* (9th edn, 1993).
3 These statutes have all been largely replaced by subsequent consolidating and amending legislation: Resale Prices Act 1976, Restrictive Practices Court Act 1976, Restrictive Trade Practices Acts 1976 and 1977 and the Competition Act 1980. See the full discussion of the effects of this legislation in *Chitty on Contract* (27th edn) vol 2, ch 10.
4 See the discussion of the nature and effect of these provisions in ch 10 below.

Prevention of unfair competition

1.03 The second aspect of the development of the law has had the opposite effect of introducing restrictions on competition of a type considered to be taking an unfair advantage of a rival trader's endeavours and thus depriving him of rewards which are justly his. It has long been recognised by English law that some forms of competition are unfair and ought to be restrained. As Chitty J said at the end of the last century:[1]

> 'there is such a thing as just and fair competition — the Court never acts to prevent that — but there is such a thing as unfair competition, and by artful wiles to take away a portion of a man's reputation, which is part of his fortune when it is embarked in a trade... [W]hen the Court finds that in substance, notwithstanding there are many things which the Defendant could do which are legitimate and within his rights, yet he is so contriving them as to take away something which belongs to another man, it is the duty of the court to interfere.'

Although it can be seen from the context of the matter he was considering that Chitty J was concerned with a classic case of passing off, it is also clear that he recognised that the foundation of the law of passing off was the desire to check unfair competition.[2] However, passing off is only one form of unfair competition. There are features of the law of copyright, registered designs, registered trade marks, patents, malicious falsehood, libel slander and breach of confidence which are concerned solely with preventing unfair competition. However, despite occasional academic suggestions to the contrary,[3] the English courts have yet to recognise a tort of unfair competition as such.[4]

---

1   *Huntley and Palmer v Reading Biscuit Co Ltd* (1893) 10 RPC 277 at 280.

2   *Erven Warnink v J Townend & Sons (Hull) Ltd (Advocaat)* [1979] AC 731 at 740, [1980] RPC 31 at 90 per Lord Diplock; see eg per Maugham J in *Cambridge University Press v University Tutorial Press* (1928) 45 RPC 335 at 346.

3   See eg Gerald Dworkin 'Unfair Competition: Is the Common Law Developing a New Tort?' [1979] EIPR 241.

4   See ch 2, para 2.39.

The scope of passing off

1.04   The tort of passing off consists essentially of a representation that a person's goods or business are connected with the goods or business of someone else. It is founded upon the acquisition by use by that other person of a reputation in the market-place in relation to his business or goods. The representation may take many forms; indeed the categories of representation are not closed.[1] Most commonly it takes the form of an implied representation made by the use of a name, mark or some other indicia distinctive of someone else's business or goods.[2] It does not depend upon the trader committing the tort being aware of such distinctiveness or intending to make the representation. Passing off has also been extended to cover the selling of a trader's own goods with a representation, express or implied, that they are of a class or quality of that trader's goods which they are not.[3] The law of registered trade marks introduced by statute has grown out of the law of passing off: it now provides[4] that a trader may register a trade mark and thus acquire property in the mark itself and a monopoly of the use of the mark in relation to the goods for which it is registered.

---

1   Per Lord Parker in *Spalding & Bros v A W Gamage Ltd* (1915) 32 RPC 273 at 284.

2   Ibid.

3   See ch 4, paras 4.19–4.25 below.

4   Trade Marks Act 1994: see ch 9 below.

Other forms of unfair competition

1.05   There are other forms of unfair competition which the law is designed to prevent. False statements about a person's business or goods are actionable as malicious falsehood if made with malice and causing damage. If they are personally defamatory, they are also actionable as libel or slander.[1] Copying a copyright work, directly or indirectly, without the permission of the copyright owner, is an infringement of copyright actionable under the Copyright, Designs & Patents Act 1988.[2] If a new and original design is registered under the Registered Designs Act 1949, the registered proprietor is entitled during the subsistence of the registration to prevent others, whether they have copied or not, from applying the same or a substantially similar design industrially to an article.[3] An invention complying with the requirements of the Patents Act 1977 may be patented, giving the patentee a monopoly of the use of the invention for the term of the patent.[4] It is actionable as a breach of confidence to use for one's own benefit a person's trade secrets, be they technical or commercial.[5] There are, however, other instances of competition which might be regarded as unfair for which the law provides no remedy.[6] It is not possible in England at least to speak of a law of unfair competition.

---

1 See ch 8 below.
2 See ch 9 below.
3 See ch 9 below.
4 See *Encyclopaedia of United Kingdom & European Patent Law* (Sweet & Maxwell).
5 See Report of the Law Commission on Breach of Confidence (Cmnd 8388).
6 See eg *Cadbury Schweppes Pty Ltd v The Pub Squash Co Pty Ltd* [1981] 1 All ER 213, (1981) RPC 429; *Cambridge University Press v University Tutorial Press* (1928) 45 RPC 335.

The need to prevent unfair competition

1.06 There is an economic value to society in preventing unfair competition, of which passing off is an example. It is in the interests of established businesses possessing valuable reputations for dependable or reliable goods and services that they should be able to promote their reputations without interference from others for, 'This is the source of their goodwill which may contribute more to their value as a firm than the factories and plants they own'.[1] It is also in the interests of the public that they should be protected from being duped by the misuse of traders' characteristics which they have come to recognise and rely upon so that 'people may take the name or mark concerned as a warranty that [the goods] have come from the particular manufacturer of goods with which they have hitherto been pleased'.[2]

---

1 Milton Friedman *Free to Choose* at 223–224.
2 Per James LJ in *Massam v Thorley's Cattle Food Co* (1880) 14 Ch D 748 at 755.

The conflict between free and unfair competition

1.07 There is, unsurprisingly, a direct conflict between the twin desires of the law both to promote free competition and yet inhibit unfair competition. This conflict was recognised by Lord Scarman in *Cadbury Schweppes Pty Ltd v The Pub Squash Co Pty Ltd*[1] in the context of a claim for passing off. There he reconciled the opposing demands of the two approaches of the law in his conclusion that 'competition is safeguarded by the necessity for the plaintiff to prove that he has built up an intangible property right'[2] before the court will intervene to restrain a competitor's activities. In the case of patents and registered designs there are specific provisions in the statutes concerned to enable a person who is threatened with unjustified proceedings for infringement to obtain a remedy[3] and, in the case of patents, to render void restrictive conditions in a patent licence which would have the effect of tying the licensee to the patentee over a broader field than is encompassed by the claims of the patent.[4] The provisions of other statutes further limit the restrictions that the proprietor of a patent or registered design may impose by virtue of these monopolies. The imposition of minimum resale prices for goods made under a patent or registered design is prevented by the Resale Prices Act 1976[5] just as it is for goods not so made although such conditions may be imposed by the patentee on his immediate licensee or assignee.[6] Pooling agreements for patents and registered designs are also governed by the Restrictive Trade Practices Act 1976.[7] It is also possible, perhaps somewhat paradoxically, to invoke the law of malicious falsehood, or even libel to restrain unfounded allegations of passing off and trade mark or copyright infringement as well as patent or registered design infringement[8] thus preventing unfair competition. Finally the Treaty of Rome can in certain circumstances be used to prevent or restrict reliance upon any form of industrial property rights.[9] By a combination of the two opposing forces available, the law seeks to strike a balance between placing undue restrictions on competition by overprotecting a trader's position on the one hand and permitting unfair advantage being taken by allowing competitors in the market to fight without restraint on the other.

1 [1981] 1 All ER 213, [1981] RPC 429.
2 Ibid at 200, 490.
3 Patents Act 1977 s 70. Registered Designs Act 1949 s 26.
4 Patents Act 1977 s 44.
5 S 10.
6 S 10(3).
7 Sch 3, para 5.
8 See ch 9 below.
9 See ch 10 below.

1.08 A number of recent cases concerning the extent of intellectual property rights have highlighted the difficulty of setting the boundaries of the conflict between free and unfair competition. In two cases the House of Lords has imposed limitations on the extent of intellectual property rights on the grounds that they would otherwise constitute an improper interference with free competition. The first was *British Leyland v Armstrong*[1] in which it was held that the plaintiff could not rely upon the copyright in drawings of parts of motor cars to prevent spare part manufacturers from competing with them in the supply of replacements. In *Coca-Cola's Application*[2] an attempt to register the shape of the Coca-Cola bottle as a trade mark was refused. Lord Templeman, whose antipathy towards intellectual property rights is well known, described the application as:

'another attempt to expand the boundaries of intellectual property to convert a protective law into a source of a monopoly.'[3]

The right relied upon in a passing off action is, however, not a monopoly.[4] The injunction granted on a successful claim will normally be limited to activities which do not adequately distinguish the defendant's goods or services from those of the plaintiff.[5] Indeed, the same shape of bottle for which a trade mark registration was refused in *Coca-Cola's Application*[2] had previously been successfully protected in a passing off action.[6] Injunctions have regularly been granted to restrain the use of packaging of a particular shape in passing off actions[7] and, in the latest case to come before the House of Lords, *Reckitt & Colman v Borden*,[8] an injunction was granted to prevent the defendant from supplying lemon juice in lemon-shaped containers 'so nearly resembling the plaintiff's JIF lemon-shaped container ... as to be likely to deceive or cause confusion without making it clear to the ultimate purchaser that it is not of the goods of the plaintiff'. Lord Bridge was particularly troubled by the result of this case because, on the judge's findings of fact, which could not be challenged 'however surprising they may seem', the effective result was 'to give the [plaintiffs] a de facto monopoly of the container as such which is just as effective as a de jure monopoly'.[9] Lord Oliver did not accept this and said that in any event 'the principle that no man is entitled to steal another's trade by deceit is one of at least equal importance'.[10] These cases show that there is always a balance between free and unfair competition. They also show that the balance is not the same in all circumstances and that individual judges may not always agree where the balance lies. The results in individual cases may be surprising and to some even repugnant but the courts must always try to strike the balance between protecting the goodwill of individual traders and ensuring that the public interest in competition between traders is served.

---

1   [1986] 1 All ER 850, 2 WLR 400, RPC 279.
2   [1986] 2 All ER 274, RPC 421. This decision has now been statutorily reversed by the enactment of the Trade Marks Act 1994 which brings UK trade mark law into concordance with the EC Directive on Harmonisation of Trade Mark Laws. Under the new law a trade mark may now consist of the shape of goods or their packaging: see s 1(1).
3   Ibid at 275, 456.
4   See ch 2, paras 2.07–2.09.
5   See ch 7, paras 7.47–7.50.
6   *Coca-Cola v Barr* [1961] RPC 387.
7   See ch 3, para 3.46.
8   [1990] 1 All ER 873, RPC 341.
9   Ibid at 877, 402.
10   Ibid at 889, 416.

The Trade Descriptions Act

1.09   Criminal penalties have also long been imposed for the application of a false trade description to goods. Trade descriptions legislation started with the Merchandise Marks Act 1862 which was replaced by the Merchandise Marks

Act 1887.[1] This was itself replaced by the Trade Descriptions Act 1967, the present governing statute. The Act does not give a right of civil action for breach of statutory duty to the trader whose mark is falsely appropriated[2] and thus it is not properly regarded as a measure intended to prevent unfair competition. Its purpose is the protection of consumers and thus a detailed consideration of its provisions is not within the scope of this book. However, since the recognition in the law of passing off of rights to 'descriptive' trade marks,[3] there will be cases where the civil remedy of passing off overlaps with criminal remedies available to deceived customers in such circumstances.

---

1 Subsequently amended in 1891, 1911, 1926 and 1953.
2 *Bollinger v Costa Brava Wine Co Ltd* [1960] RPC 16.
3 'Champagne' passing off is considered in paras 2.30 and 2.31, and 4.10 and 4.11 below.

Coincidence of remedies for unfair competition

1.10 The various forms of unfair competition considered above are not distinct and separate but coincide to a significant event. The same set of facts may well give rise to a cause of action for more than one of the torts which are primarily means of engaging in unfair competition. It is, therefore, not possible to deal with passing off entirely in isolation from the various other wrongs which may also be committed in the same circumstances. Thus, although the principal topic of this book is the law and the practice of passing off, chapters on the relevant aspects of registered trade mark, registered and unregistered design and copyright infringement, malicious falsehood, libel and slander have been included to put the many facets of a passing off action in context and to assist practitioners in deciding whether there are also other causes of action in a particular case. As contempt of court often involves the making of untrue statements about opposing litigants, it has been found helpful to include a passage on this subject in the chapter dealing with malicious falsehood and libel. There is, however, much less direct coincidence between passing off and the other torts, such as patent infringement, breach of confidence and procuring breach of contract, in which there is sometimes an aspect of unfair competition; reference should therefore be made to appropriate works on these topics.[1] Finally a chapter on the effect of the Treaty of Rome is included in view of its overriding importance in competition law generally.

---

1 See eg *The Encyclopaedia of United Kngdom and European Patent Law*, Gurry *Breach of Confidence* (2nd edn due shortly), Street *On Torts* (9th edn, 1993).

CHAPTER 2

The nature of the tort of passing off

The origin of the tort

2.01 The term 'passing off' first appears in 1842 in *Perry v Truefitt*[1] to describe the wrong now commonly referred to by that name. However, the origin of the action appears to go back at least as far as 1618, where Doderidge J is reported as saying of a case decided in 1580:

> 'An action upon the case was brought in the Common Pleas by a clothier, that whereas he had gained a great reputation for his making of cloth, and by reason whereof he had great utterance to his great benefit and profit, and that he used to set his mark to the cloth, whereby it should be known to be his cloth, and another clothier perceiving it, used the same mark to his ill-made cloth on purpose to deceive him, it was resolved that an action will lie.'[2]

The wrong was justiciable in the common law courts as an action on the case for deceit. To succeed it was necessary to show that the defendant had deliberately adopted the plaintiff's mark or a colourable imitation of it in order to deceive the public.[3]

---

1 (1842) 6 Beav 66.
2 *Southern v How* (1618) Poph 143 at 144; see *Hirst v Denham* (1872) LR 14 Eq 542 at 549 and *Magnolia Metal Co v Tandem Smelting Syndicate Ltd* (1900) 17 RPC 477 at 484. The report of *Southern v How* Cro Jac 468 at 471 records Doderidge J's remark in a rather different form and the report at 2 Roll Rep 26 at 28 omits it altogether.
3 *Edelsten v Edelsten* (1863) 1 De GJ & Sm 185 at 199.

2.02 By 1810 it was established that the Court of Chancery would intervene to grant an injunction to restrain the defendant's activities in such a case. Lord Eldon LC set out the principle on which the court acted in the following terms:

> 'There can be no doubt that the Court would interpose against that sort of fraud which has been attempted by setting up the same trade in the same place, under the same sign or name, the party giving himself out as the same person.'[1]

---

1 *Crutwell v Lye* (1810) 17 Ves 335.

2.03 Two cases brought shortly after this in the common law courts show advances which the courts were prepared to make in protecting a trader's reputation in his mark. In *Sykes v Sykes*[1] in 1824 the defendant sold shot belts and powder flasks of inferior quality to those of the plaintiff's make

and marked them with the words 'Sykes Patent', a mark which the plaintiff
had used for many years to denote his goods. The defendant sold his goods
to retailers who, it appeared from the evidence, were not themselves in the
least deceived. The jury found that the defendant had indeed adopted the
mark 'for the purpose of inducing the public to suppose the articles were
manufactured . . . by the plaintiff' and this was held sufficient fraud to found
the action. Thus the law had developed to the point where putting the article
into circulation with the intention that it should subsequently be used to
deceive purchasers was enough to establish the tort. In *Blofeld v Payne*[2] in
1833 the defendant wrapped hones for sharpening razors in envelopes bearing
directions for their use and other matter similar to that used by the plaintiff
on wrappers for his hones and intended to distinguish them from others. The
plaintiff alleged (but failed to prove) that the defendant's hones were inferior
to his and that he had suffered special damage. The jury awarded the plaintiff
one farthing damages. Nonetheless, on a motion to enter a nonsuit on the
ground that special damage was of the essence of the action, the court held
that the plaintiff was entitled to recover general damages: 'the circumstances of
the defendants' having obtained the plaintiff's wrappers and made this use of
them, entitles the plaintiff to some damages.'[3] The Court was clearly prepared
to accept that some damage was inevitable and that this alone entitled the
plaintiff to relief.

---

1   (1824) 3 B & C 541.
2   (1833) 4 B & Ad 410.
3   Ibid per Taunton J at 411.

2.04   The foundation of the modern law of passing off is probably *Perry v
Truefitt* where Lord Langdale MR made the statement of principle which has
subsequently been widely adopted:

> 'A man is not to sell his own goods under the pretence that they are the goods of
> another man; he cannot be permitted to practise such a deception, nor to use the
> means which contribute to that end. He cannot therefore be allowed to use names,
> marks, letters, *or other indicia*, by which he may induce purchasers to believe that the
> goods which he is selling are the manufacture of another person.'[1]

This expression of the nature of the tort if passing off is of course narrower
than the principles on which the courts act today. However, it is the basis of
the many types of passing off which are now recognised to exist.

---

1   (1842) 6 Beav 66 at 73; referred to with approval by Lord Scarman in *Cadbury Schweppes Pty Ltd
v The Pub Squash Co Pty Ltd* [1981] 1 All ER 213, [1981] RPC 429; and by Lord Jauncey in *Reckitt
& Colman v Borden* [1990] 1 All ER 875 at 889, [RPC] 341 at 416.

2.05   In *Wotherspoon v Currie*[1] in 1872 a further substantial development took
place in the recognition that an accurate indication of a geographical location

might be misleading. In *Frank Reddaway & Co Ltd v George Banham & Co Ltd*[2] in 1896 this principle was further extended; it was held that a true description by a trader of the nature of his goods was actionable if the description carried with it the implication in the marketplace that the goods were made by another trader. The way was now open for actions based on misrepresentations made by using accurate descriptive terms which had acquired a secondary meaning in the market denoting a particular trader. In *Reddaway v Banham* Lord Halsbury LC expressed the principle to be applied concisely in the following words: 'Nobody has any right to represent his goods as the goods of somebody else.'[3]

---

1   (1872) LR 5 HL 508, 42 LJ Ch 130.
2   [1896] AC 199, 13 RPC 218.
3   Ibid at 224.

2.06   The use of the term 'passing off' seems to have become fully accepted by 1887[1] although the extent of its application continued to develop steadily. This development has continued up to the present day. It was with good cause that Lord Diplock described the tort of passing off as the most protean form of action in English law available to a trader who wishes to complain of unfair trading.[2]

---

1   See eg *Lever v Goodwin* (1887) 36 Ch D 1 at per Cotton LJ.
2   *Warnink v Townend* [1979] AC 731 at 740.

The nature of the right

2.07   It was recognised by the courts at an early stage[1] in the development of the law of passing off that the right to protect against piracy of a plaintiff's name or trade mark was not linked to the name or trade mark itself but to the 'property' which the plaintiff had acquired in that name or mark by the use which he had made of it. To obtain relief the plaintiff must show that he has obtained a unique and exclusive recognition amongst a significant section of the trade or the public for his goods or services by reference to the distinguishing indicia he claims to be entitled to monopolise. The precise nature of this right was the subject of considerable judicial consideration during the latter part of the nineteenth century and the early part of this century. The following examples indicate the consensus to which the courts moved:

1   'The word "property" has been sometimes applied to what has been termed a trade mark at common law. I doubt myself whether it is accurate to speak of there being property in such a trade mark, though no doubt some of the rights which are incident to property may attach to it.' Per Lord Herschell in *Reddaway v Banham*.[2]

2   'If an injunction be granted restraining the use of a word or name, it

is no doubt granted to protect property, but the property, to protect which it is granted, is not property in the word or name, but property in the trade or goodwill which will be injured by its use.' Per Parker J in *Burberrys v J C Cording & Co Ltd*.[3]

1 See eg *Blanchard v Hill* (1742) 2 Atk 484.
2 [1896] AC 199 at 209, 13 RPC 218 at 288.
3 (1909) 26 RPC 693 at 701.

2.08 In *Spalding & Bros v A W Gamage Ltd*[1] in 1915, Lord Parker reviewed the authorities and reached the following conclusion:

'There appears to be considerable diversity of opinion as to the nature of the right, the invasion of which is the subject of what are known as passing off actions. The more general opinion appears to be that the right is a right of property. This view naturally demands an answer to the question — property in what? Some authorities say property in the mark, name or get-up improperly used by the defendant. Others say, property in the business or goodwill likely to be injured by the misrepresentation. Lord Herschell in *Reddaway v Banham* . . . expressly dissents from the former view; and if the right invaded is a right of property at all, there are, I think, strong reasons for preferring the latter view.'

Lord Diplock in *Star Industrial Co Ltd v Yap Kwee Kor*[2] clarified the matter further by formulating the nature of the right in the following terms:

'A passing off action is a remedy for the invasion of a right of property not in the mark, name or get-up improperly used, but in the business or goodwill likely to be injured by the misrepresentation made by passing off one person's goods as the goods of another. Goodwill as the subject of proprietary rights is incapable of subsisting by itself. It has no independent existence apart from the business to which it is attached.'[3]

This makes plain that a claim can only be made in relation to a goodwill which subsists in relation to an identifiable business. Although goodwill has no existence independent of that business, it may continue to subsist in connection with a business which is no longer carried on and remain capable of being revived for some time.[4]

1 (1915) 32 RPC 273 at 284.
2 [1976] FSR 256 (PC).
3 Ibid at 269.
4 See ch 3, para 3.15.

2.09 Lord Parker's formulation has often been expressly endorsed as a correct analysis. Lord Diplock himself did so in *Erven Warnink BV v J Townend & Sons (Hull) Ltd*.[1] Lord Jauncey, in *Reckitt & Colman v Borden*[2] referred to and adopted both passages. It is, therefore, clear that it is injury to the goodwill in a business which is actionable in a claim for passing off.

1 [1979] AC 731 at 741.
2 [1990] 1 All ER 873 at 889, [RPC] 341 at 417.

The nature of the tortious act

2.10 As with the tort of deceit, on which the action for passing off is based, the tortious act is a misrepresentation of fact. The form which the misrepresentation can take may vary widely. As Lord Jauncey put it in *Reckitt & Colman v Borden:*[1]

> '[I]t is not essential to the success of a passing off action that the defendant should misrepresent his goods as those of the plaintiff. It is sufficient that he misrepresents his goods in such a way that it is a reasonably foreseeable consequence of the misrepresentation that the plaintiff's business or goodwill will be damaged. Thus a misrepresentation by B that his inferior goods are of a superior quality which is that of A's goods, whereby people buy B's goods instead of A's, is actionable.'

A misrepresentation that deceives others into believing that B's goods or business are in fact A's goods or business is merely a specific example of the general nature of the wrongful act. In the action for passing off, the misrepresentation is actionable at the suit of the person whose business is injured by the misrepresentation, not (as in the action for deceit itself) the person deceived.

---

1 [1990] 1 All ER 873 at 890, [RPC] 341 at 417.

2.11 The misrepresentation may be direct but is more usually indirect, or implied, and made by the use of a mark, name or other indicia the same as, or confusingly similar to, a mark, name or indicia distinctive of the plaintiff. In *Spalding v Gamage* Lord Parker put the position thus:

> 'The basis of a passing off action being a false representation by the defendant, it must be proved in each case as a fact that the false representation was made. It may, of course, have been made in express words, but cases of express misrepresentation of this sort are rare. The more common case is where the representation is implied in the use or imitation of a mark, trade name, or get-up with which the goods of another are associated in the minds of the public. In such cases the point to be decided is whether, having regard to all the circumstances of the case, the use by the defendant in connection with the goods of the mark, name, or get-up in question impliedly represents such goods to be the goods of the plaintiff, or the goods of the plaintiff of a particular class or quality, or, as it is sometimes put, whether the defendant's use of such mark, name, or get-up is calculated to deceive. It would, however, be impossible to enumerate or classify all the possible ways in which a man may make the false representation relied on.'[1]

---

1 (1915) 32 RPC 273 at 284.

The requirement for fraud

2.12 At common law, fraud was an essential element in passing off, as in deceit. Equity, however, came to take rather a different view. It was stated by Lord Cottenham LC in *Millington v Fox*, as early as 1838, that:

'It does not appear to me that there was any fraudulent intention in the use of the marks. That circumstance, however, does not deprive the Plaintiffs of their right to the exclusive use of those names.'[1]

Despite this broad statement there were subsequently a number of cases decided in the Chancery Court which appeared to require either a fraudulent intention on the part of the defendant or at least knowledge on his part that his customers would sell on to others fraudulently.[2]

---

1 (1838) 3 My & Cr 338 at 352.
2 See eg *Perry v Truefitt* (1842) 6 Beav 66 at 73; *Croft v Day* (1843) 7 Beav 84; *Farina v Silverlock* (1855) 1 K & J 509, 24 LJ Ch 632. Cf *Sykes v Sykes* (1824) 3 B&C 541 for the common law approach.

2.13 However, by 1863 it was clear that the Court of Chancery would intervene and grant an injunction to restrain a defendant who had acted entirely innocently and in ignorance of the plaintiff's rights. Lord Westbury LC in *Edelsten v Edelsten* stated the principle as follows:

'At law the proper remedy is by an action in the case for deceit, and proof of fraud on behalf of the defendant is of the essence of the action: but this court will act on the principle of protecting property alone and it is not necessary to prove fraud in the Defendant.'[1]

---

1 (1863) 1 De GJ & Sm 185 at 199.

2.14 The question of whether the defendant's use of the plaintiff's trade mark was made with the knowledge of the plaintiff's rights remained material in the Chancery Courts in relation to the remedies available to the plaintiff: an innocent user of the plaintiff's mark would be subject to an injunction but not an account of his profits unless he continued the user complained of after the plaintiff's claim was brought to his notice.[1]

---

1 Ibid; see also *Moet v Couston* (1864) 33 Beav 578 at 580; *Cartier v Carlile* (1862) 31 Beav 292 at 298.

2.15 After the Judicature Acts 1873 the equitable rule prevailed and fraud ceased altogether to be an essential element in passing off. In *Singer Machine Manufacturers v Wilson* Lord Westbury said:

'A man may take the trade mark of another ignorantly, not knowing it was the trade mark of the other, or he may take it in the belief, mistaken but sincerely entertained, that in the manner in which he is taking it he is within the law, and doing nothing which the law forbids, or he may take it knowing it is the trade mark of his neighbour and desiring to injure his neighbour by so doing.'[1]

Nevertheless the defendant's knowledge remained material in relation to the question of whether or not a plaintiff could recover an account of profits or damages after judgment as well as an injunction restraining further passing off. It was not possible to recover any monetary compensation from a person who innocently passed off his goods or devices as the plaintiff's.[2]

---

1 (1877) 3 App Cas 376 at 391.
2 See *Slazenger v Spalding* [1910] 1 Ch 257.

Reputation

2.16 In order to succeed in an action for passing off, the first essential is for a plaintiff to prove the existence of a business in which there is goodwill and that the goodwill or part of it resides in the exclusive association of the name mark or other indicia relied on with that business. In *Leahy, Kelly and Leahy v Glover*, Lord Herschell LC put the requirement this way:

> 'What is the foundation of a claim of this description? It is that the party alleging it should prove in the first instance that any name which he claims as his trade name has been so exclusively used in connection with his manufacture, or with the goods which he sells, that his goods have come to be known in the market by that name: that anyone using that name would intend to refer to his goods and that anyone to whom the name was used would understand that his goods were referred to.'[1]

---

1 (1893) 10 RPC 141 at 155.

2.17 This exclusive association continues to exist only for so long as the plaintiff continues to use the mark in his business.[1] Lord Parker in *Spalding v Gamage* emphasised its ephemeral nature and the need to prove in each case that by reason of continuing use by the plaintiff the reputation subsisted at the relevant time:

> 'Even in the case of what are sometimes referred to as Common Law Trade Marks the property, if any, of the so-called owner is in its nature transitory, and only exists so long as the mark is distinctive of his goods in the eyes of the public or a class of the public.'[2]

---

1 See ch 3, para 3.15 for consideration of 'residual' reputation persisting after use of a mark has ceased.
2 (1915) 32 RPC 273 at 284, 31 TLR 328.

The distinguishing indicia

2.18 The features of a plaintiff's business or goods which serve to distinguish it from the businesses or goods of other traders vary widely. A brief resume of the most important distinguishing indicia is given below.

TRADE MARKS

2.19 The practice of marking goods with a name, device or some other unique feature to distinguish them from the goods of someone else is almost universal. It was probably the first type of distinguishing feature to be recognised as giving rise to a cause of action in passing off and is still a common basis for a passing off action on the footing that the mark represents part of the goodwill of the plaintiff's business. The term 'trade mark' is used only for such marks when used for goods. An early example of the recognition of this type of passing off appears in *Seixo v Provenzende* where Lord Cranworth LC stated:

> 'Where a manufacturer has been in the habit of stamping the goods which he has manufactured with a particular mark or brand, so that thereby persons purchasing goods of that description know them to be of his manufacture, no other manufacturer has the right to adopt the same stamp.'[1]

---

1   (1866) 1 Ch App 192.

2.20 In order to assist plaintiffs in legal proceedings, a registration system was introduced for trade marks for goods by the Trade Marks Act 1875 and regulated by this Act and subsequent Acts up to and including the current Act of 1994. Under these Acts registered trade marks have become a statutory form of personal property enforceable by the wholly distinct action for infringement of registered trade mark. The right to bring actions for passing off based on trade marks, whether registered or unregistered, was unaffected by the coming into force of the Trade Marks Acts[1] and there are still certain advantages in relying on passing off rather than the action for infringement of a registered mark.[2]

---

1   See Trade Marks Act 1994, s 2(2).
2   See ch 9, para 9.12 below.

SERVICE MARKS

2.21 A trader in the business of providing services rather than goods often adopts a name or other mark to distinguish his business and services from similar services offered by others. For a long time English law did not permit registration of marks for services. This was rectified in 1986 under the old law of trade marks with the introduction of a separate category of 'service mark' registrations[1] and the new law of trade marks[2] also provides that marks may be registered for services as well as goods.[3]

---

1   By the Trade Marks (Amendment) Act 1984 and the Patents, Designs and Marks Act 1986 which came into force on 1 October 1986.
2   The Trade Marks Act 1994.
3   See generally ch 9 below.

2.22 Trade marks and service marks are not necessarily in the form of words. They may be in the form of pictures signs or symbols, or combinations of pictures, signs or symbols with words as well as the shape of goods or their packaging. Such marks are usually referred to as 'device marks' and, like any other trade marks, can form the basis of an action for passing off. Any sign capable of being represented graphically, which is capable of distinguishing the goods or services of one trader from those of another, may now be registered.[1]

---

1 Trade Marks Act 1994 s 1(1). See ch 9.

GET-UP

2.23 In the marking of goods the compendious term 'get-up' is used for any combination of distinctive features not easily fitted into one of the other classes. The term 'get-up' seems to have been first used in *Lever v Goodwin* in 1887 where Lindley LJ referred to 'what is called the general "get-up" which is an expression used by some of the witnesses'.[1] In *J B Williams Co v H Bronnley & Co Ltd*, Fletcher Moulton LJ defined get-up as 'a capricious addition to the article itself — the colour or shape it may be, of the wrapper, or anything of that kind'.[2] Get-up alone can be relied on as a basis for an action for passing off although it is generally more difficult to establish the requisite reputation and confusion than in the case of marks or trade names.[3] Get-up falling within the definition of a trade mark is also registrable.[4]

---

1 (1887) 36 Ch D 1 at 8, 4 RPC 492 at 507.
2 (1909) 26 RPC 765 at 773.
3 See ch 3 para 3.43–3.49 and ch 4, para 4.17 below.
4 See eg *SmithKline & French Laboratories v Sterling-Winthrop Group* [1975] 2 All ER 578, (1976) RPC 511: the old law. See ch 9 for the new law.

NAMES

2.24 In a passing off action a plaintiff can of course rely upon the name under which he carries on his business as the distinctive feature which has been appropriated by the defendant so as to cause members of the public to think the defendant's business is that of the plaintiff. A plaintiff can also rely on any name under which he trades to identify his goods or services specifically. In *Singer Manufacturing Co v Loog* Lord Blackburn said:

'There is another way in which goods not the plaintiff's may be sold as and for the plaintiffs, though it is not, and never was, impressed on the goods, or on the packages in which they are contained, so as to be a trade mark, properly so called, or within recent statutes. Where it is established that such a trade name bears that meaning, I think the use of that name, or one so nearly resembling it as to be likely to deceive, as applicable to goods not the plaintiff's, may be the means of passing off those goods as and for the plaintiff's just as much as the use of a trade mark; and I think the law (so far as not altered by legislation) is the same.'[1]

---

1 (1882) 8 App Cas 15 at 32, 52 LJ Ch 481 at 491.

2.25 If a trader carries on a business in his own name he can rely on this name in a passing off action as the trade name which is associated with his business in which there is goodwill. However, in relation to both passing off and registered trade marks there are special rules protecting bona fide use by the traders of their own names which would otherwise be infringement of the rights of others.[1]

---

1 In relation to registered trade marks, see the Trade Marks Act 1938 s 8(a); Trade Marks Act 1994 s 11(2) ch 9, para 9.08 below. In relation to passing off, see ch 4, paras 4.36–4.40 below.

2.26 With the advent of the limited company, businesses became known by the name of the company which owned the business concerned and the goodwill in the business was related to that company name. The same is true of other forms of corporate body and of trading and professional associations. Passing off actions can therefore be brought by any such company, body or association in reliance on their own names.[1]

---

1 See ch 3, paras 3.03–3.05, and 3.40 below.

Goodwill

2.27 As noted in para 2.07 above, the goodwill in a plaintiff's business has been identified as the property right which the action for passing off protects. Perhaps somewhat strangely the only comprehensive definition of goodwill which has been attempted, and the one which is generally accepted today, appears in a tax case. In *IRC v Muller*, Lord MacNaghton described goodwill in the following terms:

'It ... is the benefit and advantage of the good name, reputation and connection of a business. It is the attractive force which brings in custom. It is the one thing which distinguishes an old established business from a new business at its first start ... However widely extended or diffused its influence may be, goodwill is worth nothing unless it has power of attraction sufficient to bring customers home to the source from which it emanates.'[1]

In the same case Lord Lindley, expressed himself in essentially the same vein:

'Goodwill regarded as property has no meaning except in connection with some trade, business or calling. In that connection I understand the word to include whatever adds value to a business by reason of situation, name and reputation, connection, introduction to old customers, and agreed customers, and agreed absence from competition, or any of these things, and there may be others which do not occur to me.'[2]

---

1 (1901) AC 217 at 223–224.
2 Ibid at 235. For a modern endorsement of this view see *Star Industrial Co Ltd v Yap Kwee Kor* [1976] FSR 256 at 269 per Lord Diplock, cited in para 2.08 above.

2.28 As had been noted above in relation to the reputation attaching to a trader's distinguishing indicia, goodwill is essentially ephemeral. However, it is recognised as a species of personal property and can be transferred with the sale of a business, the purchaser being entitled at a later date to rely on the goodwill built up by his predecessor in title.[1]

---

1 See ch 3, para 3.50 below.

SHARED GOODWILL

2.29 In *Aerators Ltd v Tollitt* Farwell LJ said that a plaintiff must show that his name 'is exclusively identified with his own manufacture'.[1] There have nevertheless been cases where goodwill was shared by more than one plaintiff.

---

1 [1902] 2 Ch 319 at 325; see also *Reddaway v Banham* [1896] AC 199, 65 LJ QB 381.

2.30 The scope for actions based on shared goodwill was greatly extended by Dankwerts J in *Bollinger v Costa Brava Wine Co Ltd*[1] ('the *Champagne* case') to include cases where goodwill was shared by several independent enterprises engaged in the same line of business. In the *Champagne* case it was held that the plaintiffs were entitled to rely on a form of goodwill in the word 'champagne' which was derived from the fact that the sparkling wine they sold was produced from grapes grown in the Champagne district of France and which was shared by the several shippers of the wine to England. The defendants were restrained from applying the word 'champagne' to the wine they imported (as 'Spanish Champagne') from Spain. The *Champagne* case was followed by Cross J in *Vine Products Co Ltd v Mackenzie & Co Ltd*[2] ('the *Sherry* case') in which the judge accepted that there was a goodwill in the word 'sherry' shared by the importers of sherry from Spain. The defendants were restrained from using the word sherry in connection with their fortified wines except in the context of 'British Sherry'. The *Champagne* case was also followed by Foster J in *John Walker & Sons Ltd v Henry Ost & Co*[3] ('the *Scotch whisky* case').[4]

---

1 [1960] RPC 16 and [1961] RPC 116 and Appendix A below.
2 [1969] RPC 1.
3 [1970] RPC 489.

4   For forms of the injunctions granted, see ch 7, paras 7.47–7.50 and Appendix A below.

2.31   In *Warnink v Townend*[1] ('the *Advocaat* case') the House of Lords approved the *Champagne, Sherry* and *Scotch Whisky* cases and went further in holding that the rights enjoyed by a class of traders including the plaintiffs to describe their product as Advocaat applied to a specific egg and spirit drink of an identified recipe and constituted a valuable part of their goodwill. Accordingly the defendants were restrained from applying the mark 'Advocaat' to a drink not made according to that recipe.[2]

---

1   [1979] AC 731.
2   For forms of injunctions see ch 7, paras 7.47–7.50 and Appendix A below.

Damage

2.32   In order to succeed in a passing off action it is necessary for a plaintiff to prove that he has suffered damage or is likely to suffer damage in the future. In *Borthwick v Evening Post* Cotton LJ summed up the position as follows:

'In order to justify the court in granting an injunction we ought to be satisfied that there probably will be injury to the pocket of the plaintiff ... we must have evidence to satisfy us that there is reasonable probability that in fact there will be damage to the party complaining.'[1]

Although the need to prove damage can undoubtedly be an obstacle to a plaintiff in a passing off action (as it was in *Borthwick*) the courts (particularly in other common law countries) have often shown themselves prepared to exercise considerable flexibility in deciding whether damage to the plaintiff is likely to result from the defendant's activities.[2]

---

1   (1888) 37 Ch D 449 at 462–623. See also para 2.03 and n 3 thereto, above.
2   See ch 5 below.

The modern law

2.33   In *Advocaat* Lord Diplock confirmed the view that the action for passing off is based on a property right in the goodwill attached to the plaintiff's business. He went on to identify five characteristics which must be present in order to crease a valid cause of action for passing off as:

'(1) a misrepresentation (2) made by a trader in the course of trade, (3) to prospective customers of his or ultimate consumers of goods or services supplied by him, (4) which is calculated to injure the business or goodwill of another trader (in the sense that this is a reasonably foreseeable consequence) and (5) which causes actual damage to a business or goodwill of the trader by whom the action is brought or (in a quia timet action) will probably do so.'[1]

Having identified the necessary characteristics, Lord Diplock went on to warn that they might nevertheless not be sufficient to establish the cause of action:

'In seeking to formulate general propositions of English law, however, one must be particularly careful to beware of the logical fallacy of the undistributed middle. It does not follow that because all passing off actions can be shown to present these characteristics, all factual situations which present these characteristics give rise to a cause of action for passing off.'[1]

This comment, taken at face value, is somewhat unhelpful to those subsequently endeavouring to discover whether a particular set of circumstances gives rises to an action for passing off. Fortunately, however, Lord Diplock clarified what he meant in his conclusion on the facts of the *Advocaat* case:

'The presence of those characteristics is enough unless there is also present in the case some exceptional feature which justifies, on grounds of public policy, withholding from a person who has suffered injury in consequence of the deception practised on prospective customers or consumers of his product a remedy in law against the deceiver. On the facts found by the judge, and I stress their importance, I can find no such exceptional feature in the instant case.'[2]

Lord Diplock did not specifically identify any matters of public policy which would justify the withholding of a remedy. However, some matters in this category are not in principle difficult to recognise. Thus the courts would not for example protect the reputation of a trader whose trade was immoral or illegal or whose goods could only be used for illegal or immoral purposes although it is not certain that today's judges would necessarily consider immoral what was considered immoral 50 to 100 years ago.[3] There is some doubt as to how much further the courts would go in depriving a plaintiff of relief to which he would otherwise be entitled.

---

1 [1979] AC 731 at 742.
2 Ibid at 748.
3 Analogously to the operation of the Trade Marks Act 1938 s 11, and Trade Marks Act 1994 s 3(3), in relation to registered trade marks: see ch 9 below.

2.34 The five characteristics enumerated by Lord Diplock cover all the previously identified instances which could give rise to passing off, for example, the case where the defendant is selling the plaintiff's goods but making a misrepresentation about their quality, as in *Spalding v Gamage* in which Lord Parker said:

'The proposition that no one has a right to represent his goods as the goods of somebody else must, I think, as has been assumed in this case, involve as a corollary the further proposition, that no one, who has in his hands the goods of another of a particular class or quality has a right to represent these goods to be the goods of that other of a different quality or belonging to a different class. Possibly, therefore, the principle ought to be restated as follows: A cannot, without infringing the rights of B, represent goods which are not B's goods or B's goods of a particular class or quality to be B's goods or B's goods of that particular class or quality. The wrong for which relief is sought in a passing off action consists in every case of a representation of this nature.'[1]

Lord Diplock's five characteristics also cover cases where the plaintiff's and defendant's business are not the same but where the plaintiff has a basis for contending that the defendant's activities will cause his business damage or are likely to do so.[2] They also cover the case where the plaintiff is a professional association having no business (in the narrow commercial sense) but which can provide proof of damage or likely damage.

---

1   (1915) 32 RPC 273 at 284. For a modern application of the principle see *Wilkinson Sword v Cripps & Lee* [1982] FSR 16.
2   See ch 5, paras 5.04 ff below.

2.35   Lord Fraser in the only other substantive speech in the *Advocaat* case also formulated a set of five principles which in his view underlie any action for passing off.[1] Unhappily, these principals appear to be difficult to reconcile with those enunciated by Lord Diplock. In particular Lord Fraser's analysis defines a tort of passing off in terms much narrower in scope not merely than Lord Diplock's speech but also narrower than many earlier decisions which establish a tort of passing off of much wider application. Lord Fraser's principles have, however, been adopted in a number of subsequent cases of passing off goods, in particular as an authority for the proposition that goodwill is strictly local.[2] It has since been said that Lord Fraser's formulation was not intended to lay down essential requirements of the tort which would exclude from its ambit cases of a kind not under consideration in *Advocaat* itself.[3] Thus the leading analysis is now simply that of Lord Diplock.

---

1   [1979] AC 731 at 755–756, [1980] RPC 31 at 105, 106.
2   *Anheuser-Busch Inc v Budejovicky Budvar Narodni Podnik* [1984] FSR 413.
3   *Bristol Conservatories Limited v Conservatories Custom Built Limited* [1989] RPC 455 at 460 (CA), endorsing the view of Falconer J in *Lego System A/S v Lego M Lemelstrich* [1983] FSR 155 at 185 and disapproving the comment of Oliver LJ in *Anheuser-Busch Inc v Budejovicky Budvar Narodni Podnik* (above) that 'the two statements of principle complement one another'.

2.36   In the ten years following the decision in the *Advocaat* case, the courts universally followed the formulation of Lord Diplock of the essence of the tort sometimes, as in *Budweiser*, combining that formulation with the ingredients as delineated by Lord Fraser. Those formulations were of course devised in the course of considering a particularly unusual form of passing off and it is not surprising that, whilst they are well suited to the circumstances then before the court, they are often of little assistance in deciding whether there is in fact a proper claim for passing off in the more ordinary circumstances normally encountered. We noted in the final paragraph of ch 2 of the first edition of this work that, whilst Lord Diplock's five characteristics were the yardstick by which any passing off claim is to be tested, it is still convenient to consider the tort in the three facets of (1) reputation, (2) misrepresentation and (3) damage.

The judicial rebellion came in 1990 in *Reckitt & Colman v Borden*[1] when both Lords Oliver and Jauncey essayed a reconsideration of the essential elements of the tort of passing off. Lord Jauncey, after reciting Lord Diplock's formulation in *Advocaat* summarised the general law in the following simple passage:

'In a case such as the present where what is in issue is whether the goods of A are likely to be passed off as those of B, a plaintiff, to succeed, must establish (1) that his goods have acquired a particular reputation amongst the public, (2) that persons wishing to buy his goods are likely to be misled into buying the goods of the defendant and (3) that he is likely to suffer damage thereby.'[2]

Lord Oliver did not refer to earlier authority but set out the nature of the tort in detail in the following passage:

'Although your Lordships were referred in the course of argument to a large number of reported cases, this is not a branch of the law in which reference to other cases is of any real assistance except analogically. It has been observed more than once that the questions which arise are, in general, questions of fact. Neither the appellants nor the respondents contend that the principles of law are in any doubt. The law of passing off can be summarised in one short general proposition — no man may pass off his goods as those of another. More specifically, it may be expressed in terms of the elements which the plaintiff in such an action has to prove in order to succeed. These are three in number. First, he must establish a goodwill or reputation attached to the goods or services which he supplies in the mind of the purchasing public by association with the identifying "get-up" (whether it consists simply of a brand name or a trade description, or the individual features of labelling or packaging) under which his particular goods or services are offered to the public, such that the get-up is recognised by the public as distinctive specifically of the plaintiff's goods or services. Secondly, he must demonstrate a misrepresentation by the defendant to the public (whether or not intentional) leading or likely to lead the public to believe that goods or services offered by him are the goods or services of the plaintiff. Whether the public is aware of the plaintiff's identity as the manufacturer or supplier of the goods or services is immaterial, as long as they are identified with a particular source, which is in fact the plaintiff. For example, if the public is accustomed to rely upon a particular brand name in purchasing goods of a particular description, it matters not at all that there is little or no public awareness of the identity of the proprietor of the brand name. Thirdly, he must demonstrate that he suffers or, in a *quia timet* action that he is likely to suffer, damage by reason of the erroneous belief engendered by the defendant's misrepresentation that the source of the defendant's goods or services is the same as the source of those offered by the plaintiff.'[3]

Lord Jauncey's formulation is expressly restricted to passing off of goods whilst Lord Oliver's formulation endeavours to encapsulate all possible forms of passing off. They both, however, adopt the traditional division of the tort into its three basic facets.

---

1   [1990] 1 All ER 873, RPC 341.
2   Ibid at 890, 418.
3   Ibid at 880, 406.

2.37   The following year Nourse LJ, in *Consorzio del Prosciutto di Parma v Marks & Spencer Plc*,[1] emboldened by those observations expressed the following view on the formulations of Lords Diplock and Fraser in Advocaat:

'Although those speeches are of the highest authority, it has been my experience, and it is now my respectful opinion, that they do not give the same degree of assistance in analysis and decision as the classical trinity of (1) a reputation (or goodwill) acquired by the plaintiff in his goods, name, mark, etc., (2) a misrepresentation by the defendant leading to confusion (or deception), causing (3) damage to the plaintiff.

I might not have thought it appropriate to give expression to this opinion had it not been, first, for the the recent speeches in the House of Lords in *Reckitt & Colman v Borden* and, secondly, for a belief that the classical approach is of real assistance in the analysis and decision of the present case.'

He then quoted the observations of Lords Oliver and Jauncey cited above and commented that they:

'signal a welcome return to the classical approach to the elements of a passing off action.'

We wholeheartedly endorse these comments which support our approach of considering the elements of the tort in the following chapters in the form of the classical trinity.

---

1   [1991] RPC 351 at 368–369.

2.38   There are still important limits to the scope of the action for passing off. In *Cadbury-Schweppes Pty Ltd v The Pub Squash Co Pty Ltd* ('the *Pub Squash* case'). Lord Scarman described the extent of the modern law of passing off in these terms:

'The width of the principle now authoritatively recognised by the High Court of Australia and the House of Lords is, therefore, such that the tort is no longer anchored as in its early nineteenth century formulation, to the name or trade mark of a product or business. It is wide enough to encompass other descriptive material, such as slogans or visual images, which radio, television or newspaper advertising campaigns can lead the market to associate with a plaintiff's product, provided always that such descriptive material has become part of the goodwill of the product. And the test is whether the product has derived from the advertising a distinctive character which the market recognises.

But competition must remain free; and competition is safeguarded by the necessity for the plaintiff to prove that he has built up an 'intangible property right' in the advertised descriptions of his product, or, in other words, that he has succeeded by such methods in giving his product a distinctive character accepted by the market. A defendant however, does no wrong by entering a market created by another and there competing with its creator. The line may be difficult to draw; but, unless it is drawn, competition will be stifled.'[1]

---

1   [1981] RPC 429 at 490–491 (PC).

Passing off as a remedy for unfair competition

2.39   It was recognised as long ago as 1893 that passing off was a remedy for a kind of unfair competition.[1] However, the courts have refused to recognise, let alone define, a tort of unfair competition per se. In *Vine Products Co Ltd v*

Mackenzie & Co Ltd, Cross J appeared to be laying the basis for a fundamental extension of passing off when he described the decision in the *Champagne* case as going 'beyond the well trodden paths of passing off into the unmapped area of "unfair trading" or "unlawful competition"'[2] and applied it to the facts of the case before him. However, in subsequent cases it has been made clear that passing off is still a remedy for certain forms of unfair competition only and is relatively limited in scope. Lord Diplock has stated the position in the following words:

> 'Unfair trading as a wrong actionable at the suit of other traders who thereby suffer loss of business or goodwill may take a variety of forms, to some of which separate labels have become attached in English law. Conspiracy to injure a person in his trade or business is one, slander of goods another, but most protean is that which is generally and nowadays, perhaps misleadingly, described as "passing off".'[3]

This analysis is essentially the same as that first formulated in the last century. Since then the courts have considerably extended the circumstances in which the action will lie for passing off but they have fallen short of creating a new tort properly described as unfair competition. There are still trading activities which can be categorised as immoral or unfair which do not give rise to an action for passing off or any other legal remedy.

---

1 *Huntley & Palmer v Reading Biscuit Co* (1893) 10 RPC 277 at 280 per Chitty J.
2 [1969] RPC 1 at 23.
3 *Advocaat* case [1979] AC 731 at 740.

CHAPTER 3

Reputation

The nature of reputation

INTRODUCTION

3.01 Whilst the title of this chapter is *Reputation* we have seen[1] that the property which is protected by a passing off action is the *goodwill* in the business. In passing off cases the two terms are often used almost interchangeably[2] and confusion arises as to the distinction between them. The difference is subtle and not always easy to see. Goodwill exists in the minds of a business's customers. It is the state of mind which makes them wish to patronise its goods or services. It can exist only in relation to a business which they are able to patronise. A reputation is the means by which something is recognised. In relation to a business which has goodwill it is the manner in which the goodwill operates on the minds of the business's customers. The difference is most acutely seen in two circumstances. Political parties undoubtedly possess reputations. However, they do not have goodwill because they carry on no business.[3] Foreign traders may well have a reputation in the sense that they are known to members of the public in this country, even though they carry on no business in here. Such a reputation, however extensive it is, will not support a passing off action unless the business's goods or services are available in this country so that the business is able to have customers here.[4]

---

1 Para 2.27 above.
2 See eg Nourse LJ in *Parma Ham* [1991] RPC 351 at 368.
3 *Kean v McGivan* [1982] FSR 119. And see paras 3.03–3.05 below.
4 Paras 2.28 above and 3.11–3.12 below.

3.02 Reputation is the first essential characteristic which the plaintiff must prove in order to bring a passing off claim. It can be summarised in these words: that the 'mark, name or other indicia'[1] on which the plaintiff relies is well known in connection with a business in which he has goodwill, or with goods connected with that business[2] and is distinctive of those goods or that business.[3] This aspect of a passing off claim raises a number of issues. In what kind of marks, names and other indicia may the plaintiff claim a reputation and goodwill? What is the nature of the reputation and goodwill which will support a claim of passing off? What must the plaintiff do to acquire the required reputation? For how long and over what area does the reputation subsist? What kinds of activities and organisations[2] are considered by the courts to constitute a business which is entitled to make a claim of passing off?[3] The purpose of this chapter is to examine these issues in detail.

1   *Perry v Truefitt* (1842) 6 Beav 66.
2   *Burberrys v J C Cording & Co Ltd* (1909) 100 LT 985, 26 RPC 693.
3   See para 2.16 above.

WHAT IS A BUSINESS

3.03   Nowadays any activity which is or may be capable of suffering some kind of loss which can be viewed in pecuniary terms will be regarded by the courts as a business capable of protection by an action for passing off. This was not always thought to be so. Lord Langdale MR in *Clark v Freeman*,[1] decided in 1848, refused to restrain the defendant from selling pills under the name 'Sir J Clark's Consumption pills' on the ground that the plaintiff, an eminent physician, had no business in the making of pills. It was held that, if a wrong had been done to the plaintiff, that wrong was a libel, which the Court of Chancery then had no jurisdiction to restrain. That decision was followed in *Williams v Hodge & Co Ltd*[2] and *Lee v Gibbings*.[3] However, doubt had frequently been expressed about its correctness[4] and in a parallel line of cases brought by professional associations to prevent the use by non-members of the associations of terms used to identify their members it was held that an injunction would lie.[5] In 1931, in *British Medical Association v Marsh*,[6] Maugham J reviewed both lines of authorities in an action by the Association to prevent the sale of a variety of proprietary remedies under the mark 'BMA' and came to the following conclusion:

> 'The professional cases are far from establishing the view which some people have held that *Clark v Freeman* is an authority for the proposition that a professional man has no remedy if a tradesman chooses to put forward some quack remedy or article of that kind as having been prescribed or been sold for the benefit of or the approval of the medical man in question. What it is necessary in such a case to prove is, either positive injury, or, in a *quia timet* action, a reasonable probability of injury, and if that is done, I for my part see no reason why such an action should not succeed.'[7]

Since that decision there has been no doubt that a professional practitioner may prevent exploitation of his reputation if he can show that his professional practice is damaged by the use made of his name. Equally, professional associations can bring actions where the association is harmed.

1   (1848) 11 Beav 112, 17 LJ Ch 142.
2   (1887) 4 TLR 175.

3   (1892) 67 LT 263, 8 TLR 773.
4   See *Re Rivière's Trade Mark* (1884) 26 Ch D 48, 53 LJ Ch 578; *Prudential Assurance Association v Knott* (1875) 10 Ch App 142; *Maxwell v Hogg* (1867) 2 Ch App 307; and *Springhead Spinning Co v Riley* (1868) LR 6 Eq 551, 37 LJ Ch 889.
5   *Society of Accountants in Edinburgh v The Corporation of Accountants Limited* (1893) 30 SLR 677; *Society of Accountants and Auditors v Goodway* [1907] 1 Ch 489, 76 LJ Ch 384.
6   (1931) 48 RPC 565.
7   Ibid at 574.

3.04   Plaintiffs have been held entitled to bring proceedings[1] for passing off based upon businesses consisting of, inter alia, associations of accountants,[2] associations of medical practitioners,[3] an ex-servicemen's association,[4] night clubs,[5] a concert hall,[6] beauty competitions,[7] bands of girl pipers,[8] films,[9] a television series,[10] theatrical sketches,[11] an operetta,[12] plays,[13] books,[14] magazines,[15] newspapers,[16] hotels,[17] restaurants,[18] gramophone records[19] and an organisation for looking after children[20] as well as commercial activities of all kinds whether concerned with providing goods or services. It has, however, been left expressly undecided whether an unincorporated association founded and conducted for charitable purposes could bring a passing off action.[21]

1   Some of these actions failed but not because of the failure to prove the existence of a 'business'.
2   *Society of Accountants and Auditors v Goodway* above; *Society of Incorporated Accountants v Vincent* (1954) 71 RPC 325.
3   *British Medical Association v Marsh* above; *British Association of Aesthetic Plastic Surgeons v Cambright Ltd* [1987] RPC 549.
4   *British Legion v British Legion Club (Street) Ltd* (1931) 48 RPC 555.
5   *Ad-Lib Club v Granville* [1971] 2 All ER 300, [1972] RPC 673; *Annabel's (Berkeley Square) Ltd v Schock* [1972] RPC 838.
6   *Hall of Arts and Sciences Corp v Albert Edward Hall* (1934) 50 TLR 518 51 RPC 398.
7   *Miss World (Jersey) Ltd v James Street Productions* [1981] FSR 309; *Morecombe and Heysham Corporation v Mecca Ltd* [1962] RPC 145 (interlocutory injunction), [1966] RPC 423 (trial).
8   *Dagenham Girl Pipers Ltd v Vishnu Pather* (1951) 69 RPC 1.
9   *Raleigh v Kinematograph Trading Co* (1914) 31 RPC 143.
10   *Hexagon Pty v Australian Broadcasting Commission* [1976] RPC 628 (an Australian case).
11   *Samuelson v Producers Distributing Co Ltd* (1931) 48 RPC 447, 580 (CA).
12   *Loew's Inc v Littler* (1955) 72 RPC 166.
13   *Twentieth Century Fox Film Corporation v Gala Film Distributors Ltd* [1957] RPC 105.
14   *Archbold v Sweet* (1832) 1 Mood & R 162.
15   *Hulton Press Ltd v White Eagle Youth Holiday Camp Ltd* (1951) 68 RPC 126.
16   *Borthwick v Evening Post* (1888) 37 Ch D 449, 57 LJ Ch 406.
17   *Sheraton Corporation of America v Sheraton Motels Ltd* [1964] RPC 202.
18   *My Kinda Town v Soll* [1983] RPC 407 (CA).
19   *Pickwick International (GB) Inc v Multiple Sound Distributors* [1972] 3 All ER 384, 1 WLR 1213.
20   *Deane v Schofield* [1962] RPC 179.
21   *Workman and Persson v Johns* (the '*Canine Defence League*' case) [1960] RPC 265.

3.05   Cases where the plaintiff has failed to establish the existence of a business have been few and have been restricted to circumstances in which it is clear that there is no commercial activity in any real sense carried on by the plaintiff. In *Day v Brownrigg*,[1] a case decided in 1878, the plaintiff

27

sought to restrain the defendant from adopting as a name for his house the name of the plaintiff's adjoining house, 'Ashford Lodge'. It was held that there was no basis for a passing off action. A modern example is *Kean v McGivan*, where the plaintiff brought proceedings on behalf of a small political party called the Social Democratic Party. It was held that this was not capable of being a 'business' having goodwill and Ackner LJ put the essential requirement in these terms: 'the plaintiff must establish that in some sense he is carrying on a business with which the trade or public will be led to associate the defendant's activities'.[2] This does not mean, however, that the business must necessarily be one which is carried on for profit. A number of the cases referred to above concerned charitable or non-profit making bodies.[3]

---

1 (1878) 10 Ch D 294, 48 LJ Ch 173.
2 [1982] FSR 119 at 120 (CA).
3 See the cases cited in notes 2, 3, 4 and 21 to para 3.04.

DISTINCTION BETWEEN REPUTATION IN BUSINESS AND GOODS

3.06 There is in principle no difference between a passing off action brought to protect a reputation in a business and one brought to protect a reputation in goods. However, whilst a trader in goods can sue either on the reputation of his business or on that of his goods, a trader in services can only protect the reputation of his business. This leads to some slight practical differences. A claim to protect the reputation of a business must necessarily involve an allegation that the business is recognised in some way by the public. This will usually be by a trading or corporate name or logo. The key is that the use of the name or logo indicates to the public the particular business behind it. In the case of a trader in goods, all that is required is to demonstrate that the public recognises his goods as emanating from a particular trade source. It is not necessary to show that the public is aware of the name or identity of the source of the goods. This has long been recognised. The point was argued in *Birmingham Vinegar Brewery Co v Powell*[1] (the *'Yorkshire Relish'* case) where Lord Herschell dealt with the submission in this way:

'I think the fallacy of the appellants' argument rests on this: that it is assumed that one trader cannot be passing off his goods as the manufacture of another unless it be shown that the persons purchasing the goods know of the manufacturer by name, and have in their mind when they purchase the goods that they are made by a particular individual. It seems to me that one man may quite well pass off his goods as the goods of another if he passes them off to people who will accept them as the manufacture of another, though they do not know that other by name at all.'[2]

This approach was apparently taken a stage further in *Bristol Conservatories Ltd v Conservatories Custom Built Ltd*[3] where the Court of Appeal held that by using photographs of the plaintiff's products with a claim that they were products of the defendant the defendant simultaneously created goodwill to the plaintiff in the mind of the person to whom the photographs were shown and misappropriated it by the implicit claim that the skill and experience of the plaintiff in making the product was properly attributable to the defendant.

---

1   [1897] AC 710.
2   Ibid at 715. The same point is also made in *Oertli v Bowman* [1959] RPC 1; *Jarman & Platt v Barget* [1977] FSR 260 at 272; *William Edge & Sons Ltd v Niccolls & Sons Ltd* [1911] AC 693, 80 LJ Ch 744; *Hoffman la Roche v DDSA Pharmaceuticals* [1969] FSR 410 at 419 and *Plomien Fuel Economiser Co Ltd v National School of Salesmanship Ltd* (1943) 60 RPC 209 at 214.
3   [1989] RPC 455.

SHARED OR DIVIDED REPUTATION AND GOODWILL

3.07   The traditional form of statement of claim in a passing off action alleges that the identifying characteristic means to the the public the goods or business of 'the plaintiff *and none other*'. However, there is no authority for the proposition that this is an essential requirement of the action.[1] Indeed, in a variety of circumstances reputation and goodwill in a name, mark or get-up may be shared or divided amongst a number of different people. The best known form of shared goodwill is that which subsists in descriptive 'class' marks such as *Champagne,*[2] *Sherry,*[3] *Advocaat*[4] or *Scotch Whisky.*[5] In such cases the essence of the reputation and goodwill is that the mark is descriptive of a defined class of products which are identified by its use. There are two principal problems likely to be encountered by claimants wishing to bring such proceedings. The first is to arrive at an exposition of the nature of the product which is both clear (ie the boundaries of which are clearly defined) and covers all the accepted members of the class. It is no coincidence that in the first three cases of this type the goods came from a precisely determined geographical area. This makes it easy to see that anyone who uses the description on goods from another locality must be misusing it. In the subsequent extension of the principle in the *Advocaat* case to a class of goods defined only by its ingredients and method of manufacture, the facts were extremely clear and there could be no doubt whether the proper ingredients and process were being used. It is not difficult to find examples of product descriptions which, whilst prima facie clear, turn out to have very flexible boundaries. In such cases the courts will probably conclude that it is not possible to divide those entitled to benefit from the goodwill from those who are not. The second problem is that unless the members of the class act effectively to protect their descriptive name, it is likely to be used by others not properly entitled to do so, destroying the exclusivity of use by the true class members. Both the *Champagne* and *Sherry* litigation arose from such misuse on a substantial scale. Indeed the *Sherry* case was an action brought by the producers of 'British Sherry' for a declaration that they were entitled to continue to use that designation on products not emanating from Jerez in Spain which was granted on the ground that the Spanish sherry producers were held to have lost their right to complain of the use of that term as a result of their acquiescence over a long period.[6] In such cases the defendants will of course only be prevented from applying the name to goods not of the appropriate description.[7]

---

1 Farwell J's statement in *Aerators Ltd v Tollitt* [1902] 2 Ch 319 at 325 that the plaintiff must show his name is 'exclusively associated with his own manufacture' which has been thought to support the proposition is in fact not to the point being concerned only with the question whether the name in issue was descriptive or distinctive.
2 [1960] Ch 262, [1960] RPC 16; (No 2) [1961] 1 All ER 561, [1961] RPC 116.
3 [1969] RPC 1; (No 2) [1968] FSR 625.
4 [1979] AC 731, [1980] RPC 31.
5 [1970] 2 All ER 106, [1970] RPC 489.
6 See paras 2.30–2.31 and 4.10 for further discussion of these cases.
7 See para 7.49 for a discussion of the relief granted.

3.08 Descriptive class marks are not the only examples of divided goodwill. In *Dent v Turpin*[1] two separate firms of watchmakers were held to be entitled to prevent a third firm from using the name 'Dent'. In *Shell-Mex & BP Limited and Aladdin Industries Ltd v Holmes*[2] the plaintiffs were engaged in a joint venture to market paraffin coloured pink under the name 'Aladdin'. It was held that they were entitled jointly to bring suit. In other circumstances goodwill may be divided between different traders, operating for example in different geographical areas. In *Parker & Son (Reading) Ltd v Parker*[3] the plaintiff, an estate agent, was held entitled to an interlocutory injunction to prevent the defendant's use of the the name 'Parkers' notwithstanding the existence of other estate agents called 'Parker' in different towns (who might also have goodwill in the name 'Parker' in those towns). Where goodwill is shared, plaintiffs may bring proceedings jointly,[1] separately[3] or in a representative capacity.[4]

---

1 (1861) 2 John & H 139, 30 LJ Ch 495.
2 (1937) 54 RPC 287.
3 [1965] RPC 323.
4 *Bollinger SA v Goldwell Ltd* [1971] RPC 412, [1971] FSR 405. This approach has also been followed in many other subsequent cases.

Acquisition, extent and duration of reputation

ACQUISITION

3.09 The only way to acquire a reputation in a mark, name or other 'indicium' is to use it in connection with the carrying on of a business. Having said this it is not possible to lay down hard and fast rules as to the extent of the use required to establish a reputation which will support a passing off claim. With sufficient effort it is possible to acquire an extensive reputation in a very short period of time. Large-scale national advertising can bring a trader's goods to the notice of most of the public in a matter of days. However, that is not necessary to bring a claim. There have been many cases in which relatively little use of a name by the plaintiff has been held sufficient to support a claim in passing off. In *Stannard v Reay*[1] a mere 3 weeks' use of the words 'Mr Chippy' for a mobile fish and chip business was held sufficient for the granting of interlocutory relief. In *W H Allen & Co v Brown Watson Ltd*[2] a month and a half's heavy advertising was held to be sufficient to have rendered the title of a book distinctive of the plaintiff. And in *Elida Gibbs v Colgate-Palmolive*[3] the court was prepared to grant relief even before the plaintiff's advertising campaign had been launched to the public on the basis of pre-launch trade publicity. Equally there have been many cases in which limited user has been held to be insufficient to support a claim. Unsurprisingly in *Licensed Victuallers Newspapers Ltd v Bingham*[4] 3 days' circulation of a magazine with the title 'The Licensed Victualler's Mirror' was held insufficient and in *Maxwell v Hogg*,[5] 3 months' advertising was held not to have made the magazine title 'Belgravia' distinctive. More recently, in *County Sound v Ocean Sound*,[6] 8 months' use of the descriptive title 'The Gold AM' for a radio programme playing old pop songs was held insufficient to render the name distinctive.

---

1   [1967] RPC 587.
2   [1965] RPC 191.
3   [1982] FSR 95.
4   (1888) 38 Ch D 139, 58 LJ Ch 36.
5   (1867) 2 Ch App 307, 33 LJ Ch 433. Applied in *Marcus Publishing plc v Hutton-Wild Communications Ltd* [1990] RPC 576.
6   [1991] FSR 367.

EXTENT

3.10   Reputation may be acquired by user restricted to a small geographical area. Generally this will mean that the reputation is correspondingly restricted.[1] However, this is not necessarily so. If customers travel large distances to avail themselves of the plaintiff's goods or services the reputation may extend over a wider area.[2] Even if the plaintiff's reputation is geographically limited it is possible that to protect that reputation an injunction extending over a wider area is necessary.[3]

---

1   This is usually the case with businesses such as local restaurants and hotels. Examples are *The Clock Ltd v The Clock House Hotel Ltd* (1936) 53 RPC 269 and *Clouds Restaurant Limited v Y Hotel Ltd* (1982) Dillon J (unreported but referred to in *Chelsea Man Menswear Ltd v Chelsea Girl Ltd* [1987] RPC 189 at 199).
2   See eg *Brestian v Try* [1958] RPC 161 and ch 7, para 7.49 below.

3 See *Chelsea Man Menswear Ltd v Chelsea Girl Ltd* supra. This point is fully considered in para 7.49 below.

THE NEED FOR GOODWILL TO BE IN THIS COUNTRY

3.11 It has always been a fundamental requirement of passing off that the plaintiff establishes that he has a reputation residing in goodwill which exists in this country. That can only be acquired by user here. Jenkins LJ, giving the judgment of the court in *Oertli AG v Bowman (London) Ltd*, gave the classic exposition of the requirement in these terms:

'It is of course essential to the success of any claim in respect of passing off based upon the use of a given mark or get-up that the plaintiff should be able to show that disputed mark or get-up has become by user in this country distinctive of the plaintiff's goods so that the use in relation to any goods of the kind dealt in by the plaintiff of that mark or get-up will be understood by the trade and the public in this country as meaning that the goods are the plaintiff's goods.'[1]

However, this does not mean that a manufacturer or importer of foreign made goods has to have a place of business in this country. It is sufficient that the goods are available here and that accordingly there are customers in whom the goodwill can reside. In *Anciens Etablissements Panhard et Levassor SA v Panhard-Levassor*,[2] at the beginning of this century, the plaintiffs were French motor car manufacturers. They had not themselves exported cars to this country or sold them here. Despite this it was held that the use of the name on cars bought by other people abroad and brought by them into this country was sufficient to establish the plaintiffs' reputation here on the footing that as a result of such importation 'England was one of their markets'. Twenty years later, in *Poirot v Jules Poirot and Nash*,[3] Lawrence J said: 'Paul Poirot is in my judgment in the circumstances of this case entitled to protect his goods and the reputation he has acquired in this country notwithstanding the fact that he has not got a place of business here.' A further sixty years later Walton J, in *Athletes Foot Marketing Associates v Cobra Sports Ltd*,[4] reached virtually the same conclusion saying:

'... it would appear to me that, as a matter of principle, no trader can complain of passing off against him in any territory — and it will usually be defined by national boundaries, although it is well conceivable in the modern world that it will not — in which he has no customers, nobody who is in trade relation with him. This will normally shortly be expressed by saying that he does not carry on any trade in that particular country (obviously, for present purposes, England and Wales) but the inwardness of it will be that he has no customers in that country: no people who buy his goods or make use of his services (as the case may be) there.'[5]

He expressed this view before going on to carry out a comprehensive review of the authorities at the end of which he concluded that they led to the conclusion that:

'It does not matter that the plaintiffs are not at present actually carrying on business in this country provided that they have customers here. Equally, it is of no moment, if they have no customers here, that they have a reputation in the general sense of the word in this country. It is also of no moment that that reputation may have been brought about by advertising: this can be of no moment unless (as it did in the *C & A* case) it brings in customers, when, of course, once again there is no need to rely upon it.'[6]

The members of the Court of Appeal in the *Budweiser*[7] case regarded the presence of customers in this country as the key to the question whether the requisite goodwill had been established and Oliver LJ in particular thought Walton J's finding helpful but pointed out that it:

'... needs, in the light of authorities, to be approached with the caveat that "customers" must not be read restrictively as confined to persons who are in a direct contractual relationship with the plaintiff, but includes the persons who buy his goods in the market.'[8]

---

1 [1957] RPC 388 at 397 (CA); affirmed on appeal to the House of Lords at [1959] RPC 1.
2 [1901] 2 Ch 513, 18 RPC 405.
3 (1920) 37 RPC 177.
4 [1980] RPC 343.
5 Ibid at 350.
6 Ibid at 357.
7 *Anheuser-Busch Inc v Budejovicky Budvar Narodni Podnik* [1984] FSR 413.
8 Ibid at 465.

3.12   The cases discussed in the previous paragraph were all concerned with traders in goods. In such cases the question of whether a trader has a business here is ultimately answered by determining whether his goods are available in this country. The problem of what constitutes the carrying on of a business here arises in its most acute form in relation to providers of services. It is difficult as a matter of logic to see how a person who provides services only outside this country can be said to be carrying on a business here, even if some of his customers are habitually resident here. They must travel abroad to obtain the service. What is required to constitute a business in this country has been addressed in a number of cases. In *Sheraton Corporation of America v Sheraton Motels*,[1] the plaintiffs were hoteliers whose hotels were all situated abroad. The name 'Sheraton' was known in this country in connection with hotels only through people travelling abroad, advertisements circulating here and bookings taken through an office they maintained in London and through travel agencies. Buckley J was prepared on the basis of these facts to grant an interlocutory injunction restraining the use of the name Sheraton by the defendants. Shortly afterwards Pennycuick J, distinguishing the *Sheraton* case, refused to grant an interlocutory injunction restraining the use of the name 'The Crazy Horse Saloon' at the suit of the proprietor of a place of entertainment of that name in Paris notwithstanding the fact that the plaintiff had advertised in England for many years and presumably derived significant custom from recipients of that advertising who travelled to Paris.[2] The distinction between these two cases is more apparent than real. Although it appears now to be firmly established as English law, there has been considerable judicial dissatisfaction with it, particularly in other common law jurisdictions. In an Australian case, *Fletcher Challenge v Fletcher Challenge Pty*,[3] Powell J held that: 'the relevant question is, "does the plaintiff have the necessary reputation?," rather than "does the plaintiff itself carry on business here?" ' and refused to follow *Crazy Horse*. In an Irish case, *C & A Modes v C & A (Waterford) Ltd*,[4] Findlay J said specifically:

> 'I would disapprove the distinction arising in *Alain Bernadin et Cie v Pavilion Properties Ltd* [the *Crazy Horse* case] between user arising from some actual commercial activity carried out within the jurisdiction of the court and user arising from advertisement and publicity distributed within the jurisdiction of the court and resulting in the attraction of persons from there to make use of the business or services of the plaintiff company. Therefore, I am satisifed that the absence of a retail outlet or agency within the Republic of Ireland owned or operated by the plaintiffs is not a bar to their action for passing off.'

Until recently, in England only Graham J[5] had expressed a dislike for the distinction. However, Browne-Wilkinson VC further reviewed the position in *Pete Waterman Ltd v CBS United Kingdom Ltd*.[6] As he pointed out:

> 'The changes in the second half of the 20th century . . . have produced worldwide marks, worldwide goodwill and brought separate markets into competition one with the other. Radio and television with their attendant advertising cross national frontiers. Electronic communication via satellite produces virtually instant communication between all markets. In terms of travel time, New York by air is as close as Aberdeen by rail. This has led to the development of the international reputation in certain names, particularly in the service fields, for example Sheraton Hotels, Budget Rent A Car.
> In my view, the law will fail if it does not try to meet the challenge thrown up by trading patterns which cross national and jurisdictional boundaries due to a change in technical achievement.'[7]

In the light of this he took the view that, untrammelled by authority, he could see no reason why the courts of this country could not protect the trading relationship between a foreign trader and his customers here, wherever his goodwill is situated. However, he then considered in full the cases cited above and concluded that there was binding authority to the effect that the basis of the plaintiff's claim must be a goodwill locally situate in England. As to that he said:

> 'The presence of customers in this country is sufficient to constitute the carrying on of business here whether or not there is otherwise a place of business here and whether or not the services are provided here. Once it is found that there are customers, it is open to find that there is a business here to which the local goodwill is attached.'[8]

He specifically commented that to the extent that the *Crazy Horse* case is authority to the contrary he preferred not to follow it. The Hong Kong High Court has also taken a similar approach.[9]

---

1 [1964] RPC 202.

2 *Alain Bernadin et Compagnie v Pavilion Properties Ltd* [1967] RPC 581, [1967] FSR 341. Followed in *Amway Corporation v Eurway International Limited* [1974] RPC 82. See also the discussion of this point in *Globelegance BV v Sarkissian* [1974] RPC 603.

3   [1982] FSR 1.
4   [1978] FSR 126 at 135; approved by the Irish CA at 139, 141.
5   See his decisions in *Baskin-Robbins Ice Cream Co v Gutman* [1976] FSR 545 and *Maxim's v Dye* [1977]
    1 WLR 1155, [1978] 2 All ER 55. The latter is a particularly unsatisfactory authority being an
    application for judgment in default of defence on which the defendant was unrepresented and
    in which all the facts pleaded in the statement of claim must be presumed to be true.
6   [1993] EMLR 27.
7   Ibid at 50–51.
8   Ibid at 58.
9   *Tan-Ichi Co Ltd v Jancar Ltd* [1990] FSR 151.

REPUTATION AS BETWEEN FOREIGN MANUFACTURER AND IMPORTER

3.13   It follows that in the case of imported goods, the reputation in the
trade marks used is in all cases the reputation acquired in this country and
not abroad.[1] Disputes not infrequently arise between the manufacturer and
importer over who is entitled to the reputation in England. At common law
as a general rule the owner of the reputation is the foreign manufacturer and
not the importer[2] even if the importer is the sole agent or distributor in this
country of the goods in question.[3] Thus in *Goodfellow v Prince*[4] the plaintiff, who
was the sole importer of champagne under the label 'Le Court et Cie, Reims',
was held not to have a reputation in that name which enabled him to prevent
others importing champagne of the same manufacture under it.[5] Similarly in
A/B Manus v R J Fullwood & Bland Ltd[6] it was held that the reputation in the
word 'Manus' belonged to the Swedish manufacturer and not to the importer
of his goods into England.

1   See also, for a much earlier statement of the principle, *Sturtevant Engineering Co Ltd v Sturtevant Mill
    Co. of USA Ltd* [1936] 3 All ER 137, 53 RPC 430.
2   Ibid; *Suhner & Co AG v Suhner Ltd* [1967] RPC 336. Many of the cases referred to in the preceding
    two paragraphs are examples of this phenomenon although the dispute there was not with the
    importer of particular goods. See in particular *Poirot v Poirot, Anciens Etablissements Panhard et Levassor
    v Panhard-Levassor* and *Sheraton*.
3   *Dental Manufacturing Co Ltd v De Trey & Co* [1912] 3 KB 76, 29 RPC 617; *Roberts Numbering Machinery
    Co. Ltd v Davis* (1935) 53 RPC 79.
4   (1887) 35 Ch D 9, 56 LJ Ch 545.
5   See also *Van Zeller v Mason Cattley & Co* (1908) 25 RPC 37.
6   [1949] Ch 208, 1 All ER 205.

3.14   However, in some cases the importer has been held to be entitled
to the reputation in the mark concerned. This will generally only occur in
unusual circumstances, such as where the importer is perceived by the public
as the true source of the goods, the fact that they have been manufactured by
someone else being unknown to the purchasers and thus irrelevant. Thus, in
J Defries & Sons Ltd v Electric and Ordnance Accessories Co Ltd[1] the defendants
had acquired the business of the importers of lamps made to the importers'
order in the USA and sold under the mark 'Stewart'. In an action brought
by the US manufacturers it was held that the defendants and not the
plaintiffs were entitled to the reputation in the mark. A case similar in

principle — although here the goods were made in England under licence from the foreign manufacturer — is *Oertli v Bowman*,[2] where the plaintiffs had granted the defendants an exclusive manufacturing licence to make and sell machines under the mark 'Turmix' without first having imported any significant quantities of machines made by them abroad. The plaintiffs exercised no control over the manufacture of machines by the defendants during the term of the licence[3] and it was held that the plaintiffs had accordingly acquired no reputation in the name, nothing having been done by the parties to make the mark distinctive of the plaintiffs. The defendants were accordingly entitled to continue to use the mark after termination of the licence for non-payment of royalties. It has also been held that where the right to marks belonging to foreign manufacturers passed to the Custodian of Enemy Property in the Second World War, the reputation and goodwill is enjoyed by the purchaser of the goodwill in the British business, not the foreign manufacturer (or any person who has acquired his business).[4] The modern approach to such problems is of course potentially considerably affected by the provisions of EC law[5] and the now commonplace activity of parallel importation of goods made by multinational companies.[6]

---

1   (1906) 23 RPC 341.
2   [1959] RPC 1 (HL).
3   Rendering the UK trade mark registration invalid under the provisions of section 28 of the Trade Marks Act 1938.
4   *R J Reuter Co Ltd v Muhlens* [1954] Ch 50, 70 RPC 235 (CA); *Adrema Werke Maschinenbau GmbH v The Custodian of Enemy Property* [1957] RPC 49.
5   This subject is dealt with in ch 10.
6   See paras 4.26–4.27 below.

RESIDUAL REPUTATION

3.15   Reputation is essentially ephemeral. As Lord Parker put it in *Spalding Bros v A W Gamage*:

> 'Even in the case of what are sometimes referred to as common law marks the property if any of the so-called owner is of its nature transitory and only exists so long as the mark is distinctive of the goods.'[1]

However, unless the trade under the mark has been positively abandoned,[2] the reputation attached to it does not die immediately the business ceases to be carried on. Generally there will continue to be a reputation and goodwill under any mark which has been substantially used for some time after the cessation of its user. That residual goodwill can be relied upon to support an action for passing off. The residual goodwill may subsist for a considerable period if the plaintiff takes specific steps to keep it alive. In *Ad-Lib Club v Granville*,[3] the plaintiffs successfully relied upon the reputation in the name of their night club 4 years after it had been forced to close because of the nuisance caused by the noise it made, there being evidence that publicity had been given to the fact that the plaintiffs were seeking to re-open the club. And in *Thermawear v Vedonis*[4] the plaintiffs' residual reputation in the mark 'Thermawear' acquired through extensive use of the mark up to a date 5 years before the date of the writ was held sufficient to support a claim for passing off where the name remained part of the plaintiff's corporate title. However, in *Norman Kark Publications v Odhams Press Ltd*[5] it was held that the plaintiffs had made no effort to preserve any reputation in their title *Today* which had therefore become *communis juris.*

---

1 [1914] 2 Ch 405, 31 RPC 421, 83 LJ Ch 855.
2 In which case the trader will be taken to have abandoned the goodwill also. See *Star Industrial Co Ltd v Yap Kwee Kor* [1976] FSR 256 (PC).
3 [1971] 2 All ER 300, [1972] RPC 673.
4 [1982] RPC 44.
5 [1962] RPC 163.

The distinguishing indicia

INTRODUCTION

3.16 In principle the distinguishing indicia upon which a trader can rely in a passing off claim may consist of almost any aspect of the presentation of his products or services. The indicia may, however, be conveniently divided into a number of classes. First, and most obviously, are trade and service marks. The expression 'mark' is defined in The Trade Marks Act, 1938[1] as including:

'a device, brand, heading, label, ticket, name, signature, word, letter, numeral, or any combination thereof'

and that definition is equally applicable to unregistered trade and service marks. A trade or service mark is also defined for the purposes of the Trade Marks Act, 1938.[1] With slight modification the definition is also appropriate for unregistered marks:

'A mark used ... in relation to goods [or services] for the purpose of indicating, or so as to indicate, a connection in the course of trade between the goods [or services] and some person having the right ... to use the mark, whether with or without any indication of the identity of that person.'

For simplicity the categories of marks which require separate consideration are words, letter and numbers, and devices. These are each considered separately below. The remaining categories of mark mentioned in the definition are either ways of presenting marks of those principal types or alternatively fall to be considered as part of the get-up of the goods or services. Word marks may consist either of fancy or invented words, that is existing or newly coined words which have no direct reference to any characteristic of the goods or services to which they are applied or of words which are more or less descriptive. Word marks of these two types are treated very differently by the courts, as is explained below. Other than marks, a trader may also rely upon the get-up of his goods or services. Get-up is a wide ranging and flexible concept covering the appearance of almost any aspect of a product, or its packaging and other promotional and business documents. The nature of get-up and the manner of its protection are also examined in detail.

---

1 S 68(1). Whilst these definitions have now been superseded by the definition in s 1 of the Trade Marks Act 1994 (see ch 9, para 9.03), they are entirely sufficient for present purposes.

WORD MARKS

Fancy and invented words

3.17 If a word mark is a 'fancy' word (that is one having no reference to the character or quality of the goods) or an invented word (that is one devised for the express purpose of distinguishing the plaintiff's goods from those of other traders) it is relatively easy to prove a reputation in the mark. The same is true of surnames. There can be little or no purpose in another trader adopting such mark save to obtain the benefit of the plaintiff's reputation. The position is of course different in relation to marks which refer either to the geographical origin of the goods or to some aspect of their character or quality. The acquisition of a reputation in such marks is discussed in detail below but it is self evident that, prima facie, the effect of such terms in relation to particular goods will be to identify their qualities or geographical origin rather than to designate a particular trade origin for them. This inherent ability of fancy or invented words to distinguish the goods of one trader from those of others has often been remarked upon by the courts. In *Cellular Clothing Co v Maxton and Murray*,[1] Lord Shand put it this way:

> 'There is a vital distinction in cases of this class between invented or fancy words or names, or the names of individuals such as 'Crowley' or 'Crowley Millington' attached by a manufacturer to his goods and stamped on the articles manufactured, and words or names which are simply descriptive of the article manufactured or sold. The idea of an invented or fancy word used as a name is that it has no relation, and at least no direct relation, to the character or quality of the goods that are to be sold under that name. There is no room whatever for what may be called a secondary meaning in regard to such words. . . . The word used and attached to the manufacture being an invented or fancy name, and not descriptive, it follows that if any other person proceeds to use that name in the sale of his goods it is almost, if not altogether, impossible to avoid the inference that he is seeking to pass off his goods as the goods of the other manufacturer.'

Whilst it is easy in principle to divide marks into the different classes mentioned by Lord Shand, his reference to 'at least no direct relation' highlights the fact, almost axiomatic in marketing, that the best marks to choose are those which, whilst not overtly descriptive of the goods to which they are applied, nevertheless make a 'covert and skilful allusion'[2] to their character. There is frequently considerable debate into which class of marks a particular word falls.[3] Nevertheless, the courts are relatively willing to find that a reputation has been acquired in relation to marks which are not directly descriptive of the goods to which they are applied.

---

1 [1899] AC 326 at 338–339.
2 Per Lord Macnaghton in *Eastman Photographic Materials Co Ltd v Comptroller-General of Patents Designs and Trade Marks (Re Solio* trade mark) [1898] AC 571 at 583.
3 See eg *Thermawear v Vedonis Ltd* [1982] RPC 44.

Proper names

3.18 Traders often adopt proper names, sometimes not their own, as trade marks or trading names. These are of course the epitome of marks intended to denote trade origin. They are inherently distinctive, at least as regards distinguishing people of the same name from people of other names and will readily be found by the courts to be distinctive of the particular trader by whom they have been used. There are many such claims and the following are merely examples: 'Annabel's' for a night club,[1] 'Albert Hall' for the concert hall,[2] 'Wright's' for a shop[3] and 'Osborne House' for a cheesemongers.[4] Because proper names do not in themselves distinguish between persons of the same name peculiar difficulties arise if the defendant's name is the same as the plaintiff's.[5] Individuals carrying on a profession or vocation are entitled to protect their names by making a claim of passing off.[6] This has been specifically held in the case of authors,[7] artists,[8] broadcasters,[9] journalists,[10] cartoonists[11] and actors.[12] Whilst there are no examples of other professions bringing proceedings for passing off in their own names, there is no reason in principle why individual doctors, lawyers, architects and others should not also do so. This will apply even in cases where the plaintiff may have assigned other rights in works put out under his name. In *Archbold v Sweet*[13] the plaintiff was able to prevent a publisher from using his name for an inaccurate edition of his work even though the publisher owned the copyright in it.

---

1   *Annabel's (Berkeley Square) v Schock* [1972] RPC 838.
2   *Hall of Arts and Sciences Corporation v Hall* (1934) 50 TLR 518.
3   *Wright, Layman and Umney v Wright* (1949) 66 RPC 149.
4   *Hudson v Osborne* (1869) 39 LJ Ch 79, 21 LT 386.
5   See paras 4.36–4.40 below.
6   Some of the cases referred to in this paragraph concern assumed names which are dealt with specifically in para 3.20 below. The principles are the same.
7   *Lord Byron v Johnson* (1816) 2 Mer 29.
8   *Martin v Wright* (1833) 6 Sim 297.
9   *McCulloch v Lewis A May (Produce Distributors) Ltd* [1947] 2 All ER 845, 65 RPC 58.
10 *Forbes v Kemsley Newspapers Ltd* [1951] TLR 656, 68 RPC 183.
11 *Marengo v Daily Sketch and Sunday Graphic Ltd* (1948) 65 RPC 242 (HL); the CA judgment in this case was recently reported at [1992] FSR 1.
12 *Hines v Winnick* [1947] Ch 708, 64 RPC 113.
13 (1832) 5 C & P 219, 1 Mood & R 162.

3.19 Where the name chosen is that of a particular person employed or engaged in the trading enterprise, the question not infrequently arises whether he or the enterprise is entitled to the goodwill in the name after he leaves it. This is always a question of fact and no general rule can be laid down although there are many examples of such cases. In *Birmingham Vinegar Brewery Co v Liverpool Vinegar Co*[1] the plaintiffs made and sold 'Holbrook's Sauce', the deviser of which had been a Mr Holbrook, one of the plaintiffs' employees. He left the plaintiff's employment and joined the defendants who sought to sell a sauce to the same recipe under his name. It was held that the reputation in the name belonged to the plaintiffs and not to Mr Holbrook.[2] However, in *Franke v Chappell*[3] the plaintiffs had organised a number of concerts known as 'Richter's Concerts' and conducted by Herr Richter. It was held that they had no right to that name which meant concerts conducted by Herr Richter and not concerts organised by them. *Ward v Beeton*[4] was a similar case in which Beeton was employed by the plaintiff following the sale to him of Beeton's publishing business. This business had published a work called 'Beeton's Christmas Annual' which continued to be published after the sale of the business. The terms of Beeton's employment gave the plaintiff the right to use his name for present and future publications and obliged him not to grant permission for its use to others without the plaintiff's consent. It was held that the plaintiff was entitled to publish under that name a work in whose preparation Beeton had not been concerned.

---

1   (1888) WN 139, 4 TLR 613.
2   There are many other similar cases. See for example: *W H Dorman & Co Ltd v Meadows Ltd* [1922] 2 Ch 332, 91 LJ Ch 728; *Bentley Motors v Lagonda Ltd and Bentley* (1946) 64 RPC 33; *Dence v Mason* (1878) WN 42, 41 LT 573; *Warner v Warner* (1889) 5 TLR 327 at 359.
3   (1887) 57 LT 141, 3 TLR 524.
4   (1874) LR 19 Eq 207.

3.20 *Assumed names and noms-de-plume.*   There is no difference in principle between real proper names and assumed names, nicknames or noms-de-plume if these have been adopted or used in the course of trade. Authors, composers, artists and actors can and do rely upon their stage or professional names in precisely the same way as they would be entitled to if they used their real names in the course of the business. There are many examples of such actions and the following are illustrative: 'Kim' for a cartoonist,[1] 'Dr Crock' (of 'Dr Crock and his Crackpots') for an actor on a radio programme,[2] 'Ben Sarto' for an author[3] and 'Aunt Naomi',[4] 'Mary Delane'[5] and 'Pierpoint'[6] for journalists. In such cases the dispute is often between a writer, usually a journalist, and his or her employer as to who owns the reputation in the name. The cases referred to establish that in the absence of special terms the reputation will accrue for the benefit of the author. Publishers who wish to ensure that they gain the benefit of such reputation should ensure that their contracts of employment are drawn appropriately.

---

1 *Marengo v Daily Sketch and Sunday Graphic Ltd* (1948) 65 RPC 242 (HL); the CA judgment in this case is reported at [1992] FSR 1.
2 *Hines v Winnick* [1947] Ch 708, [1947] 2 All ER 517.
3 *Modern Fiction Ltd v Fawcett Ltd* (1949) 66 RPC 230.
4 *Landa v Greenberg* (1908) 24 TLR 441.
5 *Forbes v Kemsley Newspapers Ltd* (1951) 68 RPC 183.
6 *Sykes v Fairfax & Sons* [1978] FSR 312 (an Australian case).

Considerations common to fancy and invented words and proper names

3.21 *Acquired descriptive meaning.* The fact that a word, when originally adopted, bore no descriptive meaning in relation to the goods to which it is applied does not mean that it cannot over time acquire a descriptive meaning. There are many well-known examples of words which started life as invented trade marks for novel goods but were then used descriptively by the public for goods of that type. *Aspirin, Hoover, Formica* and *Jeep* readily spring to mind. The proprietors of such marks often expend considerable time and effort in ensuring that the descriptive use does not deprive them of the distinctiveness the names originally possessed but they are not always successful. In *Linoleum Manufacturing Co v Nairn*[1] the plaintiffs used the invented word 'Linoleum' as the name of their new product. Fry J held that this word had become descriptive of the product and thus no longer distinctive of the plaintiff's goods:

> 'The plaintiffs have alleged . . . that having invented a new substance, namely, the solidified or oxidised oil, they gave it the name of "Linoleum" and it does not appear that any other name has ever been given to this substance. It appears that the defendants are now minded to make, as it is admitted they may make, that substance. I want to know what they are to call it. This is a question I have asked, but I have received no answer for this simple reason, that no answer could be given, except that they must invent a new name. I do not take that to be the law. I think that if *Linoleum* means a substance which may be made by the defendant, the defendants may sell it by the name which that substance bears.'

There were similar results in cases concerned with the fancy or invented words 'Chlorodyne' for a medicine,[2] 'Dolly Blue' for a laundry blue,[3] 'Star' for bicycles[4] and 'Magnolia' for a metal alloy.[5] There are equally many examples of proper names used as trade marks which have become associated with the type of goods rather than their trade source. In *Lazenby v White*[6] the name 'Harvey's Sauce' was held to have become descriptive of the type of sauce supplied by the plaintiff and not distinctive of the plaintiff as supplier. A similar result was obtained for the name 'Lieutenant James' Horse Blister' (a liniment for treating horses)[7] although the defendant was restrained from claiming his was the 'original' or signing it with the actual name of the inventor of the product even though that was his name too. Other examples of cases in which apparently distinctive marks have been held to be descriptive, at least in some circumstances, are 'Leibig's extract of beef',[8] 'Armstrong Oiler' (descriptive when used as 'Armstrong type oiler')[9] and 'Winser's Interceptor' (for a particular design of sewer trap).[10] A mark originally distinctive will inevitably become descriptive of the type of goods to which it is applied if others are licensed to manufacture and sell them under the mark unless the use of the mark is controlled so as in fact to associate the licensed goods with the licensor. This happened to the name 'Bowden Wire'.[11]

1   (1878) 7 Ch D 834 at 866.
2   *Browne v Freeman* (1864) 12 WR 305; *(No 2)* [1873] WN 178.
3   *Edge & Sons Ltd v Gallon & Son* (1899) 16 RPC 509, affd (1900) 17 RPC 557 (HL).
4   *Star Cycle Co v Frankenburgs* (1907) 25 RPC 405.
5   *Magnolia Metal Co v The Atlas Metal Co* (1897) 14 RPC 389; *Magnolia Metal Co v Tandem Smelting Syndicate Co* (1898) 15 RPC 701, 17 RPC 477 (HL).
6   (1870) 6 Ch App 89, 19 WR 291.
7   *James v James* (1872) LR 13 Eq 421.
8   *Leibig's Extract of Meat Co Ltd v Hanbury* (1867) 17 LT 298.
9   *Armstrong Oiler Co v Patent Axlebox and Foundry Co* (1910) 27 RPC 362.
10 *Winser v Armstrong & Co* (1899) 16 RPC 167.
11 *Bowden Wire Ltd v Bowden Brake Co Ltd* (1913) 30 RPC 45, 580 (CA), (1914) 31 RPC 385 (HL).

3.22   In *Ford v Foster*,[1] the Court of Appeal considered and rejected the defendants' argument that the plaintiffs' mark 'Eureka' had become descriptive of a particular shape of shirt and had thus ceased to be distinctive of the shirts of the plaintiff's manufacture. Mellish LJ set out the test for determining whether or not this was so in the following passage:

> 'The question is, has [the mark "Eureka"] become *publici juris*?. There is no doubt, I think, that a word which was originally a trade mark to the exclusive use of which a particular trader, or his successors in trade may have been entitled, may subsequently become *publici juris*. ... Then what is the test by which a decision is to be arrived at whether a word which was originally a trade mark has become *publici juris*? I think the test must be, whether it may still have the effect of inducing the public to buy goods not made by the original owner of the trade mark as if they were his goods. If the mark has come to be so public and in such universal use that nobody can be deceived by the use of it, and can be induced from the use of it to believe that he is buying the goods of the original trader, it appears to me ... that the right to the trade mark must be gone.'

There are many other cases in which originally distinctive fancy or invented word marks have been challenged on the ground that they have become descriptive and thus free for public use. In *Treasure Cot v Hamleys*[2] Harman J, following the approach set out by Mellish LJ in *Ford v Foster*, held that the word 'Treasure' remained a fancy word in relation to a cot, although perhaps descriptive of the inmate. Similar arguments were also rejected in *Wellcome (t/a Burroughs Wellcome & Co) v Thompson & Capper*[3] in relation to the word 'Tabloids' for compressed drugs and in *Procea Products Ltd v Evans & Sons Ltd*[4] for 'Procea' for processed bread. There are also many examples of unsuccessful arguments that proper names applied to the plaintiff's goods have become associated with the particular type of goods supplied by the plaintiff rather than the plaintiff's manufacture. In *Massam v Thorley's Cattle Food*,[5] James LJ rejected a claim that the term 'Thorley's cattle Food' used by the plaintiffs had come to denote a particular recipe rather in the following terms:

> 'The recipe is said to have been purchased by the original Thorley and "Thorley's Food for Cattle", according to my view does not mean food consisting of particular ingredients, or made up according to a particular recipe, because no purchaser would know or care about that. "Thorley's Food for Cattle" means that food which for many years was manufactured at works belonging to Joseph Thorley, and afterwards was manufactured by his executors carrying on business at the same works. . . . That, in truth, is the meaning and object and result of a trade mark. It indicates this, that you may take this as a warranty that it has come from the particular manufacturer of the goods with which you have been hitherto pleased.'

Similarly in *Bechstein v Barker and Barker*[6] and *Edison Storage Battery Ltd v Britannia Batteries Ltd*[7] claims that the words 'Bechstein' and 'Edison' had become associated with particular types of piano and electric battery respectively were rejected. In *Burberrys v Raper and Pulleyn*,[8] the name 'Burberry' was held to be distinctive of the plaintiffs' manufacture and not descriptive of the type of raincoat. The last three cases have now become striking examples of the potential value and longevity of effectively used proper name marks.

---

1   (1872) 7 Ch App 611 at 628.
2   (1950) 67 RPC 89.
3   [1904] 1 Ch 736.
4   (1951) 68 RPC 210.
5   (1880) 14 Ch D 748 at 755.
6   (1910) 27 RPC 484.
7   (1931) 48 RPC 350.
8   (1906) 23 RPC 170.

3.23 *Acquired descriptive meaning as an accessory or part.*   Particular problems arise with durable goods which are habitually used together with consumable items. Ribbons and toner cartridges for typewriters and printers, film cartridges for cameras and till rolls are all examples of items which generally have to be made in a specific configuration to be suitable for use with any particular manufacturer's product. To enable pattern spares manufacturers and vendors to carry on their trade it is necessary for them to identify the equipment with which their consumables are designed to be used. This almost inevitably requires that equipment to be identified by its trade mark. The Trade Marks Acts make specific provision for such use.[1] However, in passing off cases the problem appears to have been dealt with more pragmatically, although there are no modern examples. In *Gledhill & Sons Ltd v British Perforated Toilet Paper Co*[2] the plaintiffs were manufacturers of cash tills sold under the trade mark 'Gledhill'. It was held that the word 'Gledhill' when applied to paper rolls for tills meant merely rolls suitable for fitting into 'Gledhill' tills and not rolls made or supplied by the plaintiffs. Similarly in *Neostyle Manufacturing Co Ltd v Ellam's Duplicator Co*[3] it was held that 'Neostyle' was distinctive of the plaintiff's duplicating machines but, when applied to paper or accessories for use with those machines, meant simply that such items were suitable for that use and not necessarily that they were supplied by the plaintiffs. However, in *Kodak Ltd v London Stereoscopic and Photographic Co Ltd*[4] the court rejected the argument that 'Kodak' and 'Brownie' when applied to photographic films merely meant films suitable for Kodak and Brownie camera and not necessarily films made by the plaintiff.

---

1 The old law is section 4(3)(b) of the Trade Marks Act 1938, the new section 11(2)(a) of the Trade Marks Act 1994.
2 (1911) 28 RPC 429 and 714 (CA).
3 (1904) 21 RPC 185 and 569 (CA).
4 (1903) 20 RPC 337.

3.24 *Retrieval of distinctiveness.* Because the plaintiff's reputation in his mark depends upon the circumstances of its user at any particular time, it is possible for a mark to lose its distinctive character and become descriptive. It is equally possible that, having done so, the circumstances change again and the mark re-acquires its former distinctiveness. Thus, while in *Singer Machine Manufacturers Co v Wilson*[1] and *Singer Manufacturing Co v Loog*[2] (decided in 1877 and 1882 respectively) it was held that the name 'Singer' was descriptive of the type of sewing machine made by the plaintiffs, when the same plaintiffs later brought an action against British Empire Manufacturing Co[3] in 1903 it was held that, notwithstanding the earlier judgments, the name 'Singer' had again become distinctive of the plaintiffs' goods. Accordingly the defendants were enjoined from using the word 'Singer' for sewing machines not of the plaintiffs' manufacture. Similarly in *Daimler Motor Co (1904) Ltd v London Daimler Co Ltd*[4] the plaintiff having failed in its previous actions to establish the distinctiveness of the word 'Daimler' succeeded and obtained an injunction against the defendants' use of it.

---

1 (1877) 3 App Cas 376, 47 LJ Ch 481.
2 (1882) 8 App Cas 15, 52 LJ Ch 481.
3 *Singer Manufacturing Co v British Empire Manufacturing Co Ltd* (1903) 20 RPC 313.
4 (1907) 24 RPC 379 (CA).

Descriptive words

3.25 *The secondary meaning.* Claims to reputation in words which are in some way descriptive of the goods or services to which they are applied form by far the largest single class of passing off cases. There are two primary categories of descriptive marks, those which refer to some characteristic or quality of the goods or services and those which refer to their geographical origin. Although these might be thought to present fundamentally different legal problems, they in fact have a great deal in common as the development of the case law in relation to shared goodwill in such marks has shown.[1] The most important common characteristic is that to acquire a reputation in descriptive marks it is always necessary to show that the mark has acquired a secondary meaning denoting the trade connection with a particular trader apart from its usual or primary descriptive signification. In his renowned judgment in *Burberrys v Cording*,[2] Parker J expressed the requirement in these words:

'If [the word] has come to distinguish their [ie the plaintiffs'] goods from those of others, it has done so by acquiring a secondary meaning without losing its descriptive character. Though I do not agree with the argument that a word cannot be at the same time both descriptive and distinctive, I think the fact that it retains its *prima facie* descriptive signification increases the difficulty of proving that it is distinctive of the goods of any particular manufacturer.'

It is crucial that Parker J did not think that the word must lose its primary signification before it could become distinctive of the plaintiff. It is this dual ability of such marks both to denote origin and to describe that renders them so valuable. Lord Herschell in *Reddaway v Banham*[3] expressed the same point in this way:

'... a word may acquire in a trade a secondary signification differing from its primary one, and ... if it is used to persons in the trade who will understand it, and be known and intended to understand it in its secondary sense, it will nonetheless be a falsehood that in its primary sense it may be true.'

During the development of the tort the courts were particularly wary of such claims. Lord Shand, in *Cellular Clothing Co v Maxton*[4] put it this way:

'If a person employing a word or term of well-known signification and in ordinary use — though he is not able to obtain a patent for his manufacture, and although he has not got the protection of a registered trade mark for the goods he is proposing to sell — is yet able to acquire the right to appropriate a word or term in ordinary use in the English language to describe his goods, and to shut others out from the use of this descriptive term, he would really acquire a right much more valuable than either a patent or a trade-mark; for he and his successors in business would gain the exclusive right, not for a limited time as in the case of a patent, but for all time coming, to use the words as applicable to goods which others may be desirous of manufacturing, and are entitled to manufacture and sell as much as he is. That being so, it appears to me that the utmost difficulty should be put in the way of anyone who seeks to adopt and use exclusively as his own a merely descriptive term.'

In *Burberrys v Cording & Co Ltd*,[5] Parker J (refusing to hold that the term 'Slip-on' was distinctive of the plaintiff's coats) likened the problem to that facing a trader whose invented name becomes the name of the goods to which he has applied it pointing out that:

'It is dangerous for a trader to allow the word he chooses to become the popular name of the article to which it is applied, and it is dangerous to choose a descriptive word. If the word is descriptive or becomes the name of the article, it will be difficult, if not impossible, to prove that it is distinctive of his own goods, or that there will be any deception in its use by others, and apart from the Trade Marks Act, the right of anyone to the exclusive use of a word is always limited by the possibilities of its use by others without any risk of deception.'

That statement of principle remains as true today as it was when it was made and explains the need to establish that the word has a 'secondary meaning'. The first case in which this principle was expressly applied to geographical marks was *Wotherspoon v Currie*, decided in 1872, where the plaintiffs sold their starch under the name 'Glenfield Starch', Glenfield being where it was made. Lord Westbury explained how the plaintiffs became entitled to a reputation in that name in these terms:[6]

> 'I take it to be clear from the evidence, that long antecedently to the operations of the defendant the word 'Glenfield' had acquired a secondary signification or meaning in connection with a particular manufacturer, in short it had become the trade denomination of the starch made by the plaintiff. It was wholly taken out of its ordinary meaning, and in connection with starch had acquired that peculiar secondary signification to which I have referred.'

It can be seen from this that there is no distinction in principle between the approach to marks directly descriptive of the characteristics of goods or services and those descriptive of geographical origin.

---

1 See paras 2.30–2.31 and 4.10.
2 (1909) 26 RPC 693 at 704.
3 [1896] AC 199 at 213.
4 [1899] AC 326 at 338–339. This passage immediately follows the passage from Lord Shand's speech quoted in para 3.17 above. The two contrast the differing principles to be applied when dealing with fancy or invented words on the one hand and descriptive words on the other.
5 Ibid at 708.
6 (1872) LR 5 HL 508 at 521.

3.26 *Words descriptive of nature or quality*   It is in relation to claims based upon words (and to some extent get-up) descriptive of the goods or services to which they are applied that the traditional refuge of the lawyer that 'passing off cases depend peculiarly upon their own facts' is used most often. There is no logic or principle which can be derived from the varying results of the many cases brought to protect reputations claimed in descriptive words. All one can say for certain is that in the cases which succeeded there was evidence which persuaded the court that deception would occur and in those which failed there was not. The message for the practitioner is clear: credible evidence that the words are recognised by the public as denoting the plaintiff's goods or services is crucial to a successful claim. Often such cases turn upon whether the defendant uses the plaintiff's descriptive term alone or in conjunction with his own name. In a series of cases around the turn of the century actions were brought to protect the name 'Camel Hair Belting'. The best known of these is *Reddaway & Co v Banham* in which Lord Herschell said:[1]

> 'What right, it was asked, can an individual have to restrain another from using a common English word because he has chosen to employ it as his trade mark? I answer that he has no such right, but he has a right to insist that it shall not be used without explanation or qualification if such a use would be an instrument of fraud. Who suffers injury by such a conclusion, or would be the worse if the defendant is thus restrained?'

Two points should be borne in mind in connection with the finding in *Reddaway v Banham* that the words 'Camel Hair Belting' were distinctive of the plaintiff's goods. First, the plaintiff did not obtain a monopoly in those words. The defendant was only enjoined from using them without the addition of other words to distinguish their goods from those of the plaintiff. Lord Morris explained the principle in this passage:[2]

> 'A representation deceiving the public is and must be the foundation of the appellants' right to recover; they are not entitled to any monopoly of the name "camel hair belting" irrespective of its deceiving the public, and every one has a right to describe truly his article by that name, provided he distinguishes it from the appellants' make. In this case the respondents did not so distinguish it, because they omitted to state that it was their own make.'

Second, the courts were much influenced by a letter (called by Vaughan Williams LJ in *Hommel v Bauer*[3] the 'celebrated letter') in which the defendants admitted that by using the words 'Camel Hair Belting' simpliciter they expected to be able to pass off their goods as the plaintiffs' goods. As frequently happens in passing off cases, fraud, if present, tends to override all other considerations.[4] In other cases Reddaway successfully relied upon the words 'Camel Hair Belting' against defendants who did not distinguish their goods but he failed against defendants who were shown to have been acting bona fide and adding their own names to the description 'camel hair belting'.[5]

---

1 [1896] AC 199 at 214–215.
2 Ibid at 222.
3 (1905) 22 RPC 43.
4 See para 4.48 below.
5 *Reddaway & Co v Ahlers* (1902) 19 RPC 12; *Reddaway & Co v Benham Hemp Spinning Co* [1892] 2 QB 639, 9 RPC 503; *Reddaway & Co v Frictionless Engine Packing Co Ltd* (1902) 19 RPC 505; *Reddaway & Co v Irwell and Eastern Rubber Co Ltd* (1906) 23 RPC 621, affd (1907) 24 RPC 203 (CA); *Reddaway & Co v Stevenson & Brother* (1902) 20 RPC 276. These cases are considered further in para 4.35 below.

3.27 *Reddaway v Banham* was followed in *Faulder & Co Ltd v O and G Rushton Ltd*[1] in which the trade mark 'Silver Pan' for jam was chosen because the jam concerned was made in silver vessels, such vessels also being used by other jam manufacturers. Nevertheless it was held that the plaintiff had made sufficient use of the trade mark 'Silver Pan' to make it distinctive of his jam. In *Iron-Ox Remedy Co Ltd v Co-operative Wholesale Society Ltd*[2] the mark 'Iron-Ox' for tablets was held distinctive of the plaintiff's tablets which did not in fact contain iron oxide. The adoption of 'Iron-Ox' by the defendants for their tablets, which did contain iron oxide, was held to constitute passing off, again primarily because of the defendants' fraudulent intention. In *Island Trading Co v Anchor Brewing Co*[3] an injunction was granted restraining the defendants from using the term 'steam' in relation to beer although it was accepted that the plaintiffs' use of the term was primarily to give the impression that their product was strong, pure and old-fashioned. Examples of highly descriptive names for business establishments which have been held distinctive are 'The Brine Baths',[4] 'Bodega' for a wine tavern[5] and 'Credit Management' for a business carrying on precisely that activity.[6] However, as a general rule it has been difficult for plaintiffs to prove that a mark descriptive of the nature or quality of their goods or services has acquired a secondary distinctive meaning and there are many examples of such claims which have failed. The following are good examples: 'Flaked Oatmeal',[7] 'Spanish Graphite' for pencils,[8] 'Shredded Wheat',[9] 'Naphtha' for soap,[10] 'Haematogen' for a medicine,[11] 'Bile Beans' for a laxative,[12] 'Erect Form' for corsets,[13] 'Oval Blue' for a cake of laundry soap,[14] 'Health' for cocoa,[15] 'Universal' for textile machines,[16] 'Native Guano' for artificial manure,[17] 'Classic' for stationery[18] and 'Prophylactic' for toothbrushes.[19] Similar examples of non-distinctive business names are 'International' for a hotel[20] and 'Tape Recorder Centre' for a shop selling tape recorders.[21] These cases emphasise the point that relatively few marks are wholly descriptive. Many have an element of descriptiveness either manipulated or combined with something else to provide the quality of distinctiveness. Whether, and, if so, to what extent, a mark is descriptive of the goods or services to which it is applied is always a matter of fact and degree depending both upon the use of language and the evidence of recognition by the public.

---

1 (1903) 19 TLR 452, 20 RPC 477.
2 (1907) 24 RPC 425.
3 [1989] RPC 287a.
4 *Hesketh Estates (Southport) Ltd v Droitwich Brine Baths Ltd* (1934) 52 RPC 39.
5 *Bodega v Owens Co Ltd and Rivière* (1890) 7 RPC 31.
6 *Credit Management Co Ltd v Credit Management Ltd* [1961] RPC 157.
7 *Parsons v Gillespie* [1898] AC 239, 67 LJPC 21.
8 *Wolff & Son v Nopitsch* (1900) 18 RPC 27.
9 *Shredded Wheat Co Ltd v Kellogg (GB) Ltd* (1940) 57 RPC 137.
10 *Fels v Christopher Thomas & Bros Ltd* (1903) 21 RPC 85.
11 *Hommel v Bauer* (1904) 21 TLR 80, 22 RPC 43.
12 *Bile Beans Manufacturing Co v Davidson* (1906) 23 RPC 725.
13 *Weingarten Bros v Bayer & Co* (1905) 92 LT 511, 22 RPC 341.
14 *Ripley v Bandey* (1897) 14 RPC 591, affd at 944 (CA).
15 *Thorne & Co v Sandow Ltd* (1912) 28 TLR 416, 29 RPC 440.
16 *Universal Winding Co v Hattersley & Sons Ltd* (1915) 32 RPC 479.
17 *Native Guano Co v Sewage Manure Co* (1891) 8 RPC 125.
18 *Sharpe Ltd v Solomon Bros Ltd* (1914) 84 LJ Ch 290, 32 RPC 15.
19 *Cordes v Addis & Son* (1923) 40 RPC 133.
20 *Park Court Hotel Ltd v Trans-World Hotels Ltd* [1970] FSR 89.
21 *Sypha Sound Sales Ltd and Tape Recorder Centre Ltd v Tape Recorders Ltd* [1961] RPC 27.

3.28 The results of passing off actions based upon descriptive company or trading names have varied. Again the caution that such cases are frequently illustrative of little more than the quality of the evidence is applicable. Successful claims have been made to 'Midland Dairy' for a dairy,[1] 'Efflu-ent' for a waste disposal business,[2] 'Music Corporation' for a musical and entertainment agent,[3] 'Buttercup' for a margarine vendor,[4] 'Southern' for a music publisher,[5] 'General Radio' for a radio business,[6] 'Reliance' for a dealer in rubber tyres,[7] 'Salaried Persons Personal Loans' for a business arranging such loans,[8] 'Radio Rentals' for the business of hiring radios[9] and 'Heels Stafford' for a manufacturer of shoe heels.[10] Many unsuccessful claims can also be found. The following were unsurprisingly held non-distinctive for businesses dealing in goods or services of which the words are more or less an accurate description: 'Aerator',[11] 'Vacuum Cleaner',[12] 'Industrial Furnace',[13] 'American Shoe',[14] 'Electromobile',[15] 'Buttons'[16] and 'Drive Yourself Hire'.[17] 'Premier' for motor vehicle dealing,[18] 'Colonial' for insurance[19] and 'Index' for betting[20] have also been held to be descriptive. Many of these cases also highlight a variety of other points, such as the effect of added distinguishing matter and the difficulties of claiming a reputation in descriptive words used in conjunction with distinctive words or establishing the likelihood of confusion or damage where businesses are not in direct competition.

---

1   *Midland Counties Dairy Ltd v Midland Dairies Ltd* (1948) 65 RPC 429.
2   *Effluent Disposal Ltd v Midlands Effluent Disposal Ltd* [1970] RPC 238.
3   *Music Corporation of America v Music Corporation (Great Britain) Ltd* (1947) 64 RPC 41.
4   *Ewing v Buttercup Margarine Co Ltd* [1917] 2 Ch 1 [1916–17] All ER Rep 1012.
5   *Southern Music Publishing Co Ltd v Southern Songs Ltd* [1966] RPC 137.
6   *General Radio Co v General Radio Co (Westminster) Ltd* [1957] RPC 471.
7   *Reliance Rubber Co Ltd v Reliance Tyre Co Ltd* (1924) 42 RPC 91.
8   *Salaried Persons Personal Loans Ltd v Postal and Salaried Loans of Glasgow Ltd* [1966] RPC 24.
9   *Radio Rentals Ltd v Rentals Ltd* (1934) 51 RPC 407.
10 *Heels Ltd v Stafford Heels Ltd* (1927) 44 RPC 299.
11 *Aerators Ltd v Tollitt* [1902] 2 Ch 319, 19 RPC 418.
12 *British Vacuum Cleaner Co Ltd v New Vacuum Cleaner Co Ltd* [1907] 2 Ch 312, 24 RPC 641.
13 *Industrial Furnaces Ltd v Reaves* [1970] RPC 605.
14 *H E Randall Ltd v E Bradley & Son* (1907) 24 RPC 657, affd 773 (CA).
15 *Electromobile Co Ltd v British Electromobile Co Ltd* (1907) 98 LT 258, 25 RPC 149.
16 *Buttons Ltd v Buttons Covered Ltd* (1920) 37 RPC 45.
17 *Drive Yourself Hire Co (London) Ltd v A G Parish (trading as Self Drive Cars)* [1957] RPC 307.
18 *Premier Motor Co (Birmingham) Ltd v Premier Driving School (Birmingham) Ltd* [1962] RPC 222.
19 *Colonial Life Assurance Co v Home and Colonial Assurance Co Ltd* (1864) 33 Beav 548, 4 New Rep 129.
20 *Coral Index Ltd v Regent Index Ltd* [1970] RPC 147.

3.29   There is as a matter of legal principle no word or group of words so descriptive that it is impossible to acquire a distinctive reputation in them. However, the more descriptive the name chosen the harder it is to persuade the court that a secondary meaning has been acquired and the smaller the differences between the plaintiff's name and that of the defendant which will be required to establish that the defendant has properly distinguished his goods or services from those of the plaintiff. The high water mark of such cases is undoubtedly *Office Cleaning Services Ltd v Westminster Window and General Cleaners Ltd.*[1] In the Court of Appeal Luxmoore LJ pointed out that a name might consist of words each of which was descriptive but which in combination possessed a certain degree of distinctiveness.[2] The House of Lords upheld the Court of Appeal's decision that the plaintiff was not debarred from obtaining relief merely because the name was descriptive. However, the members of the committee took account of the fact that the words 'Office Cleaning Services' were ordinary English words in common use 'apt and more apt than any other words to describe the service rendered'.[3] It was also pointed out that, although the court should take due consideration of long use of a descriptive name, it should not forget that since it is descriptive, 'small differences may suffice to avoid passing off'.[4] In the result it was held that the defendant's trading name 'Office Cleaning Association' was sufficiently different from the plaintiff's name to prevent confusion. In *Legal and General Assurance Society v Daniel*,[5] Lord Denning considered the question of the degree of descriptiveness, particularly of a combination of words, and held that the words 'Legal and General' were distinctive of the plaintiffs. He contrasted this combination of words with those used by the plaintiffs in the *Office Cleaning* case saying:

> 'It seems to me that, although these words "Legal and General" are descriptive words, nevertheless they have acquired such a connotation, such a significance in business and elsewhere, that they have become especially associated with the plaintiff company. The words are very different from the words "office cleaning" which were considered in the House of Lords in *Office Cleaning Services Ltd v Westminster Window and General Cleaners Ltd.* Those words "office cleaning" were very common, ordinary descriptive words. These words "Legal and General" are less common, less descriptive, more specialised and rarely used in combination except by the plaintiff.'

Another example of ordinary descriptive words being used in an unusual combination is *Computervision Corp v Computer Vision Ltd*[6] in which Plowman J held that the two words, not having been used in conjunction except by the plaintiff, were distinctive of the plaintiff's business and that an injunction should be granted restraining their use by the defendant. However, in *Furnitureland Ltd v Harris*,[7] Browne-Wilkinson VC held that 'Furnitureland' and 'Furniture City' were not confusingly similar when used as the names of retail furniture outlets.

---

1   (1946) 63 RPC 39.
2   [1944] 2 All ER 269 at 271, 61 RPC 133 at 136.
3   Ibid at 42.
4   Ibid at 43.
5   [1968] RPC 253 at 258.
6   [1975] RPC 171, [1974] FSR 206.
7   [1989] FSR 536.

3.30   It will be particularly difficult to demonstrate that a descriptive name has become distinctive of the plaintiff's goods or services if it has in fact been used wholly or primarily in conjunction with another, distinctive name. In *Horlick's Malted Milk Co v Summerskill*[1] the plaintiffs sought to restrain the use of the term 'Malted Milk', which they had used exclusively with their name 'Horlicks'. It was held that the term 'malted milk' was simply descriptive and that which distinguished the plaintiffs' product was the name 'Horlicks'. In *W Woodward Ltd v Boulton Macro Ltd*[2] the plaintiff was the first person to offer a proprietary remedy for infant wind under the name 'Gripe

Water'. It was sold under that name with a label which said 'prepared only by *W Woodward Ltd*' and generally known as 'Gripe Water' or 'Woodward's Gripe Water'. The term gripe water was, however, applied by pharmacists to preparations made up extemporaneously and it was held that the term was properly to be regarded as descriptive. More recently, in *McCain International v Country Fair Foods Ltd*,[3] the plaintiffs devised a novel product consisting of oil impregnated potato chips suitable for cooking in the oven. They sold these as 'McCain's Oven Chips'. The term oven chips had not previously been used for any product and was described by Templeman LJ as 'an ingenious and apt description'[4] of such goods. It was held that the name 'McCain' served to distinguish the plaintiff's goods from those of other traders whilst the term 'oven chips' merely identified the product.

---

1 (1916) 86 LJ Ch 175, 34 RPC 63.
2 (1915) 87 LJ Ch 27, 32 RPC 173.
3 [1981] RPC 69 (CA).
4 Ibid at 72.

3.31 *Words descriptive of unique goods*   More or less descriptive terms are often coined by manufacturers of new types of goods so that the public will be able to tell from the name the nature of the novel product. Both 'malted milk' and 'oven chips'[1] are examples of the phenomenon. In such cases, even the absence of an additional distinctive name used by the plaintiff may not be enough to cause the name to become distinctive through use. The danger is that the newly-coined term is the only term available or at least the most obvious and attractive term to describe the nature of the goods.[2] Once this has happened it is almost impossible to establish that the term is distinctive of the plaintiff's goods rather than descriptive of the type and free for use by other competing manufacturers of such goods.[3] The position was comprehensively summed up by Lord Oliver in the *Jif* case where he said, pointing out that confusion alone is not sufficient to establish passing off:

> 'The application by a trader to his goods of an accepted trade description or of ordinary English terms may give rise to confusion. It will probably do so where previously another trader was the only person in the market dealing in those goods, for a public which knows only of A will be prone to assume that any similar goods emanate from A. But there can be no cause of action in passing off simply because there will have been no misrepresentation. So the application to the defendants' goods of ordinary English terms such as "cellular clothing"[4] or "Office Cleaning"[5] or the use of descriptive expressions or slogans in general use such as "Chicago Pizza"[6] cannot entitle a plaintiff to relief simply because he has used the same or similar terms as descriptive of his own goods and has been the only person previously to employ that description.'[7]

---

1 See the previous para.
2 See the passage from Parker J's judgment in *Burberry v Cording* quoted in the text to n 5 to para 3.25 above.
3 See *Cellular Clothing Co v Maxton and Murray* [1899] AC 326 at 343–344, (1899) 16 RPC 397 at

408–409; *Siegert v Findlater* (1878) 7 Ch D 801 at 813; *Canadian Shredded Wheat Co v Kellogg Co of Canada Ltd* (1938) 55 RPC 125 at 146; *British Vacuum Cleaner Co Ltd v New Vacuum Cleaner Co Ltd* [1907] 2 Ch 312, 24 RPC 641.
4   *Cellular Clothing Co v Maxton and Murray* above.
5   *Office Cleaning Services Ltd v Westminster Window and General Cleaners Ltd* (1946) 63 RPC 39.
6   *My Kinda Town Ltd v Soll* [1983] RPC 407.
7   *Reckitt & Colman Products Ltd v Borden Inc* [1990] RPC 341 at 412.

3.32 *Geographical marks*   Geographical names as such merely identify the area in which goods or services are made or provided. In order to support a claim for passing off, it must again be shown that the name has come to have the secondary signification of identifying the plaintiff's goods or services.[1] With geographical marks also it is difficult to glean any clear legal principles from the many decided cases other than that in some the evidence supports the contention of distinctiveness and that in others it does not. Successful claims have been made in relation to the following geographical names: 'Glenfield' for starch,[2] 'Stone Ale' for beer,[3] 'Worcester' for china,[4] 'Reading' for biscuits,[5] 'Yorkshire Relish' for sauce,[6] 'Crystal Palace' for fireworks,[7] 'London' for candles,[8] 'Brereton' for foundry sand,[9] 'Angostura' for bitters,[10] 'Dundigal' for cigars,[11] 'Oxford' for marmalade,[12] 'Banbury' for buildings,[13] 'Radstock' for a colliery there,[14] 'Apsley' for paper mills there[15] and 'Olympia' for the Ideal Home Exhibition.[16] In all these cases the place of manufacture or trading was the area or locality indicated by the name. 'Chartreuse' was held to be distinctive of products made by monks belonging to the Monastery of the Grande Chartreuse, although it had moved from its original location there;[17] and 'Berkeley' was held distinctive of the business carried on at a hotel originally cited in Berkeley Street, Mayfair when, after it had been demolished and the proprietor was about to open a new hotel under that name in Knightsbridge, the defendant sought to open the hotel it was building on the old site under the name 'Berkeley International'.[18] Equally the following claims to have acquired a secondary meaning for geographical names failed: 'Apollinaris' for salts,[19] 'Hopton Wood Stone' for stone,[20] 'Rugby Portland' for cement,[21] 'Whitstable' for oysters[22] and 'Anatolia' for licorice.[23] Where an injunction is granted it is frequently necessary for it to be limited so as to enable the defendant to mark his goods with their place of origin provided that this is done in such a way as not to indicate that the goods are the plaintiff's goods.[24]

---

1   See para 3.25 above.
2   *Wotherspoon v Currie* (1872) LR 5 HL 508, 42 LJ Ch 130.
3   *Montgomery v Thompson* [1891] AC 217, 60 LJ Ch 757.
4   *Worcester Royal Porcelain Co Ltd v Locke & Co Ltd* (1902) 18 TLR 712, 19 RPC 479. The plaintiff also used the name Worcester as part of 'Royal Worcester' and 'Grange Worcester' as well as 'Worcester' alone.
5   *Huntley & Palmer v Reading Biscuits Co* (1893) 10 RPC 277.
6   *Birmingham Vinegar Brewery Co v Powell* [1897] AC 710, 66 LJ Ch 763.
7   *C T Brock & Co v James Pain & Sons* (1911) 28 RPC 461, affd 697 (CA).
8   *Re Price's Patent Candle Co* (1884) 27 Ch D 681, 54 LJ Ch 210.

9 *Smith Ltd v Fieldhouse Ltd* [1961] RPC 110.
10 *Siegert v Findlater* (1878) 7 Ch D 801, 47 LJ Ch 233.
11 *Bewlay & Co Ltd v Hughes* (1898) 15 RPC 290.
12 *CPC (United Kingdom) Limited v Keenan* [1986] FSR 527.
13 *Banbury Buildings Ltd v Sectional Concrete Buildings Ltd* [1970] RPC 463.
14 *Braham v Beachim* (1878) 7 Ch D 848, 47 LJ Ch 348.
15 *John Dickinson & Co v Apsley Press Ltd* (1937) 157 LT 135, 54 RPC 219.
16 *Associated Newspapers Ltd v Lew Barclay Exhibitions Ltd* (1955) 72 RPC 278.
17 *Rey v Lecouturier* [1910] AC 262, 79 LJ Ch 394.
18 *Berkeley Hotel Co Ltd v Berkeley International (Mayfair) Ltd* [1972] RPC 237.
19 *Apollinaris Co Ltd v Duckworth & Co* (1906) 22 TLR 744, 23 RPC 540.
20 *Hopton Wood Stone Firms Ltd v Gething* (1910) 27 RPC 605.
21 *Rugby Portland Cement Co Ltd v Rugby and Newbold Portland Cement Co Ltd* (1891) 9 RPC 46.
22 *Whitstable Oyster Fishery v Hayling Fisheries Ltd* (1900) 17 RPC 461.
23 *McAndrew v Bassett* (1864) 4 De GJ & Sm 380.
24 See paras 7.46–7.49, esp. 7.48 below.

3.33 *Partly descriptive marks*   It sometimes happens that a trade mark has a meaning which is both distinctive of the plaintiff and descriptive of some characteristics of the goods to which it is applied. Such marks may be used both descriptively and distinctively. To some they will identify the goods or services of the plaintiff. To others they describe the goods. In such cases the practice of the courts has generally been to protect the reputation the plaintiff has when the mark is used distinctively but to limit any injunction granted to permit the mark to be used descriptively. This practice appears to have had its origin in *Havana Cigar and Tobacco Factories Ltd v Oddenino*[1] in which the word 'Corona' was found to be used by some to identify the plaintiff's cigars and by others simply to identify a cigar of a particular size and shape. An injunction was granted in what became known as 'Corona' form[2] to enable cigars of that size and shape to be supplied where the plaintiff's cigars were not being sought by the customer. A similar form of injunction has been granted in subsequent cases.[3] However, in *Pete Waterman Ltd v CBS United Kingdom Ltd*,[4] Browne-Wilkinson VC rejected a claim by the plaintiffs to a reputation amongst only a section of the public in the name 'The Hit Factory' even though it was clear on the evidence that to some members of the public that name was indeed distinctive of them, saying:

'In my judgment this attempt to carve out a section of the public which will be misled is not legitimate. It seems to me impermissible in cases of this kind to split the relevant public so as to define sections of the public by reference to their state of knowledge. . . . Even if I am wrong in that view, I have made the classification which I have[5] merely for the purposes of exposition. There is in fact no hard and fast boundary between those groups. People will be on the borderlines between one and the other. Their state of knowledge and their understanding of the meaning of "The Hit Factory" will have a number of gradations inherent in it. It is impossible objectively to define a section of the public which is the section where [the plaintiff] has an exclusive right.'

Whilst on the facts of the case this approach was entirely unobjectionable, there being a number of organisations to which the term 'The Hit Factory' had been applied and the public varying in its state of knowledge of these matters, it may be thought to imply that it must be shown that all members of the public who are liable to come into contact with the plaintiff's goods or services identify the mark in issue with the plaintiff for there to be a claim in passing off. Such an approach is in direct conflict with previous authoritative statements of the law,[6] which do not appear to have been considered, and is wrong. A variation of the usual approach is where a normally distinctive mark is used descriptively in limited circumstances, for example to explain that goods have been designed as spare parts or accessories for other goods sold under a particular mark.[7] There are other unusual circumstances in which a mark may be descriptive to a limited extent. In *A V Roe & Co Ltd v Aircraft Disposal Co Ltd,*[8] the defendant was permitted to dispose of a number of aircraft made by others to the plaintiff's design under direction of the Ministry of Munitions during the war as 'Avro type', the mark 'Avro' otherwise being entirely distinctive of the plaintiff for aeroplanes.

1 [1924] 1 Ch 179, 93 LJ Ch 81.
2 See para 4.32 below and Appendix A for the form of injunction.
3 See *Purefoy Engineering Co Ltd v Sykes Boxall & Co Ltd* (1955) 72 RPC 89 and *Bostitch Inc v McGarry & Cole Ltd* [1964] RPC 173.
4 [1993] EMLR 27 at 49.
5 Ie into groups of people having different understandings of the name 'The Hit Factory'.
6 See eg Lord Maugham in *Saville v June Perfect* (1941) 58 RPC 147 at 175–176. See also ch 4, para 4.04.
7 See para 3.21 above.
8 (1920) 37 RPC 249.

Names of fictional characters

3.34 There are two distinct circumstances in which reliance may be placed upon the name of a fictional character. The first is where someone other than the original creator of the character wishes to publish further stories about it. In such a case there is no English authority supporting the possibility of such a claim. In *Conan Doyle v London Mystery Magazine Ltd,*[1] it was held in interlocutory proceedings that the plaintiff (the author's executor) had no right other than goodwill in the actual stories written by Sir Arthur Conan Doyle and thus no right to prevent the defendant from publishing further stories about the fictional character 'Sherlock Holmes'. However, in *Shaw Bros (Hong Kong) Ltd v Golden Harvest (HK) Ltd,*[2] the Hong Kong Full Court, relying upon a number of American decisions,[3] held that the author who created a fictional character (in this case 'the One Armed Swordsman') is entitled to goodwill in that character and can restrain others from using it. The second circumstance is the now common trade practice of character merchandising. This is dealt with below.[4]

1 (1949) 66 RPC 312.
2 [1972] RPC 559.
3 The American cases are *Patten v Superior Talking Pictures Inc* (1934) 8 F Supp. 196; *Lone Ranger Inc v Cox* (1942) 124 F. 2d. 650; and *Lone Ranger Inc v Currey* (1948) 79 F Supp 190.
4 See para 3.53 below.

Titles[1]

3.35 *Passing off is the only form of protection*   There is normally no copyright or any other form of property right in a title. Accordingly passing off is generally the only form of action which can be used to prevent the adoption by someone else of a confusingly similar title for a book, magazine, film, play or television programme. There is no doubt that such a claim may, in principle, be made. Lord Wright stated the principle as follows:

> 'A title may be used in the case of a book or newspaper under such conditions that a person may be deceived into buying the defendant's book or newspaper under the impression that they are buying that of the plaintiff. Similarity of name may be strengthened by similarity of make up, and in subject-matter, and by other circumstances. Nor is such a claim limited to things sold, though it is commoner in that class of case. It is not impossible that there might be "passing off" of such a nature that persons might pay to go to a performance of the defendant's work under the impression that they were going to witness the plaintiff's work.'[2]

Thus, as with all claims for passing off, it is necessary to show that the plaintiff has a reputation in the title relied upon which is attached to a business having goodwill. This can be extremely difficult. Titles are often highly descriptive for the obvious reason that they are intended to tell the consumer what is to be found within. Equally they are often used with other plainly distinctive material, such as the name of the author of the work, which is in fact the name by which the source of the work is recognised. Again, all the cases which follow should be read with a degree of caution. The underlying facts have often influenced the courts' decisions.

---

1   'Kinquering Kongs their titles take' per Rev William Spooner (attrib).
2   *Francis Day and Hunter Ltd v Twentieth Century Fox Corp Ltd* [1940] AC 112, [1939] 4 All ER 192. See also the further passage from this speech cited in para 3.39 below.

3.36 *Book titles*   A book title is not normally a trade mark because it does not ordinarily give any indication of trade origin. This is particularly so with descriptive titles.[1] In such circumstances no goodwill will be generated in the title. Accordingly, in *Mathieson v Sir Isaac Pitman & Sons Ltd*[2] the plaintiff claimed that the title 'How to Appeal Against Your Rates' was distinctive of a book of that name published by it. Unsurprisingly the court held that the title was entirely descriptive and could not be relied upon. Equally, in *Pet Library v Walter Ellson & Son*[3] the plaintiff failed to establish a secondary distinctive meaning for the title 'Pet Library' for a series of books about pets and the defendants were therefore entitled to use the title 'Ellson's Pet Library' for a similar series. However, in *W H Allen & Co v Brown Watson Ltd*[4] the title 'My Life and Loves by Frank Harris' was held to have become distinctive of a book published by the plaintiff and the defendant was restrained from publishing an abbreviated and expurgated version of the same work, which had previously been published under a different name, under the same name.

Most recently, the Court of Appeal considered that the title 'Dark Future' used as a series title for a number of novels published to accompany a role-playing game of imagination set in the future was arguably used to denote trade origin and enjoined the defendant from using it on a series of adventure novels of similar type.[5] All the novels published by both parties had individual subsidiary titles.

<hr />

1   See *Mothercare UK Ltd v Penguin Books Ltd* [1988] RPC 113 (CA).
2   (1930) 47 RPC 541.
3   [1968] FSR 359.
4   [1965] RPC 191.
5   *Games Workshop Ltd v Transworld Publishers Ltd* [1993] FSR 705 (CA).

3.37   *Magazine and newspaper titles*   Few claims for passing off brought to restrain the use of magazine and newspaper titles have succeeded. Many magazine and newspaper titles or parts of titles have been held to be simply too descriptive to be capable of distinguishing one trader's goods from another's. Examples are 'Today',[1] 'Athletics' for a magazine about athletics,[2] 'Post' in the newspaper title 'Morning Post',[3] 'Advertiser' in the newspaper title 'Maidenhead Advertiser',[4] 'Herald' in the title 'Tamworth Herald',[5] 'Rubber and Plastics' in the title 'Rubber and Plastics Age'[6] and 'Magazine of Fiction'.[7] The position on newspaper titles was recently summarised by Aldous J:

> 'in each case the court has to decide whether the defendant, by reason of the name that it is using for its newspaper, is representing that its paper is the plaintiffs', or is connected or associated with it. When considering the question the court will accept that, where well known words such as "Post", "Advertiser", "Star" and I include "Herald", are used the mere fact that some confusion may arise will not mean that there is necessarily the required misrepresentation to establish passing off.'[8]

This is frequently compounded by a relatively short period of user by the plaintiff.[9] Even where this is not the case, largely descriptive titles will generally be denied protection, if not on the ground of lack of sufficient reputation, then on the ground that what the defendant is doing is not sufficiently close in title or type to what the plaintiff is doing to cause confusion. It is often difficult to discern from the cases which consideration was uppermost in the court's mind. In *Ridgeway Co v Hutchinson*[10] the plaintiff's goodwill in the title 'Adventure' was held to be only 'of a shadowy and trivial character' and the defendant was not prevented from publishing under the title 'Adventure Story Magazine'. In *Ridgeway Co v Amalgamated Press Ltd*[11] the title 'Everybody's Magazine' was held to be 'somewhat descriptive' and the defendant's title 'Everybody's Weekly' not confusingly similar to it. In *Newsweek Inc v BBC*[12] the magazine title 'Newsweek' was held to be 'little removed from two descriptive words' and it was found that there was no possibility of the defendant's television programme being thought to be associated with it. In *Thomson v Kent Messenger and South Eastern Newspapers,*[13] Megarry J inclined to the view that the title 'The Sunday Post' was merely descriptive for a Sunday newspaper. Following the approach of the House of Lords in *Office Cleaning* he held that the defendant's title 'South East Sunday Post', coupled with differences in appearance, price and circulation, made a claim of passing off 'doomed to failure' and refused an interlocutory injunction. One of the more notorious failures in the annals of such claims is that by the 'Morning Star' against the 'Daily Star' when it was launched.[14] Foster J held that, when shortened to 'Star', as was customary, the title was descriptive, having a long established meaning in general use for a newspaper. Further, having regard to the numerous differences between the appearance, content, price and methods of sale of the two newspapers there was so little similarity between the two publications that even a 'moron in a hurry' could not be confused.

1   *Norman Kark Publications v Odhams Press* [1962] 1 All ER 636, [1962] RPC 163.
2   *World Athletics and Sporting Publications Ltd v A C M Webb (Publishers) Co.* [1981] FSR 27.
3   *Borthwick v Evening Post* (1888) 37 Ch D 449, 57 LJ Ch 406.
4   *Baylis & Co v Darlenko* [1974] FSR 284.
5   *Tamworth Herald Co Ltd v Thomson Free Newspapers Ltd* [1991] FSR 337.
6   *Rubber and Technical Press Ltd v Maclaren & Sons Ltd* [1961] RPC 264.
7   *William Stevens Ltd v Cassell & Co Ltd* (1913) 29 TLR 272, 30 RPC 199.
8   *Tamworth Herald v Thomson Free Newspapers* supra at 342.
9   See para 3.05 above and in particular the cases cited at notes 4 and 5.
10 (1923) 40 RPC 335.
11 (1911) 28 TLR 149, 29 RPC 130.
12 [1979] RPC 441.
13 [1975] RPC 191, [1974] FSR 485.
14 *Morning Star Co-operative Society v Express Newspapers Ltd* [1979] FSR 113.

3.38   Instances of plaintiffs succeeding in claims based upon magazine and newspaper titles are more difficult to find, although there are, particularly since the advent of the *American Cyanamid* criteria, a number of cases in which the plaintiff's claim to reputation and consequent confusion has been held to be arguable. The title 'Management Today' used for a long established and largely controlled circulation[1] magazine was held to have sufficient reputation that it was possible that a new publication called 'Security Management Today' might be thought to be from the same stable[2] although an interlocutory injunction was refused on the balance of convenience. The common phrase 'What's New In . . . ' used as the introduction to a series of ten titles of trade magazines was held to be sufficiently distinctive to prevent the publication of a magazine under the title 'What's New In Training' even though the plaintiff did not publish a magazine in this field.[3] The following magazine and newspaper titles have all been held distinctive: 'Punch',[4] 'Evening News',[5] 'Eagle',[6] 'Bradshaw',[7] 'Morning Mail'[8] and 'The Grocer'.[9]

1   These are magazines distributed free of charge to a particular group of people to whom the advertisers in the magazine wish to have access and also sold to members of the public, usually in fairly small numbers. Many trade and professional magazines are published in this way.
2   *Management Publications Limited v Blenheim Exhibitions Group plc* [1991] FSR 550 (CA).
3   *Morgan-Grampian plc v Training Personnel Ltd* [1992] FSR 267.
4   *Bradbury v Beeton* (1869) 39 LJ Ch 57, 18 WR 33.

5 *George Outram & Co Ltd v London Evening Newspaper Co. Ltd* (1911) 27 TLR 231, 28 RPC 308.
6 *Hulton Press v White Eagle Youth Holiday Camp* (1951) 68 RPC 126.
7 *Henry Blacklock Ltd v Bradshaw Publishing Co* (1926) 43 RPC 97.
8 *Walter v Emmott* (1885) 54 LJ Ch 1059, 53 LT 437.
9 *Reed v O'Meara* (1888) 21 LR IR 216.

3.39 *Other titles* Titles have been held to be distinctive in other areas. 'Top of the Pops' was held to be distinctive of a record.[1] 'Miss World'[2] and 'Miss Great Britain'[3] have been held distinctive for beauty competitions, 'Anastasia' for a play[4] and 'The New Car' for a dramatic sketch.[5] There are equally many instances where titles of a similar nature have been held not to be distinctive. 'The Merry Widow' was held not to be distinctive for an operetta[6] and a claim to 'The Younger Generation' failed for a play.[7] The title 'Irish and Proud of It' was also held insufficiently distinctive of a particular play to prevent a film being promoted under the same name.[8] The user given to each of these titles failed to overcome their prima facie descriptive content. And in *Francis Day and Hunter Ltd v Twentieth Century Fox Corp Ltd*,[9] the plaintiff failed in a claim that the title of the song 'The Man Who Broke the Bank at Monte Carlo' was sufficiently distinctive to prevent the use of that name for a film in which none of the words or music of the song were used. Having set out the principles relevant to such claims in the passage cited in para 3.35 above, Lord Wright applied them to the facts in this way:

> 'it is enough to state these elementary principles to see how inapplicable they are to the subject-matter of this appeal. . . . The two things [the song and the film] are completely different, and incapable of comparison in any reasonable sense. The thing said to be passed off must resemble the thing for which it is passed off.'[10]

1 *Pickwick International (GB) Ltd v Multiple Sound Distributors Ltd* [1972] 3 All ER 384, [1972] RPC 786.
2 *Miss World (Jersey) Ltd v James Street Productions Ltd* [1981] FSR 309.
3 *Morecambe and Heysham Corporation v Mecca Ltd* [1962] RPC 145.
4 *Twentieth Century Fox Film Corp v Gala Film Distributors Ltd* [1957] RPC 105.
5 *Samuelson v Producers Distributing Co Ltd* (1931) 48 RPC 580.
6 *Loew's Inc v Littler* (1955) 72 RPC 166.
7 *Houghton v Film Booking Offices Ltd* (1931) 48 RPC 329.
8 *O'Gorman v Paramount Film Services Ltd* [1937] 2 All ER 113.
9 [1940] AC 112, [1939] 4 All ER 192.
10 Ibid at 126, 199.

Company names

3.40 If a business belongs to a company, the company name can be relied upon. Unlike a person's name, however, a company name is chosen by the owners of the business. There are several types of company name.[1] First, a company name may be a proper name or a combination of proper names, usually of the business's founder or founders (for example 'Dunhill'[2]). Second it may be an invented or fancy word having no direct connection with the business activities of the company (such as 'Kodak'[3]). Third, it may be a name descriptive of the company's business activities (such as 'Office Cleaning Services Limited'[4]). The last kind of name is often abbreviated to initials (ie 'OCS'), which sometimes become better known than the original descriptive words (such as 'BSA'[5]) or an abbreviated word (such as 'Unitex'[6]). Company names, particularly if of the second type, are also frequently used as the company's trade or service marks. Company names are treated essentially the same way as the equivalent type of name or word when used as a trade or service mark.[7]

---

1   See W Olins (1978) *The Corporate Personality*, ch 11, Design Council.
2   See *Alfred Dunhill Ltd v Sunoptic SA* [1979] FSR 337 at 351 (CA).
3   See *Kodak Ltd v London Stereoscopic and Photographic Co Ltd* (1903) 19 TLR 297, 20 RPC 337.
4   See *Office Cleaning Services Ltd v Westminster Window and General Cleaners Ltd* [1946] 1 All ER 320n, 63 RPC 39.
5   See *Re Birmingham Small Arms Co's Application* [1907] 2 Ch 396 the full name now being now largely forgotten.
6   See *Unitex Ltd v Union Texturing Co Ltd* [1973] RPC 119.
7   See paras 3.16–3.33 above.

LETTER AND NUMBER MARKS

3.41 A plaintiff may rely upon combinations of letters or numbers provided that he can establish his reputation in them. Such marks are often the result of abbreviation of or calculation from terminology describing features of the goods or services to which they are applied. However, the process of conversion usually serves to obscure the descriptive origin of the mark so that it is treated more like an invented word. Such a case is *A Boake Roberts & Co Ltd v W A Wayland & Co*,[1] where the plaintiff succeeded in claiming that the letters 'K M S' were distinctive of its products despite the fact that the product in question was 'Kalium Meta Sulphite'. Other examples of successful claims to letter marks are 'L L' for whisky,[2] 'F M T & Co' for a business selling wines and spirits and the goods sold by the business,[3] 'B S A' for a wide variety of goods,[4] 'J L' for a business in golf clubs[5] and 'H A C' for lifts.[6] The letters 'A G S' were held distinctive of the plaintiff's business in making aeroplane parts even though those letters, when used in relation to the parts themselves stood for 'Aeronautical General Schedule' which was an official list of parts produced by the Royal Aircraft Factory, Farnham.[7] The professional association cases often involve initials: 'BMA',[8] 'CA'[9] and 'FSAA'[10] have all been protected. A case which shows the limits of such a reputation is *IDW Superstores Ltd v Duncan Harris & Co Ltd*,[11] where the plaintiff, which used the name 'I D W', failed to prevent the defendant from trading from the plaintiff's former premises under the name 'Ideal Discount Warehouses', the court holding that such confusion as there had been was caused by the occupation of the premises and not the similarity of name. And a claim to prevent the use of the initials 'BP' on proprietary medicines failed on a variety of grounds including an absence of evidence that the public understood that those initials stood for 'British

Pharmacopoeia'.[12] Beyond the notorious '4711' and 'Chanel No 5', claims to distinctive number marks are rare. In *Hymac Ltd v Priestman Bros Ltd*[13] the plaintiff successfully relied upon the model number '580' for a mechanical excavator. The defendant's argument that the term was derived from and therefore descriptive of the bucket capacity failed on the ground that it was at best a coded description and not recognisable unless one knew the code.[14]

---

1   (1909) 26 RPC 249.
2   *Kinahan v Bolton* (1863) 15 Ir Ch 75.
3   *Findlater, Mackie, Todd & Co v Newman & Co* (1902) 19 RPC 235.
4   *Birmingham Small Arms Co's Application* [1907] 2 Ch 396.
5   *John Letters & Co v J Letters (Craigton) Ltd* [1967] RPC 209.
6   *Hammond and Champness v HAC Lifts Ltd* [1975] FSR 131.
7   *AGS Manufacturing Co Ltd v Aeroplane General Sundries Co Ltd* (1918) 35 RPC 127.
8   *British Medical Association v Marsh* (1931) 47 TLR 572, 48 RPC 565.
9   *Society of Accountants in Edinburgh v Corporation of Accountants Ltd* (1903) 20 R (Ct of Sess) 750, 30 Sc LR 677.
10 *Society of Incorporated Accountants v Vincent* (1954) 71 RPC 325.
11 [1975] RPC 178, [1974] FSR 114.
12 *A-G and General Council of Medical Education v Barrett Proprietaries* (1932) 50 RPC 45.
13 [1978] RPC 495.
14 See also *Ainsworth v Walmsley* (1866) LR 1 Eq 518.

DEVICE MARKS

3.42 Reputation may be claimed in any form of device, that is a picture, sign or symbol, either alone or in combination with words or other devices or get-up. Devices can take almost any form and it should not be forgotten that a stylised word logo is strictly speaking a device for it may be identified with a particular trader only when written in the form in which it is used. There are many famous examples of device marks: the golden arch 'M' of MacDonalds being one of the currently most universally recognised. *Laura Ashley Ltd v Coloroll Ltd*,[1] a trade mark case, provides a good modern example of a device mark and the court's approach to them. *Celine's Trade Mark*,[2] a trade mark opposition appeal, provides clear and helpful guidance on the approach to take when trying to determine whether two devices are so similar that there is likely in practice to be confusion between them. It is possible, though unlikely, that a device mark could be descriptive of the product, for example by consisting of a picture or other representation of the appearance of the product. However, as has been pointed out,[3] in such cases the issue of descriptiveness is not the same as that which arises with descriptive words. The appearance of the product is a feature of it and the question in each case is, therefore, whether the appearance of the product is distinctive of its manufacturer. Such cases therefore fall to be approached in the same way as claims to distinctive get-up.

---

1 [1987] RPC 1.
2 [1985] RPC 381.
3 Per Hoffman J in *Unilever Ltd's (Striped Toothpaste No 2) Trade Marks* [1985] RPC 13.

GET-UP

3.43 Claims to distinctive get-up must always be approached with great care as must the decided cases. The first and most important reason for this is that it is rare indeed to find circumstances in which the only visible features of an article or its packaging consist of get-up. Nearly everything is packed or presented with some form of descriptive or explanatory text and usually a name. Claims to passing off by the taking of get-up are therefore unusually prone to fail by reason of additional distinguishing matter on the defendant's goods.[1] In such circumstances it is also more difficult to demonstrate that the get-up alone has come to be recognised as distinctive of a particular source of manufacture. It is of course essential to demonstrate this.[2] Successful get-up claims also tend to arise from unusual trade circumstances. Sometimes the way in which the goods are sold or supplied is odd.[3] Sometimes the nature of the article and the circumstances of its purchase combine in a way which causes the get-up to have an exaggerated importance to the purchaser.[4] It is therefore important in considering any decision of the courts to look closely at the specific reasons for the claim having succeeded or failed before endeavouring to draw any legal principle from it. Taken incautiously, decisions in particular get-up cases are apt to mislead.

---

1   See paras 4.34 – 4.35 below.
2   See *Tavener Rutledge Ltd v Specters Ltd* [1959] RPC 355 at 362 and, for an example of the difficulties which can arise in determining which, if any, features of get-up are distinctive of a business, *My Kinda Town Ltd v Soll* [1983] RPC 407 (CA).
3   The drug capsule cases cited in para 3.47 below are examples of this.
4   See the explanation of the *Jif* case in para 4.05 below.

3.44 There have over the years been two distinct approaches to claims based upon get-up. The first, which is epitomised by *William Edge & Sons Ltd v William Niccolls & Sons Ltd*[1] at the beginning of the century, and by *Reckitt & Colman Products Ltd v Borden Inc*[2] (the *Jif* case) at the end, is that any feature of the appearance of a product can become distinctive of its manufacturer and thus form part of its get-up. The other is to be found in cases such as *J B Williams & Co v Bronnley & Co Ltd*[3] where get-up is said to be limited to some characteristic of the appearance of the goods, which is in some way extraneous to the function or nature of the goods themselves. In that case Fletcher Moulton LJ gave what has often been thought of as the classic definition of get-up as:

> 'a capricious addition to the article itself — the colour, or shape, it may be, of the wrapper, or anything of that kind; but I strongly object to look at anything, that has a value in use, as part of the get-up of the article. Anything which is in itself useful appears to me rightly to belong to the article itself.'[4]

In the light of this it is hardly surprising that practitioners faced with a particular problem can find cases to support almost any view of the nature of get-up and its ability to distinguish the goods of one trader from the goods of another. And as Lord Oliver commented in *Jif*:

> ... this is not a branch of the law in which reference to other cases is of any real assistance except analogically. It has been observed more than once that the questions which arise are, in general, questions of fact.'[5]

It now seems likely that the decision in the *Jif* case marks a change of approach to passing off in two areas,[6] one of which is what is capable of constituting get-up as a matter of law. Accordingly the reasoning of the leading speeches of Lords Oliver and Jauncey, with both of whom all the other members of the House agreed, merits careful consideration.

---

1 [1911] AC 693.
2 [1990] RPC 341.
3 (1909) 26 RPC 765 (CA). This case has been regularly followed until the decision in *Jif*. See for example *Jarman & Platt v I Barget Limited* [1977] FSR 260 (CA), *Cadbury Ltd v Ulmer GmbH* [1988] FSR 385.
4 Ibid at 773.
5 [1990] RPC 341 at 406.
6 The other being the analysis of the tort. See paras 2.36 and 2.37 above.

3.45 Lord Oliver found it unnecessary to decide the question finally — the issue in the case being whether the package used for *Jif* lemon juice was distinctive — but nevertheless said this:

> 'Whether in fact the particular shape or configuration of the very object sold by a trader is incapable as a matter of law of protection in a case where it has become associated exclusively with his business is a proposition which is at least open to doubt. The decision of Buckley J in *R J Elliott & Co Ltd v Hodgson*[1] suggests the contrary, although it has been doubted: see *Cadbury Ltd v Ulmer GmbH*.[2] It is clear from the decision of this House in *William Edge & Sons Ltd v William Niccolls & Sons Ltd*[3] that where the article sold is conjoined with an object which, whilst serving the functional purpose of enabling the article to be more effectively employed, is of a shape or configuration which has become specifically identified with a particular manufacturer, the latter may be entitled to protection against the deceptive use in conjunction with similar articles of objects fashioned in the same or a closely similar shape.'[4]

Lord Jauncey went rather further. Having considered *Edge v Niccolls* he went on to deal with *British American Glass Co Ltd v Winton Products (Blackpool) Ltd*,[5] a case which has often been said to be authority for the proposition that the appearance of an article itself is not protectable, and held that Pennycuick J in that case 'was clearly recognising that the shape and configuration of the article could be protected against deception'.[6] In the light of this he concluded that:

> 'these two cases are merely examples of the general principle that no man may sell his goods under the pretence that they are the goods of another. This principle applies as well to the goods themselves as to their get-up.'[6]

The law must, therefore, now be taken to be that the appearance of an article itself as well as its packaging or other non-functional additions to it may be protected as get-up if the facts support the claim that the appearance of the product is itself distinctive. This does not, however, mean that it will be easy to demonstrate that the appearance of the article is distinctive. *Jif* followed a series of cases in which such claims had failed.[7]

1 [1902] 19 RPC 518.
2 [1988] FSR 385.
3 [1911] AC 693.
4 *Reckitt & Colman Products Ltd v Borden Inc* [1990] RPC 341 at 411.
5 [1962] RPC 230.
6 *Reckitt & Colman v Borden* ibid at 426.
7 Examples of these are *Rizla v Bryant & May* [1986] RPC 389, *Scott v Nice-Pak* [1989] FSR 100 and *Drayton Controls v Honeywell* [1992] FSR 245, *Jarman & Platt v Barget Ltd* [1977] FSR 260.

3.46 In the light of the decision in *Jif* the earlier cases on get-up are now of less relevance in determining the law. However, as Lord Oliver noted,[1] such cases turn very much on their own facts and reference to them is of considerable assistance in understanding what the courts are likely to accept as effectively distinctive get-up. Unusually shaped packaging is regularly relied upon. *Jif* itself is an example of this. There are many others. In *Coca-Cola v Barr*[2] and *John Haig & Co v Forth Blending Co*[3] the plaintiffs relied successfully upon the unusual and fanciful shape of the bottles in which their beverages were sold. The unusual appearance of articles themselves has also been successfully relied upon. *Edge v Niccolls*[4] (laundry blue on a stick) and *Elliott v Hodgson*[5] (flat-ended cigars) are two such cases, both of which were considered by the House of Lords in *Jif*, although Dankwerts J's comment[6] that *Elliott v Hodgson* was 'the very limit of cases of this kind' was noted. However, attempts to rely upon articles which do not have unusual features of appearance have always failed. In *Benchairs v Chair Centre*[7] and *George Hensher Ltd v Restawile Upholstery (Lancs) Ltd*[8] the plaintiffs claimed that the shapes of their chairs were distinctive. In both cases those claims failed and only the alternative claims for infringement of registered design and copyright respectively were pursued. A claim that the flint facing of a house was distinctive was rejected in *Charles Church Developments plc v Cronin*.[9] This was a particularly weak claim and was only an adjunct to a perfectly sound copyright claim.

1 See para 3.44 above.
2 [1961] RPC 387.
3 (1952) 69 RPC 8.
4 [1911] AC 693.
5 (1902) 19 RPC 518.
6 In *Hawkins and Tipson v Fludes Carpets Ltd* [1957] RPC 8.
7 [1972] FSR 397.
8 [1972] FSR 557, [1975] RPC 31, [1973] 1 WLR 144.
9 [1990] FSR 1.

3.47 Colours and colour schemes are frequently said to be distinctive of a particular manufacturer. There are a number of cases in which the colours of particular drug capsules have been held to be distinctive. In *Hoffman la Roche v DDSA*,[1] green and black capsules were held distinctive of the plaintiffs, the defendant's argument that these colours merely denoted the nature of the drug contained in them being rejected. However, in *Roche Products Ltd v Berk Pharmaceuticals Ltd*[2] a claim to distinctiveness of plain yellow and white tablets (the different colours being used for different doses) was rejected. The use of pink paper for printing the 'Financial Times' has been held to be distinctive of that paper[3] although the passing off claim failed on the particular facts of the case. And in *Sodastream v Thorn Cascade*[4] the plaintiffs somewhat surprisingly succeeded in a claim that the colour grey was distinctive of their carbon dioxide capsules. A claim that get-up consisting of the colours red, green and blue as individually applied to different grades of cigarette papers was distinctive was rejected in *Rizla Ltd v Bryant & May Ltd*.[5] All of these cases need to be approached with particular care as they depend substantially upon the particular circumstances of the trades with which they are concerned.

---

1 [1969] FSR 410. See also *The Boots Company Limited v Approved Prescription Services Limited* [1988] FSR 45 where the claim was held arguable but an interlocutory injunction refused on the balance of convenience.
2 [1973] RPC 473. See also *John Wyeth & Brother Limited v M & A Pharmaceuticals Limited* [1988] FSR 26.
3 *The Financial Times Ltd v Evening Standard Co Ltd* [1991] FSR 7.
4 [1982] RPC 459, Com LR 64.
5 [1986] RPC 389.

3.48 Features of articles or packaging which are common to the trade in the sense of being used by a number of different traders cannot form a distinctive get-up.[1] However, this does not mean that such features, together with other distinctive features, cannot form a get-up which overall distinguishes the plaintiff's goods. Generally get-up must be considered as a whole, although, if it appears on the evidence that some aspect of the appearance of a product is disregarded by purchasers, that part should not be taken account of.[2]

---

1 *J B Williams v Bronnley* (1909) 26 RPC 481 and 765 (CA).
2 The fact that the evidence disclosed that customers did not pay attention to the label attached to the neck of the plastic lemon in *Jif* is the primary reason for the initially rather surprising outcome of the case: see para 4.05 below.

3.49 One finds in the reported cases many examples of both successful and unsuccessful claims to a wide range of distinctive get-up. With two cautions such cases are helpful in seeing what kinds of features, marking and the like the courts have considered and what approach they have taken to them. The first warning is that one should not seek to derive any legal principle from a decision on particular facts. The second is that many of the cases turn on peculiarities of the particular trade under consideration. This is especially so with the older decisions. Methods of trading now are far removed from 100 years ago. With that introduction the following decisions provide some guidance. In *Lever v Goodwin*[1] the plaintiff successfully relied upon the combination of markings, words and decorations on a soap wrapper. In *J & J Colman v Farrow & Co*[2] the plaintiff claimed that the entire arrangement of a yellow wrapper for a mustard tin on which appeared a fancy red typeface for the name, 'Colman's', was distinctive of its mustard. It was held that this was so and that the defendant's wrapper was confusingly similar notwithstanding the fact that the defendant used the name 'Farrow's'. In *Masson Seeley & Co Ltd v Embossotype Manufacturing Co*[3] the defendant copied the contents of the plaintiff's price lists and catalogue with the intention of diverting the plaintiff's business. Unsurprisingly it was held that the defendant had succeeded and it was restrained both in passing off and copyright. A wide variety of other get-up claims have failed. Bubble gum in the form of false teeth,[4] a picture of a particular fruit to indicate flavour of jelly crystals,[5] the pattern of matting,[6] the shape and colour of tins of harness compositions (only part of which was taken),[7] the advertising style and pictures used for garden seeds,[8] the whimsical and flowery style of drawings on greetings cards,[9] a buff-coloured velveteen polishing cloth,[10] the appearance of a Rubik cube,[11] blue tubs for baby wipes[12] and the configuration of a thermostatic radiator valve[13] have all been held not to be distinctive. In New Zealand the use of polythene bags with a check pattern to package bread has been held common in the trade and thus not distinctive.[14] Cases of business get-up are less common. The overall appearance of a shop-front appears to have been regarded as capable of protection[15] and it has even been held that the internal arrangements and decor of a restaurant were distinctive although the first instance judgment was reversed on appeal on the ground that this type of confusion was not relied upon in the pleadings and was probably inevitable given that the parties ran similar styles of restaurants.[16] The presentation of a fleet of buses and their operators' uniforms has also been successfully relied upon.[17]

---

1 (1887) 36 Ch D 1, 4 RPC 492.
2 (1897) 15 RPC 198.
3 (1924) 41 RPC 160. See also *Purefoy Engineering Co Ltd v Sykes Boxall & Co Ltd* (1955) 72 RPC 89.
4 *Blundell v Margolis Ltd ('Toofy's')* (1951) 68 RPC 71.
5 *White Tompkins & Courage Ltd v United Confectionery Ltd* (1914) 31 RPC 286.
6 *Hawkins and Tipson v Fludes* (1957) RPC 8.
7 *Jamieson & Co v Jamieson* (1898) 14 TLR 160, 15 RPC 169.
8 *Wertheimer v Stewart Cooper & Co* (1906) 23 RPC 481.
9 *Gordon Fraser Gallery Ltd v Tatt* [1966] RPC 505.
10 *Jones Bros Ltd v Anglo-American Optical Co* (1912) 29 RPC 1 and 361 (CA); *Jones v Hallworth* (1897) 14 RPC 225.
11 *Politechnika Ipari Szovertkezet v Dallas Print Transfers* [1982] FSR 529.
12 *Scott Ltd v Nice-Pak Products Ltd* [1989] FSR 100.
13 *Drayton Controls (Engineering) Ltd v Honeywell Control Systems Limited* [1992] FSR 245.
14 *Klissers Farmhouse Bakeries Limited v Harvest Bakeries Limited* [1989] RPC 27.
15 *Laraine Day v Kennedy* (1952) 70 RPC 19.

16 *My Kinda Town v Soll* [1983] RPC 15, 407 (CA), particularly per Oliver LJ at 424 ll 44 ff.
17 *London General Omnibus Co Ltd v Felton* (1896) 12 TLR 213.

Dealing in reputation and goodwill

TRANSFER OF RIGHTS

3.50 It has long been recognised that, unless registered as a trade or service mark or protected by copyright or registered design, there is no right of property in a name or get-up. It follows that the name or get-up cannot be assigned separately from the goodwill in the business in which it is used. Conversely the transfer of the goodwill in a business normally carries with it the right to use the names and get-up used in that business. Romer J put the matter thus in 1894 in *Thorneloe v Hill*:[1]

> 'speaking generally, a purchaser of a business if he continues it has the right to use the trade name and trade-marks of the business in any way he pleases which is not calculated to deceive.'[2]

He went on to contrast this with the position of 'a mere assignee in gross of the right to use [a] name' saying:

> 'the right merely to use a name as a property in itself cannot be validly assigned so as to confer rights as against the public, nor can any advantage whatever as against the public attach to any attempted assignment of the sort.'[3]

These principles were not new. As early as 1865, before it had been clearly stated that there was no right of property in a name or mark as such, Lord Cranworth held that there was a right to sell and transfer a trade mark 'upon a sale and transfer of "the manufactory of the goods on which the mark has been used to be affixed" '.[4] However, if the goodwill is personal or closely associated with a particular individual, it cannot be transferred in this way. Lord Kingsdown, in the same case, drew this distinction:

> 'Though a man may assign his business and the use of his firm, and of his trade mark as belonging to it, that proceeds, in my opinion, upon the ground which I have stated, that the use of the name of the firm is not understood in trade to signify that certain individuals, and no other are engaged in the concern. Though a man may have property in a trade mark, in the sense of having a right to exclude any other trader from the use of it in selling the same description of goods, it does not follow that he can in all cases give another person a right to use it, or to use his name. If an artist or an artisan has acquired by his personal skill and ability a reputation which gives to his works in the market a higher value than those of other artists or artisans, he cannot give any other person the right to affix his name or mark to their goods, because he cannot give them the right to practise a fraud upon the public.'[5]

It is clear from this passage that it was already recognised that a trade mark could only be assigned with the business in which it was used even though it had not then been fully appreciated that the only property in law was the goodwill in the business. It is now clearly established that only the assignment of a business, or at least its goodwill, can carry with it the right to exclude others from using a name or get-up.[6]

1 [1894] 1 Ch 569, 11 RPC 61.

2 Ibid at 574, 70.

3 Ibid at 577, 72.

4 *Leather Cloth Co Ltd v American Leather Cloth Co Ltd* (1865) 11 HL Cas 523 at 534. In so saying Lord Cranworth was treating the right to a mark as analogous to copyright and 'as property or as an accessory of property'.

5 Ibid at 544–545. This passage was specifically approved and followed by Lord Esher MR in *Pinto v Badman* (1891) 7 TLR 317, 8 RPC 181 at 192.

6 The modern law is clearly stated by Lord Diplock in *Star Industrial Co Ltd v Yap Kwee Kor* [1976] FSR 256 at 269–270. See also *Pinto v Badman* (1891) 7 TLR 317, 8 RPC 181; *Kingston, Miller & Co Ltd v Thomas Kingston & Co Ltd* [1912] 1 Ch 575, 29 RPC 289; *Fine Cotton Spinners and Doublers Association Ltd v Harwood Cash & Co Ltd* (1907) 2 Ch 184, 24 RPC 533; *Tussaud v Tussaud* [1890] 44 Ch D 678, 59 LJ Ch 631.

LICENSING OF RIGHTS

Franchising[1]

3.51 Franchising, as that term is nowadays used, is a relatively new method of distributing goods, know-how and marketing techniques which has gained rapidly in popularity over the last 20 years. It is now commonplace in commercial areas such as fast food restaurants and a wide variety of retailing activities. This increasing popularity stems from the fact that it enables relatively small organisations acting as franchisors to develop large and widely-spread distribution networks at relatively little expense and risk; and gives small businesses operating as franchisees the opportunity to become part of a large network operating under common marks and to common standards and thus to obtain the benefit of a much larger goodwill than they could themselves generate. The essential hallmarks of a franchising system are as follows. It is a system of commercial cooperation between independent traders which is governed by contracts under which the franchisor grants franchisees the right to use his trade name, mark or get-up in the distribution of goods or the provision of services in accordance with the standards and other terms laid down by the contract under a marketing scheme or concept developed by the franchisor. The franchisor supervises the use of the name and the conduct of the business carried on by the franchisees to ensure that the standards laid down by the franchise agreement are maintained so that the public can be sure of a uniform standard of goods and service from all franchisees, and generally provides them with marketing and advertising support. Franchisees will normally be given exclusive areas of operation to enable them to take the maximum benefit from being a member of the scheme. In return for these rights the franchisor takes a royalty on all sales made by the franchisees. Thus the franchisees, whilst remaining commercially independent of the franchisor, become for marketing purposes part of a large uniform network of outlets. There is no legislative definition or control of franchise agreements, apart from normal contractual considerations, so their operation is governed entirely by the terms of the agreement between them and any restriction which may be imposed, for example by competition law, upon those terms.

---

1 It is beyond the scope of this book to cover franchising law in any detail. There are now a number of works devoted specifically to the subject. The reader is referred to *Franchising* by Adams and Pritchard Jones 3rd edn (1990, Butterworths) for a full treatment of this topic.

3.52 Franchising contracts should provide that the goodwill in the name, mark or get-up under which the scheme operates accrues to the franchisor. However, provided that the scheme operates in such a way as to make the franchisee's operations an arm of the franchisor's business, that will occur even without specific provision.[1] Accordingly the franchisor alone is entitled to bring proceedings for passing off although the relevant franchisees may be joined as co-plaintiffs. It follows that in general the franchisees' rights to use the name and get-up of the franchisor are wholly dependent upon the franchisor's permission and will cease when the permission is withdrawn. In practice franchise agreements make specific provision for precisely this to occur and often include in addition post termination non-competition covenants.

---

1 See *J H Coles Pty Ltd v Need* [1934] AC 82 (PC); *North Shore Toy Co Ltd v Charles L Stevenson Ltd* [1974] RPC 545 (a New Zealand case).

Character merchandising

3.53 Character merchandising is another modern form of marketing which derives its value from the public's apparently insatiable appetite for goods marked with the 'stamp' of well-known real or fictional characters. Such goods can be sold for substantially higher prices than the same goods without such markings. English law has been slow to recognise the practice and for a long time English courts took the view that there was simply no exploitable goodwill in fictional characters as the marking of goods with their names or representations did not imply any trade connection with the deviser of the character. In a series of cases brought in the mid-1970s[1] it was held that the use on products of names of well known characters did not suggest to consumers that the manufacturer of the products had a licence from the deviser of the character to use the name. It was also held in these cases that for an action in passing off to lie it was necessary to prove not only this but also that consumers recognised the licence as a guarantee of the quality of the licensed products. One of the key factors in all these cases was the fact that all that was claimed to be licensed was the name of the character. There was neither any underlying copyright or other proprietary right nor any commercial activity of the licensor in which there was relevant goodwill which could be said to support the licence. In those circumstances Walton J described such licences as being 'writ in water'.[2] It remains the case today that the owner of a name or the deviser of a fictional character has no right under the law of passing off to prevent the use of the character for merchandising goods unless (i) he has acquired a reputation in the name in connection with a business and (ii) he can prove the likelihood of damage to the goodwill in the business as a result of the use of the name of which he complains. Accordingly character merchandising cases are indistinguishable in principle from any other form of passing off action. However, there is no doubt that the increased prevalence of the practice of character merchandising has enabled the evidence which was conspicuously lacking in the early English cases to be put forward, and in both Australia[3] and South Africa[4] the courts accepted some time ago that the public generally expects products bearing the names and representations of well-known fictional characters to be licensed and controlled by the deviser of the characters. Accordingly the relevant goodwill and damage could be shown and actions for passing off would lie. Until recently, despite passing judicial comment,[5] there was no equivalent recognition in England. However, in *Mirage Studios v Counter-Feat Clothing Co Ltd*,[6] Browne-Wilkinson VC held that such an action would lie in relation to pictures of the well-known cartoon characters, Teenage Mutant Ninja Turtles. The manner in which he did so is both interesting and important.

---

1   *Tavener Rutledge Ltd v Trexapalm Ltd* [1975] FSR 479; *Lyngstad v Anabas Products Ltd* [1977] FSR 62; *Wombles Ltd v Wombles Skips Ltd* [1975] FSR 488, [1977] RPC 99.
2   *Tavener Rutledge Ltd v Trexapalm Ltd* supra at 486.
3   *Children's Television Workshop Inc v Woolworth (NSW) Ltd* [1981] RPC 187; *Fido Dido Inc v Venture Stores (Retailers) Pty Ltd* 16 IPR 365.
4   *Lorimar Productions Inc v Sterling Clothing Manufacturers Pty* [1982] RPC 395.
5   See the comments of Lord Bridge in *Holly Hobbie Trade Mark* [1984] RPC 329 at 351.
6   [1991] FSR 145.

3.54 Having considered the elements of the tort of passing off as set out by Lord Diplock in *Advocaat*,[1] he applied them to the facts turning first to whether there was a misrepresentation and saying:

'The critical evidence in this case is that a substantial number of the buying public now expect and know that where a famous cartoon or television character is reproduced on goods, that reproduction is the result of a licence granted by the owner of the copyright or other rights in that character.... If, as the evidence here shows, the public mistake the defendants' turtles for those which might be called genuine plaintiffs' Turtles, once they have made the mistake they will assume that the product in question has been licensed to use Turtles on it. That is to say, they will connect what they mistakenly think to be the plaintiffs' Turtles with the plaintiffs. To put on the market goods which the public mistake for the genuine article necessarily involves a misrepresentation to the public that they are genuine. On the evidence in this case, the belief that the goods are genuine involves a further misrepresentation, namely that they are licensed.'[2]

Thus, it is clear that the foundation of the judge's conclusion that an action for passing off lay was the finding that the evidence showed the public expectation of licence by the owner of the 'copyright or other rights in the character'. Clearly the misrepresentation was being made by the defendants in the course of trade to customers and prospective customers: they were selling T-shirts with pictures of turtles on them. These aspects of Lord Diplock's formulation of the tort therefore presented no difficulty and the judge turned to the question of damage to the plaintiffs' business and goodwill, summarising the facts in the following terms:

'What is the plaintiffs' business or goodwill? Mirage Studios are plainly in business as the creators and marketers of cartoons, videos and films of their characters, the Ninja Turtles. But the evidence is quite clear that that is only part of their business: their business also includes the turning to profit of those characters by licensing the reproduction of them on goods sold by other people. A major part of their business income arises from royalties to be received from such a licensing enterprise. In relation to the drawings of Ninja Turtles as they appear in cartoons, *etc.*, there is a copyright which can be infringed. If one wishes to take advantage of the Ninja character it is necessary to reproduce the Ninja Turtle and thereby the concept, bizarre and unusual as it is, of the Teenage Mutant Ninja Turtle becomes a marketable commodity. It is in that business that the plaintiffs are engaged.'[3]

Those findings of fact, in particular that the plaintiffs were engaged in the business of licensing Turtle reproductions, were also critical to his conclusion that the claim was made out for he went on to conclude that, in the light of them:

'if others are able to reproduce or apparently reproduce the Turtles without paying licence royalties to the plaintiffs, they will lose the royalties. Since the public associates the goods with the creator of the characters, the depreciation of the image by fixing the Turtle picture to inferior goods and inferior materials may seriously reduce the value of the licensing right. This damage to an important part of the plaintiffs' business is therefore plainly foreseeable.'[3]

In other words the goodwill being protected by the action for passing off in a character merchandising case is that in the business of licensing or merchandising the character. However, it is presumably only a matter of time before the court takes this approach to its logical conclusion and accepts that it is also proper to protect the prospective business of the creator of a character who proposes to merchandise it but has not yet done so.[4] Browne-Wilkinson VC considered and approved the Australian cases[5] saying of them:

'In my judgment the law as developed in Australia is sound. There is no reason why a remedy in passing off should be limited to those who market or sell the goods themselves. If the public is misled in a relevant way as to a feature or quality of the goods as sold, that is sufficient to found a cause of action in passing off brought by those people with whom the public associate that feature or that quality which has been misrepresented.'[6]

Having concluded that this represented the present law, the judge went on to distinguish the older English cases on the basis that they were concerned with licensing of a mere name and that there was no underlying copyright or other right to support the public perception of licence. Accordingly he held that they were not relevant to the facts of the case before him. However, he did comment in relation to them that:

> 'those cases may, given the change in trading habits, require reconsideration on a future occasion if the evidence before the court is different.'[7]

The way is therefore open for the bringing of passing off claims in relation to pure name licensing if the evidence supports the claim that the public expects the goods to be licensed. Indeed, it is submitted that, understandable though the judge's desire may have been to distinguish rather than appear to disapprove the decisions in the earlier cases, the real difference between the old cases and this one is that there was clear evidence of the fact that the public perceived and expected the goods to be licensed. It is this difference which in fact provides the relevant distinction. The presence or absence of an underlying right to form the subject of the licence does not matter. The misrepresentation is that the goods are licensed. That arises because and only because the public believes that they are licensed in the sense of being official or approved by the plaintiff. If that is the public's belief, nothing else matters.

---

1 See para 2.33 above.
2 *Mirage Studios v Counter-Feat Clothing Co Ltd* [1991] FSR 145 at 155.
3 Ibid at 156.
4 Following in effect Falconer J's approach to the extent of goodwill in *Lego System A/S v Lego M Lemelstrich Ltd* [1983] FSR 155 at 190.
5 See n 3, to para 3.53 above.
6 Ibid at 157.
7 Ibid at 158.

Other forms of licensing

3.55 The decision in the *Ninja Turtles* case also appears at least in principle to open the way to passing off actions brought on a rather broader basis than has hitherto been thought possible. It seems from the approach there that it is possible to protect a business in licensing. The question is whether the courts will ultimately accept that that business can stand alone and apart from anything else. This may have a considerable impact upon the possibility of actions by sports stars and other public figures to prevent false claims that they use or have endorsed particular products. There is as yet no contested case in which such a claim has succeeded[1] although claims have been made and settled in recent years. There seems to be no reason now why, with the appropriate evidence, public figures should not be able to claim that they have an exploitable goodwill in their names giving endorsement or approval to particular goods which is protectable by an action for passing off. There are other circumstances in which the same approach may be applied. A variety of organisations, including football and other sports clubs, arrange for the marketing of a wide variety of approved goods bearing the club's logo or emblem. Often the emblem is of some antiquity. It may well not be possible to establish that there is copyright in it or who owns the copyright. Unless there is copyright or design right in some other aspect of the article which has been infringed, passing off will be the only remedy available. The decision in the *Ninja Turtles* case will greatly facilitate such claims.

---

1   The cases in which such claims have failed are examined at para 5.15 below.

CHAPTER 4

The misrepresentation

Introduction

4.01 At the heart of every case of passing off is the act committed by
the defendant which is alleged to constitute the misrepresentation that the
defendant's goods[1] or business are in fact the plaintiff's. As has been seen, the
nature of the reputation which the plaintiff is entitled to protect can take many
forms.[2] The same is also true of the act of misrepresentation committed by the
defendant.[3] Additionally, the use by a trader of names, marks, or get-up which
would by themselves be confusingly similar to those of another trader, so as
to give rise to an improper misrepresentation, may be offset by combination
with other material which distinguishes the goods or business of the one from
those of the other. Thus, it is always necessary in a case of potential passing
off to consider the totality of what the defendant is doing in order to determine
whether or not there is a likelihood of confusion.

---

1   Or the plaintiff's goods of a different class or quality: see paras 4.19 ff. below.
2   See ch 3 above.
3   See eg per Lord Parker in *AG Spalding & Bros v A W Gamage Ltd* (1915) 32 RPC 273 at 284, lines 29–30.

THE MEANING OF 'MISREPRESENTATION'

4.02   In referring to the term 'misrepresentation' in this context it is necessary
to take care to ensure that it is being used consistently. When a trader marks
his goods in a particular way or adopts a particular trading style, he is always
making a representation of some kind to his customers. That representation
only becomes a misrepresentation if, because of another trader's reputation
in the identifying features adopted, it connotes that other trader's goods or
business in some way. Throughout this chapter it will be assumed that the
plaintiff has shown in one of the ways set out in the previous chapter that
the features relied on are normally associated with him. In this chapter we
consider the variety of ways in which a defendant may be found to have
appropriated the plaintiff's identifying features and thus pass off his goods
or business as the plaintiff's and also how the defendant may escape liability
for an act which at first sight appears to amount to passing off.

4.03   *The misrepresentation*

GENERAL CONSIDERATIONS

Whose confusion is relevant

4.03   The persons whose possible deception or confusion is to be considered are the plaintiff's own customers or the ultimate consumers of the goods or services in question[1] and it is important to identify the class or types of likely customers and consumers in each case. There are two reasons for this. First, the extent of the differences required to prevent confusion between the plaintiff's goods or services and the defendant's goods or services will depend substantially on the type of purchaser concerned and the circumstances of their sale. For example, some articles are habitually purchased in self-service shops by members of the general public who select them from a shelf without devoting great attention to what they are buying. Thus an objectively slight similarity between two packages may well give rise to confusion.[2] Indeed, if the evidence shows that they do not read the labels on goods, then even the provision of labels which do clearly distinguish if they are read may be insufficient.[3] Other articles, such as motor cars, are only purchased after careful thought and even very substantial overall similarities between rival brands may not be confusing.[4] Second, some cases of passing off arise in relation to goods or services for which there is a specialised limited market. The customers in such cases are often better informed about the products or services they are buying than members of the general public and may not be likely to be confused by what might appear prima facie to be a misrepresentation as to the origin of the goods. In the limiting case, it may never be possible for a defendant to pass off his goods as the plaintiff's simply because all potential consumers of those goods buy only directly from the plaintiff and would never think that goods from another source were the plaintiff's.[5] In such a case, while there may be unfair competition in the sense described in ch 1, above, there can never be passing off. Where the defendant sells to dealers or wholesalers who sell on to members of the public it is irrelevant that the dealer is not confused if the purchasing public will be confused.[6]

---

1   Lord Diplock's third characteristic set out in *Erven Warnink v Townend & Sons* [1979] AC 731 at 742, [1980] RPC 31 at 93.

2   Cases where purchasers have been held to be easily confused are: *Johnston v Orr-Ewing* (1882) 7 App Cas 219, 51 LJ Ch 797 and *Wilkinson v Griffith* (1891) 8 RPC 370 (both cases where label get-up imitated with different English wording marketed in India and confusing to non-English speaking purchasers); *William Edge & Sons Ltd v William Niccolls* [1911] AC 693, 80 LJ Ch 744 (many purchasers illiterate and addition of D's name insufficient to distinguish the goods where get-up otherwise identical); *Saville Perfumery Ltd v June Perfect Ltd* (1941) 58 RPC 147; *White Hudson & Co v Asian Organisation Ltd* [1965] 1 All ER 1040, [1965] RPC 45 (customers not familiar with Roman alphabet).

3   See the findings of fact in *Reckitt & Colman v Borden* [1990] 1 All ER 873, RPC 341, which are summarised in the speech of Lord Oliver at 882, 408.

4   See *Claudius Ash Son & Co Ltd v Invicta Manufacturing Co Ltd* (1911) 28 RPC 597, CA, (1912) 29 RPC 465, HL. See also *Lancer Trade Mark* [1987] RPC 303 at 325 (a trade mark case).

5   A case in which just this occurred is *John Hayter Motor Underwriting Agencies Ltd v RBHS Agencies Ltd* [1977] 2 Lloyds Rep 105, [1977] FSR 285. The plaintiff traded as 'JSB Motor Policies at Lloyds'. The defendant commenced trading as 'BJS Motor syndicate at Lloyds'. The only direct customers

74

of the defendant were insurance brokers who were fully aware of the existence of the plaintiff and the defendant as different organisations. There was thus no reasonable prospect of actual confusion and an interlocutory injunction was refused.
6 See para 4.29 below.

How many people must be confused

4.04 It is not and never has been necessary to show that all or substantially all the persons to whom the misrepresentation is made will be confused. It is sufficient that a substantial proportion of persons who are probably purchasers of the goods of the kind in question will in fact be confused.[1] Nor is it necessary to show that the act complained of is a misrepresentation to all potential customers or consumers. Where a mark is used distinctively by some people but descriptively by others the court will grant an injunction to prevent passing off but the injunction will be limited so as to permit the defendant to supply goods not the plaintiff's provided that it is made clear that the goods supplied are not the plaintiff's.[2] In *Pete Waterman Limited v CBS United Kingdom Limited*[3] Browne-Wilkinson V-C rejected an argument that it was sufficient for the plaintiff to show that a section of the public would be misled by the defendant's activities. However, the argument appears to have been advanced in response to criticisms of the evidence put forward by the plaintiffs in support of their claim to reputation and the judge rejected it on the ground that it was not open on the pleadings. It also appears that the authorities referred to here were not cited. The decision is, therefore, of doubtful value on this point and the traditional approach is to be preferred.

1 Per Lord Maugham in *Saville Perfumery Ltd v June Perfect Ltd* (1941) 58 RPC 147 at 175, HL. See also *J Bollinger and others v The Costa Brava Wine Co Limited* [1961] RPC 116 at 125–127 and the cases cited in para 4.05, n 12.
2 See *Havana Cigar and Tobacco Factories Ltd v Oddenino* [1924] 1 Ch 179, 41 RPC 47 discussed at para 4.32 below.
3 [1993] EMLR 27. The same judge has also in other cases accepted without demur that the test is whether 'a substantial number of members of the public' will be deceived: see eg *Associated Newspapers Group v Insert Media Limited* [1991] FSR 380 at 384.

How confusion must arise

4.05 Most passing off cases are concerned with the ordinary member of the general public and the likelihood of his being confused by a product or business. The question must then be asked: how much care is such a person expected to take in distinguishing between rival goods or businesses? The appropriate test has been considered in a number of cases, all of which lead to the same conclusion. In *Newsweek Inc v BBC*,[1] Lord Denning stated the principle in the following terms:

'The test is whether the ordinary, sensible members of the public would be confused. It is not sufficient that the only confusion would be to a very small, unobservant section of society: or, as Foster J put it recently, if the only person who would be misled would be "a moron in a hurry".'

Such a test has been accepted as appropriate since the middle of the last century[2] and has been adverted to in a number of modern cases. For example, in *Bar's Leaks (NZ) Ltd v Motor Specialities Ltd*,[3] Richmond J in the Supreme Court in New Zealand, considering the get-up of the defendant's product stated that 'one disregards the careless or indifferent person who fails to treat the label fairly'. He then went on specifically to apply the test set out by Haslam J in *Hansells (NZ) Ltd v Baillie*[4] that the person to be considered is the 'average prudent person with proper eyesight and reasonable apprehension'. In *Norman Kark Publications Ltd v Odhams Press Ltd*[5] Wilberforce J, relying upon *Ridgeway Co v Hutchinson*,[6] stated 'that careless or indifferent persons may be led into error is not enough'. On the other hand, there are authorities which suggest that lack of care on the part of prospective purchasers is not sufficient to avoid passing off. In *Johnston v Orr Ewing*[7] Lord Blackburn stated that if purchasers were shown to have been deceived, 'it could be no answer [to the claim of passing off] that the purchasers, so deceived, were incautious'. Equally, in *Reckitt & Colman v Borden*,[8] one of the key findings of fact which led to the plaintiff succeeding in a claim to prevent the defendant from marketing lemon juice in lemon-shaped containers was that 'virtually no, if any, attention is paid to the label which that lemon bears' so that the appearance of the defendant's label became irrelevant to the question of confusion. Lord Oliver expressed the principle to be applied in the light of that finding as follows:

> 'The essence of the action for passing off is a deceit practised on the public and it can be no answer, in a case where it is demonstrable that the public has been or will be deceived, that they would not have been if they had been more careful, more literate or more perspicacious. Customers have to be taken as they are found.'[9]

This passage is preceded by a reference to the passage in the speech of Lord Halsbury LC in *Schweppes v Gibbens*[10] which suggests that customers must 'treat the label fairly' and followed by citation of the remarks referred to above in *Johnston v Orr Ewing* as part of the conclusion that such comments must be considered in the context of the particular facts of the cases and not as establishing any 'principle of law that there must always be assumed a literate and careful customer'. In any event, there is no doubt that a defendant cannot escape liability by showing that a close inspection of his goods would disperse any misapprehension which might initially have arisen: 'The imitation of a man's trade mark in a manner liable to mislead the unwary, cannot be justified by shewing ... that a person who carefully and intelligently examined and studied it might not be misled'.[11] In the light of these conflicting authorities it is difficult to be categorical about the level of carelessness amongst customers which will lead the court to conclude that their confusion should be disregarded. Perhaps the most one can say is that, if all customers for a particular type of product are careless, then deception of them is passing off whilst the deception of customers whose carelessness is untypical for that type of product is not. This is a powerful illustration of the point made by Lord Oliver in *Reckitt & Colman v Borden*,[8] that the questions which arise in passing off actions are ones of fact and that reference to other cases is of assistance only analogically. It is of course always necessary that the person confused is one who is aware of material which is commonly used in the trade and what the distinguishing characteristics of the plaintiff's goods are. If he does not know this the court cannot take his view into account.[12] All these statements of approach have been made in cases where the ordinary member of the public is the person at whom the business or goods are aimed. It is submitted that the appropriate standard of care of the relevant member of the public is the same whether the public is general or specialised.

---

1 [1979] RPC 441 at 447 and citing *Morning Star Co-operative Society Ltd v Express Newspapers* [1979] FSR 113 at 117.
2 Eg two statements of Lord Cranworth: 'ordinary purchasers using ordinary caution' in *Seixo v Provezende* (1866) 1 Ch App 192 at 196: and 'such a resemblance as to deceive a purchaser using ordinary caution' in *Leather Cloth Co Ltd v American Leather Cloth Co Ltd* (1866) 35 LJ Ch 53 at 61.
3 [1973] RPC 21 at 28.
4 [1967] NZLR 774 at 783.
5 [1962] RPC 163 at 168.
6 (1923) 40 RPC 335.
7 (1882) 7 AC 219 at 229
8 [1990] 1 All ER 873, RPC 341.
9 Ibid at 888, 415.
10 (1905) 22 RPC 601 at 606.
11 Per Lord Selborne LC in *Singer Manufacturing Co v Loog* (1882) 8 App Cas 15 at 18.
12 *Payton & Co Ltd v Snelling, Lampard & Co Ltd* (1900) 17 RPC 48 at 57 per Romer LJ adopted by Whitford J in *Imperial Group plc v Phillip Morris Ltd* [1984] RPC 293 at 299: see also per Lord Maugham in *Thomas Bear & Sons (India) Ltd v Prayag Narain and Jagennarth* (1941) 58 RPC 25 at 28, PC.

What kind of confusion is necessary

4.06 To succeed in a passing off action it must always be shown, not only that there has been confusion, but also that the confusion has been caused by the appropriation by the defendant of the plaintiff's identifying indicia. Confusion not so arising is irrelevant. As Lord Greene MR put it in *Marengo v Daily Sketch*:[1]

> 'No one is entitled to be protected against confusion as such. Confusion may result from the collision of two independent rights or liberties, and where that is the case neither party can complain; they must put up with the results of the confusion as one of the misfortunes which occur in life. The protection to which a man is entitled is protection against passing off, which is a quite different thing from mere confusion.'

That passage was cited with approval in *County Sound plc v Ocean Sound Limited*[2] as establishing that:

> 'before it is actionable, confusion has to be shown to be such as is caused by a misrepresentation by the defendant that his goods or services are the goods or services of the plaintiff.'

In most cases this point does not cause any difficulties as that is the only available source of confusion. However, where there is a risk of confusion inherent in the general circumstances of competing trades being carried on, particularly under descriptive titles, it is necessary for the plaintiff to demonstrate that the use by the defendant of the matter complained of is the 'primary or operative cause'[3] of the confusion. If he does not show this the action fails.[4]

1 [1992] FSR 1 at 2 (CA) decided on 17 May 1946.
2 [1991] FSR 367 at 376 (CA).
3 Per Oliver LJ in *My Kinda Town Ltd v Soll* [1983] RPC 407 at 425.
4 *My Kinda Town Ltd v Soll*, see n 1, above; *Cadbury Schweppes Pty Ltd v The Pub Squash Co Pty Ltd* [1981] 1 All ER 213, [1981] RPC 429; see also *Gor-Ray Ltd v Gilray Skirts Ltd* (1952) 69 RPC 199 at 202–204 where the Court of Appeal considered the effect of evidence of confusion arising when the plaintiff's stockists were asked for the defendant's goods and supplied the plaintiff's and held that this was not relevant.

The literal truth of the statement is irrelevant

4.07   Even if what a trader says about his goods is literally true, he may still be restrained if there is implied by the statement made a misrepresentation which causes deception.

In *John Brinsmead & Sons Ltd v Brinsmead and Waddington & Sons Ltd*[1] Buckley LJ said:

'The law, as I understand it, is this: if a man makes a statement which is true, but which carries with it a false representation and induces the belief that his goods are the plaintiffs' goods, he will be restrained by injunction. He cannot rely on the fact that his statement is literally and accurately true, if, notwithstanding its truth, it carries with it a false representation'.[2]

1 (1913) 29 TLR 706, 30 RPC 493.
2 Ibid at 506.

Types of misrepresentation

4.08   The misrepresentation complained of may be made in many different ways and may be either explicit or implicit.[1] Obviously, the most direct way to misrepresent goods as coming from a particular source when they do not would simply be to mark them falsely as 'made by John Smith'.

Unsurprisingly, such direct misrepresentations are rare but are easily recognised and dealt with when they occur. However, there are a number of other ways in which a trader may overtly misdescribe or mark his goods without being so blatant which may or may not amount to passing off. Equally, there are many ways in which a trader can get-up or mark his goods or identify his business so as falsely to suggest by implication that they are what they are not.

What is and is not actionable as passing off in each case is now considered.

1 See *Spalding v Gamage* (1915) 32 RPC 273 at 284.

DIRECT MISREPRESENTATIONS

Representations as to quality or type of goods

4.09 It is not actionable for a trader to describe his goods as being 'similar to',[1] 'the same as',[2] 'as good as',[2] 'a substitute for'[3] or even 'better than'[4] the goods of a competitor. This is so even if the statement is untrue and causes damage to the competitor[5] unless it amounts to trade libel or malicious falsehood.[6]

Such a misrepresentation may, however, be actionable as passing off where there is a goodwill attached to the type or description of goods as, for example, in the *Champagne, Sherry* and *Advocaat* cases discussed below.[7] In *Cambridge University Press v University Tutorial Press*[8] a false statement that the defendant's book was one prescribed for an examination was held to be merely a representation as to quality and not actionable. Cases of this kind must, however, be distinguished from cases where the plaintiff's product has some special quality and the defendant's goods are marked in such a way as to suggest falsely that they too have that quality. In such circumstances the court is likely to find that there is passing off.[9]

---

1   *Magnolia Metal Co v Tandem Smelting Syndicate Ltd* (1898) 15 RPC 701.
2   *Bismag Ltd v Amblins (Chemists) Ltd* (1940) 57 RPC 209 at 228.
3   *Irving's Yeast-Vite Ltd v F A Horsenail* (1933) 50 RPC 139.
4   *Bismag v Amblins*, above, n 2, and per Lord Diplock in *Warnink v Townend* [1979] AC 731 at 742, [1980] RPC 31 at 91.
5   *Hubbuck & Sons Ltd v Wilkinson, Heywood and Clark Ltd* [1889] 1 QB 86, 68 LJ QB 34.
6   See ch 8 below.
7   See para 4.10 below.
8   (1928) 45 RPC 335.
9   *Combe International Limited v Scholl (UK) Limited* [1980] RPC 1. And see para 4.13 below for claims to praise properly belonging to the plaintiff.

Improper use of a descriptive class designation for goods

4.10 This type of passing off is a direct misdescription of the goods concerned. It can usefully be considered as having two features not present in what Lord Diplock described as the 'classic form of misrepresenting one's goods as the goods of someone else'.[1] First, there must exist a definable class of goods of which the name used is a correct description. Second, there must have become attached to that description a reputation and goodwill in that the public must expect to get the product correctly described by the name used. In the *Champagne* case, the first case of this type, Danckwerts J put it this way:

'There seems to be no reason why such licence (sc. To do a deliberate act which causes damage to the property of another person) should be given to a person who seeks to attach to his product a name or description with which it has no natural association so as to make use of the reputation and goodwill which has been gained by a product genuinely indicated by the name or description. In my view, it ought not to matter that the persons truly entitled to describe their goods by the name and description are a class producing goods in a certain locality, and not merely one individual. The description is part of their goodwill and a right of property.'[2]

In the *Champagne* case the class of traders entitled to the goodwill was limited to those in the Champagne region of France producing the particular sparkling wine known by that name. Two subsequent cases, *Vine Products Ltd v McKenzie & Co Ltd*[3] (the *Sherry* case) and *John Walker & Sons Ltd v Henry Ost & Co Ltd*[4] (the *Scotch Whisky* case) showed that the class of trader entitled to the goodwill might be rather wider provided that the class of goods was itself clearly defined. In both cases the designation in which there was held to be goodwill was one with a principally geographical connection. The term 'sherry' was held to denote wine produced by the solera method in the Jerez region of Spain. The traders entitled to the goodwill in the UK were the English shippers of that wine. In the *Scotch Whisky* case, the product in issue was blended whisky and it was held that the term could properly be applied to whisky blended anywhere provided that the original distillation of the components of the blend was carried out in Scotland. Any supplier of such goods was held to be entitled to a share in the goodwill attaching to the term 'Scotch whisky'.

It was not until the *Advocaat*[5] case was decided that there was a definitive statement of the extent to which such goodwill can spread. In that case Lord Diplock considered both the nature of the identity of the class of goods and that of the class of traders who are entitled to the goodwill in this type of passing off. Dealing with the class of traders he said this:

> 'the principle must be the same whether the class of which each member is severally entitled to the goodwill is large or small. The larger it is the broader must be the range and quality of products to which it has been applied, and the more difficult it must be to show that the term has acquired a public reputation and goodwill as denoting a product endowed with recognisable qualities which distinguish it from others of inferior reputation that compete with it in the same market. The larger the class the more difficult it must be for an individual member to show that the goodwill of his own business has sustained more than minimal damage as a result of deceptive use by another trader of the widely-shared descriptive term. As respects subsequent additions to the class, mere entry into the market would not give any right of action for passing off; the new entrant must have himself used the descriptive term long enough on the market in connection with his own goods and have traded successfully enough to have built up a goodwill for his business.'[6]

Thus, if the class of traders entitled to the goodwill is wide it may be difficult to show damage to each individual member. As damage is an essential element in the tort of passing off, this might lead to the conclusion that there is no cause of action in such a case. However, if the class as a whole is suffering damage, it seems illogical that the mere size of the class of traders claiming the right should act as a bar to the action. The courts have dealt with this by permitting actions to be brought by a single member of the class of traders entitled to the goodwill in a representative capacity.[7] Because the procedural rule permitting actions to be brought in a representative capacity requires that the representative and those he represents have the same interest[8] in the proceedings, this approach is not applicable where the parties have differing claims. Thus, where a number of cider producers claimed that they were entitled to the benefit of an estoppel against the Champagne houses, the representative claim was struck out on the grounds that each individual's entitlement to the benefit of any estoppel was different and depended on his own activities.[9] Equally, an action brought by a trade association on behalf of its producer members is not properly constituted.[10] The representative plaintiff must be one of the producers although the association can clearly also join as a plaintiff.

---

1 *Warnink v Townend* [1979] AC 731 at 741B.
2 *Bollinger v Costa Brava Wine Co Ltd* [1960] Ch 262 at 283–284 as adopted by Lord Diplock in *Warnink v Townend* [1979] AC 731 at 744G.
3 [1969] RPC 1.
4 [1970] 2 All ER 106, [1970] RPC 489; followed in *White Horse Distillers Ltd v Gregson Associates Ltd* [1984] RPC 61.
5 *Warnink v Townend*, above, n 1.
6 Ibid at 744.
7 *J Bollinger SA v Goldwell Limited* [1971] RPC 412. See also *H P Bulmer Ltd v J Bollinger SA* [1978] RPC 79. This has also been held to be appropriate in Bermuda: *Testut Frères (Representative Plaintiff) v J E Lightbourne & Co Limited* [1981] FSR 458. A similar approach is adopted in actions by a group of traders who have the same interest in enforcing copyrights belonging to all members of collection associations: see *EMI Records Limited v Riley* [1981] 1 All ER 838, [1981] 1 WLR 923. There are many similar subsequent cases.
8 RSC Ord 15, r 12(1).
9 *J Bollinger SA v Goldwell Limited* (above).
10 *Consorzio del Prosciutto di Parma v Marks & Spencer plc* [1991] RPC 351.

4.11 In the *Advocaat* case Lord Diplock also dealt with the nature of the class of goods in relation to which collective goodwill can arise. He considered the *Champagne, Sherry* and *Scotch Whisky* cases and made it clear that the same principles apply as much to a misdescription of other qualities of the goods as to a misdescription of their origin. He put the general proposition as follows:

'the fact that in each of these first three cases the descriptive name under which the goods of a particular type or composition were marketed by the plaintiffs among others happened to have geographical connotations is in my view without significance. If a product of a particular character or composition has been marketed under a descriptive name and under the name has gained a public reputation which distinguishes it from competing products of different composition, I can see no reason in principle or logic why the goodwill in the name of those entitled to make use of it should be protected by the law against deceptive use of the name by competitors, if it denotes a product of which the ingredients come from a particular locality, but should lose that protection if the ingredients of the product, however narrowly defined, are not restricted to their geographical provenance.'[1]

Since the proposition that a misdescription of goods by attaching to them a name in which there is goodwill is actionable as passing off is of general application, the exact nature of the description in each particular case is, it is submitted, irrelevant. If Lord Diplock's essential elements of passing off are present, there will be a cause of action.

---

1 *Warnink v Townend* [1979] AC 731 at 745.

Direct representations as to business connection

4.12 Just as it is actionable to make a direct misstatement as to the origin of goods, so it is actionable to state that a business is a part of or connected with a rival trader's business when it is not.[1] In the case of *Sony K K v Saray Electronics Ltd*[2] the defendants were restrained from representing that they were authorised dealers of the plaintiff because to do so represented that they were able to give customers the benefit of the manufacturer's guarantee. Similarly in *Nishika Corporation v Goodchild*[3] the defendants were restrained by an interlocutory injunction from selling the plaintiffs' cameras unless a label was attached to them making it clear that the defendants were not one of the plaintiffs' authorised dealers. However, there is no restriction on a trader advertising or promoting his skills by reference to his previous employment or business connection, provided that in so doing he does not falsely represent in some way that he is still part of the previous business.[4] As with all other types of passing off it is in each case a question of fact whether what has been done by the defendant is proper or whether it in fact gives rise to a misrepresentation that there is a trade connection which does not exist. In *Glenny v Smith*,[5] a tailor who had been employed by Thresher & Glenny left and set up in business on his own account. He put his own name above his shop premises but on the sun awning and under the window he placed signs saying 'from Thresher & Glenny' with the word 'from' being in much smaller type than the name. On proof that a number of people had been confused into believing that his shop was part of the plaintiff's business an injunction was granted restraining him from using his former employer's name in such a way as to confuse members of the public into believing that his shop was part of the plaintiff's business.

Similarly, the vendor of a business will not be allowed to use the name of the business he has sold in such a way as to represent that he is its successor in title.[6]

---

1 *Burgess v Burgess* (1853) 3 De G M & G 896, 22 LJ Ch 675; *Scott v Scott* (1866) 16 LT 143; *May v May* (1914) 31 RPC 325.
2 (1983) FSR 302, CA.
3 [1990] FSR 371.
4 *Cundey v Lerwell & Pike* (1908) 99 LT 273, 24 TLR 584; *Hookham v Pottage* (1872) 8 Ch App 91, 27 LT 595; *Williams v Osborne* (1865) 13 LT 498: *Goodman v Way* (1892) 36 Sol Jo 830; *Rickett, Cockerell & Co Ltd v Nevill* (1904) 21 RPC 394.
5 (1865) 2 Drew & Sm 476, 6 New Rep 363, and see *Wheeler & Wilson Manufacturing Co v Shakespear* (1869) 39 LJ Ch 36: former agent restrained from continuing to use name so as to represent continuance of agency.
6 *Scott v Scott* (1866) 16 LT 143: *May v May* (1914) 31 RPC 325; *Wood v Hall* (1915) 33 RPC 16.

References to publicity or praise given to the plaintiff

4.13 A defendant who applies to his goods or services praise, publicity or comment in fact given to those of the plaintiff will be restrained if upon proper analysis the result is to claim for himself something properly attributable to the plaintiff. Thus, in *Copydex Limited v Noso Products Limited*[1] the defendants were restrained from falsely advertising their product 'as shown on television' when in fact it was the plaintiff's product which had been shown. In *National Starch Manufacturing Co v Munn's Patent Maizeona Co*[2] the defendants were restrained from making a false claim to a prize which had in fact been awarded to the plaintiff's product; and in *Samuelson v Producers Distributing Co Limited*[3] the defendants were restrained from using press notices relating to the plaintiff's theatrical sketch, 'The New Car', as if they applied to the defendant's film 'His First Car'. In *Plomien Fuel Economiser Ltd v National School of Salesmanship Limited*[4] the defendants, who were former agents of the plaintiffs, represented that tests carried out on the plaintiff's fuel economisers had in fact been carried out on theirs. This was held to be impermissible and restrained. Even a claim to work which has in fact been done by the defendant may be prevented if made misleadingly. In *John Henderson Ltd v A Monro*,[5] the defendant, who had been manufacturing director of the plaintiff and had left to set up his own business, published a circular about work done 'by our Mr Monro' without saying that it was done when he worked for the plaintiff. It was held that this would be taken to refer to work done by the defendant's new business and was thus misleading.

---

1   (1952) 69 RPC 38.
2   [1894] AC 275, 11 RPC 281.
3   (1931) 48 RPC 580.
4   (1943) 60 RPC 209.
5   (1905) 7 F 636 (Scottish Court of Session).

Reverse passing off

4.14 The cases referred to in the previous paragraph were all cited and relied upon by the Court of Appeal in *Bristol Conservatories Limited v Conservatories Custom Built Limited*[1] where it was held that use by the defendant of albums of photographs of conservatories made by the plaintiff as if they had been conservatories made by the defendant in order to promote the defendant's products was capable of constituting passing off.[2] The basis for the decision is rather unusual in that it was held that the use of the photographs both created and misappropriated the plaintiff's reputation. Giving the only reasoned judgment, Ralph Gibson LJ put the matter as follows:

'No person affected by the misrepresentation in *Samuelson's* case, or in the *Plomien* case, or in the *Henderson* case would have known who the plaintiff in any of those cases was. That did not stop the plaintiff being injured in his property rights in his business

83

or goodwill. Nor would it matter if there was nothing in any photograph to link the conservatory there depicted with the plaintiffs in any way. Next it would not matter that there was no allegation that there would be any confusion in the minds of the public. The concept of confusion is in my view irrelevant when the misrepresentation leaves no room for confusion. The prospective customer here is not left to perceive the difference between allegedly similar products, he is told simply and untruthfully that Custom Built designed and constructed the conservatories which provide the evidence for the experience, skill and reputation of the plaintiffs . . . In truth, . . . the goodwill was asserted and demonstrated as the photographs were shown and was at the same time misappropriated by Custom Built.'[3]

This analysis is rather surprising in a number of respects but it should not be thought to establish that it is unnecessary to show confusion in a case of direct misrepresentation. What appears to have been intended is that a direct misrepresentation prevents the possibility that there will be no confusion because it does not permit the representee to make a comparison with the absent truth. The most difficult aspect of the case to understand is how the use by the defendant of the plaintiff's photographs could create the necessary reputation or goodwill in the plaintiff. It is hard to see how this is distinguished from the case in which the defendant is saying simply 'if you order a conservatory from me you will get one just like the one in this photograph'. Even if that statement is false, it ought not be to be actionable as passing off on the classical approach without the plaintiff being able to show that there is some feature of the product shown in the photograph which results in it being identified with a particular trade source rather than merely indicating the nature and quality of the goods supplied. However, the decision has since been followed[4] and it would appear that it is good law.

It has been suggested that cases of this type constitute a form of 'reverse passing off' in that what is being claimed is not that the defendant's goods are the plaintiff's but that the plaintiff's goods are the defendant's. In fact, proper analysis of the misrepresentation alleged in each case shows that what was being claimed was that the defendant was supplying goods or services which carried a benefit truly belonging to those of the plaintiff. This is no different from the nature of the misrepresentation alleged in any other kind of passing off claim and it is doubtful that the concept of reverse passing off is of any value.

---

1 [1989] RPC 455.
2 The decision was made on an application to strike out the claim as disclosing no cause of action which failed. The court accordingly did not decide that the defendant's conduct was passing off, but merely that the contention that it was was arguable.
3 Ibid at 464–465.
4 *Toye & Company plc v Ian Allen Regalia Limited* Aldous J, 19 May 1994 (unreported).

INDIRECT MISREPRESENTATIONS

4.15 These differ from direct misrepresentations only in that the falsehood is implied in the adoption by the defendant of indicia the same or confusingly similar to those which connote the plaintiff rather than being overtly expressed. As Lord Parker stated in *Spalding v Gamage*:

'In such cases the point to be decided is whether, having regard to all the circumstances of the case, the use by the defendant, in connection with the goods[1], of the mark, name, or get-up in question impliedly represents such goods to be the goods of the plaintiff... Or, as is sometimes put, is calculated to deceive.'[2]

Most cases of passing off involve an 'indirect' misrepresentation by the adoption of some indicia the same as or confusingly similar to features distinctive of the plaintiff's goods or business which remind the public of those features as used by the plaintiff.

---

1 Or business: the case was concerned only with goods.
2 (1915) 32 RPC 273 at 284.

Adoption of the plaintiff's mark

4.16 The commonest form of misrepresentation is simply use of a mark which is the same as or confusingly similar to that used by the plaintiff for his goods or business. The allegation by the plaintiff is of course that the mark appropriated by the defendant is distinctive of the plaintiff's goods or business.

Adoption of the plaintiff's get-up

4.17 The claim by the plaintiff in such a case is that the public recognises his goods by certain features of their appearance or packaging.[1] Once this is established, the real question in such cases is whether the get-up adopted by the defendant is sufficiently deceptively similar to that of the plaintiff to give rise to confusion.[2] It is only in cases of deliberate and fraudulent copying that there is likely to be identity of get-up.

---

1 See paras 3.43–3.49 above.
2 See the discussion of deceptive resemblance at paras 4.45–4.47 below, and para 4.35 below, and the cases cited at notes 7, 8 and 9 thereto.

Adoption of the plaintiff's business or company name

4.18 The use by the defendant of a business or company name which is the same as or confusingly similar to a widely-used name of the plaintiff and which thereby gives rise to deception of customers will be restrained.[1] Such deception will be readily established where the plaintiff's trading name is not descriptive of his business. However, in many cases business or company names are chosen for their descriptive qualities and then it will be much more difficult to show that there is a real likelihood of deception if there is any significant difference between the plaintiff's and the defendant's trading names. The *Office Cleaning*[2] case is probably the high water mark of what the courts will accept as sufficiently distinguishing two businesses by a small difference in name. In that case the difference between 'Office Cleaning Services' and 'Office Cleaning Association' was held to be sufficient to distinguish the two businesses. In other more recent cases such small differences have been held insufficient even where the trading name adopted by the defendant was largely descriptive. In *Legal and General Assurance Society Ltd v Daniel*[3] the defendant was restrained from using the name 'Legal and General Enquiry Bureau' and in *Effluent Disposal Ltd v Midlands Effluent Disposal Ltd*[4] the addition of the word 'Midlands' to the defendant's title was held by the court to be of no significance because that was the area in which both businesses operated.

---

1   *Lloyds and Dawson Bros v Lloyds Southampton Ltd* (1912) 28 TLR 338, 29 RPC 433; *Harrods Ltd v R Harrod Ltd* (1924) 41 RPC 74.
2   *Office Cleaning Services Ltd v Westminster Window and General Cleaners (trading as Office Cleaning Association)* (1946) 63 RPC 39, HL.
3   [1968] RPC 253, CA.
4   [1970] RPC 238.

MISREPRESENTING THE NATURE OF THE PLAINTIFF'S OWN GOODS

4.19   The promotion by the defendant of the plaintiff's own goods with a misleading indication of their class or quality is an actionable misrepresentation. This type of action was first recognised in *Spalding v Gamage*[1] where Lord Parker, in a statement of the law with which the other members of the House agreed, set out the principle on which such actions are founded in the following terms:

> 'The proposition that no one has a right to represent his goods as the goods of somebody else must, I think, as has been assumed in this case, involve as a corollary the further proposition, that no one, who has in his hands the goods of another of a particular class or quality, has a right to represent these goods to be the goods of that other of a different quality or belonging to a different class.'[2]

To succeed the plaintiff must of course establish that there are two distinct classes of his goods and that one is being represented as the other.[3] Additionally, since the plaintiff must establish that he has suffered or will suffer damage as a result of the defendant's activities,[4] it will normally be the case that the defendant is putting forward an inferior class of the plaintiff's goods as a superior one. In any other case it may be difficult for a plaintiff to demonstrate that he is suffering any damage. There are, however, circumstances in which this can be shown, as for example where the formulation of the goods for marketing in one country is different from the formulation in another because of differences of climate or usage.[5]

1   (1915) 84 LJ Ch 449, 32 RPC 273.
2   Ibid at 284.
3   *Harris v Warren & Phillips* (1918) 87 LJ Ch 491, 35 RPC 217; *Revlon v Cripps & Lee* [1980] FSR 85, CA.
4   See ch 5 below.
5   As happened in *Castrol Ltd v Automotive Oil Supplies Ltd* [1983] RPC 315: the defendant imported motor oil from Canada which was differently formulated from the oil sold in the UK because of the substantially different climatic conditions: it was not suggested that the oil was inferior, merely that it was unsuitable for use in the UK. Although this was a case of registered trade mark infringement, it appears that the plaintiff would also have succeeded in passing off.

4.20   A modern example of how both the above difficulties can defeat a plaintiff's claim is the case of *Revlon Inc v Cripps & Lee*[1] where the plaintiffs complained that the defendants had imported into the UK 'Flex' shampoo admittedly made by a US associated company of the plaintiffs but not sold here and allegedly falling into a different class of product from the types sold in this country. The product imported by the defendants was 'medicated' anti-dandruff shampoo and the plaintiffs alleged that this was of a different class from the products sold by them in Britain under the Flex name which were unmedicated shampoos for use on dry, normal or greasy hair respectively and therefore 'cosmetic'. The court entirely rejected this argument largely, it would appear, because the evidence put forward to support it was unconvincing.

1   [1980] FSR 85.

Representing second-hand goods as 'new'

4.21   To make such a representation is one way of putting forward one class of the plaintiff's goods as something different and superior to what they in fact are. It is of course a question of fact in each case whether there has been a representation that the goods are new. In the case of *Gillette Safety Razor Co and Gillette Safety Razor Ltd v Franks*,[1] where the defendant sold in the plaintiff's wrappers worn out razor blades of the plaintiff's manufacture which he had repackaged, it was clear that such a representation was being made and an injunction was granted. However, in the contrasting case of *GEC v Pryce's Stores*[2] the defendant was selling used electric lamps of the plaintiff's manufacture at a price well below the plaintiff's recommended price. The lamps in the defendant's shop were simply piled unpackaged in a basket. The court held that the circumstances of the sale were such that there was no representation that the goods were new and the action failed.

1   (1924) 40 TLR 606, 41 RPC 499; see also *Gillette Safety Razor Co v Diamond Edge Ltd* (1926) 43 RPC 310.
2   (1933) 50 RPC 232.

4.22 New goods are generally simply unused. However, there are cases where 'new' has a particular meaning. Because of the special obligations adopted by a dealer selling new motor cars to make good under the manufacturer's warranty any defects in the cars he sells it has been held that a car ceases to be new as soon as it is registered, sold and driven out of the showroom.[1] Because of the special meaning which new has in relation to cars, the form of the injunction granted must make clear precisely what is prohibited[2] for to describe a car as 'brand new' does not necessarily carry with it the implication that it is 'new' in that particular way.[3] It may sometimes be proper to describe a car as new when it has been damaged in transit between manufacturer and dealer provided that the damage has been completely made good.[4] However, these cases were decided at a time when the manufacturer's warranty was not transferred to a subsequent purchaser of the car. It is submitted that the above approach is of limited application nowadays when the manufacturer's warranty obligations are usually transferred to any subsequent purchaser and (in principle at least) will be met by any duly appointed dealer.

1 *Morris Motors Ltd v Lilley* [1959] 3 All ER 737, [1959] 1 WLR 1184.
2 *Morris Motors Ltd v Phelan* [1960] 2 All ER 208n, [1960] RPC 209.
3 *Standard Motor Co v Grantchester Garage* [1960] RPC 211.
4 *R v Ford Motor Co Ltd* [1974] 3 All ER 489, [1974] 1 WLR 1220 (a trade description case).

4.23 Where the plaintiff's goods are perishable or subject to deterioration with time, it is actionable to sell old stock as freshly manufactured goods. In *Wilts United Dairies v Thomas Robinson Sons & Co Ltd*[1] the defendants bought at a very low price quantities of old stock of the plaintiff's condensed milk, which had previously been disposed of by the Ministry of Food for use only as animal food, in manufacturing or for export. The defendants resold the stock to grocers with no warning as to its age and a recommendation to sell it at the price in force for the plaintiff's fresh stock before a recent rise. The evidence showed that condensed milk deteriorates with age and should be sold and used less than six months after manufacture but that it was not possible to distinguish old stock from new without opening the tin. Stable J, affirmed by the Court of Appeal, held that the defendants must have known from the price they paid that the goods were old stock and that in selling them as they did they were representing them as fresh stock. Such reasoning it is submitted also applies to superseded models of durable goods as it does to perishable goods. To sell them without indicating that they are not the current model must be to represent that they are.

1 [1958] RPC 94.

4.24 Generally, it is submitted that to sell as unused goods which have been used, however little, is actionable. This would seem to apply just as much to goods which have simply been used for the purposes of demonstration or testing by the dealer who is selling them as to goods which have been previously sold and used by someone else.

Additions to the plaintiff's products

4.25 It is reasonably self-evident that if a defendant materially modifies the plaintiff's goods and then presents them to the public as having originated from the plaintiff in that form, there will be a misrepresentation. It has been held that this is so for insertions bound into publications[1] and, in rather unusual circumstances, for motor cars.[2] More recently, in *Associated Newspapers Group v Insert Media Limited*,[3] it has even been held that the insertion of loose inserts into newspapers which are then sold by newsagents with those inserts in is passing off. The court in this case did not, however, suggest that this would always be so, Browne-Wilkinson V-C saying:[4]

> '... where an original product has been altered and resold under its original name such activity is capable of constituting a misrepresentation. Whether it does in fact constitute a misrepresentation must, in my judgment, depend upon the facts of each individual case. It must depend upon the nature of the product, the alterations made to it and the circumstances in which the altered product is put before the public. For example, in the present case if it were to be widely thought by the public that advertising inserts were put into newspapers by newsagents and not by the publishers, the activities of the third defendant would not constitute any actionable misrepresentation. The question whether or not there has been a misrepresentation causing confusion or deception must depend upon the perceptions of the matter by the public at large. If a substantial body of persons assume that such inserts are made by the publishers, then the insertion of the inserts into the newspaper by newsagents will be calculated to misrepresent the position to the public. In my judgment therefore the mere fact that the inserts have been made without the plaintiffs' consent does not establish the existence of a misrepresentation. One has to go on to ask whether a substantial number of persons will believe that an advertisement inserted between the pages of the *Daily Mail* is authorised by the *Daily Mail*.'

As always, therefore, the legal principle is simple and the question at the heart of the action is one of fact.

---

1 *Illustrated Newspapers Limited v Publicity Services (London) Limited* [1938] Ch 414.
2 *Rolls-Royce Motors Limited v Zanelli* [1979] RPC 148.
3 [1991] FSR 380, [1991] 3 All ER 535.
4 Ibid at 384, 541.

Parallel imports

4.26 In modern trading conditions it is often possible for a trader to obtain supplies of the plaintiff's goods abroad at a price which enables him to sell them more cheaply in Great Britain than the price at which such goods are normally sold. This practice is generally referred to as 'parallel importation'. In general, the question of whether or not parallel importation of the plaintiff's goods gives rise to passing off is posed by asking the usual *Spalding v Gamage*[1] question: is there or is there not a misrepresentation as to the nature or quality of the goods which are being sold? If so, there is passing off. If not, there is no passing off. The fact that the goods are imported is irrelevant.[2] The two opposing possibilities are well illustrated by two recent cases involving the same firm of parallel importers. These are *Revlon Inc v Cripps & Lee*[3] and *Wilkinson Sword v Cripps & Lee*.[4] In both cases the goods being marketed by the defendants in this country were as marketed by the plaintiff abroad under a brand name used by the plaintiff in this country, with no alterations to their packaging. In the *Revlon* case the product was 'Flex' shampoo of a variety not sold by the plaintiffs in this country and in fact complementary to their range as marketed here. In the *Wilkinson Sword* case the products were razor blades sold under the designation 'XCN' which was in use both in this country and in the USA where the imported blades were from. However, in the USA the name was applied to blades of a lower quality than those for which the name was used in Britain. In the *Revlon* case it was held on an application for an interlocutory injunction that there could be no passing off.[5] In the *Wilkinson Sword* case, on an application to strike out the statement of claim as disclosing no cause of action on the basis of the decision in the *Revlon* case, it was held that there could be. The question in each case is whether there is in fact a misrepresentation. In *Colgate Palmolive Limited v Markwell Finance Limited*,[6] an appeal from a final trial, the legal principles underlying these claims were fully considered. It was held that cases of this kind are no different in principle from those where a manufacturer puts onto the market two distinct qualities of goods in which case he is entitled to prevent anyone from representing that the inferior quality is the superior. It was also held that since goodwill is territorial, a manufacturer is entitled to decide what quality of goods is distributed under his mark in different territories and to prevent the movement of his goods from one territory to another if that leads to confusion. It is only where the plaintiff himself causes the confusion by, for example, circulating two different qualities of goods in one territory, that this will not apply.

---

1 (1915) 32 RPC 273 at 284.
2 *Champagne Heidsieck et Cie v Scotto and Bishop* (1926) 43 RPC 101: continental quality champagne sold as plaintiff's English quality; held there was passing off; contrast *Champagne Heidseick et Cie Monopole SA v Buxton* [1930] 1 Ch 330, 47 RPC 28, where the plaintiff's claim was rejected on substantially the same facts.
3 [1980] FSR 85.
4 [1982] FSR 16. Followed in Malaysia in *Winthrop Products v Sun Ocean* [1988] FSR 430.
5 The facts as found are set out in para 4.20 above.
6 [1989] RPC 497.

Goods imported from EEC countries

4.27 One of the objects of the Treaty of Rome, the governing treaty of the EEC which became part of English law on Britain's entry into the Community, is to prevent distortion or restriction of competition in trade between member states, inter alia, by reliance on trade mark or analogous rights. However, from the preceding paragraph it is clear that EEC objections to the prevention of parallel imports are unlikely to arise in a pure passing off case. As the right to relief depends upon there being a misrepresentation as to the class or quality of the goods being sold, there is no cause of action if there is no such misrepresentation (which is of course the usual case in relation to other species of intellectual property upon which plaintiffs have relied to prevent importation). On the other hand, if there is a misrepresentation, it cannot be said that the plaintiff is trying to use his right to prevent passing off to inhibit the free movement of goods within the EEC contrary to the Treaty of Rome, arts 30–36. The plaintiff is entitled to prevent their sale in this country unless they are so marked as to indicate their true nature. If they are so marked he cannot object in any event because there is no misrepresentation. The case will of course be different if the plaintiff is so manipulating his use of his marks in various member states of the EEC as to ensure that goods marketed in one country will be misleadingly marked if imported into another member state, for example by pursuing a policy of marketing differing qualities of goods under the same mark in different member states. Such conduct is precisely the disguised restriction on free movement of goods that the principles of the Treaty of Rome are intended to prevent. The impact of EEC law on such conduct in relation to the law of passing off is fully considered in ch 10, below.

ADOPTION OF THE PLAINTIFF'S STYLE OF MARKETING

4.28 In principle, the appropriation by the defendant of almost any aspect of the plaintiff's marketing of his goods or business in which there is shown to be goodwill, can give rise to the right to sue for passing off. In a recent authoritative statement of the law, Lord Scarman put it thus:[1]

> '[Passing off] is wide enough to encompass other descriptive material, such as slogans or visual images, which radio, television or newspaper advertising campaigns can lead the market to associate with the plaintiff's product, provided always that such descriptive material has become part of the goodwill of the product.'

The older cases on this topic which suggested that copying a system or style of advertising was not passing off,[2] are accordingly no longer good law although they might well be decided the same way today on their facts.[3]

---

1 *Cadbury Schweppes Pty Ltd v The Pub Squash Co Pty Ltd* [1981] 1 WLR 193 at 200, [1981] RPC 429 at 490; see also *Elida Gibbs Ltd v Colgate-Palmolive Ltd* [1982] FSR 95.

2 See *Wertheimer v Stewart, Cooper & Co* (1906) 23 RPC 481 and cases on styles of shop premises such as *Plotzker v Lucas* (1907) 24 RPC 551 and *J Lyons & Co v G and K Restaurants Ltd* (1955) 72 RPC 259.

3 In *My Kinda Town v Soll* [1983] RPC 407 the Court of Appeal held that confusion caused by the similar styles of two restaurants was inevitable although the action in fact failed because such confusion was not complained of in the pleadings.

ENABLING PASSING OFF BY OTHERS

4.29 It is no answer to an allegation of passing off for a defendant to say that his direct customers would not be confused if his goods when placed by such customers on the open market will cause deception amongst the public.[1] Perhaps the earliest case of the law affording relief in such a case is *Sykes v Sykes* discussed above.[2] In *Lever v Goodwin* Cotton LJ put the matter in the following terms:

> 'It still remains a wrongful act, because it put into the hands of the middlemen the means of committing a fraud on the Plaintiffs by selling the soap of the Defendants as the soap of the Plaintiffs.'[3]

And in *Singer Manufacturing Co v Loog* James LJ stated the general proposition which has since been approved by the House of Lords as follows:

> 'No man is permitted to use any mark, sign or symbol, device or other name, whereby, without making a direct false representation himself to a purchaser who purchases from him, he enables such purchaser to tell a lie or to make a false representation to somebody else who is the ultimate customer.'[4]

This principle extends even to cases where the supply is to someone to enable him to pass off outside the jurisdiction.[5] For a tort to be committed in England in such a case the English exporter must not only supply the goods but also play a part in the deceptive marketing.[6] It is insufficient to show only that the supplier has not taken reasonable steps to ensure that passing off will not occur, even where it is clear that, unless there is proper supervision abroad, that is the likely result.

However, it is not actionable simply to sell goods to a retailer which, if fairly marketed would not deceive where the retailer himself acts fraudulently.[7] Of course, in such a case the retailer will himself be guilty of passing off.

---

1 *Lever v Goodwin* (1887) 36 Ch D 1, 4 RPC 492; *John Walker & Sons Ltd v Douglas McGibbon & Co Ltd* [1975] RPC 506; see per Lord Maugham in *Saville Perfumery Ltd v June Perfect Ltd* (1941) 58 RPC 147 at 175–176.
2 See para 2.03 above.
3 (1887) 36 Ch D 1 at 7.
4 (1880) 18 Ch D 395 at 412 approved by Lord MacNaghten in *Frank Reddaway & Co Ltd v George Banham & Co Ltd* [1896] AC 199 at 215.
5 *John Walker & Sons Ltd v Henry Ost & Co Ltd* [1970] 2 All ER 106, [1970] RPC 489.
6 *White Horse Distillers v Gregson Associates* [1984] RPC 61 at 75 explaining *Walker v Ost*, above, n 5. See paragraphs 4.50–4.55 below for a discussion of whether activities committed wholly abroad can be litigated as passing off in the English court.
7 *Payton & Co v Snelling. Lampard & Co* [1901] AC 308, 17 RPC 628.

Defences

4.30 When it has been shown that the defendant has adopted some indicia the same as or confusingly similar to that used by the plaintiff to denote the plaintiff's goods, there are still a number of further matters to be considered before it can be decided whether the defendant is acting so as to pass off his goods as the plaintiff's. In some cases the matter taken by the defendant may not be distinctive of the plaintiff's goods but in truth descriptive of the type of goods in question. Sometimes a defendant may use, in conjunction with the plaintiff's mark, further material indicating the true origin of the goods, such as the defendant's own name and address. The defendant may even say that he too is entitled to use the distinguishing matter complained of. Often, the mark used by the defendant is not wholly identical to the plaintiff's mark and the question arises as to whether the similarity is such that confusion will arise. This is usually put in the form: is there a deceptive resemblance between the defendant's and the plaintiff's marks? Deceptive resemblance is dealt with in paras 4.45–4.47 below.

The other ways in which a defendant may escape liability are now considered in detail.

PARTIALLY DESCRIPTIVE MARKS

4.31   There are a number of ways in which a mark can be descriptive rather than distinctive. It can consist simply of ordinary English words descriptive of some aspect of the goods which the plaintiff fails to show has acquired the requisite secondary meaning denoting the plaintiff.[1] In such a case the plaintiff fails *in limine* as he does not establish the essential quality of distinctiveness at all.[2] More difficult to deal with are cases where the plaintiff's mark is in part descriptive and in part distinctive. The question to be answered in such cases is whether the matter taken by the defendant is apt to distinguish the plaintiff's goods or is purely descriptive. A good example of this is *Horlick's Malted Milk Co v Summerskill*[3] where the plaintiffs had for a number of years sold a preparation under the name 'Horlick's Malted Milk'. The defendant started to sell a similar preparation under the name 'Hedley's Malted Milk'. The plaintiff asserted that the term 'Malted Milk' alone was distinctive of it. No evidence was adduced of any case of actual deception. Earl Loreburn summed the position up in the following terms:

> 'The question which we really have to consider is what is the meaning of the words "Malted Milk"? In my opinion ... That expression is merely descriptive of milk which is combined or prepared with malt or extract of malt. The claim really is for part of a designation which the plaintiffs have been in the habit of using. They have been in the habit of using the term "*Horlick's* Malted Milk". They now eliminate the word "*Horlick's*" and ask that the remainder of their description shall be prohibited to the defendant. On the ground that they are descriptive words I do not think that that can be done.'[4]

A modern example of the same approach is *McCain International Ltd v Country Fair Foods Ltd*[5] where the designation in question was 'Oven Chips' which Templeman LJ described as 'an ingenious and apt description of the contents, namely potato chips prepared for cooking in the oven'.[6] The plaintiffs used the designation 'McCain's Oven Chips' on their product and in their advertising.

The defendants proposed to market their competing product under the names 'Country Fair Oven Chips' and 'Birds Eye Oven Chips'. Again the court held that the part of the name taken by the defendants was apt simply to describe the product: the distinctive element was the name preceding it. There are many further recent examples of similar results. In *County Sound plc v Ocean Sound Limited*[7] it was held that the title 'The Gold AM' was descriptive. It was only the prefix County Sound which was distinctive of the plaintiff. In *Tamworth Herald Co Limited v Thomson Free Newspapers Limited*[8] it was held that the word 'Herald' was said to be commonly used for newspapers and its adoption as part of a name for a newspaper could not be complained of. A slightly different case is found in *Mothercare UK Limited v Penguin Books Limited*,[9] where the plaintiff, the well-known chain of shops catering to the needs of mothers and young children, complained of the publication by the defendant of a book entitled 'Mother Care/Other Care' on the relative merits of children being brought up by their mothers or by paid carers. It was held that the name of the defendant's publication had to be considered as a whole and that, so considered, there was no representation at all.

> 'The name taken as a whole does not begin to suggest that the book has been issued or sponsored by, or is in any way associated with, Mothercare. . . . [A]ny potential customer who looks sufficiently far into the book to find out what it is actually about, is bound to realise that the words "Mother Care" are used descriptively to refer to the care of children by their mothers as opposed to the care of children by others, and do not refer to Mothercare or any association with Mothercare, at all.'[10]

Thus, although the plaintiff's name was undoubtedly distinctive when used as a name, the mere use of something similar as part of a longer, descriptive title did not suggest association with that name.

However, it is in each case a question of fact on the evidence whether the material taken by the defendant is merely descriptive or in some way distinctive. In *Carlsberg A/S and Carlsberg Scottish v Tennent Caledonian Breweries*[11] (a Scottish case) the petitioners had for many years marketed a strong lager under the name 'Carlsberg Special Brew'. The respondents were restrained from selling a similar lager under the name 'Tennent's Special Brew'.

---

1   A classic case of this type is *Cellular Clothing Co v Maxton & Murray* [1899] AC 326, 68 LJ PC 72 where the term 'cellular cloth' was simply an apt description in ordinary English words of the plaintiff's cloth.
2   See paras 3.25 ff above, where the question of the acquisition of a secondary meaning for prima facie descriptive terms is considered in detail.
3   (1916) 86 LJ Ch 175, 34 RPC 63.
4   Ibid at 176 and at 67.
5   [1981] RPC 69, CA.
6   Ibid at 72.
7   [1991] FSR 367.
8   [1991] FSR 337.
9   [1988] RPC 113.
10   Ibid at 116.
11   [1972] RPC 847.

Marks both descriptive and distinctive

4.32 An important category of partially descriptive marks is that where a name can be used both to indicate goods of the plaintiff's origin and also descriptively of the type or designation of the goods. In such cases the action will fail unless it is shown that some customers at least are using the name in the expectation of receiving the plaintiff's goods rather than simply goods of the type denoted by the name. Harman J put the point succinctly when he said:

> 'There is a hole in this bucket and the whole of your argument has fallen through it: if an order for "Aertex" may be using the word descriptively, then supply of material not made by the plaintiffs is not passing off, unless it is clear to the assistant that, in the case of that order, the customer wants the plaintiff's goods.'[1]

In such a case the initial request, particularly if made orally, is ambiguous. However, where it is established on the evidence that a substantial proportion of the public uses the name to identify the plaintiff's goods rather than as a descriptive term, the plaintiff will succeed, although it may well be the case that the injunction granted will be in a limited form. This was precisely what occurred in *Havana Cigar and Tobacco Factories Ltd v Oddenino*[2] where the term 'Corona' for cigars denoted the plaintiff's manufacture but was also used to denote cigars of a particular size and shape irrespective of manufacture. A number of the defendant's trade witnesses stated that they would not know whether a customer asking for 'Corona' cigars wanted specifically the plaintiff's products until they had inquired. It was held both at first instance and in the Court of Appeal that the plaintiff was entitled to an injunction restraining the defendant 'from supplying a cigar not of the Corona brand, unless it was first ascertained that the customer did not require a cigar of the Corona and no other brand, or unless it was made clear to him by word of mouth or otherwise that the cigar supplied was a brand other than the plaintiff's brand'.

---

1   *Arguendo in Cellular Clothing Co Ltd v G White & Co Ltd* (1953) 70 RPC 9 at 11.
2   [1924] 1 Ch 179, 41 RPC 47. See para 3.33 above.

4.33 This problem is particularly acute in the supply of spare parts and accessories. The use of the plaintiff's name may simply indicate that the parts are suitable for use with the plaintiff's products.[1] On the other hand, it may be that a customer expects in response to an order for a part or accessory something made by the manufacturer of the original equipment. Thus 'Brownie' was held to mean not a film suitable for use in a 'Brownie' camera but a film made by the maker of such a camera.[2] In each case it is a question of fact to be determined on the evidence whether by the use of the name the defendant is leading purchasers to believe that they are getting goods of the plaintiff's manufacture or simply goods of a type suitable for use with the plaintiff's apparatus.[3]

---

1   *Gledhill & Sons Ltd v British Perforated Toilet Paper Co* (1911) 28 RPC 714. CA.
2   *Kodak Ltd v London Stereoscopic & Photographic Co Ltd* (1903) 19 TLR 297. 20 RPC 337.
3   See para 3.23 above.

USE BY THE DEFENDANT OF ADDITIONAL MATERIAL

4.34   The question in all cases where the defendant has combined the plaintiff's mark with additional material is whether what he has added is such as adequately to distinguish his goods from those of the plaintiff and thus avoid the deception of the purchasing public which gives rise to passing off. If he has, he has a complete defence to the action for, if there is no confusion, there can be no passing off. Sir Wilfred Greene, contrasting passing off with infringement of a registered trade mark, summed the position up in the following way:

> 'It does not necessarily follow that a trader who uses an infringing mark upon goods is also guilty of passing off. The reason is that in the matter of infringement, as I have already pointed out, once a mark is used as indicating origin, no amount of added matter intended to show the true origin of the goods can affect the question. In the case of passing off, on the other hand, the defendant may escape liability if he can show that the added matter is sufficient to distinguish his goods from those of the plaintiff.'[1]

---

1   *Saville Perfumery Ltd v June Perfect Ltd* (1941) 58 RPC 147 at 162.

4.35   Again, it is always a question of fact in each case whether what the defendant has added is enough to indicate the true origin of the goods. The various cases brought by Reddaway in relation to the product known as 'Camel Hair Belting' are a striking illustration of how the courts draw the line between that which is and that which is not sufficient to distinguish the defendant's goods from those of the plaintiff. In the first case, *Frank Reddaway & Co Ltd v George Banham & Co Ltd*,[1] it was established that the descriptive name could nonetheless become distinctive of the plaintiff's goods[2] and the defendant was restrained from using the words 'camel hair' as a description of his product without clearly distinguishing it from the plaintiff's goods. Subsequently in *F Reddaway & Co v Ahlers*[3] and in *Reddaway & Co v Stevenson & Brother Ltd*,[4] the defendants were held to have passed off their goods by the use of the term 'camel hair belting' even where this use was in conjunction with the defendant's name. In the former case the addition of the defendant's name to the goods was sporadic and in the latter fraudulent intention was found and the court held on the facts that there was insufficient distinction. However, in two other cases — *F Reddaway & Co Ltd v Frictionless Engine Packing Co Ltd*[5] and *F Reddaway & Co Ltd v Hartley*[6] — where the defendants were acting bona fide, the addition of the defendant's name to the description 'camel hair belting' was held to be sufficient distinction.

The importance of looking at the entirety of the matter used and the overall impression it creates is aptly demonstrated by the case of *McDonald's Hamburgers Limited v Burger King (UK) Limited.*[7] In that case Burger King had decided to attack McDonalds by an overtly comparative advertising campaign which used posters with a picture of a Burger King 'Whopper' burger above which was the slogan 'It's not just Big, Mac', the 'Big Mac' being the well-known product of McDonalds. Underneath the picture was a considerable amount of text relating to the 'Whopper' and, in the bottom right-hand corner the Burger King name and logo. The evidence before the court confirmed the court's initial impression that the poster would lead a number of members of the public to believe that what was being advertised was an improved version of the Big Mac which they could obtain from Burger King establishments and accordingly that passing off had been demonstrated.

Get-up cases may cause difficulties. In *Schweppes Ltd v Gibbens*[8] the plaintiff's product was bottled soda water with a particular style of neck label with the name 'Schweppes' on it. The defendant marketed soda water in similar bottles with very similar neck labels but with his own name 'Gibbens' appearing in place of the plaintiff's name. It was held that this was sufficient to distinguish. On the other hand, in *J & J Colman Ltd v Farrow & Co*[9] the use by the defendant of his own name prominently on his label, which was otherwise very similar to the plaintiff's label was held insufficient to distinguish. The recent tendency of the courts has been to reject actions based purely on similarities of get-up on the basis that the presence of differing names on products is, given the sophistication of the modern public, sufficient to distinguish the goods of rival traders.[10]

The court will often find that the use by the defendant of a substantially descriptive name (even if invented) does not entitle the plaintiff to prevent the use of the same or substantially the same name by the defendant in conjunction with the defendant's own name. The *Malted Milk and Oven Chip* cases above[11] may be considered to be examples of this. In *Countess Housewares Ltd v Addis Ltd*[12] the plaintiffs ought to prevent the use of the name 'Shampoomatic' by the defendants on a carpet shampooing device. Both parties used the name in conjunction with their own trading name. It was held that this was sufficient distinction. In *Technical Reproductions v Contemporary Exhibitions*[13] a claim to prevent the use of the word 'Refrigeration' as part of the title of an exhibition devoted to that subject and taking place in direct competition with a similar exhibition by the plaintiff was refused, the remainder of the titles of the two exhibitions being different and that being sufficient to distinguish them.

In summary, therefore, the mere use of additional matter by the defendant will not provide a defence to a claim for passing off. The question in each case is whether on the evidence the additional material is such as to avoid the likelihood of confusion arising from the use of the plaintiff's identifying indicia.

---

1   [1896] AC 199, 65 LJ QB 381.
2   See the full discussion of the impact of this case in para 3.26, above.
3   (1901) 19 RPC 12.
4   (1902) 20 RPC 276.
5   (1902) 19 RPC 505.
6   (1930) 48 RPC 10 at 238, CA.
7   [1986] FSR 45.
8   (1905) 22 RPC 601, HL.
9   (1897) 15 RPC 198; and see *Birmingham Small Arms Co Ltd v Webb & Co* (1906) 24 RPC 27.
10 See for example *Fisons Ltd v Godwins (Peat Industries) Ltd* [1976] RPC 653; *Tetrosyl Ltd v Silver Paint and Lacquer Co Ltd* [1980] FSR 68, CA; *Adidas KG v O'Neill & Co Ltd* [1983] FSR 76 (Ir SC); *Scott v Nice-Pak* [1989] FSR 100; *Drayton Controls (Engineering) Limited v Honeywell Control Systems Limited* [1992] FSR 245.
11 See para 4.31 above.
12 [1964] RPC 251.
13 [1961] RPC 242.

USE BY THE DEFENDANT OF HIS OWN NAME

A. As a trade mark

4.36   The early case of *Sykes v Sykes*[1] demonstrated that a trader does not have a right fraudulently to use his own name as a trade mark if this leads to him passing off his goods as someone else's. That case was decided at a time when fraud was an essential element of the tort at common law. Following it there were many decisions, starting with *Burgess v Burgess*,[2] that, to restrain a man from selling goods under his own name, his conduct had to be shown to be fraudulent. A classic example was *John Brinsmead & Sons Ltd v Brinsmead and Waddington & Sons Ltd*.[3] The plaintiffs were piano-makers whose pianos were marked with the name 'John Brinsmead & Sons'. The defendant marked his pianos 'Stanley Brinsmead'. The plaintiffs' pianos were known generally by both trade and public as 'Brinsmead' pianos. It was held that the defendant had not acted dishonestly although he knew that he was obtaining a trading advantage from the fact that his name was the same as the plaintiffs' and accordingly the action failed.

---

1   (1824) 3 B & C 541, 5 Dow & Ry KB 292 and see para 2.03, above.
2   (1853) 3 De G M & G 896, 22 LJ Ch 675.
3   (1913) 29 TLR 706, 30 RPC 493, CA; see also *Valentine Meat Juice Co v Valentine Extract Co Ltd* (1900) 83 LT 259; 17 RPC 673, CA.

4.37   However, in subsequent passing off cases the requirement to show fraud was gradually abolished and the modern position was probably first stated in the well-known dictum of Romer J in *Joseph Rodgers & Sons Ltd v W N Rodgers & Co*:

'To the proposition of law that no man is entitled to carry on his business in such a way as to represent that it is the business of another, or is in any way connected with the business of another, there is an exception, that a man is entitled to carry on his business in his own name so long as he does not do anything more than that to cause confusions with the business of another, and so long as he does it honestly. To the proposition of law that no man is entitled so to describe his goods as to represent that the goods are the goods of another, there is no exception.'[1]

It is now established that even completely honest use of one's own name as a trade mark for goods will be restrained if the effect of such use is to pass off the goods so marked as the goods of another. In *Baume & Co v A H Moore Ltd*[2] the Court of Appeal held that

'the defence of innocent and honest user of the manufacturer's name on the watches which the Defendants have sold will not avail them as a defence if the other ingredients of an action for passing off are established.'[3]

Naturally, it follows that where the court suspects that the defendant has fraudulent motives it will readily act to restrain him.[4]

---

1 (1924) 41 RPC 277 at 291; approved by Lord Simonds in *Marengo v Daily Sketch and Sunday Graphic Ltd* (1948) 65 RPC 242 at 251 and in *Parker Knoll Ltd v Knoll International Ltd* [1962] RPC 243 at 279 (per Lord Morris) and 284 (per Lord Hodson); see also *Steiner Products Ltd v Willy Steiner Ltd* [1964] RPC 356; *Adrema Ltd v Adrema-Werke GmbH* [1958] RPC 323.
2 [1958] Ch 907, [1958] RPC 226, CA.
3 Ibid at 917, 229; see also *Wright, Layman & Umney v Wright* (1949) 66 RPC 149, CA, where use as a trade mark on goods was restrained although use of the company name did not cause confusion.
4 See eg *Alfred Dunhill Ltd v Sunoptic SA and Dunhill* [1979] FSR 337, CA, and see para 4.48 below.

B. As a trading name

4.38 Bona fide use by a trader of his own name as a trading name, rather than as a mark on goods, will not generally be restrained unless he does something more than simply trade under the name.[1] This is so even where such trading gives rise to confusion between the businesses of the rival traders: 'a man may carry on business under his own name, if he does so honestly, even though confusion may arise from the fact that some other person has long carried on business with that or a very similar name.'[2] Where, however, the confusion gives rise to deception of customers, a trader will be restrained from trading under his own name in the manner which is giving rise to the deception complained of.[3] As Lindley MR put it in *Jamieson & Co v Jamieson*:

'Now, when we are asked to restrain a man who is carrying on business in his own name, we must take very great care what we are about. The principle applicable to the case, I take it, is this: The Court ought not to restrain a man from carrying on business in his own name simply because there are people who are doing the same and who will be injured by what he is doing. It would be intolerable if the Court were to interfere, and to prevent people from carrying on business in their own names in rivalry to others of the same name. There must be something far more than that, viz., that the person who is carrying on business in his own name is doing it in such a way as to pass off his goods as the goods of somebody else.'[4]

And:

'In all cases in which a person has been restrained from carrying on business in his own name he has done something more than use his name; he has copied something from somebody else in the trade, or he has gone out of his way to make his things look like those of a rival in the trade.'[5]

Subsequently, in *Brinsmead v Brinsmead*[6] Buckley LJ went perhaps even further than the above statement when he said:

'If a trader takes a name which is not his own name, but is that of a rival trader, and uses it in his trade, no doubt that is very strong evidence that he intends to deceive, and the court will fasten upon that in any case in which it occurs; but if that is not so, if he is simply using his own name and it is proved that its use results in deception, he will be restrained even from using his own name without taking such steps as will preclude the deception which, by hypothesis, it engendered by his using his own name.'[7]

Thus it would seem that the court will in principle act to restrain the use by a trader of his own name as a trading name if this in fact results in deception. Where a man has used his name embellished so that it resembles the plaintiff's trading style, such use will also generally be restrained.[8] Whether it will go so far as totally to prevent a man from using his own name as a trading name at all is open. While in principle it would seem to follow from the statement of Buckley LJ quoted above that, if such use in any form must necessarily deceive, it will be restrained, it must be borne in mind that *Brinsmead v Brinsmead* was a case in which it was held on the facts that there was no passing off and it is submitted that cases in which the courts might think it appropriate to restrain a trader from using his own name as a trading name at all will be very rare. It should be noted that, in approving the passage from *Brinsmead v Brinsmead* cited above, the majority of the House of Lords in *Parker-Knoll Ltd v Knoll International Ltd*[9] either did not deal with the point[10] or specifically left it open,[11] although the dissenting speech of Lord Denning suggests that if deception results, then the exception does not apply.[12]

---

1 See the dictum of Romer J in *Rodgers v Rodgers* quotes in para 4.37 above.
2 Per Lord Simonds in *Marengo v Daily Sketch* (1948) 65 RPC 242 at 251; see also *Turton v Turton* (1889) 42 Ch D 128, 58 LJ Ch 677, CA; *Jay's Ltd v Jacobi* [1933] Ch 411, 102 LJ Ch 130.
3 *J and J Cash Ltd v Cash* (1902) 86 LT 211. 19 rpc 181; see also *Wright, Layman & Umney Ltd v Wright* (1949) 66 RPC 149, CA; *Parker-Knoll Ltd v Knoll International Ltd* [1962] RPC 265, HL; *Thomas Richfield v Speedy Cables Ltd* [1957] RPC 47; see Appendix A, below, for the appropriate limitation to the form of the injunction.
4 (1898) 15 RPC 169 at 181, CA.
5 Ibid at 183.
6 (1913) 29 TLR 706, 30 RPC 493.
7 Ibid at 506.
8 See eg *Parker & Son (Reading) Ltd v Parker* [1965] RPC 323.
9 [1962] RPC 265, HL.
10 Ibid per Lords Morris and Hodson.
11 Ibid per Lord Guest at 287, Lord Devlin at 291.
12 Ibid at 276.

COMPANY NAMES, FIRST NAMES, AND NICKNAMES

4.39 While the principle that a trader has a right to use his own name as a trading name may be applied where the defendant is trading under a surname which he has acquired through use,[1] it does not extend to the use of a first name or nickname which has been acquired merely by adoption.[2] Nor does it apply where a trader incorporates a company to carry on a new business, even if the company bears his own name.[3] However, if a trader has previously traded under his own name, he can transfer the goodwill in the use of the name when he incorporates a company to continue the business.[4] The right to trade under one's own name can be exercised by an established company with an established business,[5] but only in its established field, not in a new field.[6] In practice the right of a company to use its own name may turn out to be somewhat limited in scope.[7]

1　*Jay's Ltd v Jacobi* [1933] Ch 411, 50 RPC 132; *Rael-Brook Ltd v Head Shirts Ltd* [1963] RPC 6.
2　*Biba Group Ltd v Biba Boutique* [1980] RPC 413.
3　*M P Guimaraens & Son v Fonseca* (1921) 38 RPC 388; *Alfred Dunhill Ltd v Sunoptic SA and Dunhill* [1979] FSR 337.
4　*Fine Cotton Spinners and Doublers Association Ltd and John Cash & Sons Ltd v Harwood Cash & Co Ltd* [1907] 2 Ch 184, 24 RPC 533; *S Chivers & Sons v S Chivers & Co Ltd* (1900) 17 RPC 420.
5　*Parker-Knoll Ltd v Knoll International Ltd* [1962] RPC 265, HL, and *Habib Bank Ltd v Habib Bank AG Zurich* [1982] RPC 1 are examples of this type.
6　*Abel Morrall Ltd v Hessin & Co* (1903) 19 RPC 557, 20 RPC 429, CA: *Rodgers & Sons Ltd v Hearnshaw and Hearnshaw* (1906) 23 RPC 349.
7　As in *Parker-Knoll Ltd v Knoll International Ltd* [1962] RPC 243.

4.40　Sometimes cases on the borderline of merely trading under a name and using a mark for goods give rise to extreme difficulty in deciding whether or not a trader should be restrained from using his own name. A particularly difficult case is where the defendant's name has come to denote the plaintiff's article. Then, even where the defendant is not selling goods of that type, his use of his own name simply as a business name may give rise to deception. As Lord Halsbury put it in *Electromobile Co Ltd v British Electromobile Co Ltd*:[1]

'I do not deny that a person might be restrained even from using his own name. If in point of user a particular thing had become so identified with the proper name of a person who carried on business under his own name that he could establish, as a matter of fact, that the name had become associated with the particular manufacture, I do not deny that another person who set up in business under that name, although it might be that person's own proper name, might be restrained from carrying on business under that name.'

This passage and the cases cited in the previous paragraph indicate the considerable difficulty which the law has had in balancing the right of an individual to use his own name if he chooses to go into trade against the need to protect other traders and the public against the possibility of passing off. In such cases, therefore, the parties' motives will be even more important than normally.

1　(1908) 25 RPC 149 at 154, CA.

DEFENDANT'S CONCURRENT RIGHT TO USE THE MARK

4.41   In contrast to the position in relation to registered trade marks,[1] there is no specific principle or doctrine of 'honest concurrent user' in the law of passing off which entitles a defendant who has been using the matter concerned in his business to continue to do so, irrespective of whether his activities cause confusion or deception.[2] However, a trader who shows that he has been using the matter complained of in his business for some time may well be able to show that his doing so does not trespass on the plaintiff's goodwill and thus give rise to a misrepresentation.[3] As Oliver LJ said in *Habib Bank Ltd v Habib Bank AG Zurich*:[4]

> 'Where you find that two traders have been concurrently using in the United Kingdom the same or similar names for their goods or businesses, you may well find a factual situation in which neither of them can be said to be guilty of any misrepresentation. Each represents nothing but the truth, that a particular name or mark is associated with his goods or business.'[5]

The same result may follow in a modified form where the defendant has a long history of using a similar but not identical mark to that of the plaintiff. It may well be the case that, even though the mark was objectionable when first used, the extensive use by the defendant has led to it acquiring a reputation of its own or at least becoming distinct from the plaintiff's mark. This was the result in the *British sherry* case where on the facts it was held that whilst *sherry* simpliciter meant a particular type of wine from the Jerez region of Spain, long use of the expressions *British sherry* and *South African sherry* had led to those expressions having become differentiated from it.[6] The case is particularly interesting because the delay arose from the sherry producers' mistaken but reasonable belief that the law did not provide them with any right to prevent the use of the term *British sherry*.[7] However, even extensive use of a trading name or mark outside the UK will not assist a defendant in establishing a right to do so here:

> 'The use of the same name ... however honest and however much used elsewhere, constitutes a misrepresentation if it leads people to believe that [the defendant's] goods are the goods of the plaintiff.'

---

1   See para 9.05 below and the Trade Marks Act 1994 s 7(1) and (2).

2   *Habib Bank Ltd v Habib Bank AG Zurich* [1982] RPC 1 at 24, CA.

3   *City Link Travel Holdings Ltd v Lakin* [1979] FSR 653: five years' concurrent use with little or no confusion, action dismissed.

4   *Habib Bank Ltd v Habib Bank AG Zurich*, above, n 2.

5   Per Oliver LJ in *Anheuser-Busch Inc v Budejovicky Budvar Narodni Podnik* [1984] FSR 413 at 463. CA; see also *J C Penney Co Inc v Penneys Ltd* [1975] FSR 367, CA; see also the analogous problem arising through attempts to establish reputation in the UK through foreign user discussed at ch 3, paras 3.11–3.12 above.

6   *Vine Products Limited v McKenzie & Co Ltd* [1969] RPC 1.

7   The litigation followed the original decision in the *Champagne* case ([1960] RPC 16, [1961] RPC 116 (CA)) which for the first time held that a claim lay in passing off for misuse of defined product descriptions.

Acquiescence, laches and estoppel

DELAY IN PROCEEDING

4.42 We have seen in the previous paragraph that long delay by the plaintiff in bringing an action whilst the defendant is trading under the name to which objection is taken may result in a finding that there is no misrepresentation and the action accordingly failing. However, mere delay in proceeding will not bar a claim unless coupled with the elements necessary to give rise to a true case of acquiescence or estoppel. Thus, in the *Sherry case*,[1] an injunction was granted to restrain the use of the name *sherry* simpliciter, even though it was held that no objection could be taken to use of the term 'British sherry'. A further consequence of delay may be that the action will fail as a result of the plaintiff's inability to show any damage despite extensive use by the defendant of the name complained of. As it was put by Mellish LJ in *Rodgers v Rodgers*:[2]

'In order to make out a clear case where [the defendant's] use of the word complained of has lasted for such a great number of years as this, the plaintiffs need to prove satisfactorily that persons have actually been deceived.'

Thus in *Bulmer v Bollinger*[3] the failure of the champagne houses to prove any actual confusion or damage during a period of 18 years use of the term 'champagne perry' for sparkling cider was fatal to their case even though they were expressly absolved from laches or acquiescence. As Goff LJ said in that case, for the plaintiff's claim to be barred on those grounds:

'the facts must be such that the owner of the legal right has done something beyond mere delay to encourage the wrongdoer to believe that he does not intend to rely on his strict rights and the wrongdoer must have acted to his prejudice in that belief.'[4]

Despite this comment, Goff LJ considered that there might be cases in which 'inordinate delay' alone would be sufficient to bar an injunction to protect a legal right.[5] Even deliberate delay in order to strengthen the plaintiff's position in a trade mark claim will not alone bar a claim.[6]

1   *Vine Products v McKenzie & Co Ltd* [1969] RPC 1 following *Lindsay Petroleum Co v Hurd* (1874) LR 5 PC 221.
2   (1874) 31 LT 285.
3   [1977] 2 CMLR 625, [1978] RPC 79.
4   Ibid at 682, 136.
5   Ibid at 681, 135 following Jenkins LJ in *Electrolux Limited v Electrix Limited* (1954) 71 RPC 23 at 41 and Upjohn J in *Cluett Peabody v McIntyre, Hogg, Marsh & Co* [1958] RPC 335.
6   *Electrolux Limited v Electrix Limited* (above).

ACQUIESCENCE AND ESTOPPEL

4.43 The foundation of the law is the judgment of Fry J in *Willmott v Barber*[1] in which he set out the five probanda necessary to found a claim of acquiescence. However, the law of acquiescence and estoppel has developed greatly in the last 100 years. The cases referred to in the previous paragraph were decided at a time when the courts were engaged in a debate as to the difference between the effect of delay depending upon whether what is being enforced is a legal or equitable right. That debate came to a head in *Habib Bank Ltd v Habib Bank AG Zurich*[2] where Oliver LJ rejected the distinction, saying:

> 'I have to confess that I detect in myself, despite the erudition displayed by both counsel, a strong predilection for the view that such distinctions are both archaic and arcane and that in the year 1980 they have but little significance for anyone but a legal historian. For myself, I believe that the law as it has developed over the last 20 years has now evolved a far broader approach to the problem than that suggested by [counsel for the plaintiff] and one which is in no way dependent upon the historical accident of whether any particular right was first recognised by the common law or was invented by the Court of Chancery. It is an approach exemplified by cases such as *Inwards v Baker*[3] and *Crabb v Arun District Council*.'[4]

In the light of this he went on to hold that the approach of the modern law to determining whether there is an estoppel, whether called proprietary, by acquiescence or encouragement:

> 'is directed ... at ascertaining whether, in particular individual circumstances, it would be unconscionable for the plaintiff to deny that which, knowingly or unknowingly, he has allowed or encouraged another to assume to his detriment than to inquiring whether the circumstances can be fitted within the confines of some preconceived formula serving as a universal yardstick for every form of unconscionable behaviour.'[2]

The question now, therefore, depends upon the court's judgment whether the behaviour of the plaintiff in seeking to enforce his rights is unconscionable in all the circumstances. This allows the court to do justice whatever the facts rather than trying to fit them into a predetermined structure. This applies as much to a case in which all that is alleged is delay by the plaintiff as to a case in which the plaintiff is alleged to have taken some positive step.

---

1 (1880) 15 Ch D 97.
2 [1982] RPC 1 at 36.
3 [1965] 2 QB 29.
4 [1976] Ch 179.

Misconduct by the plaintiff

4.44 The broad principle which has long guided the courts is of course *ex turpi causa non oritur actio* and refusal of relief for misconduct in a passing off action by the plaintiff is no more than an example of that principle in action. It was first said in relation to a passing off action that:

> 'If the plaintiff makes any misrepresentation in connection with the property he seeks to protect he loses ... his right to claim the assistance of the Court of Equity.'[1]

In practice, however, the courts have tempered the rigour of that approach by considering whether the misrepresentation has in fact misled anyone or whether it is merely collateral. The statement quoted above was made in relation to a false claim that the plaintiff's product was patented which was held in that case to debar relief. However, in *Ford v Foster*[2] the Court of Appeal held that such a representation was merely collateral, not having deceived the defendants or anyone else, and was not a bar to relief. It is likely that such representations would be treated the same way today. The broad principle has, nevertheless been restated subsequently in a slightly different form. In *J H Coles Pty Ltd v Need*,[3] the Privy Council held that:

> 'an action will be barred where the plaintiff is using a trade mark or trade name in aid of a fraudulent trade.'

although the principle was held not to be applicable on the facts of the case. In the celebrated case of *Bile Beans Manufacturing Co Ltd v Davidson*,[4] however, it was held that the plaintiff's representations about their products went beyond a 'mere puff' and constituted 'a deliberate fraud on the public' as a result of which the plaintiffs were refused relief. The fraud in the *Bile Bean* case was particularly spectacular, consisting of a complete fiction that the plaintiff's pills were the product of the discovery of a native remedy which had been carefully scientifically tested and refined and it is hardly surprising that the claim was rejected. Less obviously fraudulent claims have, however, been held to bar relief. For example, in *Cropper Minerva Machines Co Limited v Cropper Charlton & Co Limited*[5] Farwell J held that a claim by the purchaser of an established business to be 'the old and original firm' was sufficiently false to deprive the plaintiffs of relief. Nowadays it is submitted that the court would not refuse relief unless satisfied that the way in which the plaintiff has presented his business to the public is such as itself to mislead them materially as to its nature or quality.[6]

---

1 Per Lord Westbury in *Leather Cloth Co Limited v American Leather Cloth Co Limited* (1863) 4 De GJ & Sm 137 at 142 (affirmed by the House of Lords at (1865) 11 HL Cas 523) in which a false claim that the plaintiff's goods were patented led to the denial of equitable relief. At that time, however, the plaintiff could bring a separate action at law and, having established his legal right, reapply to the court of equity for an injunction to assist it: see eg *Pidding v How* (1837) 8 Sim 477, 6 LJ Ch 345.
2 (1872) 7 Ch App 611, 41 LJ Ch 682. See also *Hudson v Osborne* (1869) 39 LJ Ch 79; *Holloway v Holloway* (1850) 13 Beav 209; *Siegert v Findlater* (1878) 7 Ch D 801 where it was held that a representation not made until after the commencement of the proceedings was immaterial.
3 [1934] AC 82, 50 RPC 379.
4 (1906) 23 RPC 725 at 734.
5 (1906) 23 RPC 388.
6 There are also, of course, now a variety of statutory and non-statutory controls on trading and advertising such as the Trade Descriptions Act 1968 and those provided by the Advertising Standards Authority which reduce the likelihood that seriously misleading material will be used.

Deceptive resemblance

GENERALLY

4.45 Deceptive resemblance is always a question of fact[1] which has to be determined by the court looking at the plaintiff's and defendant's goods or businesses in the light of the evidence relating to the surrounding circumstances.[2] In the light of such surrounding circumstances the resemblance is to be judged by the overall impression given to the eye of the viewer[3] and this impression is entirely a matter for the judgment of the court, not the witnesses.[4] Accordingly it is impossible to define as a matter of law the degree of resemblance which is necessary to give rise to a right of action.[5] Lord Cranworth put the principle succinctly when he said: 'All that can be done is to ascertain in every case as it occurs, whether there is such a resemblance as to deceive a purchaser using ordinary caution.'[6] In considering the question of deceptive resemblance it is therefore necessary for the court to take into account the nature of the purchasing public, the extent of confusion and the way in which confusion arises.[7]

---

1   There are many cases from which this is clear including the cases cited in the notes to paras 4.03–4.05 above: the following are typical: *Lever v Goodwin* (1887) 36 Ch D 1, 4 RPC 492, CA; *Johnston & Co v Orr Ewing & Co* (1882) 7 App Cas 219, 51 LJ Ch 797; *Fisons Ltd v E J Godwins (Peat Industries) Ltd* [1976] RPC 653; *Tetrosyl Ltd v Silver Paint & Lacquer Co Ltd* [1980] FSR 68.
2   *Payton & Co v Snelling, Lampard & Co* [1901] AC 308, 17 RPC 628, HL; *Perry & Co v T Hessin & Co* (1912) 29 RPC 509 at 528, CA, per Cozens-Hardy, LJ.
3   *Jones v Hallworth* (1897) 14 RPC 225 at 233.
4   *Payton v Snelling, Lampard & Co*, above, n 2, at 315 and at 635; *Spalding & Bros v A W Gamage Ltd* (1915) 32 RPC 273 at 286; *George Ballantine & Son Ltd v Ballantyne Stewart & Co Ltd* [1959] RPC 273 at 280, CA; *Parker-Knoll Ltd v Knoll International Ltd* [1962] RPC 265 at 279, 285, HL.
5   *Seixo v Provezende* (1866) 1 Ch App 192 at 196.
6   *Leather Cloth Co Ltd v American Leather Cloth Co Ltd* (1865) 11 HL Cas 523, 35 LJ Ch 53.
7   These matters are discussed in paras 4.03–4.05, above.

IMPERFECT RECOLLECTION: THE IDEA OF THE MARK OR GET-UP

4.46   The test for comparison of allegedly confusingly similar names, marks or other distinguishing indicia is not to compare them side by side but to take into account the fact that the confusion which may occur will take place when the customer has in his mind his recollection of the plaintiff's mark which may well be only an idea of the whole or actual mark:

> 'The likelihood of deception or confusion in such cases is not disproved by placing the two marks side by side and demonstrating how small is the chance of error in any customer who places his order for the goods with both the marks clearly before him, for orders are not placed, or are often not placed, under such conditions. It is more useful to observe that in most persons the eye is not an accurate recorder of visual detail, and that marks are remembered rather by general impressions or by some significant detail than by any photographic recollection of the whole.'[1]

The court must allow for such imperfect recollection and have special regard for those parts or the idea of the mark which are likely to have stuck in the memory rather than those parts which, being common place or insignificant, may well have been discarded. As Romer LJ said:

> 'It must I think be borne in mind, in this, as in other similar cases, that the ordinary purchaser has only the ordinary memory, and that a man who has been accustomed to buy the plaintiffs' material "Kleenoff" is quite likely to have forgotten the precise name.' [The defendants' product was called 'Kleenup'.][2]

In relation to word marks it has been held that the first portion or syllable of the mark is more important than the ending because of 'the tendency of persons using the English language to slur the termination of words [which] also has the effect necessarily that the beginning of words is accentuated in comparison'.[3] However, it is submitted that to treat this as a rule or principle is wrong and that in each case the comparison must be approached in the way set out by Lord Radcliffe above. In many cases the significant part of the word may well not be the beginning.[4]

1   Per Lord Radcliffe in *De Cordova v Vick Chemical Co Ltd* (1951) 68 RPC 103 at 106; see also *Saville Perfumery Ltd v June Perfect Ltd* (1941) 58 RPC 147 at 161, HL; *Seixo v Provezende* (1866) 1 Ch App 192.
2   *Bale and Church Ltd v Sutton, Parsons and Sutton and Astrah Products* (1934) 51 RPC 129 at 141, CA.
3   Per Sargant LJ in *Re London Lubricants'(1920) Ltd's Application* (1925) 42 RPC 264 at 279.
4   For example the following marks have been held confusingly similar: Rysta and Aristoc (*Aristoc Ltd v Rysta Ltd* [1945] AC 68, 62 RPC 65, HL), Babycham and Chamlet (*Showerings Ltd v HP Bulmer & Co Ltd, Re Bulmer (HP) & Co Ltd's Trade Mark* [1956] RPC 307), Watermatic and Aquamatic (*Reynold v Laffeaty's Ltd* [1957] RPC 311, CA); although it is clear that the idea conveyed by the first part of the mark was important there was phonetic similarity only in the second part.

TRADING NAMES

4.47   In the case of trading names, the court's approach to deceptive resemblance appears particularly to depend upon its own reaction to the similarity between the two trading names. In the *Office Cleaning* case[1] all the members of the House of Lords clearly thought that the name relied on was so descriptive that there would be no deception. By contrast in *North Cheshire and Manchester Brewery Co v Manchester Brewery Co*[2] where both the plaintiff's and the defendant's names might well have been held (one would think) to be highly descriptive, Lord Halsbury said this:

'I should think myself that the inevitable result would be that which appears to have happened — that anyone who saw the two names together would arrive at the conclusion without any doubt at all that the two companies, both with well-known names, both in the particular neighbourhood with which we are dealing, had been amalgamated. Indeed, there is a considerable body of evidence to shew that; every one who was called to give evidence on the subject, merely looking at the name, came to the conclusion that they had amalgamated ... For my own part I should not have required such evidence.'[3]

1   *Office Cleaning Services v Westminster Office Cleaning Association* [1946] 1 All ER 320n, 63 RPC 39, HL.
2   [1899] AC 83, 68 LJ Ch 74.
3   Ibid at 85.

The relevance of fraud

4.48   The defendant's subjective intention has for many years been irrelevant in a claim for passing off.[1] However, while fraud is no longer required to establish the tort of passing off, its presence makes the burden of proof on the plaintiff to prove confusion much lighter. Once the defendant is found to have had a fraudulent intent, the court will generally presume that deception will arise and there are many examples of cases where the defendant's fraud has persuaded the court that there will be deception where without fraud the decision would probably have gone the other way.[2] As Cozens-Hardy MR said in *Claudius Ash Sons & Co Ltd v Invicta Manufacturing Co Ltd:* 'If you find a defendant who is a knave, you may presume he is not a fool.'[3] In a perhaps even more celebrated comment, Lindley LJ expressed the view: 'Why should we be astute to say that he [the defendant] cannot succeed in doing that which he is straining every nerve to do?'[4] Indeed, far from providing a defence, the bringing in by the defendant of someone with the same name as the plaintiff and then using his name may well be treated by the court as evidence of fraud sufficient to found an allegation of passing off.[5] On the other hand, a defendant whose fraudulent intent is beyond doubt is not thereby guilty of passing off and, if no deception of customers is caused, the action will fail. In *Cadbury Schweppes Pty Ltd v The Pub Squash Co Pty Ltd*[6] it was proved at the trial, though denied by the defendants that they had intended to imitate all aspects of the plaintiffs' extremely successful product as closely as possible. The evidence nevertheless showed that there was no deception of customers and the action failed.

---

1   See ch 2 paras 2.12–2.15. The point was recently reiterated in the Court of Appeal in *Taittinger v Allbev Ltd* [1993] FSR 641 at 667.

2   See cases such as the 'Camel Hair Belting' cases cited at para 4.35, above: *Dunlop Pneumatic Tyre Co Ltd v Dunlop Lubricant Co* (1898) 16 RPC 12 contrasted with *Dunlop Pneumatic Tyre Co Ltd v Dunlop Motor Co* [1907] AC 430, 76 LJ PC 102; *Harrods Ltd v R Harrod Ltd* (1924) 41 RPC 74; *Draper v Trist* [1939] 3 All ER 513, 56 RPC 429, CA; *C & A Modes v C & A (Waterford) Ltd* [1978] FSR 126 per Henchy J at 139; *Dunhill v Sunoptic* [1979] FSR 337.

3   (1911) 28 RPC 597 at 603. In his judgment the following year in *Lloyd's v Lloyds (Southampton) Ltd* (1912) 29 RPC 433 at 439, CA, he expanded this sentiment, saying: 'If I find that a man, taking a particular name under which to trade, is a knave, I give him credit for not being also a fool, and I assume that there is a reasonable probability that his knavish purpose will succeed.'

4   *Slazenger v Feltham (No 2)* (1889) 6 RPC 531 at 538.

5   *Dunlop v Dunlop*, above n 1; *Dunhill v Sunoptic*, above n 2.

6   [1981] 1 All ER 213, [1981] 1 WLR 193.

4.49   If fraud is to be alleged it should be pleaded and proved[1] although in some circumstances the court will consider whether the defendant has acted fraudulently even when it is not raised on the pleadings.[2]

---

1   *Claudius Ash Son & Co Ltd v Invicta Manufacturing Co* (1912) 29 RPC 465: *H P Bulmer Ltd v J Bollinger SA* [1977] 2 CMLR 625, [1978] RPC 79: RSC Ord 18, r 12(1).

2   See ch 7, para 7.13 below.

Activities committed abroad

THE NATURE OF THE TORT

4.50 An interesting and, as yet, open question is whether activities committed in other jurisdictions can be sued on in England. This may arise in two ways. The first is where there are activities committed in this country which have led to the commission of a tort in another country. In that case the question is whether the activities here are such as to amount to the complete tort of passing off in the manner found in the *Scotch Whisky* cases.[1] The second type of claim is where it is alleged only that activities have taken place in another country but that they are justiciable in this country under the rules of private international law.[2] The two kinds of action raise completely different questions and, whilst there is no real doubt that the former is a proper cause of action, the latter probably does not exist. There are, however, a number of authorities in which the tort in the latter form has been held to be triable in this country[3] and the point therefore merits careful examination.

1   This is an action of the type found in the whisky cases, *John Walker v Ost* [1970] RPC 489 and *White Horse Distillers v Gregson* [1984] RPC 61, where the question is whether the exporting of the means to commit the passing off abroad constitutes the complete tort of passing off here.
2   Ie where there is simply an activity committed which is a tort in the foreign jurisdiction which is in the nature of passing off.
3   *John Walker v Ost* [1970] RPC 489; *Alfred Dunhill Limited v Sunoptic SA* [1979] FSR 337; *Intercontex v Schmidt* [1988] FSR 575.

PASSING OFF ABROAD AS A TORT IN ENGLAND

4.51 This action is simply a particular, if rather unusual, example of enabling passing off by someone else.[1] The cases in which it has arisen have both involved the export of Scotch whisky to South America.[2] In each case the defendants were exporters of genuine Scotch whisky to countries in South America which they knew was to be admixed with local spirit and sold there in such a way as to represent, untruthfully, that the combined product was Scotch whisky. The question which arose in these actions was whether the putting of the instrument of fraud into the hands of the person who was ultimately going to use it constituted the complete tort of passing off in England where the act of misrepresentation was in fact to be committed abroad.

1   See para 4.29 above.
2   *John Walker v Ost* and *White Horse Distillers v Gregson*: note 1 to para 4.50.

ACTIONABILITY OF ACTIVITIES COMMITTED IN OTHER COUNTRIES

4.52 For acts committed wholly abroad to be the subject of an action in England they must satisfy the private international law rule of 'double actionability'.[1] Under that rule, for it to be possible to bring a claim in England, it is necessary that the act complained of be:

(a)   actionable as a tort according to English law, and

(b)   actionable according to the law of the country where it was done.

It is therefore clear that, if the law of the country in which the activity in question was committed does not recognise any right analogous to passing off, there can be no claim in relation to it in England.[2] On the assumption that the law of the country where the act was committed does recognise such a right,[3] there arises the difficult question whether such activities are actionable as passing off in England, that is whether point (a) above can be satisfied. The present state of the authorities on this issue is entirely unclear and it is therefore necessary to examine in some detail the relevant legal principles.

---

1   The test appears as rule 203 in the 12th edition of Dicey and Morris *The Conflict of Laws* to which reference should be made for a full discussion of the authorities from which it is drawn.

2   It is beyond the scope of this book to consider the countries in which there are recognised analogous rights to the tort of passing off. Plainly, common law jurisdictions generally recognise such a right. However, many civil law jurisdictions also recognise similar rights which can be treated as satisfying this limb of the test.

3   It should be noted that in the absence of evidence on the question, the court assumes that the relevant foreign law is the same as that in England: see for example Evershed MR in *British Nylon Spinners Ltd v ICI Limited* [1953] Ch 19 at 27 although it has been held that this assumption is not sufficient for the grant of interlocutory relief in a claim of passing off: *Alfred Dunhill Limited v Sunoptic SA* [1979] FSR 337 applied in *Intercontex v Schmidt* [1988] FSR 575.

Transitory and local actions

4.53   The first relevant principle is the distinction between transitory and local actions. The origins of this distinction are historical and lie in the fact that issues of fact were originally tried by juries drawn from the locality or venue in which the facts arose. It was then necessary to state truly the venue of each fact in issue and, if the venues of the facts were different, each issue would be tried by a jury drawn from the place in which the facts relating to it arose. In *British South Africa Co v Companhia de Moçambique*,[1] Lord Herschell, in giving the leading speech, explained the development of the distinction between transitory and local actions from this state of affairs as follows:

'When juries ceased to be drawn from the particular town, parish or hamlet where the fact took place, that is, from amongst those who were supposed to be cognisant of the circumstances, and came to be drawn from the body of the county generally, and to be bound to determine the issues judicially after hearing witnesses, the law began to discriminate between cases in which the truth of the venue was material and those in which it was not so. This gave rise to the distinction between transitory and local actions, that is, between those in which the facts relied on as the foundation of the plaintiff's case have no necessary connection with a particular locality and those in which there is such a connection. In the latter class of actions the plaintiff was bound to lay the venue truly; in the former he might lay it in any county he pleased. . . . Where a local matter occurred out of the realm, a difficulty arose, inasmuch as it was supposed that the issue could not be tried, as no jury could be summoned from the place, and it was by the general rule essential that a jury should be summoned from the venue laid to the fact in issue. It was, however, early decided that, notwithstanding the general rule, such matters might be tried by a jury from the venue in the action, and thus the difficulty was removed and the form was introduced of adding after the statement of the foreign place the words, 'to wit at Westminster in the County of Middlesex', or wherever else might happen to be the venue of the action. . . .

My Lords, I cannot but lay great stress upon the fact that whilst lawyers made an exception from the ordinary rule in the case of a local matter occurring outside the realm for which there was no proper place of trial in this country, and invented a fiction which enabled the courts to exercise jurisdiction, they did not make an exception where the cause of action was a local matter arising abroad, and did not extend the fiction to such cases.'[2]

It can be seen from this that the courts developed a practice of allowing fictional locations to be attributed to facts the place of whose occurrence was immaterial. However, this practice was not permitted where the place of the occurrence was material. In such cases the location of the act had to be correctly stated and the action had to be tried where the events occurred; and, as Lord Herschell went on to explain, this has a profound effect upon the jurisdiction of the English courts to try matters arising from activities occurring abroad whose location is material to their nature:

'The rule that in local actions the venue must be local did not, where the cause of action arose in this country, touch the jurisdiction of the courts, but only determined the particular manner in which the jurisdiction should be exercised; but where the matter complained of was local and arose outside the realm, the refusal to adjudicate upon it was in fact a refusal to exercise jurisdiction, and I cannot think that the courts would have failed to find a remedy if they had regarded the matter as one within their jurisdiction, and which it was proper for them to adjudicate upon.'[2]

Lord Herschell went on to approve as accurately stating the law the following passage:

'It is now too late for us to enquire whether it were wise or politic to make a distinction between transitory and local actions: it is sufficient for the courts that the law has settled the distinction, and that an action *quare clausum fregit* is local. We may try actions here which are in their nature transitory, though arising out of a transaction abroad, but not such as are in their nature local.'[3]

He noted that the distinction referred to in that passage was not technical but went to the jurisdiction of the court and in the light of this he concluded that:

'the grounds upon which the courts have hitherto refused to exercise jurisdiction in actions of trespass to lands situate abroad were substantial and not technical, and that the rules of procedure under the Judicature Acts have not conferred a jurisdiction which did not exist before.'[4]

Thus, the court does not have jurisdiction to try disputes arising out of matters occurring abroad if the place in which they occurred is relevant to the dispute. This principle has since then been universally applied to land situated abroad[5] and the courts have refused to take jurisdiction over disputes involving questions of title or possession relating to such property.

---

1   [1893] AC 602.

2   Ibid at 617–618.
3   Per Buller J in *Doulson v Matthews* (1792) 4 Durn. & E 503 at 504 cited at [1893] AC 602 at 621.
4   [1983] AC 602 at 629.
5   The common law principle is summarised in Rule 77 of the 10th edition of Dicey and Morris's *The Conflict of Laws* (1980). Later editions contain the rule as modified by the Brussels and Lugano Conventions: see now 12th edition rule 116.

Movable and immovable property

4.54   The second relevant principle is the distinction between movable and immovable property. In private international law the primary division of property into types is between movable and immovable property. Land is clearly an immovable. This distinction is not the same as that between tangible and intangible property[1] and is inextricably linked with the need to establish the *situs*[2] of any property when questions arise over the jurisdiction of the English courts to determine what happens to property in another country or the law to be applied when they do so. English courts do not at common law have jurisdiction to determine the rights to foreign immovable property.[3] They do, however, have jurisdiction to consider such matters relating to foreign movable property whether it is tangible or intangible.[4] The question, therefore, whether the English court has jurisdiction over foreign intellectual property rights is governed by whether such rights are movable or immovable property. Patents, copyrights and trade marks are all creatures of statute. They are created in each country by the local legislature and are accordingly territorial.[5] They have no effect outside the territory in which they were granted. As a result the English courts have now concluded, following earlier Australian authorities,[6] that such rights are analogous to immovable property and that consequently the English courts have no jurisdiction to entertain actions relating to foreign patents, copyrights and trade marks.[7]

1   See Dicey and Morris *The Conflict of Laws* 12th edn p 918.
2   The *situs* of things is the rule which determines where things are for legal purposes. Tangible property is where it is physically. Choses in action are situated where they can be recovered or enforced. The rules relating to other intangible property, such as intellectual property are not clear: Ibid Rule 114.
3   See n 5, to para 4.53.
4   See generally Dicey and Morris Rules 118–121 for the rules which apply in such circumstances.
5   This is universally recognised and is the basis for all European jurisprudence permitting the continued unfettered existence of such rights as arising solely under the domestic laws of the member states: see ch 9.
6   *Potter v Broken Hill Proprietary Co Limited* (1906) 3 CLR 479; *Norbert Steinhardt & Sons Limited v Meth* (1961) 105 CLR 440.
7   *Def Lepp Music v Stuart-Brown* [1986] RPC 273 (copyright); *LA Gear Inc v Gerald Whelan and Sons Limited* [1991] FSR 670 at 674 (trade marks); Patents Act 1977 sections 60(1) and (2): only activities within the UK infringe.

The local nature of goodwill

4.55   The goodwill which is the foundation of the action is 'local and divisible'[1] in each country in which it arises and is connected with the business carried on in that country. It might therefore be thought that logically goodwill would be treated as immovable property and that the same result would follow for passing off. However, there is no case in which this question has formed the ratio decidendi and such dicta as there are suggest the opposite. In *Tyburn Productions Ltd v Conan Doyle*,[2] Vinelott J said:

> 'By contrast, although goodwill is local an action for passing off is an application of the tort of misrepresentation and the court can grant an injunction to restrain passing off in a foreign jurisdiction if the threatened conduct of the [defendant] is unlawful in that jurisdiction: see *Dunhill v Sunoptic SA*.'[3]

In the *Dunhill*[3] case an injunction was granted restraining passing off in Switzerland and in *Walker v Ost*[4] an injunction was granted restraining passing off in Equador. In neither case was it argued that the double actionability test could not be satisfied because of the nature of the tort of passing off. In the recent Scottish case of *James Burroughs v Speymalt*[5] Lord Cousfield struck out a case of alleged infringement of foreign trade marks but refused to strike out the parallel claims in passing off. In striking out the trade mark action Lord Cousfield said this:

> 'the *jus actionis* for breach of an Italian trade mark is a different *jus actionis* from that for breach of a United Kingdom trade mark. Each *jus actionis* is separately derived from a different statutory privilege which the trade mark holder has in the territory in question and is strictly confined to that territory. It follows, in my view, that the fact that a person holds trade marks in each of two separate countries does not satisfy the requirements of double actionability.'[6]

It is submitted that this view is correct and, if correct, is directly applicable to actions for passing off where the common law franchise which the plaintiff has is derived from a goodwill earned *in this country*. The same is true in each country in which the plaintiff has an analogous claim. It follows that the *jus actionis* in each country is different. This is simply another way of saying that the facts in an action for passing off are ones which English law categorises as local rather than transitory: they are actionable not simply because of what they are but because they were committed in a locality where the plaintiff has a goodwill. Had he not had a goodwill there, he would have had no claim.[7] Alternatively, the point can be expressed by saying that goodwill is immovable rather than movable property because it arises only where the business is carried on. However, this may not be the end of the argument. As has been seen[8] there may be a movement in the law towards recognition of 'worldwide' goodwill based upon international trade and travel. If so, then it is possible to say that the *jus actionis* in the two countries is the same goodwill and the double actionability test can be satisfied. It will be interesting to see how the courts resolve this dilemma.

1   Per Lord Diplock in *Star Industrial Co Ltd v Yap Kwee Kor* [1976] FSR 256 at 269.
2   [1991] Ch 75.

3   [1979] FSR 337.
4   [1970] RPC 489.
5   [1989] SLT 561, [1991] RPC 130.
6   Ibid at 570, 138.
7   It should also be noted that the analogy between this analysis and a claim for passing off based upon a goodwill which is localised within England is complete. In such a case an activity which is actionable where the plaintiff has a goodwill is not actionable in other parts of England where he does not.
8   See ch 3, para 3.12 above.

CHAPTER 5

Damage

The need to establish damage

INTRODUCTION

5.01 It is not sufficient for a plaintiff to succeed in an action for passing off to establish his reputation and a misrepresentation by the defendant. Damage to the plaintiff is an essential element of the tort and thus it is also necessary to establish that the plaintiff has suffered damage or, in a *quia timet* action, will probably do so as a result of the defendant's activities.[1] As with any tort in which damage is an essential element, there is no claim unless the damage constitutes *injuria* for which the law provides a remedy. In other words, the damage must be to the property which is protected by the tort. In a claim for nuisance the damage must be to real property. Correspondingly, in passing off the damage must be to the plaintiff's goodwill in his business.[2] The misappropriation of a name or address may cause extensive damage and yet not be actionable as passing off because there is no goodwill in that name or address. Thus, in *Day v Brownrigg*[3] the defendant adopted the name of the plaintiff's house for his own. Jessel MR rejected the plaintiff's claim for an injunction on the ground that there is no goodwill in the name of a house. He said:

> 'An allegation of damage alone will not do. You must have in our law injury as well as damage. The act of a defendant, if lawful, may still cause a great deal of damage to the plaintiff.'[4]

Equally, in *Street v Union Bank of Switzerland*[5] the plaintiff tried to stop the defendant from using the same telegraphic address as him. It was held that any damage to the plaintiff was a mere inconvenience for which the law provides no remedy.

---

1 See *Borthwick v Evening Post* (1888) 37 Ch D 449 at 462, 57 LJ Ch 406 at 411 (CA); *British Legion v British Legion Club (Street) Ltd* (1931) 48 RPC 555 at 563; *Erven Warnink BV v Townend & Sons (Hull) Ltd* [1979] AC 731 at 742, [1980] RPC 31 at 91.
2 See ch 2, paras 2.07–2.09.
3 (1878) 10 Ch D 294, 48 LJ Ch 173.
4 Ibid at 304, 177.
5 (1885) 30 Ch D 156, 55 LJ Ch 31.

NATURE OF DAMAGE IN A PASSING OFF ACTION

5.02 The purpose of the present chapter is to consider the various ways in which the law recognises that a plaintiff's goodwill may be damaged. These will vary considerably depending upon the nature of the plaintiff's business, the relationship between that and the business carried on by the defendant, the relative standards of the goods or services offered by the parties as well as a range of other factors. In some ways damage is perhaps the most elusive element of the tort of passing off. Whilst actual loss has to be proved on the enquiry in order for the plaintiff to recover damages,[1] in many cases the court simply presumes that some damage will follow once reputation and misrepresentation have been established and the issue of damage is not discussed. Thus, clear analysis of the grounds upon which it has been held that damage will result from the defendant's activities is rare and difficult to find. This makes the subject somewhat diffuse and awkward to categorise. A particular difficulty is the requirement found in many cases for a 'common field of activity' in which the plaintiff and defendant are both engaged before damage can be suffered. Although it is clear that this requirement is now obsolete, it is impossible to understand the courts' present position on the establishment of damage without a brief historical review of this concept. This is, therefore, considered first. We then consider the variety of ways and circumstances in which it has been held that damage can be expected to flow and turn finally to circumstances in which there has been held to be no damage.

---

1 The court may grant an injunction but refuse an enquiry as to damages unless the plaintiff shows at trial that more than nominal damages have been suffered. For a full discussion see ch 7, paras 7.51–7.53.

The 'common field of activity'

5.03 The expression 'common field of activity' was coined by Wynne-Parry J in *McCulloch v Lewis A May (Produce Distributors) Ltd*[1] (the '*Uncle Mac*' case) in which he held that its presence or absence was conclusive in determining whether or not there was passing off, saying:[2]

'there is discoverable in all those cases in which the court has intervened this factor, namely, that there was a common field of activity in which, however remotely, both the plaintiff and the defendant were engaged and it was the presence of that factor that accounted for the jurisdiction of the court.'

The requirement that a 'common field of activity is conclusive in determining whether there can be passing off has been extensively criticised, first in *Henderson v Radio Corp Pty*,[3] in which Manning J said, of the ratio of *McCulloch v May*:[4]

'I think it would be unsafe to adopt the view there expressed that what has been called a common field of activity must be established in every case to entitle the plaintiff to succeed. It is undoubtedly true to say that the existence of a common field of activity is a most cogent factor to be taken into account in considering whether the misrepresentation is calculated to deceive or likely to lead to deception and may also be a factor in considering the second question as to whether the plaintiff has suffered damage. But, in my view, it is going too far to say that the absence of this so-called common field of activity necessarily bars a plaintiff from relief.'

Evatt CJ and Myers J, in a joint judgment, expressed their criticism in the following way:[5]

'The remedy in passing off is necessarily only available where the parties are engaged in business, using that expression in its widest sense to include professions and callings. If they are, there does not seem to be any reason why it should also be necessary that there be an area, actual or potential, where their activities conflict. If it were so, then, subject only to the law of defamation any businessman might falsely represent that his goods were produced by another provided that other was not engaged, or reasonably likely to be engaged, in producing similar goods. This does not seem to be a sound general principle.'

It is now clear that there is no requirement for a common field of activity to found a claim in passing off. It is not consistent with the principles expressed by Lord Diplock in *Warnink v Townend*,[6] and in *Ames Crosta Ltd v Pionex International Ltd*[7] Walton J described *McCullough v May* as having been 'decided on far too narrow grounds', basing himself on the approach taken by Russell LJ in *Annabel's v Schock*.[8] In *Lyngstad v Anabas Products*[9] Oliver J described *Henderson v Radio Corpn Pty* as: 'to some extent based on a misconception of what Wynne-Parry J was saying in *McCullough v May*'. He went on to describe the expression 'common field of activity' as 'not . . . a term of art but merely a convenient shorthand term for indicating . . . the need for a real possibility of confusion'.[10]

More recently Browne-Wilkinson V-C said that 'the so-called requirement of the law that there should be a common field of activity is now discredited'.[11] The real question in each case is whether there is as a result of a misrepresentation a real likelihood of confusion or deception of the public and consequent damage to the plaintiff. In determining whether that is so it may well be helpful to consider whether the public would naturally regard the activities of the parties as being so similar that they are likely to be commercially connected. If so, then it follows that there is a much greater likelihood of deception or confusion than if not. Naturally, such an approach is not capable of direct application to trades such as character merchandising and endorsement for there the trade connection perceived by the public emanates from a belief that the plaintiff is licensing the defendant's activities and not from their similarity to the primary business of the plaintiff.

---

1 [1947] 2 All ER 845, 65 RPC 58.
2 Ibid at 851 and at 66.
3 [1969] RPC 218.
4 Ibid at 242.

5 Ibid at 234.
6 [1979] AC 731 at 742.
7 [1977] FSR 46 at 48.
8 [1972] RPC 838 at 844.
9 [1977] FSR 62.
10 Ibid at 67.
11 *Mirage Studios v Counter-Feat Clothing Co Ltd* [1991] FSR 145 at 157.

Kinds of damage

DIRECT COMPETITION

Loss of sales and exclusivity

5.04 If a defendant is in direct competition with the plaintiff, the court will readily infer the likelihood of damage to the plaintiff's goodwill, not merely through loss of sales but also through loss of the exclusive use of his name or mark in relation to the particular goods or business concerned, on evidence of the plaintiff's reputation in the goods or business and a relevant misrepresentation by the defendant in relation to the same or similar goods or the same or a similar business. Thus in *Warwick Tyre Co v New Motor and General Rubber Co*[1] Neville J said:

'Practically the sole asset possessed by the plaintiff is the goodwill which attaches to the name of Warwick in the tyre market, and I think the evidence shows that the goodwill is an asset of great value. It would not be doubted that the value of the trade name Warwick in the tyre market would be considerably lessened by the fact that there was another person in the market who was entitled to deal in tyres in connection with the name Warwick. In the first place it would limit the right of the owner of the name Warwick in the tyre market, to the use of his name in respect of those articles — only those actual articles — on which he had used it hitherto, and in the second place, it puts the reputation of the plaintiffs in the hands of persons over whom they have no control whatever.'

It is in the context of cases like *Warwick v New Motor* that one must consider *Draper v Trist*,[2] an inquiry as to damages in which passing off was in effect admitted, judgment on liability having been entered by consent; the Court of Appeal held that:

'the law presumes that if goodwill in a man's business has been interfered with by the passing off of goods, damage results therefrom. He need not wait to show that damage has resulted ... Because passing off is of the class of cases in which the law presumes that the plaintiff has suffered damage.'

However, as will be seen, in cases of passing off where the plaintiff and defendant are not in direct competition in the same goods or business, a plaintiff may have to prove damage or the likelihood of damage expressly.

1 [1910] 1 Ch D 248 at 255, 27 RPC 161 at 170.
2 [1939] 3 All ER 513 at 526, 56 RPC 429 at 442.

Inferiority of defendant's goods or services

5.05 It is not essential, to establish damage, to prove the goods or business of the defendants to be inferior, except in the special case where the defendants are passing off inferior quality goods of the plaintiff as good quality goods.[1] In *Singer Manufacturing Co v Loog*,[2] Lord Blackburn said:

> 'The original foundation of the whole law is this, that when one knowing that goods are not made by a particular trader sells them as and for the goods of that trader, he does that which injures that trader. At first it was put upon the ground that he did so when he sold inferior goods as and for the trader's; but it is established (alike at law: *Blofeld v Payne* and in equity: *Edelsten v Edelsten*) that it is an actionable injury to pass off goods known not to be the plaintiff's as or for the plaintiff's goods even though not inferior.'

Nonetheless an important form of injury to the plaintiff's goodwill is that resulting from a defendant's inferior reputation and this form of injury alone can be relied on. Thus in *Annabel's (Berkeley Square) v Schock*[3] it was held that the plaintiff's business, a night club, was likely to suffer damage through association with the defendant's escort agency on the basis that the plaintiff was entitled to say: 'if it is going to be thought by a sufficient number of people that we are somehow associated with the running of an escort agency, some of the tar will come off on us, and we have no tar on us at all.'[4] Similarly injunctions have been granted in cases where there was a risk (even a small risk) of the defendant 'falling on evil days',[5] or of some disaster befalling the defendants,[6] reflecting on the plaintiffs' goodwill as a result. The fact that the defendant has a good reputation may be sufficient to avoid an injunction (at any rate at the interlocutory stage) in circumstances where a plaintiff needs to prove this sort of damage in order to succeed.[7] The possible inferiority of the defendant's goods or services may itself be sufficient to establish damage. It has been said that the mere fact that the use of the plaintiff's name by the defendant is outside the plaintiff's control leads to damage because it prevents the plaintiff from controlling the reputation to which the goodwill is attached.[8] Naturally, where there is a substantial risk that the defendant's goods or services will be inferior or lead to complaints, this kind of consideration can prove overwhelming.[9] The inferiority of the defendant's goods or services can of course also be a substantial head of damage where there is no direct competition between the parties for, if the public believes that the defendant's inferior goods are in some way connected or associated with the plaintiff, then it is entirely possible that they will subsequently avoid purchasing the plaintiff's actual goods or services.

---

1 See ch 4, paras 4.19–4.25 above.
2 (1882) 8 App Cas 15, 52 LJ Ch 481.
3 [1972] RPC 838, [1972] FSR 261, CA.
4 Ibid at 845 per Russell LJ.
5 *British Legion v British Legion Club (Street) Ltd* (1931) 48 RPC 555 at 564.
6 *Hulton Press v White Eagle Youth Holiday Camp Ltd* (1951) 68 RPC 126.
7 *Unitex Ltd v Union Texturing Co Ltd* [1973] RPC 119, [1973] FSR 181, CA.

5.05 *Damage*

8 *Lego System A/S v Lego M Lemelstrich* [1983] FSR 155 at 190.

9 See *Associated Newspapers plc v Insert Media Limited* [1990] 2 All ER 803 at 814, upheld on appeal at [1991] FSR 380.

OVERLAPPING ACTIVITIES

5.06 Where the plaintiff and the defendant are not in direct competition it may nevertheless be said that their activities are so closely related that their spheres of activity overlap. As a result, there is an increased likelihood that the public will think that the defendant's goods or services are from the same source as those of the plaintiff. An extension of this approach is that the plaintiff may wish to exploit its existing goodwill by expanding into the precise area occupied by the defendant. If that is so, the plaintiff's ability to do so is reduced by the defendant's activities and, hence, the value of its goodwill depreciated. Thus, in *Eastman Photographic Materials Co Ltd v John Griffiths Cycle Corpn Ltd*[1] the plaintiffs were the well-known manufacturers of cameras and films sold under the name 'Kodak' and the defendants were using the trade mark 'Kodak' for bicycles. The plaintiffs succeeded in the action in reliance on their reputation in 'Kodak' for cameras as it extended to special cameras made and sold by them for use with bicycles. In *Dunlop Pneumatic Tyre Co Ltd v Dunlop Lubricants Co Ltd*[2] the defendant was enjoined from using the name 'Dunlop', on the footing that the plaintiffs, whose nearest activity was selling bicycle accessories, might move into selling lubricants. In both the above cases the courts were greatly assisted in coming to a conclusion in the plaintiffs' favour by the presence of fraud.[3]

---

1 (1898) 15 RPC 105.

2 (1899) 16 RPC 12.

3 See *Dunhill (Alfred) Ltd v Sunoptic SA and Dunhill* [1979] FSR 337 for a modern example of fraudulent use of the name of a member of the defendant's family (the son of the chairman) and paras 4.36–4.38 above for a full discussion of the use of the defendant's own name.

5.07 However, in *Dunlop Pneumatic Tyre Co Ltd v Dunlop Motor Co Ltd*[1] the defendant used 'Dunlop' for a retail motor business and it was held that they were not passing their business off in doing so, the plaintiff's activities being confined to the manufacturers and sale of tyres and other accessories for bicycles and cars. Likewise in *Joseph Lucas v Fabry Automobile Co Ltd*[2] the plaintiffs, relying on the name 'Lucas' for car accessories, were not able to prevent the defendants from using 'Lucas' for tyres. In both these cases there was no evidence that the defendants were fraudulent. In *Rolls Razors Ltd v Rolls (Lighters) Ltd*,[3] the plaintiffs used 'Rolls' for razors and the defendants used 'Rolls' for lighters. Harman J held that the defendants had not acted fraudulently in adopting the name 'Rolls' and said: 'in the case of a manufacturer a very strong case must be made out to entitle him to monopolise a word in a use to which he has never put it before the public'. It was held that the plaintiff had failed to make out a case of passing off.

---

1   [1907] AC 430, 24 RPC 572.
2   (1905) 23 RPC 33.
3   (1949) 66 RPC 137 at 142.

5.08   In *Lego System A/S v Lego M Lemelstrich*[1] the plaintiffs had a large business in toy plastic bricks under the name 'Lego'. The plaintiffs were extremely well known under the name. The defendants used the mark 'Lego' on plastic garden equipment which they had marketed for a number of years abroad and intended to launch in this country. Although the types of goods are at first blush rather different, Falconer J held that the combination of the notoriety of the plaintiffs' name and the fact that both parties used the name on goods made of moulded plastic would result in an association between them and that damage would flow because this would, inter alia, 'restrict the plaintiff in, or deprive him of, his ability to use his goodwill to launch other products of his own in that particular area or field'.[2]

---

1   [1983] FSR 155.
2   Ibid at 190.

ASSOCIATION OR CONNECTION

5.09   In *Ewing v Buttercup Margarine Co Ltd,*[1] Cozens-Hardy MR said:

'I can see no principle for holding that a trader may not be injured ... in his business as a trader by a confusion that will lead people to conclude that the defendants are connected with the plaintiffs or a branch of the plaintiff's business or in some way mixed up with them.'

A similar test was applied in *British Legion v British Legion Club (Street) Ltd.*[2] In *Annabel's (Berkeley Square) v Schock*[3] the plaintiff's business was a night-club and the defendant's an escort agency. In the Court of Appeal Russell LJ held that, since both the plaintiff's and defendant's business were concerned with 'night entertainment', there was:[4]

'a relevant association between the fields of activities sufficient to make it impossible to say that the general public could not be confused into thinking that Mr Schock's business under the name of "Annabel" was something to do with or was associated with the plaintiff's business also under the name of "Annabel's".'

Having established this association, it was reasonable to infer a probability of damage and injury to the goodwill of the plaintiffs.

---

1   [1917] 2 Ch 1, 86 LJ Ch 441.
2   (1931) 48 RPC 555.

3 [1972] RPC 838, [1972] FSR 261, CA.
4 Ibid at 845 and at 445.

5.10 The test of damage through association has been applied to a large variety of different circumstances in other cases. For example, in *HP Bulmer Ltd and Showerings Ltd v Bollinger SA*,[1] a case concerned with the plaintiffs' rights to use the terms 'Champagne Cider' and 'Champagne Perry' in defiance of the champagne houses, Goff LJ said:

> 'It is sufficient if what is done represents the defendant's goods to be connected with the plaintiff's in such a way as would lead people to accept them on the faith of the plaintiff's reputation. Thus for example, it would be sufficient if they were taken to be made under licence, or under some trading arrangement which would give the plaintiff some control over them.'

A further result of that misrepresentation is that the distinctiveness of the plaintiff's mark is eroded or blurred so that the plaintiff's exclusive reputation under the mark is debased and his goodwill consequently damaged. This approach was applied by the court in *Taittinger SA v Allbev Limited*[2] where the defendant was selling a carbonated soft drink as 'Elderflower champagne'. The court in that case also rejected an argument that whether the defendant's activities are of sufficient scale to affect the plaintiff's reputation should be assessed by comparison of the parties' relative sizes. In *Treasure Cot Co Ltd v Hamley Bros Ltd*,[3] Harman J commenced his judgment in the following manner:

> 'The issue in this action is whether the offer for sale by the defendants to the public under the name "Treasure Cot" of dolls' cots not supplied by the plaintiffs, constitutes a representation to the public that such cots are in some way connected with the plaintiffs.'

That was the case where the plaintiffs made and sold children's cots under the name 'Treasure Cot' but did not sell toy cots under that name. In *Morny v Ball and Rogers*[4] the plaintiff had a business in perfume, soap and toilet articles and the defendant was selling a combination of the defendant's scent and the plaintiff's perfumed foam bath in a transparent package. It was held that there was a

> 'substantially arguable case that the packaging and get-up represent that the plaintiff has authorised the scent to be sold in conjunction with its own foam bath and also strongly arguable that such a representation carries with it, a consequent likelihood of damage to the plaintiff's goodwill.'[5]

In *Harrods Ltd v R Harrod Ltd*[6] the plaintiff owned the famous Harrods department store and the defendant was in the business of moneylending. The plaintiff, however, had a banking department in its store and this was a sufficient similarity in activity to enable the plaintiffs to succeed. This was a case in which the defendant's clear fraudulent motive was of assistance in persuading the Court to grant an injunction. In the Court of Appeal Warrington LJ said:[7] 'Can anyone doubt that if this is allowed to continue it will probably cause not mere annoyance but probable serious injury to (the plaintiffs) in their reputation in their business ... as bankers?'

---

1   [1978] RPC 79 at 117.
2   [1993] FSR 641 (CA).
3   (1950) 67 RPC 89.
4   [1978] FSR 91.
5   Ibid at 93.
6   (1924) 41 RPC 74, CA.
7   Ibid at 86.

5.11 Sometimes the association arises from people thinking that the defendant is a subsidiary, branch or agency of the plaintiff.[1] In *Ames Crosta Ltd v Pionex International Ltd*[2] the plaintiffs were in the business of environmental control and the defendants in the business of protective clothing. Walton J held that there was 'a sufficient association between the fields of activities of the two companies that the defendants' reputation 'might rub off on the plaintiffs sufficiently to cause them damage'.[3] In *John Walker & Sons v Rothmans,*[4] which concerned the use by the defendants of the name 'Red Label' for cigarettes, it was held that the use of a plaintiff's well-known name or get-up, in 'either an associated field or even a different field may be restrained if the public may be deceived into thinking that the product or service of the other trader has the cachet of the first trader's established name or get-up'.

---

1   See, for example, *Lloyds and Dawson Bros v Lloyds Southampton Ltd* (1912) 29 RPC 433 (agency); *Ewing v Buttercup Margarine Ltd* [1917] 2 Ch 1 34 RPC 232, CA (regional agent); *Computervision Corpn v Computer Vision Ltd* [1975] RPC 171, [1974] FSR 206 (UK subsidiary of American corporation); *North Cheshire and Manchester Brewery Co Ltd v Manchester Brewery Co* [1899] AC 83, 68 LJ Ch 74 (successor in business).
2   [1977] FSR 46.
3   Ibid at 48, 49.
4   [1978] FSR 357.

5.12 *BBC v Talbot Motor Co*[1] is a case in which the association test was stretched as widely as one can imagine possible. The plaintiffs had publicised the CARFAX for a traffic information system capable of being received on a special car radio: the defendants sold cars and car spare parts, including radios. It was held that a party was entitled to complain about his injury

'even if that injury is caused by some means other than filching trade or damaging his reputation ... It is the injury to the goodwill rather than the precise method of inflicting that injury that matters.'

Another case in which the test of 'connection' was broadly applied is *Walter v Ashton*[2] where the defendant advertised his bicycles in such a way as to lead the public to believe that the proprietors of The Times newspaper were in some way connected with his business. Byrne J held that the plaintiffs 'might be exposed to litigation and possibly be held responsible, had they

5.12 *Damage*

not taken steps to disconnect this name with the defendant's advertisements and circulars' and that this was sufficient damage to justify the granting of an injunction. In *Hulton Press Ltd v White Eagle Youth Holiday Camp Ltd*[3] the plaintiffs published a boy's magazine under the name 'Eagle' and also provided holidays for boys on a non-profit-making basis. The defendants used 'Eagle' in the name of their holiday camp. Wynne-Parry J held that there was a sufficient probability of damage to the plaintiffs to justify an injunction on the ground that if any serious accident or disaster were to occur at the defendants' camps this would seriously damage the value of any venture associated with the camp and thus the plaintiffs.

1   [1981] FSR 228.
2   [1902] 2 Ch 282, 71 LJ Ch 839.
3   (1951) 68 RPC 126.

SUGGESTION OF ENDORSEMENT OR CONSENT

5.13   As has been seen, a plaintiff can succeed in passing off in reliance on a name,[1] whether his own or a nom-de-plume or assumed name,[2] if he can prove a reputation in the name in connection with a business having goodwill,[3] a broad construction being placed on the word 'business'.[4] If, however, the defendant is using the plaintiff's name in connection with a 'business' of an entirely different sort from the plaintiff's principal business, the requirement that the plaintiff must prove damage to his goodwill relies on the suggestion that the plaintiff is in some way participating in, endorsing, licensing or otherwise lending his reputation in his principal field of business to the defendant's activities. This situation arises most commonly with well-known individuals such as entertainers or sportsmen. As will be seen, the same problem can also arise in the case of well-known fictional characters.

1   See ch 3, paras 3.18–3.20 above.
2   See eg *Hines v Winnick* [1947] Ch 708, 64 RPC 113 (actor's stage name).
3   And, of course, damage.
4   See ch 3, paras 3.03–3.05 above.

Real people

5.14   In *McCulloch v May*[1] (the *Uncle Mac* case) the plaintiff, a well-known broadcaster who used the assumed name Uncle Mac, was refused relief against the defendant, who used the same name for a breakfast cereal, on the grounds that there was no 'common field of activity' between the plaintiff and defendant. Although as has been seen this particular test is not decisive[2] the plaintiff would on the facts probably have been equally unsuccessful if the court had considered whether there would be damage to the plaintiff's goodwill. Such a case was *Lyngstad v Anabas*[3] where the plaintiff, a member of a pop group called Abba, was unable to obtain an interlocutory injunction to restrain the defendants from using his name on a variety of goods. Oliver J held that there was:

> 'no business of the plaintiffs with which the defendants' business could possible be confused . . . The evidence suggests no more than that some people might think that the plaintiffs might have granted some sort of licence for the use of the name, although why they should do so has never been explained, since it is not alleged . . . that there is any general custom for such licences . . . Indeed the available evidence is quite to the contrary.'

The plaintiffs fared better in the Australian case of *Henderson v Radio Corpn Pty Ltd*[4] where the circumstances were superficially very similar. There the plaintiffs were well-known ballroom dancers and the defendants had used the plaintiffs' names in connection with and to endorse their gramophone records. The somewhat broader approach set out above[2] was applied and the plaintiffs accordingly succeeded. However, it should be noted that there was a finding on the facts that the plaintiffs were being deprived of income from paid endorsement of other recordings as well as the ability to sell their own recordings of ballroom music[5] so that apparently the case could have been considered to be one where there was direct damage to the plaintiffs' goodwill in their business. The Australian and Canadian courts have adopted a similar approach in later cases[6] and may now do the same.[7] However, the absence of any reason to infer the existence of a licence from the plaintiff is fatal.[8]

---

1 [1947] 2 All ER 845, 65 RPC 58.
2 See para 5.03 above.
3 [1977] FSR 62.
4 [1969] RPC 218.
5 Ibid at 226, 243.
6 See *Totalizator Agency Board Inc v Turf News Pty Ltd* [1972] RPC 579; *Children's Television Workshop Inc v Woolworth (NSW) Ltd* [1981] RPC 187 [1981] 1 NSW LR 273; *Krouse v Chrysler Canada Ltd* (1973) 40 DLR (3d) 15.
7 See *Mirage Studios v Counter-Feat Clothing Co Limited* [1991] FSR 145: see ch 3, paras 3.53–3.54 above and para 5.15 below.
8 *Grundy Television plc v Startrain Ltd* [1988] FSR 11.

Fictional characters

5.15 It has been held that there is no goodwill in the name of a fictional character.[1] Not surprisingly, therefore, the use of the name of a fictional character, whether well-known or not, for commercial purposes, has produced difficulties for any deviser of the name of such a character wishing to exploit the name for profit, whether by way of 'character merchandising'[2] or in some other way. The case of *Tavener Rutledge Ltd v Trexapalm Ltd*[3] was concerned with the use of the name of a fictional character 'Kojak' well known to the public from the television series. The defendants had a licence from the owners of the rights in the television series to use the name 'Kojak' for lollipops. The plaintiffs were, however, already using 'Kojak' (as 'Kojakpop') for lollipops without permission from anyone and had established a business reputation for themselves in 'Kojak' for lollipops. It was held that the plaintiffs were entitled not merely to use 'Kojak' for lollipops but also to prevent the defendants from doing so, the defendants' licence being valueless and 'writ in water'.[4] On a similar basis, in *Wombles Ltd v Wombles Skips Ltd*[5] the plaintiffs were unable to prevent the defendants from using the name 'Wombles' for a business of hiring out skips. However, as has been seen,[2] these cases have now been distinguished if not directly disapproved in *Mirage Studios v Counter-Feat Clothing Co Limited*[6] opening the way to actions for passing off by misrepresentation of licence or authorisation. A key element in such cases is whether there is damage to the plaintiff's goodwill. In *Mirage Studios* Browne-Wilkinson V-C was greatly impressed by the fact that the plaintiffs were already involved in the business of licensing reproductions of their cartoon characters, the *Teenage Mutant Ninja Turtles*, and charging licence fees for the right to do so. As he said '[a] major part of their business income arises from royalties to be received from such a licensing enterprise'.[7] Accordingly he held that reproduction without payment would damage the plaintiffs:

> 'if others are able to reproduce or apparently reproduce the Turtles without paying licence royalties to the plaintiffs, they will lose the royalties. Since the public associates the goods with the creator of the characters, the depreciation of the image by fixing the Turtle picture to inferior goods and inferior materials may seriously reduce the value of the licensing right. This damage to an important part of the plaintiffs' business is therefore plainly foreseeable.'[7]

This approach does not directly provide authority for saying that any creator of a fictional character may bring an action for passing off by its unauthorised exploitation in other fields. The facts of the *Mirage Studios* case enabled the court to conclude that the plaintiffs had an existing business in licensing the use of their characters. The deviser of a character who is merely contemplating the possibility of doing so can at least in theory be met by the answer that he has no subsisting goodwill in such a business. However, applying the reasoning in *Lego*[8] it is difficult to see why on appropriate evidence the plaintiff should not be able to establish that his goodwill will be damaged in such a case.

---

1   See *Conan Doyle v London Mystery Magazine Ltd* (1949) 66 RPC 312, when it was held that there was no goodwill in the fictional character 'Sherlock Holmes'. A different view was, however, formed by the Hong Kong Court in considering the fictional character 'The One-Armed Swordsman' in *Shaw Bros (Hong Kong) Ltd v Gold Harvest (HK) Ltd* [1972] RPC 559.
2   See ch 3, para 3.53 above.
3   [1977] RPC 275.
4   Ibid at 281.
5   [1977] RPC 99, [1975] FSR 488.
6   [1991] FSR 145.
7   Ibid at 156.
8   See para 5.08 above.

DAMAGE TO PROFESSIONAL GROUPS AND ASSOCIATIONS

5.16 The question of damage arises acutely in the cases where professional and other groups and associations have sought to protect themselves by the action of passing off. In *British Medical Association v Marsh*,[1] the defendant was representing that he was in some way connected with the plaintiffs by using their title and/or the initials 'BMA'. It was held by Maugham J that the acts of the defendant tended to injure the plaintiffs in their business both by tending to cause existing members of the Association to leave the Association and to cause qualified men not yet members of the Association to abstain from joining. Accordingly an appropriate injunction was granted. In *Society of Accountants and Auditors v Goodway*[2] the defendant was restrained from using the words 'Incorporated Accountant' indicating membership of the plaintiff society. Warrington J said:[3]

'The (plaintiff) society has a pecuniary interest in preventing persons who are not its members, and not entitled to the status its membership confers from representing that they are its members, and are entitled to that status.'

In *British Legion v British Legion Club (Street) Ltd*[4] the plaintiffs were an ex-servicemen's organisation and the defendants were restrained from using their name for a club. Farwell J, having held that the public would think that the defendants were in some way associated or connected with the plaintiffs, said:[5]

'It is of the first importance from their point of view that they (the plaintiffs) should be above suspicion of any impropriety . . . If the defendants were to fall on evil days that might . . . reflect discredit on the plaintiffs' association and might result in damage to that association.'[6]

---

1   (1931) 48 RPC 565.
2   [1907] 1 ch 489, 24 RPC 159.
3   Ibid at 502, and at 167.
4   (1931) 48 RPC 555.
5   Ibid at 564.
6   See also *Re Dr Barnardo's Homes: National Incorporated Association v Barnardo's Amalgamated Industries* (1949) 66 RPC 103.

Cases where there is no damage

PLAINTIFF TOO WELL KNOWN

5.17   Sometimes a plaintiff's title is held to be too well known and established for damage to be likely to result from the defendant's activities, even if in the same or a similar field. Thus in *Bradbury v Beeton*[1] the court refused to accept that the well-known magazine 'Punch' was likely to be confused with, or suffer damage from, a publication called 'Punch & Judy'. In *Miss World (Jersey) Ltd v James Street Productions Ltd*[2] the plaintiffs' beauty contest was considered, somewhat paradoxically, to be too well known and respectable to be confused with the defendants' rather disreputable film made under the title 'The Alternative Miss World'. An injunction was also refused in the other 'beauty contest' case, *Morecambe and Heysham Corpn v Mecca Ltd*,[3] on the grounds that there was no real risk of damage to the plaintiff as a result of the defendant's use of the title 'Miss Britain'.

1   (1869) 18 WR 33.
2   [1981] FSR 309.
3   [1962] RPC 145.

USE OF NAME OF NON-TRADER

5.18   There is in English law no right to prevent use of a name, unless there is an established business in connection with the name in which there is goodwill or the use of the name is defamatory. In *Du Boulay v Du Boulay* Lord Chelmsford said:[1]

> 'In this country we do not recognise the absolute right of a person to a particular name to the extent of entitling him to prevent the assumption of that name by a stranger. The right to the exclusive use of a name in connection with a trade or business is familiar to our Law, and any person using that name, after a relative right of this description has been acquired by another, is considered to have been guilty of a fraud, or, at least, of an invasion of another's right, and renders himself liable to an action, or he may be restrained from the use of the name by injunction. But the mere assumption of a name, which is the patronymic of a family, by a stranger who had never before been called by that name, whatever cause of annoyance it may be to the family, is a grievance for which our Law affords no redress.'

It is a remarkable result of *Du Boulay v Du Boulay* that, under English law, a trader can with impunity (except in special circumstances) use the name of someone else, without permission, for the promotion of his business. Such use can only be prevented if it constitutes defamation[2] or passing off.

1   (1869) LR 2 PC 430 at 441, 38 LJPC 35 at 38.
2   See para 5.19 below.

Defamation

5.19   In *Tolley v J S Fry & Sons Ltd*[1] the plaintiff was a well-known golfer and the defendants were using his name without his permission to advertise their chocolate. In an action for libel, the plaintiff successfully relied on an innuendo that he was accepting payment for the advertising and therefore was no longer an amateur. The circumstances were somewhat unusual and there seem to have been no similar later cases.

1   [1931] AC 333, 100 LJ KB 328, HL.

MISCELLANEOUS CASES IN WHICH NO DAMAGE WAS SHOWN

5.20   Whatever basis the plaintiff asserts for saying that he has suffered or will suffer damage to his goodwill, it is imperative that he satisfies the court that this is a realistic prospect. There are many cases in which actions or applications for interlocutory injunctions have failed simply because the plaintiff has not persuaded the court that, even if there is confusion, his goodwill will be damaged.

The following cases are mere examples of this problem but they illustrate well the ways in which the court may resist suggestions that damage will flow from the defendant's activities. In *Unitex Ltd v Union Texturing Co*[1] the plaintiffs failed to obtain interlocutory relief in the absence of evidence of damaging or potentially damaging confusion or any evidence from which this could be inferred; it was held relevant that there was no evidence of fraud and that the defendants were of good standing. In *Granada Group v Ford Motor Co*,[2] Graham J held that there was unlikely to be confusion between the plaintiffs' business (television, theatre, cinema and publicity) and the defendants' business (motor vehicles) by the defendants' use of 'Granada' either directly or indirectly through anyone thinking that the plaintiffs had sponsored or approved the defendants' cars. Accordingly an interlocutory injunction was refused. In *Hall of Arts and Science Corpn v Albert Edward Hall*[3] the plaintiffs owned a concert hall called 'The Albert Hall' while the defendant was in the business of supplying musicians for orchestras and other musical groups. An injunction was refused on lack of evidence of damage or likely damage. In *George Outram & Co Ltd v London Evening Newspapers Co Ltd*,[4] it was held that the plaintiffs' newspaper published in Glasgow was unlikely to be confused with the defendants' newspaper published in London and that there was therefore no likelihood of the plaintiffs suffering damage. In *Walter v Emmott*[5] it was held that there was no risk of damage to the plaintiffs' newspaper 'The Mail' from a cheaper newspaper published earlier in the day under the title 'The Morning Mail'. In *Newsweek Inc v BBC*[6] there was held to be no likelihood of the plaintiff's magazine incurring damage as a result of a BBC television programme under the same title; the outcome of plans by the plaintiff to start television programmes was held too speculative to take into account. In *Stringfellow v McCain Foods (GB) Ltd*[7] the plaintiffs owned a night-club called 'Stringfellows' and the defendants were selling potato chips under the name 'Stringfellows'. The Court of Appeal, although satisfied that a small number of people might be led to believe that the defendant's chips were associated with the plaintiff, were not satisfied that the plaintiff had proved that any damage would result therefrom. Accordingly relief was refused. In the *Budweiser*[8] case the Court of Appeal held that the plaintiffs had failed to establish any damage to such business as they had in this country. Finally, in *Mothercare UK Limited v Penguin Books Limited*[9] the Court of Appeal considered whether confusion between the plaintiff and a book entitled 'Mother Care / Other Care' would in fact cause the plaintiff damage to its goodwill. Dillon LJ said this:

'[The plaintiffs] recognise that the mere fact, even if established, that the name of the book was erroneously understood as a representation that they were in some way

129

associated with the book does not, by itself, cause them any damage at all. They do not suggest that the book is in competition with the *Complete Mothercare Manual* or with any other book which they are likely to issue (since they eschew controversial subjects and do not approve of the thesis which the book seeks to make out). What they claim to fear is that potential customers for the sort of goods that Mothercare sells, who suppose from the name that Mothercare is associated with the book, will be so horrified when they realise the thesis that the book is concerned to develop, vis., in brief, that the mother-child relationship is not uniquely important for the welfare of the child, that they will refuse to have anything to do with Mothercare and in particular will insist on buying any goods they need from shops other than Mothercare's shops. In my judgment such hypothetical damage is altogether too far-fetched; it is not a reasonably foreseeable consequence, in Lord Diplock's words of the supposed misrepresentation.' [10]

This is a trenchant, but nonetheless valid, illustration of the difficulty of persuading a court that an improbable case of deception is capable of leading to any real damage to the plaintiff.

---

1   [1973] RPC 119, [1973] FSR 181, CA.
2   [1973] RPC 49.
3   (1934) 51 RPC 398.
4   (1911) 28 RPC 308.
5   (1885) 54 LJ Ch 1059.
6   [1979] RPC 441, CA.
7   [1984] RPC 501.
8   [1984] FSR 413 at 468 and 472.
9   [1988] RPC 113.
10 Ibid at 116.

CHAPTER 6

Practice and procedure: (1) interlocutory injunctions

Introduction

6.01 The interlocutory injunction is probably the single most important remedy available to the plaintiff in a passing off action. It enables him to obtain rapid relief from the court to prevent a defendant committing acts of passing off. Acting reasonably swiftly it is possible to obtain an injunction to restrain the defendant until the trial of the action within a few weeks of commencing proceedings. In cases of extreme urgency it is possible to obtain relief even more quickly by applying to the court 'ex parte', that is without giving the proposed defendant an opportunity to place evidence before the court, or even, if necessary without giving him notice of the application.[1]

---

1 Procedure is dealt with at paras 6.19 ff.

6.02 As will be seen below,[1] an interlocutory injunction is granted by the court without full consideration of the merits of the plaintiff's case. It is, therefore, a condition of its grant that the plaintiff gives a cross-undertaking to the court to pay damages to the defendant in respect of any loss suffered by reason of the existence of the interlocutory injunction in the interim period, if the defendant is successful at the trial of the action.[2] Accordingly, the court will usually need to be satisfied that the plaintiff is of sufficient financial standing to meet any likely award on, or that there is sufficient security for,[3] the cross-undertaking. However, a plaintiff whose cross-undertaking is of limited value, such as one who is legally-aided, will not be refused an injunction on this ground alone if to do justice an injunction is necessary.[4]

---

1 Paras 6.04 ff.
2 See the discussion of the nature and effect of the cross-undertaking in the judgments of the Court of Appeal in *Smith v Day* (1882) 21 Ch D 421.
3 See eg *Morning Star Co-operative Society Ltd v Express Newspapers Ltd* [1979] FSR 113; *Combe International v Scholl (UK) Ltd* [1980] RPC 1 at 9.
4 *Allen v Jambo Holdings* [1980] 2 All ER 502, [1980] 1 WLR 1252, CA.

6.03 In circumstances where it can be shown that the defendant is trading dishonestly and it is likely that, if given notice of any proceedings, he will ensure that the documents and evidence the plaintiff needs to make good his allegations are destroyed, it is possible to obtain an order for inspection of the defendant's premises and removal of incriminating material without notice.[1] Where cause is shown the courts will also freeze the defendant's assets to prevent him dissipating them or removing them from the jurisdiction, and thus prevent the plaintiff obtaining effective financial relief.[2] Interlocutory proceedings can also be used in some circumstances to obtain discovery of documents and the names of suppliers or customers.[3]

---

1 The *Anton Piller* order and the circumstances in which it is appropriate are discussed below at para 6.26.
2 This is known as a *Mareva* injunction from the name of the case in which it was first granted: *Mareva Compania Naviera SA v International Bulk Carriers SA* [1980] 1 All ER 213, [1975] 2 Lloyd's Rep 509, CA, discussed at para 6.28.
3 See para 6.29 below.

The basic principles

6.04 The principles governing the grant of interlocutory injunctions were completely reconsidered by the House of Lords in *American Cyanamid Co v Ethicon Ltd*[1] (usually referred to simply as *American Cyanamid*) in 1974. Lord Diplock, in a speech with which all the other members of the House agreed, set out the approach to be adopted by the court in all cases in which an interlocutory injunction is sought. This consists of a series of tests to be applied to the case which may be summarised as follows:

1   Has the plaintiff shown on the evidence before the court that there is a serious question to be tried? If not, then no injunction is granted.
2   If there is a serious question to be tried, then the court considers whether the damages awarded at the trial would be an adequate remedy for the plaintiff. If so, then no injunction is granted.
3   If damages would not be an adequate remedy for the plaintiff, the court then goes on to consider if damages would be an adequate remedy for the defendant: if so, then normally an injunction will be granted.
4   If damages would not be an adequate remedy for the defendant, the court goes on to consider the factors affecting the balance of convenience, ie which party will suffer more uncompensatable damage from the grant or refusal of the injunction.
5   If the balance of convenience is fairly even, then it is prudent for the court to seek to preserve the status quo.
6   Finally, where there is approximately equal uncompensatable damage to both parties, it is proper to look at the relative strength of the parties' substantive cases. Where one is disproportionately stronger than the other, this may swing the balance.

---

1 [1975] AC 396, [1975] RPC 513.

6.05 The decision in *American Cyanamid* has fundamentally altered the way in which the courts approach the granting of interlocutory injunctions. All previous authorities on the granting of interlocutory injunctions must therefore be discarded unless they deal with matters falling within the principles enunciated by Lord Diplock (or matters not considered by him at all).[1] However, the courts have considered the application of Lord Diplock's principles in a number of cases since the decision in *American Cyanamid* and the effect of the more important of these cases are considered below as they give considerable guidance to the meaning and application of the above tests. Before proceeding to carry out this analysis, it is, however, salutory to bear in mind the warning given by Kerr LJ in *Cambridge Nutrition Limited v BBC*[2] about the nature of the guidance given by Lord Diplock:

> 'It is important to bear in mind that the *American Cyanamid* case contains no principle of universal application. The only principle is the statutory power of the court to grant injunctions where it is just and convenient to do so. The *American Cyanamid* case is no more than a set of useful guidelines which apply in many cases.'

Thus, there may be circumstances in which the *American Cyanamid* guidelines are simply inappropriate and, in such cases, an alternative approach must be taken.[3]

---

1 Such as delay. See para 6.16 below.
2 [1990] 3 All ER 523 at 534.
3 See paras 6.17 and 6.18 below.

'A SERIOUS QUESTION TO BE TRIED'

6.06 Prior to *American Cyanamid* it had been held that a plaintiff seeking an interlocutory injunction had to demonstrate a prima facie case (according to some authorities a strong prima facie case) that he would ultimately succeed in the action before there was any possibility of the court granting an interlocutory injunction. In a passage which is now the governing authority in determining the strength of the substantive case the plaintiff must show, Lord Diplock stated that there is no such rule:

> 'The use of such expressions as "a probability", "a prima facie case", or "a strong prima facie case" in the context of the exercise of a discretionary power to grant an interlocutory injunction leads to confusion as to the object sought to be achieved by this form of temporary relief. The court no doubt must be satisfied that the claim is not frivolous or vexatious; in other words that there is a serious question to be tried.
>
> It is no part of the court's function at this stage of the litigation to try to resolve conflicts of evidence on affidavit as to facts on which the claims of either party may ultimately depend nor to decide difficult questions of law which call for detailed argument and mature consideration. These are matters to be dealt with at the trial.
>
> ... Unless the material available to the court at the hearing of the application for an interlocutory injunction fails to disclose that the plaintiff has any real prospect of succeeding in his claim for a permanent injunction at the trial, the court should go on to consider whether the balance of convenience lies in favour of granting or refusing the interlocutory relief that is sought.'[1]

The precise strength and nature of the substantive case which Lord Diplock required a plaintiff to establish in interlocutory proceedings has given rise to some difficulty in subsequent cases and a divergence of opinion has emerged.

---

1   [1975] AC 396 at 408.

The meaning of the test

6.07   Difficulty arises from the fact that Lord Diplock used three different phrases to define this first hurdle which the plaintiff must overcome in an application for an interlocutory injunction: is the claim 'frivolous or vexatious', is there 'a serious question to be tried' and is there a 'real prospect of [the plaintiff] succeeding ... at the trial'?[1] This is to some extent compounded by the fact that the requirement has had a gloss placed on it by being commonly referred to as the need for the plaintiff to show an 'arguable case'[2] although this phrase was not used by Lord Diplock in *American Cyanamid*. In *Smith v ILEA*,[3] Browne LJ concluded that the three phrases must all have the same meaning. Brightman J in *John Walker & Sons v Rothmans International*[4] adopted this approach and went on to say that the terminology used by Lord Diplock:

> 'recalls the almost identical wording of Order 18 rule 19(1)(b),[5] and suggests that if the test be not satisfied, the plaintiffs are at least a promising candidate for an application by the defendants to strike out the action.'[6]

However, shortly afterwards in *Mothercare v Robson Books*[7] Megarry V-C considered both the above cases and a number of others in which the point had arisen[8] and concluded that:

> 'the phrase "frivolous or vexatious" in the *American Cyanamid* case should be read and understood in a sense somewhat different from its sense as used in relation to striking out actions as being frivolous or vexatious, and as resembling, rather than affecting, the natural meaning of the other two phrases.'[9]

In the authors' view the approach of Megarry V-C is correct and the test of whether there is 'a serious question to be tried' requires the plaintiff to cross a substantially higher hurdle than that required to avoid being struck out as frivolous or vexatious.

---

1   Per Lord Diplock in *American Cyanamid* [1975] AC 396 at 541 set out in para 6.06 above.
2   See eg Browne-Wilkinson J in *Rolls-Royce Motors v Zanelli* [1979] RPC 148 at 150; per Walton J in *Newsweek v BBC* [1979] RPC 441 at 444: per Megarry V-C in *Vernon & Co (Pulp Products) v Universal Pulp Containers* [1980] FSR 179.
3   [1978] 1 All ER 411, CA.
4   [1978] FSR 357.
5   Of the rules of the Supreme Court. This is one of the grounds on which an action may be struck out.
6   [1978] FSR 357.
7   [1979] FSR 466.

8   The remaining cases reviewed were *Hubbard v Pitt* [1976] QB 142 at 189, CA; *Fellowes v Fisher* [1976] QB 122 at 138, 140, CA; *Re Lord Cable, Garratt v Waters* [1977] 1 WLR 7 at 19.
9   [1979] FSR 466 at 473.

6.08   In *Re Lord Cable*[1] Slade J added an important caveat to the requirement for the plaintiff to raise only an arguable case when he stated:

> 'in my judgment it is still necessary for any plaintiff who is seeking interlocutory relief to adduce sufficiently precise factual evidence to satisfy the court that he has a real prospect of succeeding in his claim for a permanent injunction at the trial. If the facts adduced by him in support of his motion do not themselves suffice to satisfy the court as to this, he cannot in my judgment expect it to assist him by inventing hypotheses of fact upon which he might have a real prospect of success.'[2]

Although *Re Lord Cable* was not concerned with passing off, the point raised is of particular application to it. It is not, for example, sufficient for a plaintiff, in a case of passing off, simply to assert that there will be confusion because the name used by him and by the defendant are similar. He must provide evidence to support such a conclusion. The court will, however, appreciate that, in interlocutory proceedings, it may not be possible to provide evidence of any actual confusion.[3]

---

1   [1976] 3 All ER 417, [1977] 1 WLR 7.
2   Ibid at 431 and at 19.
3   See for example, the comments of Roskill LJ in *Tetrosyl v Silver Paint and Lacquer Co* [1980] FSR 68 at 76, CA, in relation to mere assertions of confusion by the plaintiff. See also *Sirdar Ltd v Les Fils de Louis Mulliez* [1975] 1 CMLR 378, [1975] FSR 309.

THE ADEQUACY OF DAMAGES AS A REMEDY

A. For the plaintiff

6.09   If the plaintiff has established that there is a 'serious question to be tried' the court should next consider whether damages are an adequate remedy for the plaintiff for the acts committed by the defendant pending final determination of the plaintiff's rights at the trial: if so, there is no question of granting an interlocutory injunction.

> 'If damages in the measure recoverable at common law would be an adequate remedy and the defendant would be in a financial position to pay them, no interlocutory injunction should normally be granted, *however strong the plaintiff's claim appeared to be at that stage.*'[1] (Emphasis added.)

Thus if the plaintiff can be compensated in damages, then it is not right to restrain the defendant until the plaintiff has properly established his right to relief. Even if the evidence establishes that the plaintiff is bound to be successful at the trial, this is not a proper ground for the grant of an interlocutory injunction if damages are an adequate remedy. The proper course in such a case is to seek summary judgment.[2]

---

1   Per Lord Diplock in *American Cyanamid* [1975] AC 396 at 541, [1975] RPC 513 at 541.
2   Under RSC Ord 14 in the High Court or under the County Court Rules Ord 9, r 14, in the County Court; but see para 6.18, below for cases where, although there is no serious factual dispute, damages would not be an adequate remedy for the plaintiff.

6.10   *Factors determining whether damages are an adequate remedy for the plaintiff*   Where the only damage complained of by the plaintiff is confusion caused by the use by the defendant of the plaintiff's distinctive indicia leading to dilution of the plaintiff's exclusivity in those indicia, the view has been expressed in some cases (and interlocutory injunctions refused, on this ground) that this damage is entirely made good by the grant of the final injunction at the trial: the plaintiff will be restored to his previous position of exclusivity and will therefore suffer no further harm. As Whitford J put it:

'that is a position which it seems to me will be completely remedied if the plaintiffs are ultimately granted the injunction which they now seek by way of interlocutory relief.'[1]

However the more general view is that damage to reputation is not only inherently difficult to assess in money terms but also has an incalculable 'knock on' effect on the plaintiff's position even after he has had his previous exclusivity restored by the grant of the final injunction.[2] A plaintiff's case is the stronger if he can show that the defendant's goods or services are of a quality inferior to those of the plaintiff and the court will usually accept that the plaintiff's damage will be irreparable in such a case.[3] A further factor which is often relied on in passing off cases is that the defendant's activities constitute use of the plaintiff's goodwill without his consent and outside his control and hence will affect the plaintiff's reputation in a way which is necessarily difficult to assess.[4] There are of course many other individual circumstances in which it can be shown that damages would not be an adequate remedy for the plaintiff. For example, where the plaintiff complains of loss of sales it may be impossible after the event to assess how many sales have in fact been taken by the defendant because of the confusion which has arisen rather than simply as a result of competition.[5] Where, however, the only reason that damages would not be adequate compensation for the plaintiff is because there is doubt as to the ability of the defendant to pay them, the court should not grant an interlocutory injunction without giving the defendant an opportunity to pay into court a sum representing a reasonable proportion of his sales to provide security for damages.[6] It had been suggested that damages are an adequate remedy for a plaintiff who exploits his reputation merely by licensing others to produce goods or services under his name, ie a pure franchisor, unless the quality of the defendant's goods or services are shown to be poor.[7] Now, however, it is clear that where a licensor takes care to control the quality of the goods to which his mark is applied the loss of the ability to control the use of the mark together with the encouragement to others to infringe his rights constituted by a defendant's unlicensed use are harm of a kind for which damages are not sufficient recompense.[8]

---

1   *Reckitt & Colman Leisure Ltd v Children's Book Club Ltd* (30 April 1981 unreported) H Ct; see also *Sirdar Ltd v Les Fils de Louis Mulliez* [1975] 1 CMLR 378, [1975] FSR 309.
2   *Sodastream Ltd v Thorn Cascade Ltd* [1982] RPC 459 at 471, CA; *Combe International Ltd v Scholl (UK) Ltd* [1980] RPC 1 at 8.
3   *Morny Ltd v Ball & Rogers (1975) Ltd* [1978] FSR 91: plain from examination of products that defendant's of poorer quality than plaintiff's; *Tavener Rutledge v Trexapalm* [1977] RPC 275, [1975] FSR 479: defendant's product poor value for money compared with plaintiff's: *Rolls-Royce v Zanelli* [1979] RPC 148: plaintiff's reputation founded on extremely high quality.
4   *Lego System A/S v Lego M Lemelstrich* [1983] FSR 155 at 190.
5   See the cases cited in n 2, above.
6   *Brupat Ltd v Sandford Marine Products Ltd* [1983] RPC 61; see also *Vernon & Co (Pulp Products) v Universal Pulp Containers* [1980] FSR 179.
7   *Wombles Ltd v Wombles Skip Ltd* [1975] FSR 488 at 491. See the equivalent approach in relation to patents in *Minnesota Mining and Manufacturing Corporation v T J Smith & Nephew plc* [1983] RPC 92.
8   *Mirage Studios v Counter-Feat Clothing Co Limited* [1991] FSR 145.

B. For the defendant

6.11   It is only if 'damages would not provide an adequate remedy for the plaintiff in the event of his succeeding at the trial'[1] that the court should go on to consider whether to grant an interlocutory injunction at all. If, having reached this stage, the evidence shows that the defendant would be adequately compensated by an award of damages under the plaintiff's cross-undertaking and the plaintiff is able to pay such damages 'there would be no reason on this ground to refuse an interlocutory injunction'.[1] Whilst Lord Diplock stated this proposition in the negative, he clearly intended that in such cases the grant of an interlocutory injunction should follow.[2]

---

1   *American Cyanamid* [1975] AC 396 at 408.
2   The more important and frequently occurring of the factors which determine whether damages would be an adequate remedy for the defendant are considered in para 6.13 below.

THE BALANCE OF CONVENIENCE

6.12   Once the court has considered whether damages would be an adequate remedy for either of the plaintiff or the defendant, it must consider the balance of convenience. Lord Diplock said 'It is where there is doubt as to the adequacy of the respective remedies in damages available to either party or to both that the question of balance of convenience arises'.[1] The term balance of convenience is rather misleading. The court is in fact concerned to balance the risk of injustice which will result from its decision at the interlocutory stage turning out to have been incorrect. As Hoffman J put it in *Films Rover International Limited v Cannon Film Sales Limited*:[2]

'The principal dilemma about the grant of interlocutory injunctions, whether prohibitory or mandatory, is that there is by definition a risk that the court may make the 'wrong' decision, in the sense of granting an injunction to a party who fails to establish his right at the trial (or would fail if there was a trial) or alternatively, in failing to grant an injunction to a party who succeeds (or would succeed) at trial. A fundamental principle is therefore that the court should take whichever course appears to carry the lower risk of injustice should it turn out to have been 'wrong' in the sense I have described. The guidelines for the grant of both kinds of interlocutory injunctions are derived from this principle.'[3]

This passage was later cited with approval by Lord Jauncey in *R v Secretary of State for Transport ex parte Factortame Limited*[4] in which Lord Bridge expressed the same approach in these words:

'A decision to grant or withhold interim relief in the protection of disputed rights at a time when the merits of the dispute cannot be finally resolved must always involve an element of risk. If, in the end, the claimant succeeds in a case where interim relief has been refused, he will have suffered an injustice. If, in the end, he fails in a case where interim relief has been granted, injustice will have been done to the other party. The objective which underlies the principles by which the discretion is to be guided must always be to ensure that the court shall choose the course which, in all the circumstances, appears to offer the best prospect that eventual injustice will be avoided or minimised.'[5]

In assessing the risk of doing injustice the court must weigh up the damage which each party will suffer if the decision is adverse to it and then endeavour to balance them against each. Many things have to be taken into account in this often difficult task and it is impossible to formulate a comprehensive definition of the relevant factors. As Lord Diplock stated:

'It would be unwise to attempt even to list all the various matters which may need to be taken into consideration in deciding where the balance lies, let alone to suggest the relative weight to be attached to them. These will vary from case to case.'[1]

However, there are a number of factors the presence of which the courts generally accept lead to the conclusion that damages are not an adequate remedy for one or the other party. Some of the factors frequently prayed in aid by plaintiffs have been summarised in para 6.10, above.

The remaining more important factors which arise regularly in passing off actions are now considered. In approaching any individual case, it must be borne in mind that it is the relative extent and effect of those factors on the opposing parties which determines the balance of convenience. Thus, while it is possible to identify particular factors which will influence the court, the mere fact of their existence, taken alone, is not enough to swing the balance one way or the other.[6]

---

1 *American Cyanamid* [1975] AC 396 at 408.
2 [1987] 1 WLR 670.
3 Ibid at 680.
4 [1991] 1 AC 603.

5   Ibid at 659.
6   *American Cyanamid* (above) at 409.

Factors affecting the balance of convenience

6.13   It is generally accepted that damage to reputation cannot be readily assessed in money terms, particularly if the defendant's goods or services are inferior to those of the plaintiff.[1] Loss of sales by either party can be taken into account in the balance of convenience only to the extent that such loss cannot be accurately determined.[2] Other types of damage which are not readily susceptible of assessment in money terms and hence inherently germane to the question of the balance of convenience include loss of the benefit of advertising expenditure already incurred[3] and damage suffered by employees who may lose their jobs if the injunction is granted or refused.[3] If the plaintiff or the defendant is at a critical stage in establishing or expanding his business the effect of the grant or refusal of the injunction may be much more significant to him than otherwise and this will be taken into account.[4] The fact that a defendant has not yet started trading, while a factor counting against him if the question of status quo falls to be considered,[5] may increase the likelihood that his losses will be difficult to quantify because it will be impossible to assess how well his business would have done if the injunction had not been granted.[6] The inability of a party to meet a claim for damages (either in the action or on the cross-undertaking) is relevant unless the party is prepared to give adequate security in some form.[7] The likelihood of confusion in the period up to the trial is also a factor to be taken into account.[8] The reason for this is that the likelihood of confusion is directly related to the likely extent of the damage that the plaintiff will suffer pending trial.[9] In practical terms this means that in many passing off cases the court must look at the merits of the claim in assessing the balance of convenience. It is only by doing this that it can assess the real likelihood of substantial confusion and, therefore, substantial damage to the plaintiff. If the case is weak because confusion is unlikely then the risk of significant irreparable harm to the plaintiff is correspondingly small. Where the parties are involved in disparate trades and the injunction is being sought to protect the plaintiff's ability to use its goodwill to extend its sphere of operations, it may well be the case that the court is able to conclude that the likelihood of damage is small even on the assumption that there is substantial confusion. In such a case, the court will not need to assess the likelihood of confusion.[10]

---

1   See para 6.10 above.
2   *Alltransport International v Alltrans Express* [1976] FSR 13 at 15, per Whitford J.
3   *Sirdar v Les Fils de Louis Mulliez and Orsay Knitting Wools* [1975] 1 CMLR 378, [1975] FSR 309.
4   EAR *Corpn v Protector Safety Products (UK) Ltd* [1980] FSR 574 (a patent case).
5   See paras 6.14 and 6.15 below, and eg *Morny Ltd v Ball & Rogers (1975) Ltd* [1978] FSR 91.
6   *Brupat Ltd v Sandford Marine Products Ltd* [1983] RPC 61 at 65 (a patent case).
7   See paras 6.02 and 6.10 above.

8 See eg *Sirdar v Les Fils de Louis Mulliez* [1975] ICMLR 387, [1975] FSR 309; *Boot Tree Ltd v Robinson* [1984] FSR 545 at 553.
9 *The Financial Times Limited v Evening Standard Co Limited* [1991] FSR 8 at 10. An application for an ex parte injunction in which the question was asked in relation to the period pending the full hearing of the motion. The principle, however, is identical.
10 *Blazer plc v Yardley & Company Limited* [1992] FSR 501, distinguishing *The Financial Times Limited v Evening Standard Co Limited* (above).

OTHER CONSIDERATIONS

6.14 In *American Cyanamid* Lord Diplock turned finally to two further matters to be considered if the balance of convenience appears to be even. First, he said, 'it is a counsel of prudence to take such measures as are calculated to preserve the status quo'.[1] Further, it is a final step permissible to take some account of the respective merits of the parties' contentions:

'if the extent of the uncompensatable disadvantage to each party would not differ widely, it may not be improper to take into account in tipping the balance the relative strength of each party's case as revealed by the affidavit evidence adduced on the hearing of the application. This, however, should be done only where it is apparent on the facts disclosed by evidence as to which there is no credible dispute that the strength of one party's case is disproportionate to that of the other party. The court is not justified in embarking upon anything resembling a trial of the action upon conflicting affidavits in order to evaluate the strength of either party's case.'[1]

This is frequently relied upon by the court in passing off cases where it may be very difficult to reach a satisfactory conclusion on the balance of convenience.[2]

---

1 [1975] AC 396 at 409.
2 *Sirdar v Les Fils de Louis Mulliez* [1975] 1 CMLR 378, [1975] FSR 309; *Combe International Ltd v Scholl (UK) Ltd* [1980] RPC 1 at 10.

Preservation of the status quo

6.15 The term status quo is a partial quotation of the phrase 'status quo ante bellum'.[1] It is therefore necessary for the court to determine at what point in time the 'war' should be considered to have started. The House of Lords has now reconsidered this matter and Lord Diplock has said:

'The status quo is the existing state of affairs; but since states of affairs do not remain static this raises the query: existing when? In my opinion, the relevant status quo to which reference was made in the *American Cyanamid* case is the state of affairs existing during the period immediately preceding the issue of the writ claiming the permanent injunction or, if there be unreasonable delay between the issue of the writ and the motion for the interlocutory injunction, the period immediately preceding the motion. The duration of that period since the state of affairs last changed must be more than minimal having regard to the total length of the relationship between the parties in respect of which the injunction is sought; otherwise the state of affairs before the last change would be the relevant status quo.'[2]

Whilst this appears entirely determinative, it had previously been thought that the status quo should be assessed at the slightly earlier date of the letter before action. It is submitted that this is still the correct point in time to assess the status quo in a passing off action unless there is, in Lord Diplock's words 'unreasonable delay'[3] between that and the issue of the writ. If this is not taken as the point at which to assess the status quo, then any defendant can take advantage of the plaintiff's courtesy in affording him an opportunity to cease the activities complained of without recourse to litigation by redoubling his efforts between then and the issue of the writ.[4] This can be very important in modern trading conditions where a defendant can easily take orders for and distribute very large quantities of goods in the fourteen days usually allowed in the letter before action.

---

1 Per Megarry V-C in *Metric Resources Corpn v Leasemetrix Ltd* [1979] FSR 571 at 581.
2 *Garden Cottage Foods v Milk Marketing Board* [1983] 2 All ER 770 at 774–775 in a speech with which Lords Keith, Bridge and Brandon agreed.
3 Delay by the plaintiff in seeking interlocutory relief is also considered as a separate factor by the court: see para 6.16 below.
4 See, for example, *Potters-Ballotini Ltd v Weston-Baker* [1977] RPC 202, CA where the defendants commenced manufacture between the issue of the notice of motion and the hearing and it was held that the balance of convenience was consequently against the grant of the injunction.

Factors outside the *American Cyanamid* guidelines

DELAY

6.16 An interlocutory injunction is a discretionary remedy. Unexplained delay by the plaintiff has always been a bar to such relief. This has been said to be an application of the equitable maxim: *vigilantibus, non dormientibus, jura subvenient*.[1] A more modern approach is that the very fact of delay demonstrates that the plaintiff does not need the immediate and exceptional relief provided by an interlocutory injunction. Moreover, if by his delay the plaintiff knowingly allows the defendant to build up his business in the activity complained of, it would be inequitable to grant the plaintiff relief until he has fully proved his case.[2] The extent of delay necessary to prevent the grant of relief in any particular case will depend upon the individual circumstances and no hard and fast rules can be given. The court may be willing to disregard delay which is satisfactorily accounted for even though the defendant has during that time increased his activities but may hold that the balance of convenience and/or the status quo have altered to the detriment of the plaintiff's case. Delay was not a factor in *American Cyanamid*. It seldom seems to have been a factor in recent cases. Quite long periods of delay have been excused in cases decided before *American Cyanamid*[3] but it is uncertain whether the basis for the excuses would now be accepted.[4]

---

1 The law supports the vigilant and not the indolent: see 2 Co Inst 690.
2 See *Cavendish House (Cheltenham) Ltd v Cavendish-Woodhouse Ltd* [1970] RPC 234, CA.

3 Ibid: eight months' delay, five of which unexplained: injunction granted; *Effluent Disposal Ltd v Midlands Effluent Disposal Ltd* [1970] RPC 238, [1969] FSR 468: three months' delay without explanation: injunction granted.

4 *Tavener Rutledge v Trexapalm* [1977] RPC 275, [1975] FSR 479: defendant warned action would be taken then two months' delay: injunction granted; *J C Penney Co Inc v Penneys Ltd* [1975] FSR 367, CA: three months' delay whilst the defendant was fully aware of the plaintiff's objections: injunction granted; *The Great American Success Co Ltd v Kattaineh* [1976] FSR 554: five months' delay balanced against the fact that the defendant was fully aware of the complaint and the strength of the plaintiff's case: injunction granted; *Century Electronics v CVS Enterprises* [1983] FSR 1: six months' delay with no real explanation: injunction refused.

WHERE THE EFFECT OF THE INTERLOCUTORY INJUNCTION IS FINAL

6.17   In a passing off action the outcome of the interlocutory proceedings often determines the final outcome of the whole proceedings. If the defendant is restrained at the interlocutory stage, he will have to find a new name, mark or get up for his goods or business, at any rate for the time being: having done so, there is little or no incentive for him to fight on to preserve the right to do something he in reality no longer needs to do. If the application is unsuccessful, the plaintiff will have to take appropriate commercial steps to cope with the situation. This too may lead to a change of business name or trade mark and make it no longer worthwhile to continue the action.

This type of situation did not arise in *American Cyanamid* but arose subsequently, and was then considered in *NWL v Woods* where Lord Diplock said:

'*American Cyanamid* . . . was not dealing with a case in which the grant or refusal of an injunction at that stage would, in effect, dispose of the action finally in favour of whichever party was successful in the application, because there would be nothing left on which it was in the unsuccessful party's interest to proceed to trial.'[1]

He went on to say that:

'Where the grant or refusal of the interlocutory injunction will have the practical effect of putting an end to the action . . . The degree of likelihood that the plaintiff would have succeeded in establishing his right to an injunction if the action had gone to trial is a factor to be brought into the balance [of convenience].'[2]

Thus, the court is in such circumstances justified in considering the substantive case.[3] *NWL v Woods* was a case in which there was little difficulty in determining the outcome of the final trial. Lord Diplock regarded it as a 'virtual certainty'. However, the same approach has been applied and amplified in later cases in which the outcome was not so certain. In *Cayne v Global Natural Resources plc*[4] the Court of Appeal upheld a decision to refuse an interlocutory injunction where the plaintiff had a doubtful but entirely arguable case on the ground that, as to do so would put an end to the dispute, the effect of granting the injunction would be to give judgment for the plaintiff and that it was unjust to do so without giving the defendant an opportunity to dispute the plaintiff's claim. The point arose even more acutely in *Cambridge Nutrition Limited v BBC*[5] where the plaintiff sought to restrain the broadcasting of a programme critical to it on the ground that there was an oral agreement between the parties to broadcast only with the plaintiff's consent. Having referred to the above authorities, Kerr LJ said this:

'I do not consider that [this] is an appropriate case for the *Cyanamid* guidelines because the crucial issues between the parties do not depend on a trial, but solely or mainly on the grant or refusal of the interlocutory relief. The *American Cyanamid* case provides an authoritative and most helpful approach to cases where the function of the court is to hold the balance as justly as possible in situations where the substantial issue between the parties can only be resolved by a trial. In my view for reasons which require no further elaboration, the present case is not in that category. Neither side is interested in monetary compensation, and once the interlocutory decision has been given, little, if anything, will remain in practice.'[6]

Whilst that observation was made in a case concerned with a contractual right to keep information confidential, it is remarkably apt to many passing off actions. The court went on, avoiding application of the *American Cyanamid* guidelines, to take account of the relative weakness of the plaintiff's case in refusing the injunction. As Kerr LJ put it 'in such cases it should matter whether the plaintiff's chances of success are 20 % or 90 %'[7] when carrying out the balancing exercise which the court is bound to do on any application for an interlocutory injunction. Aldous J has treated the finality of the injunction as a factor in assessing the balance of convenience.[8]

---

1 [1979] 3 All ER 614 at 625, [1979] 1 WLR 1294 at 1306.
2 Ibid at 626 and at 1307. See also at 628 and at 1309, per Lord Fraser. Lord Scarman regarded this as a separate factor: see at p 633 and at 1315.
3 *BBC v Talbot Motor Co* [1981] FSR 228 at 233.
4 [1984] 1 All ER 225.
5 [1990] 3 All ER 523.
6 Ibid at 535.
7 Loc cit: the reference to percentage chances of success was taken directly from *Alfred Dunhill Limited v Sunoptic SA* [1979] FSR 337 at 373.
8 *The Post Office v Interlink Express Parcels Ltd* [1989] FSR 369.

APPLICABILITY OF *AMERICAN CYANAMID* TO PASSING OFF

6.18 It has been suggested by a number of judges, notably Lord Denning, that the *American Cyanamid* guidelines are inappropriate to passing off actions.[1] Suggestions have been made that in order to obtain an interlocutory injunction the plaintiff must do rather better than demonstrate a merely arguable case[2] and that, where the primary facts are not substantially disputed, the proper approach is simply to decide the outcome of the action.[3] Such suggestions have, however, now been authoritatively rejected in *County Sound plc v Ocean Sound Limited*[4] where Nourse LJ passed the following comment on the appropriateness of the *Cyanamid* guidelines in passing off actions:

'In some cases it can be said that a passing off action is especially suited to an application of the *American Cyanamid* principles. Take the case of an old-fashioned dispute between traders as to the get-up of their goods, which stand on either side of the judge's desk at the hearing of the motion. Sometimes he can tell at once, however well established the plaintiff's reputation in his get-up may be, that there is no real possibility that the rival get-up will confuse ordinary, sensible members of the public into believing that the defendant's goods are those of the plaintiff. Having made a decent allowance for the fuller evidence of confusion which may be available at the trial, and with a generous application of the common sense which should always be to hand in passing off cases, the judge will usually refuse to grant an interlocutory injunction. At other times the judge can see at once that the rival get-up *will* confuse ordinary, sensible members of the public into believing that the defendant's goods are those of the plaintiff. In such a case an interlocutory injunction will usually be granted. In the language of the *American Cyanamid* principles the judge holds, in the first case, that there is no serious question to be tried as to confusion, by which is meant in this context a serious question which needs a trial to decide it; and, in the second, that the balance of convenience can only be in favour of the grant of an injunction where there is no real possibility that the defence will succeed at trial. In either case the judge who hears the interlocutory application is at a special advantage. He pictures the same rival get-ups standing on either side of the trial judge. He knows that the mental processes of the trial judge, albeit more fully informed, will be the same as his own. He can see now that, whatever evidence, whether direct or through survey, is put before the trial judge there is no real possibility that he will take a different view.'[5]

There is no logical reason why the judge's analysis should be limited to cases of get-up rather than allegedly confusing names and, with great respect to him, it would appear that in reality what he was doing was to reinforce the suggestions previously made that passing off motions are often best dealt with by deciding the outcome of the trial rather than refuting them. In practical terms, whilst the *American Cyanamid* guidelines do apply generally to claims of passing off, many, if not most, passing off disputes exhibit characteristics which mean that their application is not straightforward. Where the decision on the application for the interlocutory injunction will in practice decide the dispute, the court will often approach the matter without applying the guidelines.[6] Where the likelihood of confusion is slight, the court will frequently treat this as the determinative factor in the balance of convenience[7] even though the court is not prepared to go so far as to say that there is no arguable case. This is especially so where the grant of the injunction is likely to be the end of the matter because the defendant will have to change its name or get-up. It is only in cases where the court is simply unable to determine whether the merits favour the plaintiff or the defendant that a 'classical' application of the guidelines is necessary. Even then, the court will often take refuge in the doctrine of preserving the status quo rather than make an overt assessment of the balance of convenience.[8] Thus in summary whilst there is now no doubt that the *American Cyanamid* guidelines are indeed applicable to actions for passing off, the exceptions or adjustments to their application are probably greater in number than the occasions upon which they are applied.

---

1   *Newsweek v BBC* [1979] RPC 441 at 448 where Lord Denning followed his previous comment in *Fellowes v Fisher* [1976] QB 122 that such cases should normally be decided on motion.

2   Eg per Walton J in *The Athletes Foot Marketing Associates Inc v Cobra Sports Limited* [1980] RPC 343 at 348–349 following *NWL v Woods* (above); per Whitford J in *Parnass/Pelly v Hodges* [1982] FSR 329.

3   Per Kerr LJ in *Sodastream Limited v Thorn Cascade Co Limited* [1982] RPC 459 at 467; and see the cases cited in notes 1 and 2 above.

4 [1991] FSR 367.
5 Ibid at 372.
6 See para 6.17 above.
7 See eg *Management Publications Limited v Blenheim Exhibitions Group plc* [1991] FSR 550 (CA) and 348 (Ch D); *The Financial Times Limited v Evening Standard Co Limited* [1991] FSR 8.
8 See eg *Morgan-Grampian plc v Training Personnel Limited* [1992] FSR 267; *Blazer plc v Yardley & Company Limited* [1992] FSR 501.

Procedure

6.19 The application for an interlocutory injunction is made in the course of the action. In a case of passing off, the action should be brought in the Chancery Division[1] and is started by writ. The general power of the court to grant an interlocutory injunction is given by the Supreme Court Act 1981 s 37,[2] and RSC Ord 29, r 1(1) made under the statutory power provides that application may be made 'before or after the trial of the cause or matter'.

---

1 See *McCain International v Country Fair Foods* [1981] RPC 69, CA.
2 Replacing the Judicature Act 1925 s 45.

INTER PARTES APPLICATIONS

6.20 The normal course adopted by a plaintiff seeking an interlocutory injunction is to make what is called an inter partes application.[1] This is an application made by motion in the High Court and by notice of application in the county court on notice to the defendant. Evidence on such an application is given by affidavit and the plaintiff is required to give the defendant two clear days' notice of the application.[2] In such a case it is permissible and indeed common to serve the writ and the notice of motion together.[3] Given the short period of notice, it is unlikely even where the defendant has been served with copies of the plaintiff's affidavits, that he will be prepared to put affidavits of his own in answer before the court on the first occasion when the matter is heard. If the defendant wishes to put evidence before the court, he is of course entitled to do so and the usual procedure is that the parties agree a timetable for the defendant to serve his evidence on the plaintiff and for the plaintiff to serve any evidence in reply on the defendant and for the matter then to come back before the court for a full hearing and argument. Such a timetable is of course subject to the approval of the court and, unless the case is a particularly complex one or there are special factors, such as the need to obtain information from abroad, which will inevitably cause delay, the court will normally expect the period for the defendant's evidence to be two weeks or less. It is rare for the period for the defendant's evidence to exceed three weeks. The plaintiff should not need more than a further week for his evidence in reply and applications for longer are frequently met with little sympathy although there is nowadays a tendency to relax time constraints. The interim period pending the full hearing can be dealt with in a number of ways. Where the application is *quia timet* the defendant may be prepared to undertake to the court that he will not do the acts complained of pending the full hearing. Such an undertaking has the same effect for the purposes of imposing penalties for its breach as the grant of an injunction. If the defendant is not prepared to give such an undertaking, the plaintiff will either have to apply 'ex parte on notice'[4] for an injunction pending the full hearing or simply allow the defendant to continue for the period before the full hearing.

---

1   This may be preceded by a letter before action, except in really urgent cases. See ch 7, para 7.08 below.
2   RSC Ord 8, 4 2(2).
3   RSC Ord 8, r 4.
4   See para 6.22 below.

EVIDENCE

6.21   The matters which must be dealt with by the affidavit evidence are, as regards the substantive case, the same as those which arise in the action[1] and should in principle be approached in the same way. However, because of the speed with which evidence on interlocutory applications must be prepared, it is necessarily less complete than that which would be adduced at a full trial. Hearsay evidence is admissible[2] provided that the sources of the information and the grounds for believing it is true are given but the court may well decline to give it the same weight as direct evidence. Although the court has the power to give leave to cross-examine a deponent on his affidavit[3] such leave is not usually given and, as the affidavit evidence is not normally subject to cross-examination, the court will not be able to resolve direct conflicts of evidence and will generally make no attempt to do so. Public opinion survey evidence is in principle admissible although the recent tendency of the court is to give it little weight.[4] In addition to the substantive issues arising in the action, the evidence must also cover the matters which are relevant only on the application for interlocutory relief: the adequacy of damages as a remedy, the balance of convenience, the preservation of the status quo and any question of delay by the plaintiff in seeking relief.[5]

---

1   As to which see ch 7, paras 7.25–7.42 below.
2   RSC Ord 41, r 5(2).
3   RSC Ord 38, r 2(3); the form of affidavits is regulated by RSC Ord 41.
4   See the approach of Whitford J in *Imperial Group v Philip Morris* [1984] RPC 293 at 303 but contrast the approach of Falconer J in *Lego System A/S v Lego M Lemelstrich* [1983] FSR 155.
5   These matters are considered in detail in paras 6.09–6.18 above.

EX PARTE APPLICATIONS

6.22   Strictly speaking ex parte applications are those made completely without notice to the defendant. Such applications are made either in cases where there is such extreme urgency that there is no opportunity to notify the defendant of what is being done[1] or in cases where the need for the court order is to prevent the defendant defeating the ends of justice.[2] However, a practice has grown up of making applications which, although inter parties in the sense that the required two clear days' notice of the application has been given to the defendant, are ex parte in the sense that the plaintiff seeks interim relief from the court straightaway without giving the defendant an opportunity to put in evidence in answer to the application. Such applications are often referred to as being 'ex parte on notice'. At such a hearing the defendant may be represented and, if successful, may be awarded his costs.[3] Relief will normally only be granted until the full hearing of the motion when the evidence is complete. Such applications are made in the normal way by motion.[4]

---

1 Such applications may be heard before the writ is issued: RSC Ord 29, r 1(3).
2 That is where relief of *Anton Piller* or *Mareva* type is sought: see paras 6.26 ff, below.
3 *Pickwick International Inc (GB) Ltd v Multiple Sound Distributors Ltd* [1972] 3 All ER 384, [1972] 1 WLR 1213, [1972] RPC 786.
4 RSC Ord 8, r 2(1).

THE RELIEF GRANTED

6.23 The relief sought by the plaintiff will be framed in his notice of motion or application. The court will often modify the relief sought after hearing what the parties say and, in the county court, the injunction is required by the rules to be settled by the judge hearing the application.[1] It is now the normal practice to frame interlocutory injunctions in terms of the precise acts complained of without reference to the nature of the wrong. This avoids any question of trying the substantive issues if there is an application to punish or remedy a contempt. Broadly framed injunctions in a form such as restraining 'passing off' are therefore inappropriate at the interlocutory stage.[2] It is also important to ensure that all types of acts sought to be prevented are specified precisely in the injunction sought. An injunction restraining 'offers for sale' does not include placing advertisements in a catalogue[3] or other acts which amount only to 'an invitation to treat'. Nor is it possible to seek further interlocutory relief from the court if the plaintiff accepts an undertaking which is later discovered to be insufficient to protect him[4] although it would seem that the position is otherwise if the application was contested and further evidence later shows the relief to have been insufficient. Similarly a defendant will not be released from an undertaking given to the court unless there has been an intervening change of circumstances, which does not include a subsequent judgment affecting the law as the defendant could have taken the point himself rather than give the undertaking.[5]

---

1 County Court Rules Ord 13, r 6(6)
2 *Hepworth Plastics Ltd v Naylor Bros* [1979] FSR 521, CA.
3 *C A Norgreen & Co v Technomarketing* (1984) Times, 3 March.

4   *GCT Management Ltd v Laurie Marsh Group Ltd* [1973] RPC 432, [1972] FSR 519.
5   *Chanel Ltd v F W Woolworth & Co Ltd* [1981] FSR 196.

APPEALS

6.24   An appeal lies to the Court of Appeal but, since October 1993, only with the leave of the court from the decision of the High Court[1] or the County Court[2] to grant or refuse an interlocutory injunction. Appeals to the House of Lords lie only with leave.[3] Although the appeal is 'by way of rehearing'[4] and fresh evidence may be adduced,[5] it should be noted that appeals in interlocutory injunction applications are solely for the purpose of correcting errors of principle made by the judge at first instance and are not to enable the parties to have 'a second bite at each interim cherry'.[6] In particular the Court of Appeal will not interfere with the exercise by the judge of his discretion unless he is shown to have exercised it on wrong grounds or taken into account irrelevant matter.

1   Supreme Court Act 1981 Sections 18(1) and (1A) as amended by the Courts and Legal Services Act 1990 section 7 and Schedule 20; RSC Ord 59, r 1 B(1)(f).
2   Ibid and County Courts Act 1984, s 77.
3   Administration of Justice (Appeals) Act 1934 s 1.
4   RSC Ord 59, r 3(1).
5   RSC Ord 59, r 10(2).
6   Per Donaldson MR in *Elan Digital Systems Ltd v Elan Computers Ltd* [1984] FSR 373.

FURTHER COURSE OF THE PROCEEDINGS

6.25   The grant of an interlocutory injunction is an interim measure only. Unless settled in the meantime, as is often the case, the action continues until the trial and final determination of the parties' rights. If an interlocutory injunction is granted and the plaintiff fails to prove his case at the trial, the defendant will be entitled to proceed with an enquiry as to the damages suffered by him as a result of the wrongful grant of the interlocutory injunction and payable by the plaintiff on his cross-undertaking in damages to the court. The interlocutory injunction is normally granted after a full inter partes hearing until judgment in the action or further order. The parties may, however, apply at any time to the court for the modification or discharge of the order. An application to vary an order granted by consent will not be entertained by the court unless there has been a significant change of circumstances since the original order was granted or the applicant has become aware of facts which it could not have found out before the original hearing[1] unless the consent is made expressly subject to the defendant's right to apply for a variation without a change of circumstances.[2] A mere change in or clarification of the law since the order was made is not sufficient since the defendant could himself have taken the point which has since been decided.[1] A plaintiff may elect not to move his motion, standing the matter over to trial. It is unclear whether he has an absolute right to do so once the defendant has served evidence in answer.[3] Where a motion is stood over, the court has discretion as to how to dispose of the costs but will normally reserve them to the trial judge[4] unless it is of the view that the motion was unjustified in which case it may take the exceptional step of ordering the plaintiff to pay the defendant's costs in any event and, in appropriate circumstances, even make them payable forthwith.[5]

---

1   *Chanel Limited v F W Woolworth & Co Limited* [1981] FSR 196, [1981] 1 All ER 745.
2   *Butt v Butt* [1987] 1 WLR 1351.
3   See *Simon Jeffrey Limited v Shelana Fashions Limited* [1977] RPC 103; *Société Française d'Applications Commerciales et Industriales SARL v Electronic Concepts Limited* [1976] 1 WLR 51.
4   *Simons Records Limited v WEA Records Limited* [1980] FSR 35.
5   *Kickers International SA v Paul Kettle* [1990] FSR 436.

Other interlocutory orders

ANTON PILLER ORDERS

6.26   The *Anton Piller* order is named after the case in which the type of procedure it embodies was first sanctioned by the Court of Appeal.[1] Under an *Anton Piller* order the defendant is ordered to permit the plaintiff to enter his premises and to take away documents and other evidential material relating to the complaint made against him. The order is made ex parte as the basis for granting it is that, if the defendant is notified that there are proceedings against him, there is 'grave danger of property being smuggled away or of vital evidence being destroyed'.[2] Whilst in some respects it appears to resemble a search warrant, it is crucial to realise that it is not, for the court has no power to grant such a thing.[3] The order granted by the court only permits entry to and inspection of documents upon the defendant's premises with his consent. If he refuses to consent to the relief set out in the order he does so at his peril and at risk of penalties for contempt which, if he uses the interval to destroy documents or other material, may be very grave.[4] This is so even if the order is later discharged although the subsequent discharge of the order is a circumstance relevant to the appropriate penalty.[5] Additionally, the court may well subsequently draw an adverse inference against the defendant when the substantive issues come before the court.

The *Anton Piller* order has been described, with the *Mareva* injunction as 'one of the law's two "nuclear" weapons'[6] and as such must be used with great circumspection. It will only be granted where the plaintiff shows 'an extremely strong prima facie case'.[7] As with all ex parte orders, the plaintiff is under an absolute duty to disclose all relevant facts within his knowledge to the court upon the application.[8] If he fails to do this, even through inadvertence, the order will subsequently be discharged without consideration of the merits.[9] The plaintiff is also under a duty to make proper investigations of the defendant's circumstances to ascertain whether in fact it is appropriate to apply for such an order[10] and to be meticulous in its execution.[11] Failure by the plaintiff or his solicitors to comply with these duties will result in the discharge of the order with costs which, depending upon the gravity of the failure, may be on the indemnity basis. Where it is clear that there has been a material non-disclosure by the plaintiff on the application for the order, the court may discharge it on the inter partes interlocutory hearing.[12] Otherwise, the court will not normally deal with an application to discharge an *Anton Piller* order until the trial of the action as the purpose of the inter partes interlocutory application is to consider what will happen in the future and not what has happened in the past.[13] Where, however, delay in dealing with the application to discharge might result in a substantial injustice to the defendant by being deprived of costs to which he is entitled, the court may investigate the merits of the application at the interlocutory stage.[14] In appropriate cases, where it is not possible to ascertain the identity of all the defendants engaged in the wrongful activities, the court will make an order against a represented class of defendants.[15] Copies of the evidence on which the order was obtained together with copies of the photocopiable exhibits must be served with the order.[16]

---

1   *Anton Piller KG v Manufacturing Processes Ltd* [1976] Ch 55, [1976] 1 All ER 779, CA.
2   Ibid at 61F per Lord Denning.
3   Ibid at 60B per Lord Denning.
4   *WEA Records Ltd v Visions Channel 4 Ltd* [1983] 2 All ER 589, [1983] 1 WLR 721 per Sir John Donaldson MR.
5   *Wardle Fabrics v Myristis* [1984] FSR 263.
6   *Bank Mellat v Nikpour* [1982] Com LR 158, CA per Donaldson LJ.
7   *Anton Piller KG v Manufacturing Processes Ltd* [1976] Ch 55 at 62A per Ormrod LJ.
8   *R v Comrs Kensington Income Tax ex p De Polignac* [1917] 1 KB 486, CA.
9   *Thermax Ltd v Schott Industrial Glass Ltd* [1981] FSR 289; *Wardle Fabrics v Myristis* [1984] FSR 263.
10 *Jeffrey Rogers Knitwear Productions Ltd v Vinola (Knitwear) Manufacturing Co* (1984) The Times, 5 December per Whitford J; *Bank Mellat v Nikpour* [1982] Com LR 158.
11 *AB v CDE* [1982] RPC 509.
12 *EMI Records Ltd v Kudhail* [1983] Com LR 280, [1985] FSR 36.
13 *Manor Electronics v Dickson* [1988] RPC 618.
14 *Dormeuil Frères SA v Nicolian International (Textiles) Limited* [1988] 3 All ER 197.
15 *Lock International plc v Beswick* [1989] 3 All ER 373.
16 *International Electronics Ltd v Weigh Data Ltd* [1980] FSR 423.

6.27 Once established *Anton Piller* orders were initially granted rather readily by the courts and in rapidly increasing numbers. It gradually became clear, however, that such a process necessarily results in a degree of injustice to a defendant and that accordingly the circumstances in which orders should be granted should be even more closely circumscribed and that the limitations imposed upon execution of an order should be even more severe. There have been a number of celebrated cases in which orders have been discharged with substantial penalties in costs and damages being imposed on both the plaintiffs and, on occasion, their solicitors either because the order ought never to have been sought or because it had been improperly executed. In the course of these cases the courts have laid down increasingly strict guidelines for the obtaining and execution of *Anton Piller* orders in order to safeguard the position of defendants who are made subject to them. The turning point was the decision of Scott J in *Columbia Pictures Inc v Robinson*[1] in which he said this:

> 'a decision whether or not an *Anton Piller* order should be granted requires a balance to be struck between the plaintiff's need that the remedies allowed by the civil law for the breach of his rights should be attainable and the requirement of justice that a defendant should not be deprived of his property without being heard. What I have heard in the present case has disposed me to think that the practice of the court has allowed the balance to swing much too far in favour of the plaintiffs and that *Anton Piller* orders have been too readily granted and with insufficient safeguards for defendants'[2]

As a consequence he laid down a series of limitations on the granting, scope and execution of such orders. These are:

(1)   Orders should be limited to the minimum necessary for their purpose of the preservation of documents or articles which might otherwise be destroyed or concealed. Once the plaintiff's solicitors have satisfied themselves what material exists and had an opportunity to take copies, the material should be returned to its owner. This process should occupy only a short period of time.

(2)   A detailed record of what is taken should be required to be made by the solicitors before anything is removed so as to minimise subsequent disputes.

(3)   No material should be taken unless it is clearly covered by the terms of the order. It is unacceptable to persuade the respondent to agree during the execution that other material may be taken.

(4)   The order should provide that disputed material be held pending trial not by the plaintiff's solicitors but by the defendant's.

(5)   In carrying out their duty of full and frank disclosure applicants and their solicitors should err on the side of excessive disclosure. Where material may be relevant, the judge and not the plaintiff's solicitors should decide.

The promulgation of these guidelines led almost immediately to a tightening up of the court's procedure in dealing with applications for *Anton Piller* orders. Despite this, there continued to be cases in which inappropriate applications were made or orders executed with inadequate consideration for the defendant's rights and substantial injustices were done.[3] As a result in *Universal Thermosensors Limited v Hibben*,[4] Nicholls V-C laid down yet further guidelines restricting their granting and execution. He directed that when granting such orders the court should consider whether the execution should be supervised by an experienced independent solicitor who should make a written report to the court of the conduct of the execution. As a result, of this, virtually all orders are now required to be so supervised. Whilst this significantly increases the already large cost of obtaining and executing an *Anton Piller* order, the general experience is that the presence of a supervising solicitor and the content of his report greatly reduces the scope for subsequent dispute about what occurred and that there has as a result been a very substantial reduction in applications to discharge orders for flaws in their execution. He also indicated that the order should be subject to the following further restrictions:

(1)   Execution should be permitted only in working hours when a solicitor can be expected to be available so that the defendant's right to take legal advice may be effectively exercised.

(2)   If an order is to be executed on a private house where it is at all likely that it may be occupied by a woman alone, the solicitor serving the order must be accompanied by a woman.

(3)   Orders should not be executed at business premises in the absence of a responsible officer or representative of the occupant.

(4)   Unless it is seriously impractical the defendant should be given an opportunity to check the accuracy of the detailed list of items to be removed before this is done.

(5)   If an order is to be executed at the premises of a competitor of the plaintiff, the order should prevent the plaintiff from carrying out a search of his competitor's files.

(6)   If the order is accompanied by an injunction to prevent the defendant from informing others of its existence, that restraint should last only so long as necessary to enable the further enquiries which that restraint is designed to enable to be carried out and, in any event, not for as long as a week.

Since this decision it has been suggested that the pendulum has now swung back too far the other way. The authors' view, however, is that the essentially unfair and draconian nature of the relief requires that it be accompanied by stringent controls and safeguards for defendants and that it is better to err on the side of protecting those who may in fact be innocent of any serious wrongdoing. And there is as yet no evidence that orders are now not being granted or effectively executed where they are really necessary.

---

1   [1987] Ch 38.
2   Ibid at 76.
3   See eg *Lock International plc v Beswick* [1989] 3 All ER 373.
4   [1992] 3 All ER 257.

MAREVA INJUNCTIONS

6.28   *Mareva* injunctions are granted to restrain a defendant from dealing with his assets so as to defeat the ends of justice by dissipating them or taking them out of the jurisdiction of the court before judgment[1] or between judgment and execution,[2] even where there has been no *Mareva* injunction up to the date of judgment:[3] a facet of the jurisdiction of particular importance where the plaintiff has suffered a substantial loss by an extended period of passing off.

Whilst the practice was originally devised for use in cases where the defendant was resident or domiciled out of the jurisdiction so that he could easily remove any assets within the jurisdiction, and thus defeat any judgment the plaintiff might obtain, it has rapidly widened and is now available in cases where the defendant is domiciled or resident in the jurisdiction, a change which has subsequently received legislative sanction.[4] The *Mareva* injunction cannot be used to alter the priority of the plaintiff's claim against the defendant.[5] Similar considerations apply to *Mareva* injunctions as to *Anton Piller* orders and they should be used only in grave cases. Guidelines for the operation of *Mareva* injunctions have been given in a number of cases[6] which are of similar effect to those set out above in relation to *Anton Piller* orders, with the addition that they require adequate protection to be given to innocent third parties (such as banks) who may be holding the defendant's assets and that provision be made for the defendant to have access to sufficient funds to meet normal living and business expenses and the costs of the litigation during the pendency of the injunction. In passing off cases *Mareva* injunctions are only granted in clear cases of piracy by dishonest defendants but can then be used to freeze removable and disposable chattels which are clearly shown to have been acquired as the result of the profits from the defendant's wrongful acts.[7] With appropriate safeguards and in limited circumstances *Mareva* injunctions can even extend to assets held outside the jurisdiction.[8]

1 *Mareva Compania Naviera SA v International Bulkcarriers SA (The Mareva)* [1980] 1 All ER 213, [1975] 2 Lloyd's Rep 509.
2 *Stewart Chartering Ltd v C & O Managements SA* [1980] 1 All ER 718, [1980] 1 WLR 460.
3 *Orwell Steel (Erection and Fabrication) Ltd v Asphalt and Tarmac (UK) Ltd* [1984] 1 WLR 1097.
4 Supreme Court Act 1981 s 37(a).
5 *PCW (Underwriting Agencies) Ltd v Dixon* [1983] 2 All ER 158.
6 See *Third Chandris Shipping Corpn v Unimarine SA* [1979] QB 645, [1979] 2 ALL ER 972; *PCW (Underwriting Agencies) Ltd v Dixon* [1983] 2 All ER 158; *Iraqi Ministry of Defence v Arcepey Shipping Co SA* [1980] 1 All ER 480, [1980] 2 WLR 488; *A v C* [1981] QB 961, [1981] 2 All ER 126 and others: the cases are fully summarised at paras 29/1/20 to 29/1/23 of the *Supreme Court Practice 1995*.
7 *CBS (UK) Ltd v Lambert* [1983] Ch 37, [1982] 3 All ER 237, CA: primarily a copyright action but the principle is identical.
8 *Babanaft International Co SA v Bassatne* [1989] 2 WLR 232; *Derby v Weldon (No 1)* [1989] 2 WLR 276; *Derby v Weldon (No 2)* [1989] 1 All ER 1002.

INTERLOCUTORY ORDERS FOR DISCOVERY AND LISTS OF SUPPLIERS, ETC

6.29 The court has power to order interlocutory discovery of documents even against people who are not parties to the action.[1] this power can be used in conjunction with *Anton Piller* orders and *Mareva* injunctions.[2] Such orders can be used to locate both the source and destination of falsely marked goods in cases of piracy. The court also has power to order lists of suppliers[3] and (sometimes) of customers.[4] The power to order disclosure of assets can be used in aid of a *Mareva* injunction or *Anton Piller* order and even extends to requiring disclosure of assets by those who aid others in the avoidance of judgments against them.[5]

1 *Norwich Pharmacal Co v Customs and Excise Comrs* [1974] AC 133, [1974] RPC 101.
2 As in *EMI Ltd v Sarwar and Haidar* [1977] FSR 145, CA.
3 *RCA Corpn v Reddington's Rare Records* [1975] 1 All ER 38, [1975] RPC 95.
4 *Freedman v Hillingdon Shirts Co Ltd* [1975] FSR 449; *Sega Enterprises Ltd v Alca Electronics* [1982] FSR 516.
5 *The Mercantile Group (Europe) AG v Aiyela* [1993] FSR 745.

Costs

6.30 The usual practice in the Chancery Division is to award the successful party his costs in the cause on interlocutory injunction applications. This means that if successful at the trial he will recover his costs of the application whilst if he fails at the trial he will not but that the opposite party will not recover his costs of the interlocutory application. The rationale for this practice is that a party who succeeds on an interlocutory application should recover all his costs if he also succeeds at the trial but should not have to pay the costs of the interlocutory application if he fails because failure at the trial is unconnected with the basis for the granting of the interlocutory order. The rationale is not entirely sound and assumes, for example, that there will be a trial. That assumption is often incorrect and some judges are now showing a willingness to depart from the practice.[1] An order for simple costs in cause is sometimes more appropriate where the merits of the claim are very finely balanced because it is only fair that in such a case the ultimate winner should not be disadvantaged in costs as a result of the interlocutory application. On the other hand, where it is clear that the interlocutory application will effectively decide the case, it is appropriate to make a final order that the winner should have his costs to be taxed and paid forthwith.[2] Any other order ignores the reality that the proceedings will go no further. Whilst the logic of this approach is self-evident, may judges remain reluctant to apply it.

1 See eg the discussion of the practice in *Steepleglade Limited v Stratford Investments Limited* [1976] FSR 3.
2 *Kickers International SA v Paul Kettle* [1990] FSR 436.

CHAPTER 7

Practice and procedure: (2) the action for passing off

Introduction

7.01 In this chapter we consider the substantive proceedings for passing off leading to contested trial, at which (subject to appeal) the parties' rights are determined, and the nature of the relief granted. An action for passing off follows the traditional English procedure. The action is commenced with a writ and formal pleadings. There is then discovery and a summons for directions at which the court takes control of the timetable to trial. There will be exchange of written witness statements before the trial. At the end of the trial there is judgment and the precise nature and form of the relief (if any) is determined by the court. After trial there may be an appeal by the losing party to the Court of Appeal and thereafter, with leave, a further appeal to the House of Lords. If the plaintiff succeeds, there will be a separate enquiry as to damages as these are traditionally not determined at the same time as liability in intellectual property actions.[1] This is in effect a further complete trial and the majority of actions which have proceeded to judgment are settled before the enquiry has progressed very far.[2] The process is inevitably lengthy, complex and costly.

---

1 This is not the case in Scotland where the assessment of damages takes place at the trial of the issue of liability.
2 There is therefore very little jurisprudence on the conduct of enquiries or their consequences. This is discussed further below at paras 7.52–7.55.

7.02 Over the past ten years the nature of passing off actions has changed. There is now much more emphasis on evidence from witnesses who are the actual customers for the products or services in issue and much less on evidence from the trade or from experts who have conducted market surveys on the issues arising in the proceedings.[1] There is also a much greater willingness amongst both the parties and the courts to investigate the circumstances surrounding the alleged misrepresentation in order to determine whether the defendant has in fact sufficiently distinguished his goods from those of the plaintiff. As a result there has been a considerable increase in the length and complexity of passing off trials with a consequent increase in costs. This is a cause of considerable concern. However, there is no obvious remedy.[2] One of the consequences of the steady increase in the cost of litigation is the much greater attention which is now paid to costs. The importance of offers made 'without prejudice save as to costs' is much more widely recognised and the procedure is regularly used.[3]

---

1   See paras 7.35–7.37 below for discussion of the use of survey evidence.
2   Indeed, the new law of registered trade marks imports concepts surrounding the issue of deceptive resemblance similar to those well known in passing off. It is therefore likely that the same trend will be observed even in pure trade mark infringement actions: see ch 9, paras 9.07–9.08 below.
3   See para 7.59 below.

7.03   Although the vast majority of passing off claims are effectively determined by the grant or refusal of interlocutory relief, there are nevertheless substantial numbers of claims which proceed to full trial. An understanding of trial procedure is, therefore, of considerable value. The application for an interlocutory injunction is considered in chapter 6. In the context of trial procedure it need only be noted that the application will generally be made right at the outset of the proceedings to avoid any allegations of delay. Whilst there has been a trend to defer the carrying out of the steps required to progress the substantive action whilst the application for the interlocutory injunction is proceeding, this has been deprecated by the courts on many occasions, particularly as to do so when the interlocutory hearing is heavy and may not take place for several weeks after the issue of the writ can considerably delay the progress of the action. In principle, therefore, the action should proceed in accordance with the rules of court without reference to the interlocutory application.

Commencing the proceedings

THE PARTIES

The plaintiffs

7.04   Selection of the parties is often one of the most difficult tasks. Only those who have a share in the reputation and goodwill are entitled to be plaintiffs. In actions involving shared reputation[1] it is necessary to decide whether all the members of the class should sue or whether the action should be brought as a representative action. The latter course presents special difficulties as the representative plaintiff and the parties represented must have 'the same interest'[2] in the proceedings. An action brought by an association of producers on behalf of the producers will not be properly constituted as a representative action:[3] it is necessary to appoint an individual producer as the representative of the class. Where an action is brought in relation to imported goods, it is necessary to decide whether both the manufacturer and the importer should be plaintiffs or whether in fact the goodwill resides wholly with one or other of them.[4]

---

1   See paras 3.07 and 3.08 above.
2   RSC Ord 15, r 12(1).

3   *Consorzio del Prosciutto di Parma v Marks and Spencer plc* [1991] RPC 351.
4   See paras 3.13 and 3.14 above. This can have significant consequences in relation to the giving of
    security for costs where only the foreign manufacturer has a cause of action.

The defendants

7.05   Once the plaintiffs have been selected, the defendants have to be identified. This involves the usual questions relating to joinder of individuals who control small companies [1] and also whether all those in the chain who handle the goods should be joined. It may be preferable to restrict the action to the manufacturer or importer as the wholesalers or retailers are the plaintiffs' customers. However, it may not be possible to identify the ultimate source of the goods without reference to the retailer. In such circumstances the only course may be to attack the resellers seeking information about the ultimate source. Depending upon the nature of the passing off complained of, it may be possible to join as a defendant the person who is responsible for procuring the tort.[2]

---

1   See para 7.06 below.
2   See *Belegging-en Exploitatiemaatschapij Lavender BV v Witten Industrial Diamonds Ltd* [1979] FSR 59 at 66.

7.06   *Liability of directors and employees for the activities of companies*   It is well established in all branches of the law that an employer, whether an individual or a company, is vicariously liable for the activities of his servants who are acting in the course of their employment, even though they may be acting contrary to express instructions they have been given.[1] It is also common to seek to join in an action against a small company one or more of the directors or senior employees of the company. The essential reason for this is that such companies often have few assets to meet awards of damages and costs so that it is necessary, if the plaintiff is to recover, to bind the individuals behind the company. It is, however, not always legitimate to do this. The basic principle upon which this is done was expressed by Willmer LJ in the following terms:

> 'Of recent years cases have become increasingly common in which servants sometimes as well as their company, and sometimes by themselves, have been personally sued. It is well established now that, provided you can fix the responsibility to a particular individual, a right of suit against that individual exists.'[2]

The classic statement of the principle on which directors will be held liable for the acts of their company was given by Lord Buckmaster in *Rainham Chemical Works Ltd v Belvedere Fish Guano Co*,[3] where he said:

> 'If the company really was trading independently on its own account, the fact that it was directed by Messrs Feldman and Partridge would not render them responsible for its tortious acts unless, indeed, they were acts expressly directed by them. If a company is formed for the express purpose of doing a wrongful act or if, when formed, those in

157

control expressly direct that a wrongful thing be done, the individuals as well as the company are responsible for the consequences.'

Shortly thereafter Atkin LJ cited this passage and went on to say of it:

'Perhaps that is put a little more narrowly than it would have been if it had been intended as a general pronouncement without reference to the particular case because I conceive that express direction is not necessary. If the directors themselves directed or procured the commission of the act they would be liable in whatever sense they did so, whether expressly or impliedly.'[4]

More recently there was a trend to hold that directors were only liable if they directed or committed tortious acts with a degree of *mens rea* by which the director made the act his own rather than that of the company on the ground that:

'it would seem to be irrational that there should be personal liability merely because the director expressly or impliedly directs or procures the commission of the tortious act or conduct. In the extreme, but familiar, example of the one-man company, that would go near to imposing personal liability in every case.'[5]

However, that trend has now been firmly reversed and it has been held that a director will generally be liable for a tortious act he himself commits or whose commission he directs.[6] However, it should not be forgotten that 'each case depends upon its own particular facts'[7] and that there is no simple general rule by which a director's or employee's personal liability for acts he has not himself carried out can be determined. Those who set up a company for the purposes of carrying on business which necessarily involves passing off will be liable for the activities of the company.[8] In the case of a partnership, an innocent partner who had repudiated his partner's acts has been held not to be liable for them.[9]

---

1   There are many cases on vicarious liability. Examples in the field of passing off are: *Grierson Oldham & Co v Birmingham Hotel Co* (1901) 18 RPC 158; *E Cusenier Fils Aîné et Compagnie v Gaiety Bars Ltd* (1902) 19 RPC 357; *Monro v Hunter* (1904) 21 RPC 296; *Hennessey & Co v Neary* (1902) 19 RPC 36. For a full discussion of the principles of vicarious liability in tort the reader is referred to *Clerk and Lindsell on Torts* 16th edn (1989) paras 3.01 – 3.53.
2   *Yuille v B & B Fisheries (Leigh) Ltd and Bates (The Radiant)* [1958] 2 Lloyd's Rep 596 at 619.
3   [1921] 1 AC 465 at 476, 90 LJ KB 1252 at 476, 1257.
4   *Performing Right Society Ltd v Ciryl Theatrical Syndicate Ltd* [1924] 1 KB 1 at 15.
5   Per Nourse J in *White Horse Distillers Ltd v Gregson Associates Ltd* [1984] RPC 61 at 92. See also *Mentmore Manufacuring Co Ltd v National Merchandising Manufacturing Co Inc* (1978) 89 DLR (3d) 195; *Hoover plc v G Hulme (Stockport) Ltd* [1982] FSR 565.
6   *C Evans & Sons Ltd v Spritebrand Ltd* [1985] 2 All ER 415 (CA).
7   Per Lord Salmon in *Wah Tat Bank Ltd v Chan Cheng Kum* [1975] AC 507 at 515 cited with approval by Slade LJ in *C Evans & Sons Ltd v Spritebrand Ltd* (supra) at 425.
8   *Anciens Établissements Panhard et Levassor SA v Panhard-Levassor Motor Co Ltd* [1901] 2 Ch 513, 18 RPC 405.
9   *Magnolia Metal Co v Atlas Metal Co* (1897) 14 RPC 389.

7.07 *Carriers, agents and bailees*   If goods in his possession are deceptively marked, the fact that the defendant is a mere carrier, agent or bailee of them does not afford a defence to a claim for passing off by dealing in the goods. However, a bailee who upon being challenged gives the plaintiff all the information necessary to pursue the consignor of the goods and undertakes to remove them from the jurisdiction or erase the offending marks will not be liable for any costs after the offer is made.[1]

---

1   *Upmann v Elkan* (1871) LR 12 Eq 140, 7 Ch App 130; *Moet v Pickering* (1878) Ch D 372, 47 LJ Ch 527.

THE LETTER BEFORE ACTION

7.08   It is conventional to send a letter before action seeking cessation of the activities complained of before taking the step of commencing proceedings. Many potential actions are stifled at birth in this way. If no letter before action is sent and the defendant submits to judgment on receipt of the writ, the court may refuse to award costs on the ground that the defendant should have been given the opportunity to accede to the plaintiff's claims without incurring the cost of litigation.[1] The form of the letter before action is important. Because the claim is founded upon use of the identifying indicia by the plaintiff, it should give sufficient information about that use to enable the defendant to understand the basis of the case being made against him. Absence of a proper explanation may prolong a dispute which would otherwise settle quickly. The letter should also set out concisely the nature of the activities complained of and the form of undertaking not to continue them which is required. If trap orders[2] have been made and are relied upon as showing that passing off has taken place, the letter should explain this and should give sufficient information about the orders to enable the defendant to investigate them.[3] Notice of a trap order should in any event be given promptly. Because the plaintiff will probably not know the extent of the defendant's activities at this stage, it is impossible to specify the level of damages, if any, which are claimed. A convenient formula to avoid this difficulty is to seek disclosure of the extent of the activities and an undertaking to pay such damages as are agreed between the parties or in default of agreement determined by the court in the light of such disclosure.

---

1   It is not essential to send a letter before action: see *Customagic Manufacturing Co Ltd v Headquarter and General Supplies Ltd* [1968] FSR 150. However, failure to send such a letter may result in criticism: see *Ind Coope Ltd v Paine & Co Ltd* [1983] RPC 326 at 342.
2   See para 7.32 below.
3   *C C Wakefield & Co Ltd v Board* (1928) 45 RPC 261; *Cellular Clothing Co Ltd v G White & Co* (1953) 70 RPC 9 at 14.

THE WRIT

7.09   An action for passing off is begun by writ.[1] Actions in the High Court should be brought in the Chancery Division.[2] Passing off actions may also be brought in the appropriate County Court.[3] The jurisdiction of the County Court is geographically limited[4] and it is generally only actions which involve local traders which are pursued in that forum. Although the County Court's jurisdiction is no longer financially limited,[5] in most cases the plaintiff is more concerned about the injunction than establishing substantial damages so this is not really a substantial factor. In addition there is always the possibility that costs in the County Court will be awarded on one of the scales limited to less than the full reasonable costs recoverable in the High Court. In practice it is rare for passing off claims to be made in the County Court. The writ must be either specially endorsed with the full statement of claim or generally endorsed with 'a concise statement of the nature of the claim made'.[6] It is conventional to have a general rather than a special endorsement simply because it is more convenient to amend a separate statement of claim than one endorsed on the writ. A general endorsement should set out the form of injunction sought, seek delivery up, destruction or obliteration of the offending marks, damages or an account of profits (unless the action is brought quia timet) and costs. The form of the injunction will necessarily identify the conduct which it is desired to inhibit.

---

1   RSC Ord 5, r 2: it is a claim in tort.
2   *McCain International v Country Fair Foods* [1981] RPC 69 CA.
3   A tortious act must have been committed within the geographical jurisdiction of the court although it can grant a nation-wide injunction in an appropriate case.
4   County Courts Act 1984 s 15 as amended by High Court and County Courts Jurisdiction Order 1991, para 2.
5   Ie the court in the jurisdiction of which the passing off was committed. The Patents County Court does not have jurisdiction over passing off claims: see the Patents County Court (Designation and Jurisdiction) Order 1990, SI 1990 No 1496 and *MacDonald v Graham* [1994] RPC 407.
6   RSC Ord 6, r 2(1)(a).

SERVICE OF THE WRIT OUT OF THE JURISDICTION

7.10   Service of the writ on a defendant who is not resident in the jurisdiction can be effected without leave under the Civil Jurisdiction and Judgments Act 1982[1] on defendants resident within the European Union. Leave is required to service defendants who are resident elsewhere.[2] It is beyond the scope of this text to consider in detail the rules relating to service out. They are complex and technical, and need to be carefully followed.[3]

---

1   RSC Ord 11, r 1(2).
2   RSC Ord 11, r 1(1).
3   There is a full and very helpful explanation of the operation of the rules in the notes to Order 11 in the Supreme Court Practice.

Pleadings

INTRODUCTION

7.11   Pleadings are one of the cornerstones of English legal procedure. They are the means by which the parties set out formally the case they intend to advance at the trial and they determine the scope of the dispute. All pleadings must contain a complete statement of the material facts upon which the party relies.[1] Much confusion is engendered by the distinction between facts to be proved and the evidence by which they will be proved. The evidence should not be pleaded.[1] This rule is frequently broken. On the other hand, any material fact or matter which is not pleaded cannot be proved by evidence at the trial. It is, therefore, important to ensure that the pleadings contain an averment of any fact which is necessary to support the case being advanced.

---

1   RSC Ord 18, r 7(1).

STATEMENT OF CLAIM

7.12   In all but the simplest passing off case, the manner in which the plaintiff's case is set out in the statement of claim is of considerable importance. It is on the pleaded misrepresentation that the plaintiff's entitlement to relief will be judged. As has been authoritatively stated by the Court of Appeal: 'it is for the plaintiff to specify in his pleadings what he complains about'[1] and, if the pleadings do not accurately specify the misrepresentation, it may well be that the action will fail. If the statement of claim is not endorsed in the writ, it must be served thereafter not more than 14 days after the defendant gives notice of intention to defend.[2] It should state the nature of the plaintiff's business, the name, mark or get-up relied on, the manner in which the reputation and goodwill in the name mark or get-up was acquired and the nature of the defendant's activities complained of. Particulars of the specific acts relied upon should be given[3] and individual acts of deception relied upon should be fully particularised giving the identities of the persons confused. It should be clearly specified whether the passing off is of the business or goods, or both. If the activities complained of are not themselves alleged to be directly passing off, this must be made clear and a case made out on the facts that the defendant's activities have caused or enabled passing off by others.[4] The statement of claim must allege that the plaintiff has suffered damage as a result of the defendant's activities for this is an essential element of the tort. However, no particulars of damage are conventionally given, these issues being left to the enquiry.[5] There must be an express pleading of any claim to interest on damages or an account of profits.[6] To obtain an injunction, it is necessary to assert that the defendant threatens and intends to continue to carry on the activities complained of. The statement of claim finishes with a prayer for relief which should set out every head of relief claimed clearly and concisely. The court will generally refuse to grant relief going beyond that sought in the prayer and for that reason it is conventional to include in the prayer a general claim for 'further or other relief'.

---

1   Per Oliver LJ in *My Kinda Town v Soll* [1983] RPC 407 at 419 to which reference should be made for a helpful exposition of the result of failing to prove that the misrepresentation alleged is the cause of the confusion in fact observed.

2   RSC Ord 18, r 1.
3   See *Whitstable Oyster Fishery Co v Hayling Fisheries Ltd* (1900) 17 RPC 461; *Jeyes Sanitary Compounds Co v Philadelphus Jeyes* (1929) 46 RPC 236; *Imperial Tobacco Co Ltd v Purnell & Co* (1903) 20 RPC 718; *Humphries & Co v The Taylor Drug Co* (1888) 39 Ch D 693, 5 RPC 687. These cases show the importance of pleading fully specific acts of deception if evidence of them is to be admitted at the trial.
4   See ch 4, paras 4.29 and 4.45–4.48 above.
5   Unless the plaintiff elects to take an account of profits in which case they will never be investigated.
6   RSC Ord 18, r 8(4). It is common practice to insert a paragraph in the body of the statement of claim asserting the right to interest and specifying the basis upon which the claim is made although it has been held that this rule is satisfied by a bare assertion of a right to interest in the prayer for relief: *McDonald's Hamburgers Limited v Burger King (UK) Limited* [1987] FSR 112.

Allegations of fraud

7.13   Allegations of deliberate or intentional passing off, ie fraud, are not uncommon. This is because fraud, if established, will often be decisive.[1] However, as a general rule allegations of fraudulent or deliberate intent must be fully and strictly pleaded.[2] As Lord Loreburn put it in the context of passing off:

> 'Once you establish the intent to deceive, it is only a short step to proving that the intent has been successful, but it is still a step even though it be a short one. To any such charge there must be, however, two conditions ... that it ought to be pleaded explicitly, so as to give the defendant an opportunity of rebutting the accusation of intent [and] ... that it must be proved by evidence.'[3]

If allegations of fraud are made in the statement of claim and are not properly particularised or appear incapable of being supported by evidence, they may be struck out as scandalous or an abuse of the process of the court.[4] The rule that fraudulent intent must be pleaded has not always been followed. In *Midland Counties Dairy Ltd v Midland Dairies Ltd*, Harman J found fraud in the absence of any pleading saying:

> 'A court is not bound by the form of the pleadings or by disclaimer on the plaintiffs' behalf to shut its eyes to a case of fraud if convinced that one exists.'[5]

In *H P Bulmer Ltd v J Bollinger SA* the members of the Court of Appeal considered the need to plead fraud if it is to be relied upon. Buckley LJ thought that it would be permissible to reach a finding of fraud in the absence of a pleading if the evidence supporting it was admitted without protest, particularly where it was adduced by the defendant in cross examination.[6] Goff LJ, however, doubted the correctness of Harman J's comment and considered that there should be an application to amend if evidence of intent emerged at the trial without having been previously pleaded.[7]

---

1   See ch 4, para 4.48 above and para 7.33 below as to evidence of fraud.
2   RSC Ord 18, r 12(1) which applies to all actions.
3   *Claudius Ash Son & Co Ltd v Invicta Manufacturing Co Ltd* (1912) 29 RPC 465 at 475.
4   *Cadbury v Ulmer GmbH* [1988] FSR 385.
5   (1948) 65 RPC 429 at 435. A similar course was adopted in *John Walker & Sons Ltd v Henry Ost & Co Ltd* [1970] 2 All ER 106, [1970] RPC 489 at 503–504.

6   [1977] 2 CMLR 625 at 653, [1978] RPC 79 at 107.
7   Ibid at 667, 121–122.

DEFENCE AND COUNTERCLAIM

7.14   Generally, the defendant is entitled merely to deny or not admit any facts alleged by the plaintiff which he merely says are incorrect without being required to give particulars of the denial. However, if the defendant asserts any form of positive answer to the plaintiff's allegations, then he must plead and give particulars of his case. For example, if the defendant pleads that the mark or get-up asserted by the plaintiff to be distinctive of his goods is in fact descriptive or in common use in the trade, he will normally be required to give full particulars of the use which he says has been made of it.[1] Particulars of such allegations have been ordered in many cases[2] although there have in the past been instances where particulars were refused on the defendant undertaking to confine his case to 'general knowledge'.[3] However, it is thought that the courts would now insist upon particulars being given of any general positive assertion which requires evidence of specific instances of its occurrence to be established. Other positive cases must also be pleaded. For example, if the defendant asserts that he is merely trading under his own name,[4] or if he says that the way in which his products or services are presented has sufficient added matter as to distinguish them from those of the plaintiff,[5] then he must plead this specifically and give sufficient particulars to explain the basis of the allegations.[6] Any estoppel which is alleged must be expressly pleaded[7] as must any defence arising from the operation of the Treaty of Rome, the so-called EC defences.[8]

1   *La Radiotechnique v Weinbaum* [1928] Ch D 1, 44 RPC 361; see also *Norman Kark Publications Limited v Odhams Press Limited* [1962] 1 All ER 636, [1962] RPC 163. See ch 4, paras 4.31–4.33.
2   Examples are *Schweppes v Gibbens* (1905) 22 RPC 113 (CA); *Aquascutum v Moore & Scantlebury* (1903) 20 RPC 640; *Beindorff v Chambers & Co Ltd* (1928) 45 RPC 122; *Willesden Varnish Co Ltd v Young & Marten Ltd* (1922) 39 RPC 285.
3   *A Boake Roberts & Co Ltd v W A Wayland & Co* (1909) 26 RPC 251. This is the reverse of the approach applied in patent actions where a defendant who relies solely on common general knowledge will normally have to give particulars of it so that the plaintiff knows the basis of the case being put forward.
4   See ch 4, paras 4.36–4.40.
5   See ch 4, paras 4.34–4.35.
6   The requirement to plead such matters is expressly set out in RSC Ord 18, r 8.
7   See Supreme Court Practice paragraph 18/8/5.
8   *Application des Gaz SA v Falks Veritas Ltd* [1974] Ch 381; *Pitney Bowes Inc v Francotyp-Postalia GmbH* [1991] FSR 72. See also ch 10 below.

7.15   Counterclaims are relatively rare in passing off actions. They normally arise only in two circumstances. The first is where the defendant has for some years been carrying on an activity which the plaintiff now asserts to be objectionable. In such a case, the defendant may wish to broaden the argument and seek a declaration either that what he is doing does not amount to passing off or that there is something else he is entitled to do.[1] The second is where there is a dispute between the parties as to which of them is entitled to the name or get-up in dispute.[2] The counterclaim is then simply a cross claim of passing off. It has particular dangers: a counterclaiming defendant will find it very difficult to advance both his counterclaim and a case that the name or get-up is common to the trade, and an attempt to do so may devalue both arguments leading to the court accepting the plaintiff's case. Whether such a claim should be made requires careful judgment in the light of all the facts. If the plaintiff has been making his allegations about the defendant's goods or services widely known before suing on them, it may also be worth considering a claim for trade libel or malicious falsehood. However, the burden of establishing the requisite degree of malice is high.[3] The counterclaim must be pleaded with the same degree of particularity as if it were a statement of claim.[4]

1 Such a claim was made in *Bulmer v Bollinger* [1977] 2 CMLR 625, [1978] RPC 79. In *Vine Products Ltd v MacKenzie & Co Ltd* [1969] RPC 1, the plaintiffs were in fact the natural defendants who had been threatened by the sherry houses and sued for a declaration of entitlement to use the particular designations including the word *sherry* which were in dispute.
2 A classic example is *Anheuser Busch Inc v Budejovicky Budvar Narodni Podnik* [1984] FSR 413 where both parties asserted the exclusive right to use the mark *Budweiser* for beer and both claims were rejected. See also *Chelsea Man Menswear Limited v Chelsea Girl Limited* [1985] FSR 567.
3 See ch 8, paras 8.21–8.23 for a discussion of this topic.
4 RSC Ord 18, r 18.

REPLY AND DEFENCE TO COUNTERCLAIM

7.16 If the defence raises new issues to which the plaintiff wishes to raise his own positive answer, then a reply is required.[1] In other cases, issue is joined without a further pleading.[2] Naturally, if a counterclaim is served, a defence to counterclaim is required. This must be pleaded precisely as if the counterclaim were a statement of claim.[3]

1 RSC Ord 18, r 3.
2 RSC Ord 18, r 14.
3 RSC Ord 18, r 18.

FURTHER AND BETTER PARTICULARS

7.17 Further and better particulars may be requested of any fact or matter contained in a pleading.[1] It is often the case that a party has pleaded his case in such a way that the precise scope of the allegation being made is obscure to his opponent. To avoid being taken by surprise, it is nearly always wise to seek further and better particulars of such matters. However, particulars should generally not be requested where a pleading omits to set out a material averment as the request for particulars serves merely to remind the opposing party that his pleading is defective. It is also possible to serve voluntary further and better particulars. This may well be done where it is desired to assert facts which fall within a general averment in a pleading, but which have occurred after the pleading was served or constitute the underlying support for the general averment. For example, it is not unusual in passing off actions to serve specific particulars of instances of confusion.

---

1   RSC Ord 18, r 12.

ADMISSIONS

7.18   Both the High Court[1] and the County Court[2] rules contain provisions entitling the parties to serve upon one another notices to admit facts. The primary purpose of serving such a notice is to confine the true area of the dispute as closely as possible. Facts which have been admitted do not have to be proved at the trial. The consequence of refusing to admit a fact set out in a notice is substantially the same in each case: if the fact is proved by evidence at the trial, the cost of doing so is normally borne by the party upon whom the notice was served.[3] This is the only penalty for failing to deal properly with a notice to admit facts and experience has shown that it is not usually sufficient to persuade litigants to make extensive admissions. This is extremely unfortunate when the costs of litigation are generally considered to be far too large and it can only be hoped that lawyers will learn to make more effective use of admissions. In principle it is possible to require the admission of any fact in issue in the proceedings. However, in practice the courts will not impose the costs penalty where the fact is one which the party upon whom the notice is served could not reasonably be expected to admit. This will generally be the case where the fact is wholly within the knowledge of the party seeking the admission. For example, it is unreasonable for the plaintiff to ask the defendant to admit the extent of the plaintiff's sales under a disputed mark. The defendant cannot possibly know whether the plaintiff's allegations are true until he has seen the evidence which supports them. It is often possible to overcome problems of this nature by supplying an auditor's certificate with the figures verifying that they have been independently checked.

---

1   RSC Ord 27.
2   CCR Ord 20, r 2.
3   High Court RSC Ord 62, r 6(7); County Court CCR Ord 20, r 2(2). These rules contain times by which a notice to admit facts must be served if it is to have the desired costs consequences. In the High Court the notice must be served not more than 21 days after the action is set down for trial (Ord 27, r 2(1)) and in the County Court not less than 14 days before the trial (CCR Ord 20, r 2(1)).

7.19   It is also possible for a party voluntarily to admit any part of the other's pleaded case and thus remove that area of dispute from the trial. Once a fact is admitted, no evidence should be adduced in support of it and, if an attempt is made to adduce evidence, the court should either exclude it or make an appropriate order as to the costs of the evidence.

AMENDMENT OF PLEADINGS

7.20 Any pleading may be amended at any stage of the proceedings.[1] Before the close of pleadings, one amendment may be made without the leave of the court.[2] Thereafter, amendments may only be made with leave, but before trial leave will nearly always be granted on appropriate terms. The only circumstances in which leave will not be granted are where the opposite party will be disadvantaged in a manner which cannot be corrected by an award of costs. Applications to amend during trial and even on appeal are not uncommon. Where this happens it is the invariable practice to allow the opposite party an opportunity to consider whether he wishes to adduce further evidence to deal with the new pleading.[3] As this may require an adjournment, the costs implications of amendments to pleadings at a late stage can be substantial and it is therefore wise to give close consideration to the state of the pleadings a sufficient period before the trial to ensure that this does not occur.

---

1 RSC Ord 20, r 5(1).
2 RSC Ord 20, r 3(1).
3 A full and extremely helpful discussion of the principles and practice on applications for leave to amend can be found in the notes to RSC Ord 20, rr 5–8 in the Supreme Court Practice.

Discovery

INTRODUCTION[1]

7.21 The process of discovery was created by the courts of equity to give an essential element of fairness to litigation. It is the means by which parties are forced to disclose information which damages their interests and which, left to themselves, they would almost certainly conceal. Discovery is generally obtained by the compulsory disclosure of documents but it may also be obtained by interrogating the opposite party. In either case it provides the mechanism by which a party is enabled to see the inner thoughts and workings of his opponent. Unfortunately, particularly since the advent of mass photocopying, the process of discovery is open to extensive abuse. The obligation to disclose documents is wide ranging and far reaching. Requests for extensive specific discovery are common. Vast lists of documents and sets of copies result and huge numbers of documents are frequently included in trial bundles. All this adds enormously to the costs of litigation. It is the common experience of litigation lawyers that the vast majority of documents disclosed on discovery are unused at the trial and there is a widespread view that something has to be done to curb the burden of discovery. Unfortunately, all who have considered the problem have found that there are no ready answers. There is widespread agreement that in an adversarial procedure the ability to see the opposite party's key documents is a valuable tool for achieving justice. The difficulty is how to avoid the enormous waste of time and costs that accompanies this need without allowing the party giving discovery to exercise control over what he discloses and thereby defeat the object of the exercise. It is not within our remit to address this problem and we freely confess that we do not know the answer. We merely add our voice to the many others who believe that if the English system of litigation is to remain viable an answer must be found to these problems.

---

1 Textbooks on discovery are rare. Two very good modern texts are *Documentary Evidence* by Style and Hollander (Longman 3rd edn) and *Discovery* by Matthews and Malek (Sweet & Maxwell 1992). The foreword to the latter contains an eloquent plea by Mr Justice Steyn for review of the process of discovery.

DISCOVERY OF DOCUMENTS

7.22 After the close of pleadings[1] the parties to an action must exchange lists of documents which are or have been in their possession, custody or control relating to the matters in issue between them.[2] The obligation to list documents extends to documents which no longer exist or to which the party no longer has access. Knowledge that a document existed may itself be extremely valuable. Clients should always be warned by their lawyers of this obligation at the earliest stage and made to preserve documents which may be required for discovery. It should not be forgotten that discovery is not merely a negative process for the party giving it. His documents, as the contemporaneous record of his activities, will also serve to establish many of the facets of his own case. If a party fails to comply with his obligation to give discovery, an order may be sought requiring him to do so generally[3] or to give specific discovery of particular documents.[4] An application for specific discovery must be supported by an affidavit giving the reasons why it is said that the documents sought exist and should be disclosed.[5] Discovery will only be ordered if it is necessary for disposing fairly of the action or in order to save costs.[6] Once lists of documents have been exchanged, the opposite party is entitled to inspect or have copies of all listed documents[7] unless the list states that there is an objection to disclosure of the document[8] on the ground that it is privileged. Because the trial of a passing off action is normally split into separate trials on liability and quantum, discovery will not be ordered of documents which go only to the issue of quantum until the enquiry as to damages.[9] Where the parties are competitors and the documents to be disclosed are commercially sensitive or otherwise confidential the court routinely makes orders restricting the people who may see them and the terms upon which they may be inspected.[10] Discovery can also be obtained against innocent parties who have become embroiled in the wrongdoing of others.[11]

The court's powers relating to discovery also extend to making orders for the taking of samples or the detention, preservation or inspection of property which is the subject matter of an action or as to which any question may arise in an action.[12]

---

1   This occurs 14 days after service of the reply or, if there is none, 14 days after service of the defence: RSC Ord 20, r 20(1).
2   RSC Ord 24, r 2(1). The obligation is to serve a list within 14 days of the close of pleadings.
3   RSC Ord 24, r 3.
4   RSC Ord 24, r 7.
5   RSC Ord 24, r 7(3).
6   RSC Ord 24, r 13. More active judicial intervention under this rule could save considerable sums in costs.
7   RSC Ord 24, r 9.
8   RSC Ord 24, r 5(2).
9   *Fennessy v Clarke* (1887) 37 Ch D 184; *William Gaymers & Son Ltd v H P Bulmer Ltd* (The Times) 18 January 1984; *Baldock v Addison* [1994] FSR 665.
10 See *Warner-Lambert Co v Glaxo Laboratories Ltd* [1975] RPC 354; *Roussel Uclaf v Imperial Chemical Industries plc* [1990] RPC 45; but this does not apply to evidence as opposed to discovery: *VNU Business Publications BV v Ziff Davis (UK) Limited* [1992] RPC 269.
11 The action for discovery is known as a *Norwich Pharmacal* action: see [1974] AC 133. See also para 6.29 above for the use of this type of action to obtain the discovery necessary to pursue a claim.
12 See RSC Ord 29, rr 2, 3 and 7A.

INTERROGATORIES

7.23   Discovery by interrogatories has its origins in the eighteenth-century procedures of the courts for obtaining information from persons whether parties to the litigation or not. It developed gradually into a variety of processes by which evidence could be obtained. Modern interrogatories serve the purpose of enabling a party to question his opponent before the trial about facts and matters of which there is no other way of obtaining the information. For many years interrogatories could only be administered with the leave of the court and leave would only be granted if it could be shown that the information sought was necessary to enable the party seeking to administer them to prepare his case. This greatly restricted their use as the application for leave is costly and time consuming. In 1990, the rules were altered to permit interrogatories to be administered twice without leave.[1] If this is done, the party upon whom they are served must apply within 14 days to have them set aside[2] if he does not wish to answer them. In practice applications to set interrogatories aside are often made and granted out of time. Interrogatories will be set aside unless they are necessary for disposing fairly of the action or the saving of costs.[3] Interrogatories will not normally be allowed if they are intended to prove a fact which will necessarily appear in evidence at the trial or to enable a party to see if he has a case which is better than or different from that which appears on the pleadings.[4] For example, it is not permissible to interrogate a defendant with a view to establishing whether or not he is putting an instrument of fraud into the hands of middlemen when the only claim in the pleadings is of direct passing off.

In general interrogatories should be confined to establishing facts which there is reason to believe are true and which cannot readily be obtained from discovery of documents or independent enquiries (which will in any event be necessary to obtain the evidence for the trial). Interrogatories have been allowed directed to allegations that the mark relied on was descriptive,[5] that the goods were of a pattern common to the trade[6] and as to documents not in the sole possession or power of a party.[7] However, interrogatories prior to the enquiry as to damages going to the extent of the defendant's sales have been disallowed[8] and interrogatories as to the evidence a party intends to call are routinely refused.[9]

1 RSC Ord 26, r 1.
2 RSC Ord 26, r 3(2).
3 RSC Ord 26, r 1(1).
4 See *Rockwell Corporation v Serck Industries Ltd* [1988] FSR 187: a copyright case in which interrogatories to obtain evidence in support of a defence yet to be pleaded were refused.
5 *Coca-Cola Co v Duckworth & Co* (1928) 45 RPC 225.
6 *Perry & Co Ltd v Hessin & Co* (1911) 28 RPC 108.
7 *Aubanel & Alabaster Ltd v Aubanel* (1950) 67 RPC 222.
8 *Benbow v Low* (1880) 16 Ch D 93, 50 LJ Ch 35 on ground of prematurity as with discovery of documents: see the text to n 1, in para 7.21.
9 See *Benbow v Low* above and *Supreme Court Practice* para 26/1/6.

The summons for directions

7.24   Under the rules of the High Court the plaintiff must take out a summons for directions 'with a view to providing . . . an occasion for the consideration by the court of the preparations for the trial of the action'[1] within a month after the close of pleadings in the action.[2] If the plaintiff does not do so, the defendant may take out the summons or apply to dismiss the action.[3] The summons for directions is a watershed in English civil procedure. It is the point at which the court takes control of the action. Thereafter, if the plaintiff fails to prosecute the action the court can and in extreme cases will strike the action out of its own volition. The order made on the summons should include all the directions which are necessary for the action to be taken to trial. Thus outstanding questions of discovery, amendment of pleadings and further and better particulars should be dealt with on the summons, and directions should be obtained for exchange of witness statements and expert reports and the conduct of any experiments which are necessary. Separate trial of individual issues should also be considered at this stage if appropriate. The equivalent procedure in the County Court is the pre-trial review[4] at which the same steps are taken. The current procedure in the County Court has been further streamlined so that in most actions directions are made automatically and without a hearing.[5] The order on the summons for directions or the pre-trial review always includes a direction for setting down or fixing the trial and liberty to apply for further directions.

---

1   RSC Ord 25, r 1(1).
2   Or 14 days after discovery if this is agreed or ordered to be later: RSC Ord 25, r 1(3).
3   RSC Ord 25, r 1(4). This is a power which is insufficiently used by defendants the subject of
    speculative or harassing actions.
4   CCR Ord 17.
5   CCR Ord 17, r 11.

Evidence

INTRODUCTION

7.25   It is a truism to say that every passing off case turns on its particular
facts. However, it is a truism of which it is essential to be acutely aware
when considering the evidence to be adduced in a passing off action. The
circumstances surrounding allegations of passing off vary so much that it
is impossible to give comprehensive guidance on the appropriate kind of
evidence to adduce in any particular case. The nature of evidence in passing off
actions also undergoes changes in fashion. For many years it was the practice
to call only evidence from those engaged in the trade who could speak of the
plaintiff's reputation and the likelihood of confusion and those members of
the purchasing public who had themselves been confused. For a period in
the 1970s and 1980s it was the practice to adduce evidence of public opinion
surveys. These underwent successive judicial attacks in a series of passing off
and trade mark cases until their evidential value was almost totally undermined
in all circumstances. The *Jif* case, however, brought them back to the fore.
Now it is common to seek to bring in large numbers of members of the
public to give evidence of their own knowledge of the plaintiff's reputation.
Such evidence is of course expensive to collect and the cost of passing off
actions has risen commensurately.

The onus of proving any fact lies upon the party asserting it. This is the
legal burden of proof of any fact. Thus the plaintiff must prove by evidence any
facts asserted in the statement of claim. Equally, the defendant must prove any
positive facts asserted in his defence and counterclaim. Such legal burden of
proof rests throughout the trial upon that party. However, there is in addition
a separate evidential burden which will shift during the trial as evidence is
adduced. For example, the plaintiff has the legal burden of establishing his
reputation. Once he has adduced sufficient evidence to support the claim
that there is a reputation, if the matter rests there, the court will so find.
If the defendant wishes to counter that evidence, there arises an evidential
burden upon him to adduce contradictory evidence to show that the reputation
attested to by the plaintiff's witnesses is limited or circumscribed in such a
way that, for example, there is no prospect of his activities being mistaken for
those of the plaintiff. Questions like these make the decision as to the nature
and extent of the evidence to be adduced at the trial both complex and fluid.
Particularly for the defendant, it is always wise to review the decision to call

particular witnesses at each stage. If the plaintiff's witnesses have failed to establish a pleaded fact, there is no point in calling witnesses to rebut it. To do so merely exposes the defendant to the risk that they will in cross-examination give evidence which provides support for the plea. The selection and adduction of evidence at the trial is a key topic in the conduct of a passing off action.

The issues to be addressed

7.26 The three primary issues in a passing off action are reputation or goodwill, confusion and damage. Each of these needs to be addressed by evidence although in many cases damage will be presumed once the first two have been established.[1] The evidence is in large part purely factual. Evidence is required to establish the nature, extent and manner of the plaintiff's trade and of that of the defendant. Customers who have been the victims of successful passing off may also be called and evidence may also be adduced of complaints to the plaintiff resulting from the defendant's activities.

Both reputation and confusion are often sought to be addressed by adducing public opinion surveys as evidence. Insofar as evidence is given of the analysis of such surveys and the conclusions which can be drawn from that analysis, the evidence is clearly expert opinion evidence and will be governed by the rules relating to such evidence. However, surveys are often used simply to identify prospective witnesses who have been or would be confused by the defendant's activities. Such witnesses are witnesses of fact. In the following sections we examine in detail the nature of the evidence that can be adduced, the rules and practices that govern the use which may be made of various forms of evidence, and the approach the court will take to it.

---

1 At the trial on the issue of liability. At the enquiry of course all damage sought to be recovered must be proved: see paras 7.51–7.53 below.

Admissibility

7.27 One of the major issues in passing off (and trade mark) actions is the admissibility of evidence relating to the primary issues and in particular evidence of all types going to the question of confusion. There are many conflicting authorities on the subject and it is difficult to form a clear view of the true state of the law. In this section we endeavour to examine these authorities and to give our view of the best approach to such evidence. It must, however, be recognised that the plethora of authorities pointing in different directions means that one court may receive and act upon evidence which another court would regard as inadmissible or irrelevant.

For a long time the courts were very strict in holding that evidence of whether or not there was a misrepresentation was inadmissible. As it was put by Lord Parker in a well-known passage from *Spalding v Gamage*:[1]

'It was also contended that the question whether the advertisements were calculated to
deceive was not one which your Lordships should yourselves determine by considering
the purport of the advertisements themselves, having regard to the surrounding
circumstances, but was one which your Lordships were bound to determine upon
evidence directed to the question itself. I do not take this view of the law. There
may, of course, be cases of so doubtful a nature that a Judge cannot properly come
to a conclusion without evidence directed to the point; but there can be no doubt that
in a passing off action the question whether the matter complained of is calculated to
deceive, in other words whether it amounts to a misrepresentation, is a matter for
the Judge, who, looking at the documents and evidence before him comes to his
own conclusion and, to use the words of Lord MacNaghton in *Payton & Co Ltd v
Snelling Lampard and Co Ltd*,[2] "must not surrender his own independent judgment to
any witness whatsoever".'

However, since that statement the courts have become increasingly willing to
receive evidence from various kinds of witnesses about the possibility that
there will be confusion amongst customers. The first exception was those
who have special expertise in the particular business. Lord Evershed, in *George
Ballantine & Son Ltd v Ballantyne Stewart & Co Ltd* said[3] that:

'it is in my opinion going too far to say that a witness expert in the trade which is
involved in the proceedings before the court, may not legitimately say, in giving his
evidence, that according to his experience of how the business ... is conducted, traders
or customers will adopt certain characteristics or practices.'

Although he went on to make clear that the weight to be given to evidence
of this kind was always a matter for the court.

---

1 (1915) 32 RPC 273 at 286. See also similar statements in *North Cheshire and Manchester Brewery Co
   v Manchester Brewery Co* [1899] AC 83; *Island Trading Co v Anchor Brewing Co* [1989] RPC 287a.
2 (1900) 17 RPC 628.
3 [1959] RPC 273 at 280.

7.28 Over the last 20 years the tendency to admit evidence of the likelihood
of confusion has become ever stronger. In 1972 Lord Diplock in *GE Trade
Mark*[1] was prepared to go so far as to say that:

'where goods are of a kind which are not normally sold to the general public for
consumption or domestic use but are sold in a specialised market consisting of persons
engaged in a particular trade, evidence of persons accustomed to dealing in that market
as to the likelihood of deception or confusion is essential.'

However, he contrasted this with the position in relation to goods which are
of a type sold to the general public where he said that:

'the question whether such buyers would be likely to be deceived or confused by the use
of a mark is a "jury question". By that I mean that if the issue had now, as formerly, to
be tried by a jury who, as members of the general public would themselves be potential
buyers of the goods, they would be required not only to consider any evidence of other
members of the public which had been adduced but also their own common sense and
to consider whether they would themselves be likely to be confused.

   The question does not cease to be a "jury question" when the issue is tried by a
judge alone. ... The judge's approach should be the same as that of a jury. He, too,
would be a potential buyer of the goods.'[2]

In *Sodastream Limited v Thorn Cascade Limited*,[3] Kerr LJ, speaking in relation to evidence of the way in which carbon dioxide cylinders are perceived by the general public, said this:

'It...seems to me that it is perfectly proper for someone in the trade to express opinions about the likely reaction of others in relation to matters which are within his or her sphere of work: indeed, it is part of their responsibility to form a view on such matters.'

The learned judge here appears to have confused the commercial or business responsibility of someone in a particular trade with his ability to assist the court in determining disputed questions of fact.[4] However his remarks have since been cited with favour by Browne-Wilkinson V-C in *Guccio Gucci SpA v Paolo Gucci*[5] and most recently by the Court of Appeal in *Taittinger v Allbev Ltd*[6] where Peter Gibson LJ said after citation of both these authorities in relation to the admissibility of such evidence:

'I cannot forebear to comment that the good sense of what Kerr LJ and the Vice-Chancellor said seems to me to be obvious.'

Other judges, however, have taken a much firmer view. In *Associated Newspapers plc v Insert Media Ltd*,[7] Mummery J said in relation to proposed expert evidence directed to informing the court of tastes and views of advertisers and readers on the question of inserts in newspapers:

'this appears to me to involve an expression of opinion by the expert as to the probability of confusion or deception arising from the use of unauthorised inserts. Such opinion evidence, directed to the very question for the decision of the court, would not be admissible.'[8]

In a recent decision, Blackburne J commented that it was not easy to reconcile the authorities but that he would draw the following conclusions on the question of admissibility:

'1 There is no absolute rule against admitting evidence directed to the question whether the matter complained of is calculated to deceive.
2 In cases where the goods are of a kind not normally sold to the general public for consumption or domestic use but are sold to a specialised market, evidence of persons accustomed to deal in that market as to the likelihood of deception or confusion is admissible.
3 In cases where the goods are of a kind which are sold to the general public for consumption or domestic use evidence of persons accustomed to deal in that market as to the likelihood of deception or confusion *may* be admissible. Whether in any case such evidence will be admissible will depend upon a variety of factors which it is neither possible nor desirable to define. Broadly, the test in such cases must be whether the experience which a judge must be taken to possess as an ordinary shopper or consumer will enable him, just as well as any other, to assess the likelihood of confusion. If it will, then the evidence will not be admissible. If, for whatever, reason it will not, then such evidence will be admissible. What, if any, weight the court attached to such evidence will of course depend upon its nature and quality....
4 In all cases evidence will be admissible to prove the circumstances and the places in which the goods are sold, the kind of persons who buy them and the manner in which the public are accustomed to ask for those goods.'[9]

Thus, it would seem that evidence going to the likelihood of confusion, particularly from trade witnesses, is in principle admissible in all kinds of case. The major distinction between goods sold to the general public and those sold to specialised trades being that in the former case the judge should be guided by his own common sense and only consider such evidence where his general knowledge and experience are insufficient and in the latter he should look first at the evidence. In any case, evidence of the surrounding circumstances of the trade will be admissible.

Finally, it should be noted that if objection is taken to the admissibility of evidence before the trial, it is likely that the court will not wish to rule on the question and thus circumscribe the manner in which the parties may present their cases but to leave the issue to the trial judge who may himself prefer to hear the evidence de bene esse before deciding whether it is in fact admissible. This is in principle a laudable approach but leads again to undesirable escalation of costs, for a party against whom such evidence is to be deployed must prepare as if it will be received and acted upon by the court. Greater powers and willingness of the courts to curb the parties' excesses in collating and presenting evidence would be one of the most effective ways to limit the costs of proceedings.

---

1 [1973] RPC 297 at 321.
2 Loc cit.
3 [1982] RPC 459 at 468.
4 And as was noted by Knox J in *Island Trading Co v Anchor Brewing Co* [1989] RPC 287a at 298–299 there was no objection to the admissibility of the evidence in question. On the contrary it way prayed in aid by both parties.
5 [1991] FSR 89.
6 [1993] FSR 641 at 663.
7 [1990] 2 All ER 803.
8 Ibid at 806 citing *North Cheshire and Manchester Brewery Co Ltd v Manchester Brewery Co Ltd* (above at 84–85) and *Royal Warrant Holders' Association v Edward Deane & Beal Ltd* [1912] 1 Ch 10 at 14. See also *Parker-Knoll Limited v Knoll International Limited* [1962] RPC 265 HL at 274 (Lord Denning), 279 (Lord Morris), 285 (Lord Hodson) and 291 (Lord Devlin).
9 *Dalgety Spillers Foods Limited v Food Brokers Limited* [1994] FSR 504.

EVIDENCE OF FACT

Reputation and goodwill

7.29 Reputation and goodwill are established primarily by evidence from the plaintiff and others in the trade of the nature and extent of the user of the indicia which are said to be indicative of his goods or business. This has to be coupled with evidence from his customers that they recognise those indicia as denoting those goods or business although this will readily be presumed in the case of fancy words or get-up. The fundamental evidence is that of the way in which the mark has been used on the goods or services. Examples of goods bearing the mark and packaging should always be put into evidence along with invoices, notepaper and other incidentals of business which show regular and repeated use of a mark or get-up. Details of advertising and sales, press comment and any publicity or promotion which the goods or business have received are also all relevant and helpful to establish reputation. Together they build up a picture for the court of the exposure which the mark or get-up has received. Evidence from customers as to their reaction to the plaintiff's mark or get-up is also helpful. This kind of evidence is usually given by witnesses who are also attesting to confusion. The evidence of confused purchasers or would be purchasers performs two roles: it indicates both that the witness is familiar with the plaintiff's mark or get-up and that he was (or would be) deceived by the defendant's mark or get-up into believing that he was obtaining the plaintiff's goods or services. However, there is no reason why customers should not be called simply to speak of their knowledge of the plaintiff's goods or business.[1]

---

1 In practice even witnesses who are called simply to give evidence of reputation can be used to establish the possibility of confusion. See the comment of Whitford J in *Chelsea Man Menswear Limited v Chelsea Girl Limited* [1985] FSR 567 at 576 on the reaction of witnesses shown a tie with the defendant's mark on it.

Confusion and deception

7.30 The plaintiff has to prove that there has been a misrepresentation by the defendant which has led or is likely to lead to deception or confusion. In practice, the evidence which can be produced covers both the misrepresentation and its result for it is not possible to separate them out. We have seen that it is impermissible to call witnesses to attest directly that the defendant's mark or get-up are confusingly similar to that of the plaintiff for that is the province of the court.[1] As Lord Devlin said in *Parker-Knoll Limited v Knoll International Limited*:[2]

> 'What the judge has to decide in a passing off case is whether the public at large is likely to be deceived. . . . What would the effect of the misrepresentation be upon the reasonable prospective purchaser? Instances of actual deception may be useful as examples and evidence of persons experienced in the ways of purchasers of a particular class of goods will assist the judge. But his decision will not depend solely or even primarily upon the evaluation of such evidence. The court must in the end trust to its own perception of the mind of the reasonable man.'

The role of the evidence is, therefore, to enable the court to put itself into the position of the notional reasonable prospective purchaser. Such evidence falls into two distinct categories. The first is evidence of the likelihood of confusion and the second evidence of actual confusion. In all passing off actions, there will be extensive evidence of likelihood of confusion: the reasons why the mark or get-up is likely to deceive. This will range through the nature of the goods or services themselves,[3] the circumstances and places in which they are supplied,[4] the kind of persons who buy them,[5] the manner in which they are bought,[6] the way the mark is pronounced[7] or abbreviated,[8] the phrases used by the public in asking for the goods[9] and whether the words or get-up concerned or part of them are common to the trade.[3,6] For example, the likelihood of confusion between two similar sounding names which are easily differentiated when written down is much greater if the evidence is that the vast bulk of business under the name is done over the telephone.[6] On the other hand, evidence of the similarity of the businesses may well demonstrate that confusion is inevitable simply because of this with the result that the fact that people are in fact confused establishes nothing.[10]

---

1   See paragraphs 7.27–7.28 above.
2   [1962] RPC 265 at 291. See also *Royal Warrant Holders' Association v Edward Deane & Beal Limited* [1912] 1 Ch 10 at 14–15 citing *Bourne v Swan & Edgar* [1903] 1 Ch 211.
3   See the resultant findings of fact in *Reckitt & Colman plc v Borden Inc (Jif)* [1990] RPC 341 at 408, the evidence being summarised in the judgment of Walton J at first instance.
4   *Island Trading Co v Anchor Brewing Co* [1989] RPC 287a.
5   *Taittinger SA v Allbev Limited* [1993] FSR 641.
6   *Lever v Sunniwite* (1949) 66 RPC 84 at 90; *Rizla Limited v Bryant & May Limited* [1986] RPC 389; *Smith Hayden's Application* (1946) 63 RPC 97; *Rysta Limited's Application* (1943) 60 RPC 87 at 108 (the latter two are trade mark cases); *Klissers Farmhouse Bakeries Limited v Harvest Bakeries Limited* [1989] RPC 27 (New Zealand).
7   *Picot Limited v Goya Limited* [1967] RPC 573, [1967] FSR 383.
8   *George Ballantine & Son Limited v Ballantyne Stewart & Co Ltd* [1959] RPC 273 at 280.
9   *Sales Affiliates Limited v LeJean Limited* (1947) 64 RPC 103 at 110 (referring to *Delaville (GB) Limited v Stanley* (1946) RPC 103 and *Havana Cigar and Tobacco Factories Limited v Oddenino* [1924] 1 Ch 179, 41 RPC 47).
10 The extreme example of this is *My Kinda Town v Soll* [1983] RPC 407 where the comments of Oliver LJ at 422–431 demonstrate how evidence of confusion can lead the court to entirely the wrong conclusion so far as the plaintiff is concerned.

7.31   It is important to appreciate that, as the questions which arise in determining the likelihood of confusion are pure questions of fact, resort to authority is useful only to indicate the nature of the material which the court is likely find helpful in deciding the question. The older cases are particularly dangerous because they relate to trading conditions which bear little or no resemblance to those found today. The Victorian grocer's shop and its attendant practices are no longer with us. With that caveat, there are many judicial indications of the kind of evidence which provides assistance in determining the likelihood of confusion. The following are typical examples. Luxmoore J in *Lever v Sunniwite*[1] said:

> 'It is, in my judgment, in the experience and views of the ordinary shopkeeper that the most reliable guide as to the likelihood of confusion is to be found. I had many such called before me ... In summary, they spoke of orders scrawled upon odd scraps of paper and cigarette packets, orders over the telephone, orders from persons who speak in a different dialect, purchases by children and the widespread custom of using abbreviations. They told me of lazy or unreliable assistants and of the necessity of reducing the possibility of confusion to a minimum. And, finally, they told me of their assumption of some connection between Lever products and "Sunniwite" and of their conviction that the simultaneous stocking of "Sunniwite" and "Sunlight" soapless detergents would inevitably result in confusion in their soaps and among their customers.'

Evidence of shopkeepers that they would not willingly stock two products side by side is generally highly persuasive that there is a risk of confusion. Conversely evidence from reputable shopkeepers that they envisage no difficulty in doing so is equally persuasive the other way and such evidence is frequently adduced.

The absence of actual confusion is not necessarily fatal to a passing off claim.[2] Indeed, where the plaintiff has obtained an interlocutory injunction at an early stage, the defendant may not have traded so that there can be no actual confusion. Even where the defendant has been trading it may be difficult to find instances of actual confusion. However, where the defendant has been trading for a long period without any evidence that there has been confusion, the court will generally conclude that there is none and that accordingly there is no misrepresentation.[3]

---

1 (1949) 66 RPC 84 at 87. See also *Baume & Co Limited v A H Moore Limited* [1958] Ch 907.
2 *Edelsten v Edelsten* (1863) 1 De GJ & Sm 185 at 200; *Saville Perfumery Limited v June Perfect Limited* (1941) 58 RPC 147 (HL); *Baume & Co Limited v A H Moore Limited* (above).
3 See *Rodgers v Rodgers* (1874) 31 LT 285; *Bulmer v Bollinger* [1977] 2 CMLR 625, [1978] RPC 79.

7.32 *Trap orders* The difficulty of obtaining direct evidence of confusion has led to the well-known practice of making what are known as 'trap orders'. These are orders placed by or on behalf of the plaintiff with the defendant in order to see whether the defendant in fact misrepresents what is being supplied when the order is fulfilled. The practice has a long history[1] and it has also long been the practice that, if a trap order is placed, the party on whom it has been carried out should be informed as soon as possible thereafter of the precise circumstances of the order so that he may check for himself what occurred.[2] The principles and practices upon which the court acts in dealing with trap orders and evidence of them were concisely summarised by Farwell J in *C C Wakefield & Co Limited v Purser* in the following passage:

> 'trap orders are in a case of this kind, it seems to me, quite essential. I fail to see how the plaintiffs can safeguard themselves or the public without having resort to some such method of testing the matter as is used in the present case; but, a trap order or a test order, whichever they may be called, are scrutinised by the courts with some jealousy, and rightly so, because, if, as the result of a trap order or a test order, a person is to be charged with the very serious offence of fraudulently misrepresenting the goods which he is supplying to the public, to the detriment of the public as well as the plaintiffs, the court must be satisfied that the offence has been proved strictly. Further, if a person is resorting to a test order or a trap order, even in a case of this kind, where the necessity for such a device may be a real one, that person is bound to carry out the proceeding with the utmost fairness to the prospective defendant in the action. It is essential, if the plaintiff is to succeed in the action which he ultimately brings, that he should be able to satisfy the court that he has acted throughout with the most exact fairness to the defendant and has given him every reasonable chance of investigating the matter for himself, so that he may be in a position to put forward in the action, if one follows, any and every defence properly open to him.'[3]

In *Procea Products Limited v Evans & Sons Ltd*,[4] Roxburgh J went so far as to

lay down a code of conduct for carrying out a trap order in retail premises.
He held that:

(a)   the trapper must be absolutely fair;

(b)   he must give the order in such circumstances that he has the undivided
       attention of the person to whom he is giving the order;

(c)   he must do absolutely nothing which might be calculated to induce the
       person whom he is seeking to trap to fall into the trap;

(d)   he must endeavour, so far as possible, to reproduce the conditions which
       would prevail if, instead of being a trap order, it was a genuine order.

Whilst these are not determinative rules, it is certainly the case that failing to
follow them will result in the court rejecting the evidence obtained. Conducting
a trap order necessarily involves making a misrepresentation to the defendant
about the real objective of the purchaser. However, the courts recognise that
this is often a necessary, if distasteful[5] or odious,[6] step and the plaintiff's
solicitor may be involved in advising him to place a trap order and even
in making the arrangements for it to be carried out.[7] The fact that the trap
purchaser is not deceived is irrelevant.[8] The purchase is intended to show
what will happen where the purchaser does not appreciate that he is being
given something other than the goods he ordered.

---

1   It was already well known at the turn of the century as the cases cited in the following notes demonstrate.
2   *Ripley v Griffiths* (1902) 19 RPC 590; *Truefitt Limited v Edney* (1903) 20 RPC 321; *Fitchett Limited v
     Loubet & Co* (1919) 36 RPC 296; *Smith's Potato Crisps v Paige* (1928) 45 RPC 132; *Cellular Clothing
     v White* (1953) 70 RPC 9.
3   (1934) 51 RPC 167 at 171. See also *Shell Mex and BP Limited v Holmes* (1937) 54 RPC 287 at 296.
4   (1951) 68 RPC 210 at 211–212.
5   Per Lord Upjohn in *Bali Trade Mark* [1969] RPC 472 at 497.
6   Per Harman J in *Cellular Clothing Co Limited v White & Co Limited* (above) at 14.
7   *Marie Claire Album SA v Hartstone Hosiery Limited* [1993] FSR 692. Many of the cases in which trap
     orders have been considered were cited to the court and they are listed in the report.
8   *Thomas French & Sons Limited v John Rhind & Sons Limited* [1958] RPC 82; *Showerings Limited v Blackpool
     Tower Co Limited* [1975] FSR 40.

Fraud

7.33   We have seen that proof of fraudulent intent will often lead the court
to conclude that the intent has succeeded.[1] However, evidence of fraudulent
intent is difficult to find except in cases of blatant counterfeiting because the
defendant's intention is necessarily subjective. Generally intention to pass off
has to be inferred from the extent of the plaintiff's reputation and the absence
of any other plausible motive for the defendant's conduct, and the best direct
evidence is likely to come from the defendant's discovery which will show
what it was he was trying to achieve. Even such evidence is not always
decisive. Whilst there have been several cases in which the existence of a
document demonstrating that the defendant intended to pass off have been
highly influential in persuading the court that he has succeeded,[2] there have
also been cases where this has not resulted. Recently, Walton J was entirely

persuaded in *Jif*[3] that an intention to produce a 'facsimile' of the plaintiff's product demonstrated an intention to deceive whilst a month later in *Scott v Nice-Pak*[4] he disregarded evidence that the defendant wished to produce a 'knock-off' of the plaintiff's product.

---

1   Ch 4, paras 4.48–4.49.
2   See the cases cited in paras 4.48 and 4.49; *Reddaway v Banham* [1896] AC 199; *Hommel v Bauer* (1905) 22 RPC 43.
3   [1990] RPC 341 at 360. In the Court of Appeal the finding of fraud was expressly reversed and the matter was not pursued in the House of Lords.
4   [1988] FSR 125; reported on appeal at [1989] FSR 100.

EXPERT EVIDENCE

7.34   At common law expert evidence is received by the court to prove matters which require a special degree of learning or study to understand and explain. As it was put by Browne-Wilkinson V-C:

> 'if you are in an area which requires specialist knowledge, it is the function of the expert to instruct and inform the court as to those things the court would otherwise not know, and in the process of so doing the expert is frequently asked the very question which the court has to answer.'[1]

This remains the case today although the admission of expert evidence is now governed by rules of court made under the Civil Evidence Acts 1968 and 1972. Expert evidence has been received on matters as diverse as nightclubs and the London scene[2] and the practice of franchising.[2] However, there is no such thing as an 'expert in human nature' and, save to explain the circumstances and operation of particular markets, evidence of the likelihood of confusion will not normally be regarded as appropriate.[3]

---

1   *Guccio Gucci SpA v Paolo Gucci* [1991] FSR 89 at 91.
2   *Stringfellow v McCain Foods (GB) Ltd* [1984] RPC 501, see at 532 reference to 'so-called' expert reports.
3   See paras 7.27–7.28 above.

Survey evidence

7.35   Whilst the best way to establish both reputation and confusion is to adduce direct evidence from witnesses who are familiar with the plaintiff's goods or services or who have been deceived by the defendant's conduct, this is often impractical. Where such evidence cannot readily be found, opinion polls or surveys are frequently sought to be substituted. Surveys have a chequered history in legal proceedings and the courts' approach to them has been extremely varied. It is generally recognised that surveys can have some evidential value and they have been used in passing off and trade mark proceedings for more than 60 years.[1] However, in recent years they have come under increasing attack on a variety of grounds. In the New Zealand case, *Customglass Boats Limited v Salthouse Brothers Limited*,[2] objection was made to survey evidence presented to the court as being hearsay. Mahon J, after reviewing the authorities, held that it was justifiable not to treat such evidence as hearsay, either on the ground that it proved 'a public state of mind' or alternatively 'an external fact, namely that an opinion is held by the public'. Subsequently, in *Lego System A/S v Lego M Lemelstrich Ltd*,[3] Falconer J admitted survey evidence on the second basis adopted by Mahon J.[4] However, in *Imperial Group plc v Philip Morris Limited*[5] (the *Raffles* case) Whitford J considered at some length the evidential value of public opinion surveys pointing out that:

> 'However satisfactory market research surveys may be in assisting commercial organisations as to how they can best conduct their business, they are by and large, as experience in other cases has indicated, an unsatisfactory way of trying to establish questions of fact which are likely to be matters of dispute.'[6]

He went on to consider the specific problems which arise in using surveys as evidence. One of the principal problems with surveys is that it is difficult to formulate questions which do not lead the respondents to the answer. And there is yet a further and even more fundamental obstacle for, as Whitford J went on to point out:

> 'It is very difficult in connection with an exercise such as this to think of questions which, even if they are free from the objection of being leading, are not in fact going to direct the person answering the question into a field of speculation upon which that person would never have embarked had the question not been put.'[6]

Even if these difficulties can be overcome, Whitford J laid down a series of guidelines which should be followed if a survey is to be of use. These are:

(1)   The interviewees must be selected by a method which ensures that a representative cross-section of the relevant public is interviewed.

(2)   The survey must be large enough to be statistically relevant.

(3)   The survey must be conducted fairly.

(4)   All surveys conducted must be disclosed to ensure that those relied upon are a fair representation of the totality of the results obtained and full disclosure must be made in relation to each survey.

(5)   All answers given must be disclosed to ensure that the opposing party has the opportunity of verifying that the responses have been correctly assessed and coded.

(6)   The questions must be framed so as not either to lead the respondent or to cause the respondent to speculate.

---

1   *A Bailey & Co Ltd v Clark Son & Morland Ltd* (1938) 55 RPC 253; *Treasure Cot Co Limited v Hamley Brothers Limited* (1950) 67 RPC 89; *GE Trade Mark* [1969] RPC 418, [1970] RPC 339 (CA) and [1973] RPC 297 (HL) (an application to rectify the Trade Marks Register); *Lego System A/S v Lego M Lemelstrich Limited* [1983] FSR 155; *White Horse Distiller Limited v Gregson Associates Limited* [1984] RPC 61 at 71–72; *Stringfellow v McCain Foods (GB) Ltd* [1984] RPC 501; *Anheuser-Busch Inc v Budejovicky Budvar Narodni Podnik* [1984] FSR 413.
2   [1976] RPC 589.
3   See n 1 above.
4   As a result of the Civil Evidence Act 1968 sections 1(1) and 9, a 'public state of mind' appears

no longer to be an exception to the hearsay rule and only the second basis adopted in *Customglass Boats* may now be available in this country.

5   [1984] RPC 293.
6   Ibid at 302.

7.36   Since the decision in the *Raffles*[1] case, the courts have viewed surveys presented in evidence with considerable caution and there has been far greater emphasis in passing off actions on putting individual witnesses before the court to give evidence of their own experiences with the marks or get-up in issue. In *Unilever v Johnson Wax Limited*,[2] Whitford J repeated his doubt as to the evidential value of surveys in resolving disputed questions of fact and passed a series of extremely critical comments on the surveys conducted in that case, the evidence adduced showing that they had been conducted 'in an atmosphere more akin to the atmosphere of a guessing game at a party than the atmosphere of the market'. In *United Biscuits (UK) Limited v Burtons Biscuits Limited*,[3] Vinelott J, basing himself on the observations in the *Raffles* case, rejected a series of surveys as unreliable. However, Walton J in *Reckitt & Colman v Borden*[4] was much influenced by survey evidence into accepting that hurried shoppers in supermarkets did not read the labels on *Jif* plastic lemons so that even distinctive labelling by the defendants would not prevent passing off. It follows that survey evidence must now be viewed with considerable caution although there can be no objection to using survey techniques to identify prospective witnesses and putting in evidence of the survey to establish that the manner in which the witnesses were discovered was fair.

1   *Imperial Group plc v Philip Morris Ltd* [1984] RPC 293.
2   [1989] FSR 145 at 162–167.
3   [1992] FSR 14; and see *Stringfellow v McCain Foods (GB) Ltd* [1984] RPC 501; *Anheuser-Busch Inc v Budejovicky Budvar Narodni Podnik* [1984] FSR 413 (CA); *Mothercare UK Limited v Penguin Books Limited* [1988] RPC 113.
4   [1990] RPC 341; see also *Lego System A/S v Lego M Lemelstrich Limited* [1983] FSR 155.

7.37   The preparation and presentation of surveys to the court is a matter requiring considerable expertise. Even the formulation of non-leading questions is difficult and it is almost impossible to frame a series of questions which cannot be criticised on the ground that they are leading the respondent to consider matters which would not normally enter his head.[1] The type of questions, the manner in which the respondents are introduced to the material and the circumstances of the interviews must all be specifically tailored to the particular circumstances of the case. It is, therefore, impossible to give general guidance on the formulation and conduct of surveys. It is, however, certain that any survey will be subjected to critical attack by the opposing party and there is every possibility that the court will find the results of no assistance.

1   See eg the comments of the Court of Appeal in *Scott Limited v Nice-Pak Products Limited* [1989] FSR 100 at 108 where a completely open-ended question was held to be illegitimate on the ground that

it proceeded on the false basis that the product in question was available even though this was the only way to assess whether the proposed product might lead to confusion.

7.38 *Tachistoscope tests* A particular type of survey which has sometimes been put in evidence is a tachistoscope test. This is a device in which viewers are exposed for a short period of time to a particular image and the minimum time in which they can recognise and identify it (or features of it) is measured. The exposure time is very short, in any event less than a second. The results of exposing a number of subjects to the material in issue are then compiled into a survey and conclusions drawn from those results as to their distinctiveness or deceptiveness. Tachistoscope studies are laboratory tests with a long established pedigree in perception studies of which Whitford J said in *Laura Ashley Limited v Coloroll Limited*:[1]

'It is a little bit of market research, a tool which may no doubt have great uses in some fields but has not, in my experience, proved particularly fruitful in litigation in the sense that, by and large, the results have been of but little assistance to the court.'

For, as he went on to observe:

'trade marks have to be considered in a business context and not in the context of laboratory experiments.'[2]

Having reviewed the results of the tests carried out in that case he said:

'[the impression] is made under conditions so remote from the conditions in which people are going to look at marks when they are in a shop that I regard it as a perfectly useless exercise.'[3]

These remarks have subsequently been endorsed by Vinelott J in *United Biscuits (UK) Limited v Burtons Biscuits Limited*[4] who found the results of similar tests of equally little assistance.

---

1 [1987] RPC 1 at 9.
2 Ibid at 10.
3 Ibid at 11.
4 [1992] FSR 14.

EVIDENTIAL PROCEDURE

7.39 All evidence, whether factual or expert, is now required to be put into the form of written statements or reports which are exchanged before the trial to enable the parties to prepare to deal with the evidence before the trial commences. It has for many years been the practice that any expert evidence upon which a party proposes to rely must be served before trial in the form of written reports[1] and this requirement is now imposed upon the evidence of witnesses of fact.[2]

Whilst initially the requirement for statements of witnesses of fact was permissive the practice has been so successful that it was changed at the end of 1992 to one in which the court is required to make an order for the exchange of statements.[3] The provisions applicable to experts' reports and statements of witnesses of fact will now be considered in detail.

---

1   RSC Ord 38, Part IV, rr 35–44.
2   By the creation of a new rule RSC Ord 38, r 2A governing the exchanging before trial of written statements of witnesses of fact proposed to be called at the trial.
3   RSC Ord 38, r 2A(2) as substituted by SI 1992 No 1907.

Experts' reports

7.40   The underlying purpose of the rules regulating the admission of expert evidence is that the parties should have advance notice of the nature of the evidence to be adduced and thus not be taken by surprise at the trial. To this end the rules provide that no expert evidence may be adduced at a trial without the leave of the court unless the parties agree that this should be done or an application has been made to the court for an order for the service of experts' reports.[1] This leaves open the possibility that the parties may simply agree to avoid the effect of the rules and not exchange reports but in practice this does not occur. Once an application is made, the court will, in the absence of special reasons, order exchange of reports.[2] The court may limit the number of experts who may be called at the trial[3] and may under this power limit the number of experts in a particular field of expertise. However, in large commercial disputes the court tends not to do so and attempts by inferior courts to curtail the costs of proceedings by restricting the numbers of experts in such cases have been deprecated by the Court of Appeal.[4] Once an application has been made for leave to adduce expert evidence the court may order that the parties' experts meet 'without prejudice' in order to agree such parts of their evidence as are not in dispute.[5] This is a provision which is valuable in many types of proceedings but in passing off actions it is likely that the issues as to reputation and confusion which are not in dispute will be resolved by the pleadings rather than the experts. It is normal for the order giving leave to adduce expert evidence to provide that the expert may not give evidence of any matters not in substance contained in his report.[6] At the trial the report will normally be put in evidence as the witness's evidence in chief[7] and, even if the witness is not called, any other party to the action may put in evidence a report which has been disclosed to him.[8] Depending upon the nature of the case it may be appropriate to order that expert evidence be exchanged either before or after the statements of witnesses of fact. In cases where the expert evidence depends upon what is said by the witnesses of fact, it is usual for the court to direct that the factual statements be served first.[9] This is not usually the case in actions for passing off where the expert evidence and the factual evidence are simply two different approaches to the same issue. Nor will this apply to cases in which the experts are dealing with some underlying technical issue which is independent of the evidence to be given by the witnesses of fact.

In such cases, particularly where the opposite party may wish to call expert evidence in reply, it is common for the court to order that experts' reports be exchanged before the statements of factual witnesses. Otherwise it is now common for orders to be made that both experts' reports and factual witness statements be exchanged at the same time.

---

1 RSC Ord 38, r 36(1).
2 Ord 38, r 37 (1).
3 Ord 38, r 4.
4 *Optical Laboratories Limited v Hayden Laboratories Limited* [1993] RPC 204 (CA) (a case on appeal from the Patents County Court).
5 Ord 38, r 38.
6 Ord 38, r 37(1) provides that the direction should be that 'the substance of the evidence be disclosed'.
7 See Ord 38, r 43.
8 Ord 38, r 42.
9 This is always the case in actions where the experts are commenting upon events which have occurred and therefore need to be able to comment in the knowledge of what the witnesses of fact say happened.

Statements of witnesses of fact

7.41 It is normally appropriate that statements should be exchanged rather than delivered sequentially as each party should prepare its evidence without having the benefit of seeing the evidence the other party intends to adduce. However, there will be circumstances in which it is necessary for the parties to reply to the opposite party's evidence or where it was not apparent to the opposite party that evidence of a particular kind would be required. In such cases the court has power to permit further statements to be served.[1] The order may also provide that witnesses may comment in the witness box on the statements of witnesses for the opposite party and, in practice, this is frequently done whether or not the order makes provision for it. The statements should be confined to matters relevant to the issues in the action although they clearly need to give any background information necessary to place such matters in context. They must contain the substance of all the evidence to be given by the witness as the witness may not normally supplement his evidence at the trial.[2] The service of a statement does not make that statement evidence[3] or make anything in it admissible[4] although the court will normally treat a statement as the evidence in chief of the witness. If the witness is not called, no other party may put the statement in evidence.[5] A statement which has been served may not be used for any purpose other than the proceedings in which it was served unless the party serving it consents or it has been put in evidence.[6]

---

1 RSC Ord 38, r 2A(10) and (17).
2 Rule 2A(7) requires the consent of the other parties or leave of the court unless the evidence relates to new matters which have arisen since the statement was served. In such cases it is in any event sensible to serve a supplementary statement.
3 Rule 2A(7)(a).
4 Rule 2A(8).
5 Rule 2A(6): in contrast to the provision relating to experts' reports. See n 7, para 7.40 above.

6   Rule 2A(11). The former rule which preserved the privilege in witness statements until they were
    given in evidence has been removed. The new provision is much more sensible and reflects the
    real purpose of serving witness statements. It means, for example, that a statement can be used
    in support of an application for further discovery before the trial.

7.42   The use of written witness statements has effected a considerable
change in the conduct of trials. First, witnesses no longer spend substantial
periods of time giving evidence in chief. As the giving of evidence is a highly
stressful and difficult matter, this can mean that they are initially somewhat
disorientated when subjected to cross-examination and it is common for
advocates to seek to put a few innocuous supplementary questions in
examination in chief simply to allow the witness a period to settle before
cross-examination starts. More importantly, whereas before a witness had
to give his evidence in chief orally and thus might simply fail to say what
he had indicated in his proof of evidence he was able to say, now that
material forms part of his witness statement and, unless dealt with in cross
examination, will stand as his evidence. This means that cross-examinations
have to be conducted with considerable care and attention to the details
of the witness statement. This undoubtedly extends the length of the cross
examination but the opportunity to prepare beforehand and the absence of
time taken in giving evidence in chief should lead to an overall reduction in
the length of the trial.

The trial

7.43   The conduct of the trial is in essence a straightforward matter. It is a
trial of the issue of liability only, the assessment of damages or profits being
left over to a later proceeding. The plaintiff opens the case setting out the
matters in issue and what he will prove to establish his claim. The court then
hears the evidence from both sides, taking the plaintiff's evidence first. The
defendant is entitled to open his case before adducing his evidence[1] but this
right is not usually invoked. With the extensive exchanges of written evidence
beforehand, the judge may have taken the opportunity to read the pleadings
and the evidence before the trial starts. If not, it is usual for him to take a short
period to do so before the witnesses are called to give their oral evidence. The
defendant has the right to make one speech after all the evidence is closed and
the plaintiff is entitled to a speech in reply. If the defendant decides to adduce
no evidence, the plaintiff makes his closing speech before the defendant states
his case.[2] It is becoming more and more common for the parties to provide
written skeletons of their cases to assist the court at trial. These can be used to
provide a convenient source of legal and evidential references around which
to explain their submissions. Once both parties have made their submissions
the judge gives judgment. After a full trial it is normal for the court to reserve

its decision for a short period of time and judgments are now often handed down in writing.

---

1   RSC Ord 35, r 7(4).
2   Ibid, r 7(3).

The relief granted

INTRODUCTION

7.44   A wide variety of relief is available to a successful plaintiff. He may be granted a declaration that the defendant's acts are wrongful and an injunction restraining their further commission. He is also entitled in support of an injunction to an order that articles and documents which can only be used in furtherance of the wrongful acts be delivered up or the offending markings on them permanently obliterated. He may be awarded damages or alternatively an account of the defendant's profits. In addition, he will normally be entitled to his costs. A successful (non-counterclaiming) defendant is entitled only to an order for costs. Each of these reliefs is now considered in detail.

DECLARATION

7.45   Where the plaintiff claims that the defendant intends to continue the activities complained of, it is usual to seek an injunction to restrain them. However, it is also possible to ask the court for a declaration that such acts would, if committed, be wrongful, and a declaration may be sought in addition to or in substitution for an injunction. The declaration, like the injunction, is a discretionary remedy and the court will only make a declaration where the circumstances justify it. Where there is no threat to commit the activities complained of, there is no need for a declaration and it will be refused.

Where the court is of the view that the defendant would have committed the acts held to be wrongful but will not do so once it has held them to be so, then it may refuse an injunction and grant simply the declaration with liberty to apply for an injunction.[1] However, an injunction is normally appropriate where the plaintiff's rights have been infringed and the defendant has not offered an undertaking to the court to cease the infringement.[2]

---

1   As in *Treasure Cot Co Limited v Hamley Bros Limited* (1950) 67 RPC 89. The form of the declaration granted in this case is in Appendix A, para 23.
2   *E W Savory Limited v The World of Golf Limited* [1914] 2 Ch 566 (a copyright case); *Fram Manufacturing Co Limited v Eric Morton & Co* (1922) 40 RPC 33 (a trade mark case).

INJUNCTION

7.46 The court has a general power to grant an injunction if it is just and convenient to do so[1] and the grant of an injunction normally follows a successful claim of passing off. However, it is a discretionary remedy and will not be granted unless the court is satisfied that, without it, there is a threat by the defendant to act wrongfully.[2] Even where the defendant shows that the sale complained of was a single isolated incident made by mistake or inadvertently, a refusal to apologise or undertake not to repeat the activities has been held a sufficient ground for granting an injunction.[3] The scope and form of the injunction are matters of considerable complexity. It must be framed so as to give proper protection to the plaintiff's rights but not so wide as unfairly to circumscribe the defendant's activities. Thus the form of the injunction will be very different in the case of a wholly distinctive fancy word mark from that which is appropriate to a highly descriptive word which only causes deception when used in a particular way. Consideration will also be given to the territorial scope of the injunction where the plaintiff's business is localised.[4] It is also necessary to consider whether the injunction should extend to preventing the defendant from enabling others to pass off by putting deceptive goods into the market. It is usual to ask for this form of relief in any case of passing off of goods and it is particularly important in actions against manufacturers, wholesalers or importers whose customers are members of the trade and are themselves not deceived.[5] A range of typical forms of injunction is set out in Appendix A. A defendant may choose instead of submitting to an injunction, to give an undertaking to the court not in future to commit the acts complained of. The effect of such an undertaking is identical to that of an injunction.

---

1   Supreme Court Act 1981, s 37(1).
2   See para 7.45 above.
3   *Singer Manufacturing Co v Spence* (1893) 9 TLR 536, 10 RPC 297; *Steiner Products Limited v Stevens* [1957] RPC 439.
4   See para 7.49 below.
5   See ch 4, para 4.29.

Form of injunction for wholly distinctive mark or get-up

7.47 Where the mark or get-up sued on is wholly distinctive, the injunction will normally take the form of an absolute prohibition against its use in relation to the goods or business. Typical forms of such injunction were those granted in *Eastman Photographic Materials Co Limited v Griffiths Cycle Corporation Limited*[1] (for passing off goods) and *Slazenger & Sons Limited v Feltham & Co*[2] (for passing off goods). Where the defendant's goods would confuse if marked but the nature of the defendant's business is such that people dealing with it would not be confused, the court may grant an injunction to prevent sales of goods but refuse one to prevent the use of the name in the business.[3]

---

1   (1898) 15 RPC 105; see Appendix A, form 1.
2   (1889) 5 TLR 365, 6 RPC 531; see Appendix A, form 2.
3   As happened in *Lego System A/S v Lego M Lemelstrich Limited* [1983] FSR 155; see Appendix A, form 3.

Form of injunction where there are circumstances in which the mark or get-up may be used by the defendant without deception

7.48   There are many cases in which there are limited circumstances in which the defendant may properly use the plaintiff's mark or get-up. Where the mark is descriptive and has come to denote the plaintiff's goods only by long use, it is normally appropriate for the injunction to be restricted to permit the defendant to use the mark provided that he does so with other distinguishing matter. This practice has been recognised since at least 1865 when an injunction preventing the use of the plaintiff's mark 'without clearly distinguishing' was granted in *Seixo v Provezende*.[1] This form of injunction has since been extensively used.[2] Where there are circumstances in which the defendant ought to be allowed to use the mark, it was common in the older cases to limit the injunction to a form such as use 'so as to induce the belief' that the goods are the plaintiff's.[3] However, this can simply lead to further disputes as to the propriety of the defendant's subsequent activities and the modern tendency is to grant an absolute injunction and to attach a proviso permitting use in certain specified circumstances to ensure that the precise ambit of the injunction is clear to both parties.[4] Typical cases in which the injunction is restricted are where the mark is used by some people to denote the plaintiff's goods and descriptively by others.[5] In such cases, the injunction will be limited to the circumstances of deceptive use.[6] It may even be necessary to provide that the injunction will only prevent sales where the defendant has not made appropriate enquiries to ascertain whether the mark is being used distinctively or descriptively.[7] Equally, where the defendant is using his own name as the name of his business, he is permitted to do so[8] but he is not permitted to go beyond that use and a limited form of injunction preventing only the additional activities is appropriate.[9] Where the claim is of the *Sherry* or *Champagne* type, the injunction will be restricted to preventing use of the mark in relation to goods which do not have the necessary qualities of geographical origin or manufactured type and ingredients.[10]

---

1   (1866) 1 Ch App 192, 14 LT 314; see Appendix A, form 4.
2   See Appendix A, forms 5–7, 14 and 16.
3   Such injunctions were granted in *Montgomery v Thompson* (Stone Ale) [1891] AC 217 affirming (1889) 41 Ch D 35, Appendix A, form 8, and in *Frank Reddaway & Co Limited v George Banham & Co Limited* [1896] AC 199, 65 LJQB 381, Appendix A, form 9.

4 See the injunction granted in *Walker v Ost* [1970] 2 All ER 106, [1970] RPC 489, Appendix A, form 21.
5 See ch 4, paras 4.31 and 4.32.
6 As in *Siegert v Findlater* (1878) 7 Ch D 801, 47 LJ Ch 233 where Fry J held that, whilst some people legitimately used the mark 'Angostura Bitters' to mean bitters of the kind made by the plaintiff, the defendant had done so fraudulently and should be restrained.
7 As happened in *Havana Cigar and Tobacco Factories v Oddenino* [1924] 1 Ch 179, 41 RPC 47, Appendix A, form 18.
8 See generally ch 4, paras 4.36–4.38.
9 As in *Rodgers v Rodgers* (1924) 41 RPC 277, Appendix A, form 15.
10 The forms of injunction granted in each of the *Champagne, Sherry, Scotch Whisky* and *Advocaat* cases are at Appendix A, forms 19 to 22 respectively.

Scope of injunction to protect localised goodwill

7.49   The scope of the injunction which is granted is that which is necessary to protect the subject matter of the action, the plaintiff's goodwill. In many, if not most, cases there is no dispute that the plaintiff's goodwill runs throughout the jurisdiction of the court and the injunction should, therefore, not be subject to any territorial limitation. However, there is no doubt that in appropriate cases, where the plaintiff has only a localised goodwill, the court will limit the geographical scope of the injunction. There is generally no need to protect a local goodwill for the injunction to affect the defendant's activities in areas to which it does not run[1] and it has long been recognised that in such cases a geographically limited injunction may suffice.[2] The scope of the injunction needed to protect a localised goodwill will vary depending upon the individual facts of the case and the starting point in considering this is whether the defendants' actual or threatened activities will harm the plaintiff's goodwill. As Slade LJ put it:

> '... the court would be justified in circumscribing the ambit of the injunction to narrower limits than England and Wales (which are the limits accepted by the plaintiffs) only if it were satisfied that the use by the defendants of the name "Chelsea Man" outside those limits in connection with their business *would not be likely substantially to injure the plaintiffs' goodwill.*' (original emphasis)[3]

Thus, an injunction limited in territorial scope is much more likely to be sufficient in the case of passing off of local businesses than of goods, particularly durable goods which may be taken by a purchaser to wherever he happens to travel. Even in the case of a local business, an injunction of relatively wide geographical scope may be justified if the area in which the defendant is sought to be restrained is one to which the plaintiff's customers might well go for the service in question.[4] Ultimately, the court's objective in determining the scope of the injunction must be to:

> 'provide for the reasonable protection of the plaintiff and no more, while paying due regard to the practical workings of any injunction which it grants.'[5]

It is relatively unusual for injunctions to be territorially limited. Whilst there are many examples of limited injunctions having been considered,[6] there is no reported case of a final injunction which does not run throughout the jurisdiction.

---

1   See eg *Clouds Restaurant Limited v Y Hotel Limited* (unreported, 7 July 1982, Dillon J) noted in *Chelsea Man Menswear Limited v Chelsea Girl Limited* [1987] RPC 189 (CA).
2   See *The Cellular Clothing Company v Maxton and Murray* (1899) 16 RPC 397; *Henry Thorne & Co Limited v Eugene Sandow and Sandow Limited* (1912) 29 RPC 440.
3   *Chelsea Man Menswear Limited v Chelsea Girl Limited* (above) at 202; and see *Ewing v Buttercup Margarine Company Limited* [1917] 2 Ch 1.
4   See eg *Brestian v Try* [1958] RPC 161 (CA).
5   Per Nourse LJ in *Chelsea Man Menswear Limited v Chelsea Girl Limited* (above) at 208.
6   In all the cases cited above the injunction finally granted was nation-wide.

Enforcement of injunction

7.50   Breach of an injunction is a contempt of court punishable by an order for costs,[1] a fine or even sequestration of assets or committal to prison.[2] It is a prerequisite of enforcement that a copy of the order containing the injunction has been served upon the defendant although the court can waive this requirement if satisfied that the terms of the order had been brought to the defendant's notice.[3] The breach must be established to the criminal standard of proof, that is beyond reasonable doubt, and applications for orders for contempt not infrequently fail because the court is not so satisfied. The size and nature of the penalty imposed will depend upon the court's view of the gravity of the breach committed. Where it is inadvertent or committed by accident, the court will normally be lenient and may do no more than order payment of indemnity costs[4] or grant a further injunction.[5] In *Showerings v Entam*,[6] a Babycham case, the defendants sought to add a proviso to the undertaking given to the court which would exclude accidental passing off by an employee contrary to instructions. Goff J refused to accept the proviso but added:

> 'If the defendants take the sort of steps they are proposing to take and if . . . the plaintiffs seek to commit for a breach and the evidence shows that the defendants have acted reasonably and the breach was isolated or *de minimis*, not only would there be no committal but I would have thought the court, in the exercise of its discretion, would not order the defendant to pay the costs.'

On the other hand, if the court considers that the directors of the defendant are themselves directly responsible for the breach, it may order them to pay the costs personally.[7] A mere employee may not, however, be made personally liable.[8]

---

1   Normally an order for indemnity costs to reflect the court's disapproval of the defendant's conduct.
2   RSC Ord 45, r 5(1).
3   Ibid, r 7(1) and 7(6).
4   As in *Showerings Limited v Fern Vale Brewery Co Limited* [1958] RPC 484; see also *Heaton's Transport v TGWU* [1932] 3 All ER 101 at 117; *Chelsea Man plc v Chelsea Girl Ltd* [1988] FSR 217.

5 See *Parker Manufacturing Co Limited v Cooper* (1901) 18 RPC 319.
6 [1975] FSR 45. See also *Britain v Trade and Commercial Press* [1957] RPC 319.
7 As in *Ronson Products Limited v Ronson Furniture Limited* [1966] Ch 603, 2 All ER 381.
8 *Daniel and Arter v Whitehouse* [1898] 1 Ch 685, 16 RPC 71.

PECUNIARY REMEDIES

7.51 It is normal in the prayer for relief appended to the statement of claim to seek the alternative of an enquiry as to damages or an account of profits. Once the trial of liability has been completed and if the plaintiff has succeeded, he is always entitled to nominal damages.[1] In any case in which the court is satisfied that more than nominal damage has been incurred, he is entitled to proceed to an enquiry to assess the quantum of the damage or, alternatively, to seek an account of the defendant's profits from passing off.[2] However, there is a limited discretion whether or not to order an enquiry and the court will not do so where it appears that it would be fruitless[3] although it must be very clear that there is no purpose in an enquiry before the court will refuse to grant one. In any event the plaintiff will be at risk as to costs unless a substantial sum is recovered.[4] The discretion to refuse an enquiry as to damages does not extend to refusing damages against a defendant who was unaware that his conduct was wrongful.[5] The entitlement to an account of profits arises from the principle that the defendant made them whilst under a fiduciary obligation to the plaintiff and is accordingly under an obligation to pay them to the plaintiff.[6] It is of course an equitable remedy and, therefore, entirely discretionary. An account of profits will normally only be ordered from the time at which the defendant became aware that his conduct was unlawful unless he was careless and ought to have known the true position before.[7] It may also be refused on other grounds, such as unreasonable delay in commencing the proceedings, which in the opinion of the court make it inequitable that the defendant should account for his profits.[8] The election between an enquiry or an account of profits has to be made after judgment and before the order is drawn up.[9] It is therefore made before discovery on the issue of quantum and thus without the information necessary to enable the plaintiff to assess which is likely to be the more attractive option.

1 *Blofeld v Payne* (1833) 4 B & Ad 410, 2 LJ KB 68; *Daniel and Arter v Whitehouse* [1898] 1 Ch 685, 15 RPC 134; *Draper v Trist* (1939) 56 RPC 225 at 235.
2 *Samuelson v Producers Distributing Co Limited* [1932] 1 Ch 201, 48 RPC 580; *Rose v Loftus* (1878) 47 LJ Ch 576, 38 LT 409; *Montgomerie & Co Limited v Young Bros* (1904) 21 RPC 285 (CA), reversing (1903) 20 RPC 781.
3 *McDonald's Hamburgers Limited v Burger King (UK) Limited* [1987] FSR 112 (CA).
4 See paras 7.57–7.60 below.
5 *Gillette UK Limited v Edenwest Limited* [1994] RPC 279.
6 *Electrolux Limited v Electrix Limited* (1953) 70 RPC 158 at 159.
7 *Young v Holt* (1948) 65 RPC 28; and see the cases cited in paras 2.13 and 2.14 above.
8 *Ford v Foster* (1872) 7 Ch App 611 at 633.
9 *Neilson v Betts* (1871) LR 5 HL 1, 40 LJ Ch 317.

Measure of damages

7.52   The basic principle has long been that the damages awarded to the plaintiff should put him into the position he would have enjoyed had the wrong which has been done to him not occurred. As Lord Blackburn put it more than 100 years ago:

> 'The general rule, at least in relation to "economic" torts, is that the measure of damages is to be, so far as possible, that sum of money which will put the injured party in the same position as he would have been if he had not sustained the wrong.'[1]

In the context of a passing off action Swinfen Eady LJ put the entitlement to damages in this form:

> 'The decision of the House of Lords[2] in the present case determines that the defendants have infringed a right of property in the plaintiffs' business or goodwill which was likely to be injured by misrepresentation; and the defendants are liable, in my opinion, for all loss actually sustained by the plaintiffs, which is the natural and direct consequence of the unlawful acts of the defendants; this will include any loss of trade actually suffered by the plaintiffs, either directly from the acts complained of, or properly attributable to injury to the plaintiffs' reputation, business, goodwill and trade and business connections caused by the acts complained of; in other words, such damages as flow directly, and in the usual course of things, from the wrongful acts, and excluding any speculative and unproven damage.'[3]

However, in order to determine what this is, one first has to establish the heads under which damage has been sustained. This is different from the task which faces the court at the trial of the action. There it is merely concerned to determine whether there has been *any* damage and therefore it looks at the heads under which damage may be suffered. At that stage, if it is satisfied that there has been real loss, however minor, then the tort is made out and judgment follows. However, substantial damage is often very difficult to demonstrate in a passing off action.[4] The most effective passing off never comes to light because the ultimate purchasers of the goods never become aware of the deception which has been played on them. In addition, damage to the plaintiff's reputation caused by association with inferior goods or services is almost impossible to quantify. Despite this, at the assessment of damages the plaintiff must establish actual loss under each of the heads claimed. In *Draper v Trist*, Luxmoore LJ put it thus:[5]

> 'the plaintiff must satisfy the court that the sale of the goods complained of has in fact injured him and he must also satisfy the court as to the extent of such injury.'

With that in mind, the plaintiff can claim damages under a variety of heads. He may say that the defendant's sales are ones which he would otherwise have made although the court will not presume that this is so: it must be proved.[6] If this is established, the plaintiff will be entitled to recover as damages the profit he would have made on such sales. If the plaintiff can show that he has suffered a loss of business as a result of the association of inferior goods with his business, this too is recoverable.[7] It has been held in particular circumstances where the plaintiff was kept out of the market by the defendant passing off

that an award can be made for the delay in re-entering the market.[8] There is
even some authority for the proposition that losses arising from a reduction
in price necessitated by deceptive sales may be recovered.[9] The most recent
authority suggests that to recover sums in relation to specific sales made by
the defendant the plaintiff must show that they were the cause of sales lost by
him and that he will not be entitled to recover a royalty on other sales made
by the defendant.[10] There is no case in which an award has in fact been made
upon that basis. The costs of putting the defendant's initially innocent suppliers
and customers on notice that their activities are unlawful are recoverable as
damages in the action, but further costs of pursuing them are not.[11]

---

1 *Livingstone v Rawyard Coal Co* (1880) 5 App Cas 25 at 38.
2 *Spalding v Gamage* (1915) 32 RPC 273.
3 *Spalding v Gamage* (1918) 35 RPC 101 at 117 (report of the appeal from the enquiry as to damages).
4 It is primarily for this reason that most passing off claims are brought before the court by way
   of applications for interlocutory injunctions: see ch 6.
5 Sitting as an additional judge of the Chancery Division to hear the enquiry reported at (1939)
   56 RPC 225 at 234.
6 See eg *Leather Cloth Co v Hirschfield* (1865) LR 1 Eq 299 at 301.
7 *Sykes v Sykes* (1824) 3 B & C 541.
8 *Aktiebolaget Manus v R J Fullwood & Bland Limited* (1954) 71 RPC 243: the plaintiff based its
   claim upon the profits made by the defendant during the period when it was passing off
   and the plaintiff was kept out of the market but this was rejected and a much smaller
   sum awarded. It is doubtful whether the court would take such an approach today: see para
   7.53 below.
9 *Alexander & Co v Henry & Co* (1895) 12 RPC 360 at 367. This was a trade mark case in which
   the proposition was accepted by analogy with patent infringement. It is therefore now of doubtful
   authority: see *Dormeuil Frères SA v Feraglow Limited* [1990] RPC 449.
10 *Dormeuil Frères SA v Feraglow Limited* (above), a decision on an application for interim payment
   under Ord 29, r 11 in which the court decided merely that the claim for a royalty was not 'likely'
   (the test laid down by the rule) to succeed at the enquiry.
11 Ibid, applying *Morton-Norwich v Intercen (No 2)* [1981] FSR 337.

Quantum of damages

7.53 The assessment of quantum is a factual enquiry within the bounds laid
down by the authorities as to the appropriate measure of damages. Many of
the cases cited in the previous paragraph proceed on the basis that the sums
to be awarded cannot be arithmetically calculated and have to be assessed by
forming a rough estimate of what is a fair and temperate sum to compensate
the plaintiff for the harm it has suffered.[1] However, the modern approach is
considerably more analytical[2] and the courts are now showing a willingness
to receive and act upon accounting and economic evidence in order to arrive
at more precise assessments of quantum of damages. Each case will inevitably
turn upon its own facts and it is impossible to give detailed guidance as to the
appropriate evidence to adduce in each case. However, it is essential to keep
in mind that the plaintiff must prove his loss. Accordingly, if it is alleged that
the plaintiff's business has suffered damage to its goodwill resulting in a general
reduction in trade, it will be necessary to put forward evidence which enables
the reduction to be attributed to the claimed cause and not, for example, to

general economic conditions or particular conditions unconnected with the passing off affecting the trade or the plaintiff's business.[3]

---

1   This is a précis of the approach of Dankwerts J in *Aktiebolaget Manus v Fullwood & Bland Limited* (1954) 71 RPC 243 at 250, which is typical of many of the cases cited above.
2   See the extensive calculations performed by Knox J in *Dormeuil Frères v Feraglow Limited* [1990] RPC 449 in order to arrive at figure for the interim payment. The same can be seen in the judgment of Falconer J in *Catnic Components Limited v Hill & Smith Limited* [1983] FSR 512 (a patent action).
3   Although it has been suggested that the court will presume that some damage to goodwill is inflicted if a considerable volume of deceptive trading is shown: per Sir Wilfred Greene MR in *Draper v Trist and Trisbestos Brake Linings Limited* (1939) 56 RPC 429 at 440.

The profits recoverable on an account

7.54   Authorities on the extent to which profits are recoverable are extremely rare. However, it is clear that in contrast to the enquiry as to damages, the court is not concerned with the effect which the defendant's activities have had on the plaintiff but merely with the profit which the defendant has made from them. Thus, the plaintiff will be entitled to an account of the profits made from all sales which fall within the scope of the injunction, whether or not he has suffered any loss thereby.[1] It follows that, where the plaintiff's complaint is the selling of deceptively marked goods to middlemen who are not themselves deceived, the defendant will be obliged to account for the profits on all such sales, irrespective of how the goods were subsequently dealt with.[1] Further the profits for which the defendant must account are the totality of those derived from the carrying on of the wrongful activity and not merely the additional profit attributable to the passing off.[2]

---

1   *Lever Bros v Goodwin* (1887) 36 Ch D 1 at 7.
2   *Peter Pan Manufacturing Corporation v Corsets Silhouette Limited* [1963] RPC 45 (a confidential information case).

The conduct of the enquiry or account

7.55   This is effectively an action with pleadings and discovery in the same way as the initial trial of the issue of liability. The practice is governed by RSC Ord 43 but this is in general terms and gives the court extremely wide powers to determine how the proceedings are conducted.[1] An enquiry is commenced by an application for directions by the plaintiff for its conduct. The directions usually provide for the delivery of points of claim and points in answer as the primary pleadings followed by discovery and evidence upon affidavit subject to cross-examination at the hearing of the enquiry. However, in some cases it is more sensible to have at least partial discovery, for example as to the extent of the defendant's activities, before any pleadings and such discovery may be ordered as the first step in the enquiry. An account is initially given by the accounting party and verified on affidavit.[2] The plaintiff may then challenge the account.[3] The account and the challenge then take the place of pleadings and are followed by discovery and evidence. These may be under an initial order for directions or an application made following the giving of the account. There will then be a hearing to determine the dispute.

1 See the powers given by RSC Ord 43, rr 2(1) and 3(1).
2 RSC Ord 43, r 4(1).
3 Under RSC Ord 43, r 5.

Delivery up, destruction and obliteration

7.56 Delivery up or destruction of infringing articles is available by statute in patent, copyright and trade mark actions. They are commonly sought in passing off actions and it is entirely unclear whether they are properly available. Whilst there are examples of orders for them being made[1] it is not clear from the reports whether this was by consent and, in the only reported discussion of the point Romer J stated that delivery up was not a remedy available in a passing off action.[2] Such reliefs are ancillary to the grant of the injunction and are intended not as a punishment to the defendant simply to remove from him the temptation to use goods or other materials whose use would be in breach of the injunction. The relief is, therefore, strictly limited to that which is necessary to protect the plaintiff from such a risk.[3] Such relief is discretionary and may be refused if it is unnecessary. The defendant may choose whether the goods are delivered up or destroyed.[4] Equally, if obliteration or erasure of the offending marks is possible, the defendant has the choice whether to do this or to deliver up or destroy the goods which bear them.[5]

1 *Warwick Tyre Company Limited v New Motor and General Rubber Company Limited* [1910] 1 Ch D 248, 27 RPC 161.
2 *Lissen Limited v Mutton* (1929) 46 RPC 10. However, the defendant appeared in person and indicated that he had in fact already delivered the offending items up to the plaintiff so that there was no argument on the point.
3 The principles upon which the court acts were authoritatively stated by Russell J in *Mergenthaler Linotype Company v Intertype Limited* (1926) 43 RPC 381 at 382 (a patent action).
4 *British Westinghouse Electric and Manufacturing Co Limited v Electrical Co Limited* (1911) 28 RPC 517 at 531.
5 *Slazenger & Sons v Feltham & Co* (1889) 5 TLR 365, 6 RPC 531; *Dent v Turpin* (1861) 2 John & H 139, 30 LJ Ch 495.

COSTS

7.57 The costs of any proceedings are in the discretion of the court[1] which is exercised in accordance with the principles laid down in the rules of court[2] and subject to the court's specific powers to make orders for payment of costs by third parties[3] and, in the case of 'wasted costs', for their payment by a party's legal or other representative.[4] The usual order is that costs follow the event. However, the court may depart from that order for a variety of reasons. The general principles upon which the court acts were helpfully summarised by Nourse LJ in *Re Elgindata (No 2)*:[5]

'(1) Costs are in the discretion of the court. (2) They should follow the event, except where it appears to the court that in the circumstances of the case some other order should be made. (3) The general rule does not cease to apply simply because the successful party raised issues or makes allegation on which he fails, but where that has caused a significant increase in the length or cost of the proceedings he may be deprived of the whole or part of his costs. (4) Where the successful party raised issues or makes allegation improperly or unreasonably, the court may not only deprive him of his costs but order him to pay the whole or a part of the unsuccessful party's costs. Of these principles the first, second and fourth are expressly recognised or provided for by [RSC Ord 62] rules 2(4), 3(3) and 10 respectively. The third depends upon well established practice. Moreover, the fourth implies that a successful party who neither improperly nor unreasonably raises issues or makes allegations on which he fails ought not to be ordered to pay any part of the unsuccessful party's costs.'

Costs awarded inter partes are normally ordered to be paid on the standard basis.[6] This inevitably results in a shortfall between the costs in fact incurred by a party and those which he recovers. In some circumstances the court may order payment of costs on the indemnity basis,[7] which results in little or no shortfall. However, generally the court will not make such an order, even if the litigation has been vigorously fought and wholly unsuccessful. To justify an order for indemnity costs there must be shown to have been conduct of the proceedings which verges on the improper or almost amounts to a contempt of court.[8] The costs of an enquiry normally follow the event, even if the plaintiff recovers substantially less than the sum originally claimed,[9] but the court may award the plaintiff only part of its costs if it advances extensive unsuccessful arguments as to the basis upon which damages should be awarded.[10]

---

1 Supreme Court Act 1981 (SCA), s 51(1). Clearly the discretion must be exercised judicially: see per Lord Goff in *Aiden Shipping v Interbulk Limited* [1986] AC 965 at 981.
2 RSC Ord 62, esp. Parts I and II (rules 1 to 11).
3 SCA s 51(3).
4 SCA s 51(6). Wasted costs are defined in subsection (7) as those arising from an improper, unreasonable or negligent act or omission or which it is unreasonable for a party to pay in the light of such an act or omission.
5 [1992] 1 WLR 1207 at 1214, [1993] 1 All ER 232 at 237.
6 This is defined in RSC Ord 62, r 12(1) as 'a reasonable amount in respect of all costs reasonably incurred' with any doubt as to this being resolved in favour of the paying party.
7 Defined in RSC Ord 62, r 12(2) as all costs 'except insofar as they are of an unreasonable amount or have been unreasonably incurred' with any doubt being resolved in favour of the receiving party.
8 *Marie Claire Album SA v Hartstone Hosiery Limited* [1993] FSR 692 at 697; see also *Strix Limited v Otter Controls Limited* [1991] FSR 163.
9 *Aktiebolaget Manus v Fullwood & Bland Limited* (1954) 71 RPC 243 at 250.
10 *Draper v Trist and Trisbestos Brake Linings Limited* (1939) 56 RPC 429 at 445.

7.58 Within the general principles outlined in the previous paragraph, there are many examples of the court's exercise of its discretion in particular circumstances which arise in passing off cases. If only isolated acts of passing off are established with no intention to repeat them, the court rather than dismissing the action may refuse the injunction and award no costs. There are also cases in which successful plaintiffs have recovered only a proportion of their costs where the injunction granted was much narrower than that sought,[1] the relief was otherwise substantially less than was asked for,[2] allegations of fraud have been made but not established[3] or excessive or irrelevant evidence has been introduced.[4] Where allegations of infringement of trade mark and passing off are made in one action, only one of which succeeds, the court may order the unsuccessful party to pay the costs of the successful party in each case with a set off between them.[5] Successful defendants have been penalised by having their costs reduced or refused on the ground that unfounded allegations of fraud were made,[6] having kept back 'material matters',[7] having 'provoked the action'[8] or having 'brought the action on themselves'.[9]

---

1 *Saxlehner v Appollinaris Co* [1897] 1 Ch 893, 14 RPC 645; *Rodgers v Rodgers* (1924) 41 RPC 277; *Daimler Motor Co (1904) v London Daimler Co Limited* (1907) 24 RPC 379 (CA).

2 *Hipkins & Sons v Plant* (1898) 15 RPC 294; *Fram Manufacturing Co Limited v Morton & Co* (1922) 40 RPC 33 (CA); *Findlater, Mackie, Todd & Co Limited v Henry Newman & Co* (1902) 19 RPC 235.

3 *Montgomerie & Co Limited v Young Brothers* (1903) 20 RPC 781; *Fram Manufacturing Co Limited v Morton & Co* (above) and the cases cited in n 1 above.

4 *Daimler Motor Co (1904) v London Daimler Co Limited* (above); *Montgomerie & Co Limited v Young Brothers* (above).

5 As in *Lever Brothers Limited v Bedingfield* (1898) 15 RPC 453. See also *Jenkins v Jackson* [1891] 1 Ch 59, 60 LJ Ch 206 (nuisance by two causes, only one established).

6 *Hargreaves v Freeman* (1891) 8 RPC 237 at 241.

7 *Meahy & Co Limited v Triticine Limited* (1897) 15 RPC 1.

8 *Lever Brothers Limited v Bedingfield* (1899) 16 RPC 3, affirming (1898) 15 RPC 453.

9 *Lambert & Butler Limited v Goodbody* (1902) 18 TLR 394, 19 RPC 377.

'Calderbank' offers

7.59 It has long been the case that a defendant threatened with proceedings may protect himself against the costs of the proceedings by offering the plaintiff such relief as he is properly entitled to. If, following such an offer the plaintiff pursues the action and fails to recover more than has been offered, then the defendant will normally be awarded his costs from the date of the offer. As it was put by Sargent J in *Rippingilles Albion Lamp Co Limited v Clarke's Syphon Stove Co Limited*:[1]

> 'After the letter offering to submit to an injunction or to give an undertaking, the plaintiffs ought to have accepted that offer, and as from that time forward, subject to the plaintiffs being entitled to get judgment in the cheapest and speediest possible way, the defendants ought to have their costs.'

However, the making of such an offer in open correspondence may be inimical to the defendant's interests. Because an injunction is sought, it is not possible for the defendant to protect his position on costs simply by making a payment into court. To deal with this the practice originally adopted in the Family division in *Calderbank v Calderbank*,[2] and now codified in RSC Ord 22, r 14, is commonly used. Under this practice, the defendant makes a written offer 'without prejudice save as to costs' which may only be revealed to the court after the substance of the case has been determined and there is argument over the payment of costs. This operates in precisely the same way as a payment in. If the plaintiff recovers no more than was offered, then he will be deprived of his costs from the date of receipt of the offer and the defendant will recover his costs from the same date. If he recovers more than the offer, the costs are not affected. However, such a procedure should not be used as a substitute for a payment into court where this is appropriate and, if it is proposed to offer a sum in damages, this should be paid in as part of the offer.[3]

1   (1917) 34 RPC 365. Similar orders were made in *Slazenger v Pigott* (1895) 12 RPC 439 and *Crosfield & Sons Limited v Caton* (1912) 29 RPC 47.
2   [1976] Fam 93.
3   See *Cutts v Head* [1984] Ch 290. This is contrary to the effect of *Draper v Trist* [1939] 3 All ER 513, 56 RPC 225 and 429 (CA). The later decision records the modern practice and is to be preferred.

Other specific rules as to costs

7.60   The parties may also protect themselves as to costs in other ways. For example, if admissions are sought and not given, the costs of proving the facts of which admission was sought will be given to the party who was forced to do so.[1] A party can also suggest limiting the ambit of the dispute by agreeing fact or consequences with the threat that it will seek a special order to cover any additional costs incurred if the suggestion is not taken up. Whilst such tactics may not always succeed they provide further opportunities to try and limit the spiralling costs of litigation.

1   See RSC Ord 62, r 6(7) and further discussion of this point at para 7.18 above.

Appeals

7.61   The unsuccessful party has a right of appeal to the Court of Appeal.[1] On an appeal the respondent may by a respondent's notice seek to have the judgment upheld on any further grounds not relied upon or rejected by the judge.[2] There is a further right of appeal to the House of Lords with leave either of the Court of Appeal or, if this is refused, with leave of the House of Lords upon petition for leave.[3] Leave to appeal to the House of Lords will normally only be given where it is clear that the case raises issues of considerable general importance.

1   Supreme Court Act 1981, ss 16–18.
2   RSC Ord 59, r 6.
3   Administration of Justice (Appeals) Act 1934, s 1.

STAY OF RELIEF PENDING APPEAL

7.62   The normal rule is that relief granted after trial takes effect immediately and an appeal does not act as a stay.[1] However, both the court of first instance and the Court of Appeal[2] have power to stay all forms of relief pending appeal. The principle upon which the court acts in deciding whether to stay relief pending appeal is that the stay should be granted only if it is necessary to do justice between the parties, whatever the outcome of the appeal.[3] Thus, where an injunction would destroy the defendant's business, it is normally the case that the court will grant a stay. Further, it is now commonplace for the court to require the plaintiff to give a cross-undertaking in damages if an injunction is not to be stayed[4] and, if this is not forthcoming, the injunction will be stayed.[5] The court has power to order terms as a condition of granting a stay, such as the keeping of accounts or the payment into court of funds to secure damages[6] and will ordinarily order that the stay lasts only so long as the appeal is prosecuted with due diligence. A stay of the order for delivery up, destruction or obliteration will normally follow a stay of the injunction.[7] A stay of the enquiry as to damages will normally be refused[8] unless the defendant can show that if the damages are paid he will be unable to recover them.[9]

---

1   RSC Ord 59, r 13(1)(a).
2   The Court of Appeal may only hear such an application where it has already been made to the court below and refused: RSC Ord 59, r 14(4).
3   See eg *Minnesota Mining & Manufacturing Corporation v Johnson & Johnson* [1976] RPC 139.
4   Ibid.
5   As happened in *Erven Warnink BV v J Townend & Sons Limited* [1978] FSR 1, [1980] RPC 31 at 56–59.
6   Ibid.
7   *Parker & Smith v Satchwell & Co Ltd* (1901) 18 RPC 299 at 309.
8   *Monks v Bartram* [1891] 1 QB 346, 60 LJ QB 267.
9   *Colman & Co v Smith & Co, Re Carvino Registered Trade Mark* [1911] 2 Ch 572; *Presto Gear Case and Components Limited v Orme, Evans & Co Limited* (1900) 17 RPC 218.

APPEAL AS TO COSTS ALONE

7.63   No appeal lies from an order as to costs unless leave has been given by the judge,[1] or there has been no real and proper exercise of the judge's discretion[2] or the appeal is part of a wider appeal on grounds of substance.[3]

---

1   Supreme Court Act 1981, s 18(1A) and RSC Ord 59, r 1B(1)(b).
2   *Scherer v Counting Instruments Limited* [1977] FSR 569 (where the earlier relevant authorities are reviewed); and see *Infabrics Limited v Jaytex Limited* [1987] FSR 529. It would appear that this is still good law notwithstanding the amendment to the Supreme Court Act 1981 as the prohibition on appeals without leave now contained in Ord 59, r 1B(1)(b) is in precisely the same terms as that previously contained in s 18(1)(f).
3   *Wheeler v Somerfield* [1966] 2 QB 94, [1966] 2 All ER 305. See also *Marshall v Levine* [1985] 1 WLR 814n, [1985] 2 All ER 177.

CHAPTER 8

Malicious falsehood, defamation and contempt of court

Malicious falsehood

THE NATURE OF THE TORT

8.01 An action lies for

> 'written or oral falsehoods not actionable per se, nor even defamatory, where they are maliciously published, where they are calculated in the ordinary course of business to produce, and where they do produce, actual damage.'

Bowen LJ used the term 'malicious falsehood' for such statements.[1] In an action for malicious falsehood the onus is on the plaintiff to prove the falsity of the statement, the suffering of damage, and the presence of malice.[2] The last is crucial for, as Whitford J commented in *McDonald's Hamburgers Limited v Burger King (UK) Limited*:[3]

> Passing off lies close very often to trade libel,[4] but whereas in passing off motive may be quite immaterial, to succeed in a trade libel, that is, to succeed in the allegation that there has been a publication of a malicious falsehood, malice must be established.

The tort is, therefore, in principle an extremely simple one and historically there has been little academic analysis devoted to it.

---

1   *Ratcliffe v Evans* [1892] 2 QB 524 at 527, 61 LJ QB 535 at 538.
2   See *White v Mellin* [1895] AC 154 at 167, 64 LJ Ch 308 at 318 per Lord Watson.
3   [1986] FSR 45.
4   A term often used in place of malicious falsehood: see para 8.03 below.

TERMINOLOGY

8.02 *'Slander of title'* is a form of malicious falsehood in which the falsehood constitutes denial of a person's title to a form of property. Strictly speaking the term 'slander of title' relates to titles to real property.[1] The term has, however, been widely applied, particularly in more recent times, to titles to personal property also. In *The Royal Baking Powder Co v Wright, Crossley & Co*,[2] Lord Davey used the term 'slander of title' in connection with an allegation of malicious damage to the plaintiffs in their trade, by denying their title to the use of a certain label and threatening to sue their customers. It was held that, to support such an action, it is necessary for the plaintiffs 'to prove (1) that the statements complained of were untrue (2) that they were made maliciously, ie without just cause or excuse, and (3) that the plaintiffs have suffered special damage thereby'. In *Wren v Weild*[3] Blackburne J approved the extension of 'the well-known action for slander of title in real property' to cases where 'the false and malicious assertion relates to goods and the damage results from the loss of a bargain to sell them'. The terms *'slander of goods'* and *'disparagement of goods'* have also been used for this type of malicious falsehood.[4]

---

1   *Halsey v Brotherhood* (1881) 19 Ch D 386, 51 LJ Ch 233.
2   (1900) 18 RPC 95, HL.
3   (1869) LR 4 QB 730, 38 LJ QB 88.
4   As in eg *White v Mellin* [1895] AC 154, 64 LJ Ch 308.

8.03   *'Slander of title'* and *'slander (or disparagement) of goods'* are particular types of malicious falsehood.[1] Other terms which have been used in the same wide meaning as 'malicious falsehood' are *'trade libel'*[2] and *'injurious falsehood'*.[3] As with any other type of malicious falsehood, slander of title and slander of goods can be in the form of written or oral false statements.

---

1   This is the terminology used in the Defamation Act 1952 s 3(1) where reference is made to 'an action for slander of title, slander of goods or other malicious falsehood'. This is also consistent with the terminology used in the reported cases.
2   See eg *Thorley's Cattle Food Co v Massam* (1880) 14 Ch D 763; *Hubbuck & Sons v Wilkinson Heywood & Clark* [1899] 1 QB 86, 68 LJQB 34, CA.
3   See *Shapiro v La Morta* (1923) 40 TLR 201, CA.

THE NEED TO PROVE DAMAGE AND MALICE

8.04   The need for a plaintiff to prove damage arises from the origin of the action for 'malicious falsehood' as an action on the case. The need to prove malice was considered by Lord Coleridge LCJ in *Halsey v Brotherhood*:[1]

'There must be evidence . . . that the statement was not only untrue, but was made mala fide for the purpose of injuring the Plaintiff and not in the bona fide defence of the defendant's own property . . . if a statement is made in defence of the defendant's own property, although it injures and is untrue, it is still what the law calls a privileged statement: it is a ~tatement that the defendant has a right to make, unless, besides its untruth and besides its injury, express malice is proved, that is to say, want of bona fides or the presence of mala fides.'

Malice is a state of mind.[2] It is established by proof of intention to injure and also by establishing that the defendant knew the words would injure and was reckless whether they were true or false.[3] However, it is not malice simply to be indifferent to whether the words will cause injury if they are not otherwise used with an improper motive.[4]

---

1   (1881) 19 Ch D 386 at 388.
2   See paras 8.21–8.23 below for a full discussion of the meaning of malice.
3   *Shapiro v La Morta* (1923) 40 TLR 201 (CA).
4   *McDonald's Hamburgers Limited v Burger King (UK) Limited* [1986] FSR 45 at 60.

THE DIFFERENCE BETWEEN MALICIOUS FALSEHOOD AND DEFAMATION
AS CAUSES OF ACTION

8.05 The essential difference between these two causes of action was stated by Tindall LCJ in *Malachy v Soper:*[1]

'Action for slander of title is not an action for words spoken or libel written or published but an action on the case for special damage sustained by reason of speaking or publication of the slander of the Plaintiff's title.'

In *Royal Baking Powder Co v Wright Crossley & Co*[2] Lord Halsbury LC said of the action of slander of title:

'There is a class of cases, of which this is one, the true legal aspect of which, however they may be described technically, is that they are actions for unlawfully causing damage. The damage is the gist of the action, and gives no right to an action in a court of law unless damage is proved.'

In *Young v Macrae*[3] Cockburn CJ recognised the distinction between malicious falsehood and libel and said:

'I am far from saying that if a man falsely and maliciously makes a statement disparaging an article which another manufactures or vends, although in so doing he casts no imputation on his personal or professional character, and thereby causes an injury, and special damage is averred, an action might not be maintained.'

Apart from the fact that, in cases of libel, proof of damage and (except in special cases)[4] malice are not necessary, the main differences between malicious falsehood and libel are that, in the action for libel, the right of action does not survive the death of the plaintiff[5] and there is an onus on the defendant to prove that the statement relied on is true[6] (whereas in the action for malicious falsehood the plaintiff has to prove that the statement relied on is untrue).[7] Slander, like libel, is a form of defamation, but differs from libel in that the defamatory statement is in a non-permanent form and special damage must be alleged and proved (except in special cases).[8] In all other respects the differences between malicious falsehood and libel apply.

---

1   (1836) 3 Bing NC 371.
2   (1900) 18 RPC 95 at 104.
3   (1862) 3 B & S 265 at 269.
4   Eg if a defendant relies on qualified privilege or fair comment.
5   See *Hatchard v Mege* (1887) 18 QB D 771, 56 LJQB 397.
6   See eg *Belt v Lawes* (1882) 51 LJQB 359 at 367.
7   See *White v Mellin* [1895] AC 154 at 167.
8   See Duncan and Neil *Defamation* (2nd edn, 1984) ch 3.

THE DIFFERENCE BETWEEN ACTIONABLE MALICIOUS FALSEHOODS
AND DEFAMATORY STATEMENTS

8.06 In *South Hetton Coal Co v North Eastern News Association*[1] Lord Esher gave a hypothetical illustration of the difference between a malicious falsehood and a defamatory statement:

'If the Plaintiff is a wine merchant, and you say that there is a bad vintage and the wine of that vintage is bad with him and with all merchants, that is no reflection upon the Plaintiff in his business, but is only a reflection upon the goods, and is not a libel upon the Plaintiff. If such a statement as that is made maliciously, and does injure the Plaintiff, it only gives rise to an action upon the case and not to an action for libel. If you say of a wine merchant that he has been selecting bad wine that is a reflection upon him in his business, and may be a libel upon him in his business.'

In *Evans v Harlow*[2] the plaintiff sued the defendant for libel, the gist of his complaint being that the defendant was telling the world that the lubricator sold by the plaintiff was not good for its purpose but wasted tallow. The Court distinguished between statements libellous of a tradesman personally and statements made in disparagement of his goods. Patterson J said:[2]

'This is not . . . a caution against the plaintiff as a tradesman in the habit of selling goods, which he knows to be bad; if it were, it would be a libel upon him personally; but it is a caution against the goods suggesting that the articles which the plaintiff sells do not answer their purpose, which is not actionable unless it were shown that the plaintiff by reason of the publication, was prevented from selling his goods to a particular person.'

In *Griffiths v Benn*[3] the Court of Appeal (reversing the court of first instance) held that an attack made on a system operated under a patent did not involve libellous imputations on those supplying the parts and licensing the patented system. A specific statement can, however, constitute both defamation and malicious falsehood.[4]

---

1 [1894] 1 QB 133, 63 LJQB 293.
2 (1844) 5 QB 624, 13 LJQB 120.
3 (1911) 27 TLR 346, CA.
4 See para 8.33 below.

THE FALSEHOOD

8.07 In order to be actionable, the falsehood must be a specific statement derogatory of the plaintiff's goods or business. In *Hubbuck v Wilkinson*[1] it was held that the mere statement that the defendant's paint was better than the plaintiff's was not actionable, even if untrue, made maliciously, and causing damage to the plaintiff; on the defendant's application the plaintiff's statement of claim was struck out. In *Young v Macrae*[2] it was held that a merely comparative statement, even if false, might not be a false statement about the plaintiff's goods; it might be true of the plaintiff's goods and false of the other person's goods. In *McDonald's Hamburgers Limited v Burger King (UK) Limited*[3] Whitford J held that an advertisement for Burgerking's products under the headline 'It's not just Big, Mac', which had a series of statements in small print comparing the two brands of hamburgers, would either be read as a whole or not at all so that it could not be said that it was implying that the Big Mac is not 100 % pure beef. Whilst this was essentially a decision on the facts of the particular case, it is a good illustration that false in this context means positively incorrect and not just possibly misleading. In *White v Mellin*[4] a statement in an advertisement to the effect that the defendant's goods were 'superior' was held to be 'a mere puff' and not actionable. Lord Herschell LC referred with approval[1] to the statement of Lord Denman LCJ in *Evans v Harlow*[5] that 'it would open an unduly wide door to litigation to expose every man who said his goods were better than another's to the risk of an action' and added:[6]

> 'If an action will not lie because a man says his goods are better than his neighbour's, it seems to me impossible to say that it will lie because he says that they are better in this or that or the other respect . . . Indeed the courts of law would be turned into a machinery for advertising rival productions by obtaining a judicial determination which of the two was the better.'

In *De Beers Abrasive Products Ltd v International General Electric Co of New York Ltd*[7] Walton J, after a thorough review of the authorities, suggested two alternative criteria for deciding whether a false statement was actionable: first, whether a reasonable man would take the claim being made as a serious claim; and second, in the alternative, whether the defendant had pointed to a specific allegation of some defect or demerit in the plaintiff's goods.

---

1 [1899] 1 QB 86, 68 LJQB 34. CA.
2 (1862) 3 B & S 264, 32 LJQB 6.
3 [1986] FSR 45.
4 [1895] AC 154, 64 LJ Ch 308.
5 (1844) 5 QB 624, 13 LJQB 120.
6 See *White v Mellin* [1895] AC 154 at 166.
7 [1975] 2 All ER 599; [1975] 1 WLR 972.

TYPES OF MALICIOUS FALSEHOOD

Slander of title

8.08 In many cases the falsehood complained of as a slander of title concerned the plaintiff's title to real property,[1] or to goods,[2] in the strict sense. The term 'slander of title' has, however, also been applied more broadly. In *Barrett v Associated Newspapers Ltd*[3] a statement that the plaintiff's house was haunted was treated as a case of slander of title, but the case was dismissed on the plaintiff's failure to prove damage. In other cases the term 'slander of title' has been applied to allegations of infringement of patent,[4] copyright[5] and trade mark.[6]

---

1 As in *Loudon v Ryder* [1953] Ch 423, [1953] 1 All ER 1005.
2 As in *British Rly Traffic and Electric Co Ltd v CRC Co Ltd and LCC* [1922] 2 KB 260, 91 LJQB 824 (title to a lorry).
3 (1907) 23 TLR 666, CA.
4 *Halsey v Brotherhood* (1880) 15 Ch D 514, (1881) 19 Ch D 386.
5 *Dicks v Brooks* (1879) 15 Ch D 22, 49 LJ Ch 812.
6 *Greers Ltd v Pearman & Corder Ltd* (1922) 39 RPC 406, CA.

Allegations of defects in the goods

8.09　In some cases the falsehood in question consisted of a statement that the defendant's goods were defective or inadequate in some way. Thus in *Thorley's Cattle Food Co v Massam*[1] the defendants were restrained from issuing advertisements stating that they alone were possessors of the secret of making the condiment known as 'Thorley's Cattle Foods' and that the plaintiffs were seeking to foist on the public an article which they pretended was the same as the defendants'. Similarly in *Cars v Bland Light Syndicate Ltd*[2] the plaintiffs successfully relied on a number of untrue statements alleging, inter alia, that the plaintiffs' articles were 'not genuine' and were 'a cheap imitation' of the defendants' articles; it was held that the defendants had 'persistently attempted by means of malicious and untrue statements to interfere with the plaintiffs in their trade.' The plaintiffs also successfully relied on allegations of infringement of patent under the provisions of the Patents Act.[3]

1　(1880) 14 Ch D 763, CA.
2　(1911) 28 RPC 33.
3　Relying on the 'threats section' of the then current Patents Act. See para 8.42 below.

8.10　In a somewhat similar case *Dunlop Pneumatic Tyre Co Ltd v Maison Talbot*[1] the plaintiffs successfully relied on false statements that they were not entitled to import or deal in Michelin tyres and were infringing patents. In *Alcott v Millar's Karri and Jarrah Forests Ltd*[2] a letter suggesting that the plaintiff's wooden road blocks would deteriorate and become rotten in use was held to constitute a malicious falsehood. Statements that the plaintiffs' products were 'spurious',[3] 'not genuine',[4] 'of low quality'[5] or 'inadequate'[6] have been held to be malicious falsehoods. In another case, the actionable falsehoods were in the form of specific tests in a report.[7] Malicious falsehoods of this type are sometimes called 'slander of goods' or 'disparagement of goods'.[8]

1　(1904) 20 TLR 579.
2　(1904) 91 LT 722, 21 TLR 30.
3　*Thomas v Williams* (1880) 14 Ch D 864, 49 LJ Ch 605.
4　*James v James* (1872) LR 13 EQ 421, 41 LJ Ch 353.
5　*Western Counties Manure Co v Lawes Chemical Manure Co* (1874) LR 9 Exch 218, 43 LJ Ex 171.
6　*London Ferro Concrete Co Ltd v Justicz* (1951) 68 RPC 261, CA.
7　*Cellactite and British Uralite Ltd v Robertson Co Inc* (1957) The Times, 23 July.
8　*White v Mellin* [1895] AC 154, 64 LJ Ch 308; *Lyne v Nicholls* (1906) 23 TLR 86. See para 8.03 above.

Allegations about the plaintiff's business

8.11　It is equally actionable to make false statements about a man's business as well as his goods. And, as in passing off,[1] a broad interpretation is given to the term 'business'. In an unusual case[2] it was even held that an actor who had suffered serious injuries and was recovering in hospital could bring an action for malicious falsehood against a newspaper which photographed and interviewed him when he was unable to give informed consent for the interview to protect his opportunity later to profit from the sale of the story of his injury and subsequent recovery.

---

1   See para 3.03.
2   *Kaye v Robertson* [1991] FSR 62.

Allegations of infringement of patent, trade mark or design

8.12   False allegations of infringement of patent, registered or unregistered design and trade mark, if not made bona fide, and if resulting in damage to the plaintiffs, are actionable as malicious falsehoods. In *Burnett v Tak*[1] it was held that the court must in such a case be satisfied that the allegations were untrue and that the defendants knew them to be untrue. If the statement made concerns a subsisting patent which might be infringed, it is very difficult for a plaintiff to discharge this burden.[1] Thus in *Halsey v Brotherhood*[2] Sir George Jessel MR held that

> 'a man is entitled to say: "I have a monopoly under the patent, you are infringing it, now please desist" or "I give notice that AB is infringing; he is not worth suing; I give notice to everybody not to buy of AB" in a bona fide assertion of his legal right; there is no obligation on him to bring an action . . . It is a totally different thing where a man, knowing he has no legal right, threatens proceedings for a collateral purpose. Then he may be liable to an action . . . because it is an untrue assertion and not made bona fide.'

The Court of Appeal, in upholding the judgment of the Master of the Rolls, held that, in absence of mala fides, this was 'one of the instances where the law, in the interests of society, permits injury to be done without any remedy commensurate with it'.[3]

---

1   (1882) 45 LT 743.
2   (1880) 15 Ch D 514 at 520.
3   (1881) 19 Ch D 386 at 388.

8.13   In due course the legislature took a different view from that expressed in *Halsey v Brotherhood*[1] and appropriate legislation was introduced in the Patents Act 1883 to make such statements actionable without proof of falsity, malice or damage, but providing for a defence that the statement was true.[2] There are similar provisions in subsequent Patents Acts, the Registered Designs Act 1949 and in relation to unregistered designs and trade marks.[3] A 'general warning' not to infringe is not actionable either as a malicious falsehood or a 'threat' unless it is disguisedly directed to a specific person or to specific persons.[4]

---

1   (1881) 19 Ch D 386 at 388.
2   See *Encyclopaedia of United Kingdom and European Patent Law* (Sweet & Maxwell).
3   See ch 9 paras 9.34 and 9.11 respectively.

4   See *Withers & Sons Ltd v Withers & Co Ltd* (1926) 44 RPC 19; *Johnson v Edge* [1892] 2 Ch 1, 9 RPC 142, CA.

Allegations of infringement of copyright or passing off

8.14   There are no statutory provisions concerned to prevent allegations of infringement of copyright or passing off: the action for malicious falsehood is accordingly the only action which can be relied on for this purpose. Thus in *Colley v Hart*[1] the plaintiff relied on threats of proceedings for infringement of patent and trade mark[2] but (there being no allegation of malice or damage) obtained an injunction to restrain the former threats only (in reliance on the statutory provisions in the Patents Act). Similarly it was held in *Ripley v Arthur & Co*[3] that the defendant had no cause of action under a counterclaim alleging threats of proceedings for passing off, without malice or damage being alleged. In *Royal Baking Powder Co v Wright*[4] and *Greers Ltd v Pearman and Corder*[5] the defendants had circulated false allegations of infringement of trade mark and passing off. In both cases malice was held to have been proved but in the first case the plaintiff failed to prove damage. In the latter case, however, damage was proved and the plaintiff succeeded. In *Dicks v Brooks*[6] the plaintiffs failed to prove malice or damage in an action to prevent threats of infringement of copyright. However, in *Jaybeam Ltd v Abru Aluminium Ltd*[7] Whitford J granted an interlocutory injunction to restrain threats of infringement of copyright, somewhat inconsistently with other authorities.[8]

1   (1890) 44 Ch D 179, (1888) 6 RPC 17, (1890) 7 RPC 101.
2   There was until the passing of the Trade Mark Act 1994 no action for threats in relation to an allegation of infringement of a registered trade mark.
3   (1902) 19 RPC 443; affirming (1900) 18 RPC 82.
4   (1900) 18 RPC 95, HL.
5   (1922) 39 RPC 406, CA.
6   (1880) 15 Ch D 22.
7   [1975] FSR 334.
8   See paras 8.42 and 8.43 below.

Statements concerning the outcome of past court proceedings

8.15   A person wishing to complain about untrue statements concerning the outcome of past court proceedings may prefer to rely on malicious falsehood rather than on contempt of court.[1] Thus in *Mentmore Manufacturing Co v Fomento*[2] the defendants were restrained by injunction from representing that the plaintiff's patent had been held valid without adding that the Court of Appeal had given leave to the defendant to appeal to the House of Lords and granted a stay of the injunction. The Court was prepared to grant an interlocutory injunction notwithstanding the normal reluctance to do so in a libel or malicious falsehood action.[3]

1   See para 8.26 below.

2   (1955) 72 RPC 157, (1954) 72 RPC 12.
3   See para 8.42 below.

Statements concerning the outcome of pending court proceedings

8.16   In *Incandescent Gas Light Co Ltd v The Sunlight Incandescent Gas Lamp Co*,[1] an action for malicious falsehood, proceedings were brought concerning statements in a circular about pending proceedings for infringement of patent. Apart from a particular portion of the defendant's circular (which the defendant amended on the Court's direction) the action failed, the Court holding that the circular was accurate if read carefully and that there was no evidence of malice.[2]

---

1   (1897) 14 RPC 180.
2   As to actions for contempt of court on these grounds, see paras 8.27 and 8.28 below.

Other types of malicious falsehood

8.17   Other false statements held to be actionable as malicious falsehoods have included statements that the plaintiff was employed by the defendant,[1] that the circulation of the defendant's newspaper was 20 times that of the plaintiff's,[2] that the plaintiff (a pianist) would accompany the defendant (a singer) on the piano,[3] that the plaintiff had gone out of business and the defendant had succeeded to the plaintiff's business,[4] that the plaintiff had left his business address,[5] that the defendant was the welter weight boxing champion of Trinidad[6] and (on a counterclaim) that the plaintiff was the designer of a particular yacht.[7]

---

1   *Balden v Shorter* [1933] Ch 427, 102 LJ Ch 191.
2   *Lyne v Nicholls* (1906) 23 TLR 86.
3   *Shapiro v La Morta* (1923) 40 TLR 201, CA.
4   *Worsley & Co v Cooper* [1939] 1 All ER 290.
5   *Joyce v Motor Surveys Ltd* [1948] Ch 252.
6   *Serville v Constance* [1954] 1 All ER 662, [1954] 1 WLR 487. The false statement concerned was held to be actionable (in presence of malice) but not in passing off (the action brought).
7   *Customglass Boats Ltd v Salthouse Bros Ltd* [1976] RPC 589.

COMPARISON OF THE ACTION FOR MALICIOUS FALSEHOOD WITH THAT FOR PASSING OFF

8.18   Both malicious falsehood and passing off are based on actions on the case and require proof of damage.[1] In the action for malicious falsehood the false statements relied on can relate to the plaintiff's goods, business or property, in *any* respect.[2] However, a plaintiff in an action for passing off can only rely on representations of a more restricted scope — that the defendant's goods or business are or are connected with the plaintiff's goods or business; however, it is not of course necessary to prove malice.[3]

Sometimes a malicious falsehood takes the form of passing off. Thus in

Wilts United Dairies Ltd v Robinson Sons & Co Ltd[4] the defendant was selling old stocks of tinned milk manufactured by the plaintiffs as and for the plaintiffs' good quality tinned milk. Stable J held that the defendant's conduct constituted malicious falsehood as well as passing off. On an appeal limited to the issue of passing off, the Court of Appeal upheld the judgment of Stable J. In *R Worsley & Co v Cooper*[5] Morton J held that a false statement that the defendants were successors in business to the plaintiffs constituted passing off as well as malicious falsehood, and would have constituted passing off had malice been absent.

---

1 See ch 2 and para 8.04 above.
2 See paras 8.07–8.17 above.
3 See ch 2, above and para 8.01 above.
4 [1957] RPC 220, [1958] RPC 94.
5 [1939] 1 All ER 290.

8.19 It is seldom, however, that a plaintiff relies on the action for malicious falsehood if there is also a case of passing off. This is probably mainly because of the difficulty and cost of proving malice. It is particularly unwise to rely on malicious falsehood if an interlocutory injunction is desired since the courts are reluctant to grant interlocutory injunctions in cases of defamation or malicious falsehood. Thus in *Sim v Heinz & Co Ltd*[1] the plaintiff, an actor, sought to restrain the defendant from using a voice which could be mistaken for the plaintiff's voice, by bringing proceedings for malicious falsehood and passing off. Although the first of these causes of action was abandoned, the Court of Appeal refused interlocutory relief on the grounds that this would have the effect of restraining an alleged falsehood which the defendant intended to justify.[2]

---

1 [1959] 1 All ER 547, [1959] 1 WLR 313.
2 See paras 8.42 and 8.43 below. See also *Lord Brabourne v Hough* [1981] FSR 79.

DAMAGE

8.20 Damage is the 'gist of the action' for malicious falsehood.[1] In all cases of malicious falsehood the plaintiff must therefore prove special damage.[2] Damage is not, however, limited to specific proved incidents and can be in the form of general damage to the business. In *Ratcliffe v Evans* Bowen LJ said:[3]

> 'In an action for falsehood producing damage to a man's trade which in its very nature is intended and reasonably likely to produce, and which in the ordinary course of things does produce, a general loss of business, as distinct from the loss of this or that known customer, evidence of such general decline of business is admissible.'

The task of a plaintiff in proving special damage is rendered easier nowadays by the provisions of the Defamation Act 1952 s 3(1), which provides:

'In an action for slander of goods or other malicious falsehood, it shall not be necessary to allege or prove special damage
   (a) If the words upon which the action is founded are calculated to cause pecuniary damage to the plaintiff and are published in writing or other permanent form; or
   (b) If the said words are calculated to cause pecuniary damage to the plaintiff in respect of any office, profession, calling, trade or business held or carried on by him at the time of the publication.'

It is necessary for the plaintiff to prove that the damage he has suffered results from the acts of the defendant complained of.[4] In an appropriate case, a court will have regard to the likelihood of future damage to the plaintiff and will in such a case grant injunctive relief even if the plaintiff has not yet actually suffered damage.[5]

1   *Royal Baking Powder v Wright* (1900) 18 RPC 95 at 104; *Ratcliffe v Evans* [1892] 2 QB 524 at 528.
2   *Malachy v Soper* (1836) 3 Bing NC 371; *Brook v Rawl* (1849) 4 Exch 521, 19 LJ Ex 114.
3   [1892] 2 QB 524 at 533, 61 LJQB 535.
4   *Barratt v Associated Newspapers Ltd* (1907) 23 TLR 666 at 667; *Alcott v Millar's Karri and Jarrah Forests Ltd* (1904) 91 LT 722 at 724, 21 TLR 30 at 31; *Riding v Smith* (1876) 1 Ex D 91, 45 LJQB 281.
5   *Thomas v Williams* (1880) 14 Ch D 864, 49 LJ Ch 605; *Dunlop Pneumatic Tyre Co Ltd v Maison Talbot* (1904) 20 TLR 579, CA.

MEANING OF 'MALICE'

8.21   In *Pater v Baker*[1] Maule J, relaying on *Pitt v Donovan*[2] (and relied on in turn in *Shapiro v La Morta*[3]), said that the malice which was essential to the tort was not malice 'in the worst sense' but in the sense 'with intention to injure the Plaintiff'. In *Shapiro v La Morta*[4] Atkin LJ gave (albeit obiter) what appears to be the best general definition of 'malice':

'I shall assume that a statement made by a man who knows that it is likely to injure and knows that it is false is made maliciously, and I shall make the same assumption if he knows that it is likely to injure and has no belief whether it is true or false and makes it recklessly, not caring whether it is true or false.'

1   (1847) 3 CB 831, 16 LJ CP 124.
2   (1813) 1 M & S 639.
3   (1924) 40 TLR 201, CA.
4   Ibid at 203, CA.

8.22   There have been all too many other definitions of malice in the decided cases. In *Shapiro v La Morta*[1] Scrutton LJ went so far as to say that 'the terms "malice" and "malicious" have caused more confusion in English law than any Judge can hope to dispel'. A particular cause of difficulty (expressly mentioned by Scrutton LJ) seems to have arisen from Lord Davey's enunciation of the essential elements of the tort of slander of title which included the requirement that the statement complained of 'was made maliciously, ie without just cause and excuse'.[2] As Maugham J observed in *Balden v Shorter*[3] it is possible for an act to be done without just cause and excuse without it being malicious. If it was Lord Davey's intention that his statement should serve as a definition of malice, such a definition must be rejected. In *Joyce v Motor Surveys Ltd*[4] Roxburgh J referred with approval to the definition of 'malice' in *Shapiro v La Morta* but observed that it was not easy to apply in all cases. The learned judge preferred, for the purpose of the case before him, to rely on the statement by Bowen LJ in *Ratcliffe v Evans,*[5] in which malicious falsehood was described as 'an action on the case for damage wilfully and intentionally done without just cause or excuse'.

---

1   (1924) 40 TLR 201 at 203, CA.
2   *Royal Baking Powder Co v Wright* (1900) 18 RPC 95 at 99: see para 8.02 above.
3   [1933] Ch 427 at 430.
4   [1948] Ch 252, [1948] LJR 935.
5   [1892] 2 QB 524, 61 LJQB 535.

8.23   In *Greers Ltd v Pearman and Corder Ltd*[1] Scrutton LJ said that the question of whether a statement was made maliciously had to be decided 'in the sense of it being made with some indirect or dishonest motive.' Maugham J adopted this criterion in *Balden v Shorter*[2] and held that the statement complained of was at the most 'merely careless' and not actionable.

---

1   (1922) 39 RPC 406 at 417.
2   [1933] Ch 427 at 431.

The statutory action for threats of proceedings for infringement of patent or registered design

8.24   Questions of infringement of patent are usually difficult to decide. It may, therefore, not be possible for a court even to determine whether an allegation of infringement of patent is true or false until an infringement action has been heard. Accordingly an allegation of malicious falsehood cannot usually be proved in a case where infringement of patent has been alleged, until a court has decided the questions of infringement and validity at the trial of an infringement action (after which persistence in such allegations is likely to be held malicious).[1]

The statutory action for 'threats', in which allegations of infringement of patent are actionable per se, is therefore much to be preferred if applicable to the facts concerned.[2] The same is true of registered designs.[2]

---

1   See *Halsey v Brotherhood* (1880) 15 Ch D 514 at 520.
2   See para 8.13 above.

Concurrent remedies from threats of legal proceedings

8.25 A plaintiff's statutory rights under the Patents Act 1977 s 70 and the Registered Designs Act 1949 s 26 do not operate to take away any common law rights. Accordingly a plaintiff can rely on actions for malicious falsehood or libel, if appropriate, in either separate or concurrent proceedings, in addition to the statutory action for 'threats'. There are limitations on the right to bring statutory threats proceedings which sometimes make it desirable to rely on some other cause of action. Thus 'threats' proceedings cannot be brought for threats coming within the exclusion in the Patents Act 1977 s 70(4) (which excludes threats of proceedings for infringement alleged to consist of making or importing a product for disposal or using a process) or for allegations of infringement made after the commencement of legal proceedings. In the latter situation, proceedings can be brought for contempt of court[1] in addition to, or alternatively to, proceedings for malicious falsehood or libel.[2]

---

1 See paras 8.26–8.28 below.
2 See paras 8.12 above, and para 8.34 below.

Contempt of court

STATEMENTS CONCERNING THE OUTCOME OF PAST COURT PROCEEDINGS

8.26 It was held in *Gillette Safety Razor Co v A W Gamage Ltd*[1] that a statement by the defendant that an injunction had been refused which failed to make it clear that the refusal was only at the interlocutory stage (because of the plaintiff's delay) constituted contempt of court. However in *Brook v Evans*[2] the defendants circulated an inaccurate account of interlocutory court proceedings concerning passing off. It was held that the statement, though unfair, did not constitute contempt of court.

---

1 (1906) 24 RPC 1.
2 (1860) 29 LJ Ch 616.

STATEMENTS CONCERNING THE OUTCOME OF PENDING
COURT PROCEEDINGS

8.27 In *Daw v Eley*[1] the solicitor for one of the parties to a patent action had participated, under a pseudonym, in public correspondence concerning the merits of the case. It was held that this conduct was 'highly reprehensible' and a contempt of court. Lord Romilly MR said:[2]

> 'the principle is quite established in all these cases, that no person must do anything... which might possibly induce the court... to come to any conclusion other than that which is to be derived from the evidence in the case between the parties... The Court must stop the publication where the evident result would be to affect the administration of justice even though that might not have been the intention of the person who did it.'

In *J & P Coats v Chadwick*[3] Chitty J held that parties to an action are bound to refrain during its pendency from public discussion on the merits or demerits of the case. An injunction was granted restraining publication of what the Court described as 'a strong one-sided statement on the merits of the case'. A similar view of the law was expressed in *St Mungo Manufacturing Co v Hutchinson Main & Co Ltd*[4] (a Scottish case) in which Lord Salvesen said: 'The merits of the case should not be tried or discussed in publications by interested parties.' In the earlier case of *Goulard v Lindsay*[5] Kay J went so far as to hold that, if there was an action pending, 'to advertise a positive statement that the Defendant had infringed was wrong' and the plaintiffs undertook to withdraw the advertisement complained of.

---

1 (1868) LR 7 Eq 49, 38 LJ Ch 113.
2 Ibid at 59 and at 115.
3 [1894] 1 Ch 347, 63 LJ Ch 328.
4 (1908) 25 RPC 356.
5 (1887) 4 RPC 189.

8.28 The general judicial view is, however, that the above three cases went too far. *Coats v Chadwick*[1] has twice been disapproved.[2] In *Carl-Zeiss Stiftung v Rayner & Keeler Ltd*[3] Russell J was content to distinguish these cases from the case before him and to indicate that, if not so distinguished, they went too far. In *Fenner v Wilson*[4] Kekewitch J, following *Goulard v Lindsay*,[5] granted an injunction to restrain a general warning to infringers issued by the defendants (who had started proceedings for infringement of patent): the judgment was, however, reversed by the Court of Appeal who held that 'it would be extravagant to treat these advertisements as a contempt of Court'.[6]

---

1 [1894] 1 Ch 347.
2 See *R v Payne* [1896] 1 QB 577, 65 LJ QB 426; *Re New Gold Coast Exploration* [1901] 1 Ch 860, 70 LJ Ch 355.
3 [1960] 3 All ER 289, [1961] RPC 1.
4 (1893) 9 TLR 496, 10 RPC 283, CA.
5 (1887) 4 RPC 189.
6 (1893) 9 TLR 496, 10 RPC 283, CA.

WARNINGS

8.29 In *Goulard v Lindsay*[1] Key J said 'You can warn as much as you like but can you advertise "I have brought an action against AB which is certain to succeed?" '. In later cases, however, emphasis had been placed only on the first part of this statement. Indeed in *Carl-Zeiss Stiftung v Rayner & Keeler Ltd*[2] Russell J rejected any general prohibition on such advertisements as 'very difficult to reconcile with other decisions'.

General warnings to infringers have been held not to be actionable either as 'threats' in reliance on the Patents or Registered Designs Acts or as malicious falsehoods[3] and the same principle appears to apply to contempt of court proceedings. It is, moreover, acceptable for general warnings to include references to the merits of the case, such as assertions to the effect that 'the writer is entitled to the trade marks relied on and the other people concerned are not'[4] or 'I say my patent is good and I say you are infringing it; I have commenced an action in which I am going to maintain the affirmative of that, in which of course I may be defeated and I may be wrong'.[5]

---

1   (1887) 4 RPC 189.
2   [1960] 3 All ER 289, [1961] RPC 1.
3   See para 8.13 above.
4   *Carl-Zeiss Stiftung v Rayner and Keeler Ltd* [1961] RPC 1 at 11–12.
5   *Haskell Golf Ball Co v Hutchinson and Main* (1904) 21 RPC 497 at 500.

8.30   In *Mullard Radio Valve Co Ltd v Rothermel Corpn Ltd*[1] Farwell J held that a mere statement of confidence in the success of a pending action was not a contempt of court and held that even though the document before him was 'unfortunate in its terms' and might have been construed so as to suggest (falsely) that the validity of the patent had been established (which would have been a contempt) the defendants did not intend to do anything improper: the motion failed but the defendants were not given their costs. In *Gaskell & Chambers v Hudson, Dodsworth & Co*[2] the defendant to a patent infringement action circulated a statement expressing their refusal to be intimidated by the plaintiff's action. It was held that there was no contempt. In *British Vacuum Cleaner Co Ltd v Suction Cleaners Ltd*[3] one of the parties had circulated a statement about the pending action, shortly before the case was to be heard. No order was made on the motion on the grounds that the result of the case was unlikely to be affected by the circular.[4]

---

1   (1934) 51 RPC 1.
2   [1936] 2 KB 595.
3   (1904) 21 RPC 303.
4   For other cases where contempt proceedings have failed against 'general warnings' see *Dunlop Pneumatic Tyre Co Ltd v Clifton Rubber Co Ltd* (1902) 19 RPC 527; *Selsdon Fountain Pen Co Ltd v Miles Martin Pen Co Ltd* (1948) 65 RPC 365 at 367.

Libel and slander

LIBEL

8.31   A libel is a defamatory statement in some permanent form published of and concerning the plaintiff, communicated to some other person than the plaintiff.[1] 'Defamatory' means 'damaging to a person's reputation', in particular (in the present context), disparaging of or injurious to him in his office, profession, calling, trade or business.[2]

Statements can be defamatory when made about a corporation as well as a natural person. In *South Hetton Coal Co v North Eastern News Association*[3] Lopes LJ said:

> 'Although a corporation cannot maintain an action for libel in respect of anything reflecting upon them personally yet they can maintain an action for a libel reflecting on the management of their trade or business, and this without alleging or proving special damage. The words complained of in order to entitle a corporation or company to sue for libel or slander, must injuriously affect the corporation or company as distinct from the individuals which comprise it. The words complained of must attack the corporation or company in the method of conducting its affairs, must accuse it of fraud or mismanagement, or must attack its financial position.'

The most valuable general criterion for deciding whether there has been a libel in a business sense is probably that propounded by the House of Lords in *Sim v Stretch*.[4] 'Would it tend to lower the Plaintiff in the estimation of right thinking members of society generally?' This would particularly apply to statements impugning the plaintiff's competence, honesty or financial position.[5]

---

1 See Duncan and Neil *Defamation* (2nd edn, 1984) ch 3.
2 Duncan and Neil *Defamation* (2nd edn, 1984) ch 7.
3 [1894] 1 QB 133, 63 LJ QB 293.
4 [1936] 2 All ER 1237 at 1240, 52 TLR 669 at 671.
5 See *South Hetton Coal Co v North Eastern News Association* [1894] 1 QB 133, 63 LJ QB 293.

8.32 The line between a statement made in disparagement of goods (actionable only on proof of malice and damage) and a defamatory statement (actionable per se) may be difficult to draw in a particular case. Thus in *Evans v Harlow*[1] and *Griffiths v Benn*[2] the plaintiff failed to prove that the statements complained of were defamatory of the plaintiff. However, in *Drummond-Jackson v BMA*[3] a majority of the Court of Appeal refused to strike out a statement of claim in which the alleged libel was a statement concerning a dentist's technique. In response to a submission that such a statement was comparable to a statement concerning goods, and not a personal libel, Lord Pearson said:[4]

> 'I doubt whether the analogy sought to be drawn between a trader's goods and a professional man's technique is sound. Goods are impersonal and transient. A professional man's technique is at least relatively permanent, and it belongs to him: it may be considered to be an essential part of his professional activity and of him as a professional man. In the case of a dentist it may be said: if he uses a bad technique he is a bad dentist and a person needing dental treatment should not go to him.'

---

1 (1844) 5 QB 624, 13 LJQB 120. See para 8.06 above.
2 (1911) 27 TLR 346, CA. See para 8.06 above.
3 [1970] 1 All ER 1094, [1970] 1 WLR 688.
4 Ibid at 1104, and at 698, 699.

8.33 'Defamation' and 'malicious falsehood' are not mutually exclusive terms. Thus in the *Linotype Co Ltd v British Empire Typesetting Machine Co*,[1] the House of Lords held that a particular statement could be both defamatory and in disparagement of goods. Lord Halsbury said:[2]

> 'It is quite possible to make a reflection which, by the mere form of expression, would seem to be only a criticism of goods, but nevertheless would involve a reflection upon the seller or maker. Could it be gravely argued that to say of a fishmonger that he was in the habit of selling decomposed fish would not be a libel upon him in the way of his trade?'

It was held in that case that the defendant's statement that the use of typesetting machines installed by the plaintiff was discontinued was defamatory of the plaintiff (as conveying an imputation of lack of competence and skill in their trade) as well as untrue of the goods themselves. The plaintiff succeeded on the issue of libel only, there being no evidence of special damage or malice. Similarly in *Bendle v United Kingdom Alliance*[3] the Court of Appeal held (Phillimore LJ dissenting) that a statement that the plaintiffs' wine, though advertised as 'nutritious', did not have highly nutritious properties would be understood as imputing to the plaintiffs a dishonesty or fraudulent incapacity in the way of conducting their business. Accordingly the plaintiffs succeeded on the issue of libel.

---

1 (1899) 81 LT 331, 15 TLR 524, HL.
2 Ibid at 333.
3 (1915) 31 TLR 403, CA.

Allegations of infringement of patent, trade mark, copyright, registered design or passing off

8.34 In *Thomas Withers & Sons Ltd v Samuel Withers & Co Ltd*[1] the plaintiffs brought an action for libel in reliance on the defendants' statement that the plaintiffs were deceiving purchasers and users of safes into believing that their safes were genuine 'Withers safes' and that the plaintiffs were infringing the defendants' registered trade mark 'Withers Safes'. Wright J, however, held the statement to be 'a fair general caution to purchasers' and not personally defamatory to the plaintiffs.

---

1 (1926) 44 RPC 19.

Statements concerning past or pending court proceedings

8.35 Fair and accurate reports of Court proceedings are privileged and cannot be the subject of libel proceedings. If inaccurate or misleading, however, or if published maliciously, such reports may be actionable.[1] In *Hayward & Co v Hayward & Sons*[2] a circular issued by the defendants misstating the result of an action for passing off was held to constitute a libel and the plaintiffs were granted an injunction to restrain the circulation of the document.

1   See Duncan and Neil *Defamation* (2nd edn, 1984), chs 14 and 17.
2   (1886) 34 Ch D 198. 56 LJ Ch 287. It is somewhat unclear whether libel or trade libel was being relied on.

Use of name of non-trader

8.36   In *Tolley v Fry & Sons Ltd*[1] the defendant used the name of the plaintiff, a well-known amateur golfer, in an advertisement for chocolate. The plaintiff succeeded in an action for libel on the footing of an innuendo that he was no longer an amateur, having accepted payment for the advertisement. This is one way in which a person can prevent his name being used for commercial purposes without his permission. The decline of the prominence of the amateur in sport has reduced the scope for this type of action as a means of preventing 'character merchandising' without the plaintiff's permission.[2]

1   [1931] AC 333, 100 LJKB 328.
2   See ch 3, paras 3.53–3.54 above for a discussion of how character merchandising may, however, now give rise to a claim in passing off.

SLANDER

8.37   Statements may be defamatory when not in permanent form. However, such statements are actionable only on proof of damage, with certain statutory exceptions.[1]

1   See para 8.05 above.

The action for malicious falsehood

8.38   The action for malicious falsehood is begun by writ and the general procedure is as for passing off.[1]

1   See ch 7 above.

STATEMENT OF CLAIM

8.39   The plaintiff must identify the false statement relied on and plead its falsity and the fact that the defendant made it.[1] Malice must be expressly pleaded with proper particulars of all facts relied on.[2] Since damage is 'the gist of the action' it must be pleaded, with appropriate particulars.[3] The Defamation Act 1952, s 3(1) insofar as relevant, must be pleaded.[4] If the plaintiff relies on an innuendo this should be expressly pleaded.[5]

1   See paras 8.07–8.17 above.
2   See RSC Ord 8, r 12(1)(b).

3 See Ord 18 r 12; para 18/12/32. *Anglo-Cyprian Trade Agencies Ltd v Paphos Wine Industries Ltd* [1951] 1 All ER 873 at 875.
4 See para 8.20 above.
5 Ord 82, r 3(1).

DEFENCE

8.40 A defence to an action for malicious falsehood usually consists mainly of denials. Any facts expressly relied on to refute allegations of falsity, malice or damage should, however, be pleaded.

PROOF OF MALICE

8.41 In *British Rly Traffic and Electric Co v CRC*[1] McCardie J said: 'malice is a question of motive, intention or state of mind. Apart from reliance on admissions, a Plaintiff can only prove his case of malice by means of inferences from other facts.' Such inferences may be drawn from the absence of probable cause[2] (ie an alternative honest reason for making the statement) or from knowledge that the makers of the statement knew it to be false.[3] Although honest belief in an unfounded claim is not malice,

'the nature of the unfounded claim may be evidence that there was not an honest belief in it. It may be so unfounded that the particular fact that it is put forward may be evidence that it is not honestly believed.'[4]

Persistence in a statement initially made bona fide, after the falsity of the statement becomes known, may convert a bona fide statement into a statement made maliciously: the court may grant an injunction or appropriate declaration if it appears that the defendant intends to continue to make such statements.[5]

1 [1922] 2 KB 260 at 269.
2 *Pater v Baker* (1847) 3 CB 831, 16 LJCP 1240.
3 *British Rly Traffic and Electric Co v CRC Co Ltd* [1922] 2 KB 260 at 271 (referring to *Fountain v Boodle* (1842) 3 QB 5).
4 *Greers Ltd v Pearman and Corder Ltd* (1922) 39 RPC 406, CA.
5 *Loudon v Ryder (No 2)* [1953] Ch 423 at 428; *Halsey v Brotherhood* (1880) 15 Ch D 514 at 520.

INTERLOCUTORY INJUNCTIONS

8.42 The courts are reluctant to grant interlocutory injunctions in cases of alleged libel for reasons given by the Master of the Rolls in *Fraser v Evans*:[1]

'If a Defendant relies on a defence of justification, or fair comment on a matter of public interest, the Courts will not restrain the publication of the alleged libel, on the grounds of public interest.'

As a result interlocutory injunctions are not granted in defamation cases where the defendant claims that he intends to justify unless it is clear that justification is impossible.[2] Thus interlocutory injunctions were refused where the defendant took the door of his house and paraded it around on his car with defamatory remarks as to its quality attached,[3] where a magazine accused the (female) plaintiff of having affairs with a number of prominent men even though not all could be proved as the overall sting of the allegation was one of general promiscuity,[4] or where a newspaper said it intended to justify the entire thrust of an article only parts of which were said by the plaintiff to be defamatory.[5] However, even if the words complained of are admittedly true, and therefore can be justified, their publication can be restrained by interlocutory injunction where it is shown that the purpose of publication is in furtherance of a conspiracy to inflict damage on the plaintiff.[6] It is also noteworthy that the rule against granting interlocutory injunctions in cases of defamation and malicious falsehood will not generally apply if the plaintiff can also frame his action in breach of confidence.[7] In such cases the defendant will have to show that there is a public interest in publication to avoid an injunction.[8]

1 [1969] 1 QB 349 at 360, [1969] 1 All ER 8 at 10. See also *William Coulson & Sons Ltd v James Coulson & Co Ltd* (1887) 3 TLR 846, CA; *Bonnard v Perryman* [1891] 2 Ch 269, 60 LJ Ch 617, CA; *Hubbard v Pitt* [1976] QB 142, [1975] 3 All ER 1.
2 *Tolley v J S Fry & Sons Limited* [1931] AC 333; *William Coulson & Sons v James Coulson & Co* (1887) 3 TLR 846.
3 *Crest Homes v Ascott* [1980] FSR 396.
4 *Kashoggi v IPC Magazines Limited* [1986] 3 All ER 577.
5 *Polly Peck (Holdings) plc v Trelford* [The Observer] [1986] 2 All ER 84.
6 *Gulf Oil (GB) Limited* [1987] 3 All ER 14.
7 See *Fraser v Evans* (above) at 362.
8 *Lion Laboratories Limited v Evans* [1985] 1QB 526; *R v Advertising Standards Authority Limited ex parte Vernons* [1992] 1 WLR 1289.

8.43 The courts have adopted the same principles in cases of malicious falsehood and are equally reluctant to grant interlocutory relief. In *Thorley's Cattle Food v Massam*, the Court refused to grant an interlocutory injunction[1] but later granted a final injunction after the plaintiffs had proved their case at the trial.[2] In *Sim v Heinz & Co Ltd*[3] the plaintiff's initial case was one of malicious falsehood and passing off, but malicious falsehood was abandoned: nevertheless the Court refused an interlocutory injunction. In *Bestobell Paints Ltd v Bigg*[4] Oliver J, after a thorough review of the authorities, refused interlocutory relief.[5] Where, however, it is plain that the statement is false and has been uttered maliciously an interlocutory injunction will be granted.[6] However, even in such cases, the court will take into account in assessing the balance of convenience the defendant's freedom of speech and any injunction granted by it should not interfere with that.[7]

1 (1877) 6 Ch D 582.
2 (1880) 14 Ch D 763.
3 [1959] 1 All ER 547, [1959] 1 WLR 313.
4 [1975] FSR 421. Followed in *Mainmeet Holdings plc v Austin* [1991] FSR 538.
5 See also *Lord Brabourne v Hough* [1981] FSR 79.
6 See eg *Kaye v Robertson* [1991] FSR 62.
7 *Compaq Computer Corporation v Dell Computer Corporation Limited* [1992] FSR 93.

THE TRIAL

8.44 In former times the facts were decided by a jury, as in modern defamation cases. However, the normal modern practice is for the case to be tried in the Chancery Division by a judge sitting alone.[1]

---

1 See *Bestobell Paints Ltd v Bigg* [1975] FSR 421 at 430.

THE RELIEF GRANTED

Injunction

8.45 In *Thomas v Williams*[1] Fry LJ held that the court could grant an injunction for a libel affecting property. It is customary to grant final injunctions to successful plaintiffs in appropriate cases of malicious falsehood where the falsehood is likely to be repeated.

---

1 (1880) 14 Ch D 864, 49 LJ Ch 605.

Damages and costs

8.46 Damages and costs are awarded in actions for malicious falsehood on the same basis as that generally adopted for actions in tort.[1]

---

1 See ch 7, paras 7.51–7.60 above.

CHAPTER 9

Related causes of action

Introduction

9.01 As we have seen, whilst passing off is a means of obtaining redress for
unfair competition, not all forms of unfair competition can be fitted within
the confines of that tort.[1] Conversely, an activity which does constitute
passing off, may also amount to a variety of other wrongs. Thus, it may
be that whilst there is no claim for passing off, another claim is available to
prevent other forms of unfair competition. Alternatively, it may be advisable
to add further claims to a validly constituted passing off action. Accordingly,
in any circumstances in which a claim for passing off is under consideration
it is always wise to consider whether there may also be other causes of action
which can be pursued. Until now the present work has been concerned only
to consider claims for passing off. However, no practitioner can properly
advise on a possible claim for passing off without also considering other
potential claims which may arise from the facts with which he is presented.
The purpose of this chapter is, therefore, to provide in an easily accessible
form an outline of the most directly relevant alternative claims.[2] These are
registered trade marks, copyright and registered and unregistered designs.
The present chapter should not be considered as being in any way a
substitute for a full textbook on any of these subjects, each of which is
complex and technical.[3] For example topics such as restoration of lapsed
trade marks and registered designs, compulsory licences, Crown user and
the procedures for registration and rectification of the registers are not
touched upon. What it can do is provide a sufficient indication of the
likelihood that such a claim may be relevant to enable the necessary further
research to be undertaken. The following text is concerned only with these
parallel rights insofar as they overlap with or are closely related to passing off.
All of these related causes of action also provide protection of other kinds
not considered here.

---

1 See ch 1, para 1.09.
2 Other than malicious falsehood and defamation which are so important and closely related that
   they are dealt with separately in ch 8.
3 There are excellent textbooks dealing with all these topics. Copyright is comprehensively covered
   in *The Modern Law of Copyright* by Laddie Prescott & Vitoria (2nd edn, 1995, Butterworths).
   Copinger & Skone James (7th edn, 1990, Sweet & Maxwell) is also a standard work on
   this subject. Both these also deal with industrial designs generally. A textbook devoted
   to the law of industrial designs is *The Law of Industrial Design* by Tootal   (1990, CCH
   Editions).

Registered trade marks

INTRODUCTION

9.02 The law of registered trade marks has just been completely revised and an entirely new statute enacted to bring United Kingdom law into conformity with the requirements of the EC Directive on the harmonization of trade mark laws.[1] The Trade Marks Act 1994 ('the 1994 Act') came into force on 31 October 1994. All its substantive provisions are new and there is as yet no jurisprudence on the operation of its provisions. Providing guidance as to their meaning is therefore rather difficult. To some extent one can draw upon the approach of the courts under the previous legislation. But the new law is just that. It does not follow any previous statutory language and is clearly intended to bring into effect a new scheme of registration. It makes many sweeping changes in the law. The distinction between part A and part B registrations has been abolished and there is now a single scheme for registering marks for goods and services. The requirements for obtaining a valid registration are entirely new. The scope of the protection conferred by a registration is entirely different: for the first time under English law it is possible to infringe a trade mark registration by using a mark upon goods or services outside those for which the registration has been granted. We are indeed embarking upon a new era of trade mark registration and it will be interesting to see how different in reality the new approach is from the old.

---

1   EC Council Directive number 89/104/EEC.

WHAT MAY BE REGISTERED

9.03 The new definition of a trade mark is contained in section 1(1) of the 1994 Act and is as follows:

> 'a "trade mark" means any sign capable of being represented graphically which is capable of distinguishing goods or services of one undertaking from those of other undertakings.
>
> A trade mark may, in particular, consist of words (including personal names), designs, letters, numerals or the shape of goods or their packaging.'

Thus, it can be seen that the old law that the shape of packaging was not capable of being a trade mark[1] has been reversed and that the only limitations on what may be registered are now that it be a sign capable of 'being represented graphically' and 'distinguishing goods or services' of undertakings from one another. Clearly any mark which consists of words or letters, a logo or a pictorial design or any combination of these is capable of being represented graphically. Thus any form of mark which was registrable under the old law will remain so. Rather startlingly it has been suggested in a number of texts that the requirement that the sign be capable of being represented graphically will not prevent the registration of sounds or smells.

This appears to be on the basis that a sound or a smell can be described in words which can be written down and thus the mark is represented graphically. It is difficult to understand the logic behind this approach and it is suggested that it constitutes wishful thinking rather than intellectually sound analysis. One has only to consider the difficulty that even highly trained and experienced oenologists have in accurately describing the taste and smell of wine to realise that to permit registrations in such a form would be to open the door to hopeless difficulties of interpretation in any action for infringement. We venture to suggest that the courts will take a rather less adventurous approach to this requirement and allow registration only for signs which can directly be written, drawn or photographed. Nevertheless, the effect of this broadening of the scope of the definition of a mark is in effect to allow to be registered in principle almost anything which is capable of being a distinguishing indicium for the purposes of a claim for passing off.

---

1 See *Coca-Cola Trade Mark* [1986] RPC 421.

9.04 The requirement that the sign be 'capable of distinguishing' the goods or services of undertakings from one another is identical in language to the requirements of the former s 10[1] which determined the registrability of marks in part B of the Trade Marks Register. It seems reasonable to assume that the legislature's intention was to equate this part of the definition with the requirements of that provision. It would therefore seem to follow that it will not be sufficient to permit registration that a mark has the capacity to distinguish in fact. It must also be capable of distinguishing in law.[2] This seems to be confirmed by the provisions of the 1994 Act which lay down a series of 'absolute grounds' for the refusal of a registration which exclude from registration any trade marks which are 'devoid of any distinctive character'[3] or which:

> 'consist exclusively of signs or indications which may serve, in trade, to designate the kind, quality, quantity, intended purpose, value, geographical origin, the time of production of goods or rendering of services, or other characteristics of goods or services.'[4]

The effect of this exclusion is, however, restricted by the qualification that registration shall not be refused on the above grounds if a mark has before the date of application for registration 'in fact acquired a distinctive character as a result of use made of it'.[5] The precise intention of the legislature is not entirely easy to determine from the statutory language. It is, for example, difficult to see how something which is devoid of *any* distinctive character can acquire distinctiveness by use. Logically, however, the position now seems to be that a mark which is devoid of any distinctive character or which consists exclusively of signs or indications of the type indicated may nonetheless be registered if, by use, it has become distinctive. Taken with the broader definition of what constitutes a mark, the reduction in the standard of distinctiveness required to enable the grant of a registration should mean that it becomes very much easier to obtain registrations than was previously the case.

---

1 Of the Trade Marks Act 1938.
2 See *York Trade Mark* [1984] RPC 231 (HL).
3 S 3(1)(b) of the 1994 Act.
4 S 3(1)(c) of the 1994 Act.
5 Loc cit.

9.05 Registration is also prohibited on a series of other absolute grounds. Thus, the shape of goods may not be registered insofar as it results from the nature of the goods themselves, is necessary to obtain a technical result or gives substantial value to the goods.[1] Nor may marks which are contrary to public policy or morality, or which are deceptive or whose use is prohibited by law be registered.[2] There is also a specific prohibition on registration of an application to register made in bad faith.[3] The 1994 Act contains conventional restrictions on registering marks which consist of Royal or national emblems and the like.[4] Registration is also prohibited on a number of what are referred to as 'relative' grounds. In essence relative grounds consist of conflict with existing rights. Thus a mark which is identical to an earlier registered mark registered for the same goods or services or so similar to it in appearance and scope as to give rise to a likelihood of confusion may not be registered.[5] Nor may a mark which is identical to a previous registered mark be registered for any goods or services if the later registration would 'take unfair advantage of or be detrimental to the distinctive character of' the previous registration.[6] This is presumably intended to prevent the registration of famous marks by people other than the proprietor. It is an exception to refusal on relative grounds that there has been honest concurrent user of the later mark[7] and honest concurrent user is specifically defined as having the same meaning as under the 1938 Act.[8] A registration will be invalid if it has been granted in contravention of any of the restrictions referred to above and accordingly it is a ground of invalidity that this is so.[9] Anyone may apply to have a registration declared invalid.[9]

---

1 S 3(2) of the 1994 Act.
2 S 3(3) and (4) of the 1994 Act. This closely parallels the prohibition on registration contained in s 11 of the 1938 Act and it is likely that the courts will apply the same principles in determining its effect.
3 S 3(6) of the 1994 Act. This is the corollary to the requirement of s 32(3) that the application shall contain a statement that the applicant is using or has a bona fide intention to use the mark and gives the registrar or the court the power to refuse or revoke a registration where such a statement has been falsely made. The wording is very similar to that in s 26(1)(a) of the 1938 Act and, again, it is likely that the result is intended to be much the same.
4 S 4.
5 S 5(1) and (2) of the 1994 Act.
6 S 5(3) of the 1994 Act.
7 S 7(1) of the 1994 Act.
8 S 7(2) of the 1994 Act which expressly provides that the term means the same as the same term used in s 12(2) of the 1938 Act.
9 S 47 of the 1994 Act.

9.06   Registrations are granted within classes[1] of goods and services. The Registrar's decision as to within which class particular goods or services fall is final.[2] Both these provisions continue a long-standing practice. An application must specify the scope of goods or services for which a registration is sought[3] and those goods or services must all fall within a single class. If they do not, separate registrations are required. Registrations are granted initially for ten years.[4] They may be renewed thereafter every ten years upon payment of renewal fees.[4] A registration can be revoked if a mark is not used for a period of five years.[5] It may also be revoked if it has become the common name for the product or service for which it is registered or has become deceptive as a result of the proprietor's activities.[6]

---

1   S 34(1) of the 1994 Act.
2   S 34(2) of the 1994 Act.
3   S 32(2)(c) of the 1994 Act.
4   Ss 42 and 43 of the 1994 Act. The old law provided that the initial registration lasted for seven years and subsequent renewals for fourteen.
5   S 46(1)(a) and (b) of the 1994 Act.
6   S 46(1)(c) and (d) of the 1994 Act.

RIGHTS OBTAINED BY REGISTRATION

9.07   The proprietor of a registered trade mark has exclusive rights in the trade mark and those rights are infringed by the activities specified in the 1994 Act.[1] It is in relation to the width of the infringement provisions that the new law of trade marks is most strikingly different from the old. Until now only use of an identical or deceptively similar mark on goods or services which were within the specification of goods or services for which a registration had been granted could infringe that registration. This is no longer the case.[2] It is now an infringement of a trade mark registration to use an identical mark on goods or services for which it is registered[3] or to use an identical or similar mark on similar goods or services where that use gives rise to a likelihood of confusion.[4] The likelihood of confusion includes the conventional concept of confusion with the goods or services of the registered proprietor[5] and also 'the likelihood of association with the trade mark'.[4] It is far from clear what this adds to the conventional concept. It is reasonably plain that comparative advertising is no longer prevented[6] so that association with the trade mark must cover something else. No doubt in time the courts will determine what. It is also an infringement of a registration to use a trade mark on goods or services which are not similar to those for which it is registered where the mark has a reputation and the use takes unfair advantage of it or is detrimental to its distinctive character or repute.[7] This provision too is entirely new and it is difficult to predict precisely what will be considered to fall within it although it is reasonably plain that it is aimed at giving a greater ambit of protection to famous marks. Overall the test for infringement is now much closer to that for

225

passing off: will there really be confusion. The primary exception to this is that it remains an infringement to use a mark identical to that registered on goods for which it is registered without consideration of the likelihood of confusion. Such a case is, however, generally very simple. The former advantage of a trade mark action (at least for infringement of a part A registration) that it was possible to present an action as involving only the simple issue whether the registered mark and the alleged infringement were confusingly similar has gone. This means that the circumstances in which summary judgment is available in a trade mark action have been greatly curtailed. This was one of the major advantages of possessing a registered trade mark, particularly as the validity of an established registration in part A could only be challenged on very limited grounds[8] with the result that it was frequently possible to say that there was no real defence to a claim for infringement.

---

1   S 9(1) of the 1994 Act.
2   The transitional provisions, however, provide that it is not an infringement of an existing registration to continue activities which were not an infringement before the 1994 Act came into force: see ch 3 para 4(2).
3   S 10(1) of the 1994 Act.
4   S 10(2) of the 1994 Act.
5   This is not expressly stated but is clearly intended.
6   S 10(6) permits the use of a mark to identify the goods or services of the registered proprietor except insofar as that use is not 'in accordance with honest practices in industrial or commercial matters'. What this means only the courts can tell us. Reference to Parliamentary debates indicates that comparative advertising is intended to be lawful under the new regime.
7   S 10(3) of the 1994 Act.
8   See s 13 of the Trade Marks Act 1938.

9.08   There are of course limits to the effect of a trade mark registration. The old law that use of one registered trade mark cannot infringe another registration has been preserved.[1] Equally, the use of a trader's own name and address[2] and indications about the nature of the goods which are excluded from registration[3] are not infringements. Nor is it an infringement to use a trade mark where this is necessary to indicate the intended purpose of goods or services, particularly where they are designed to be used as accessories to or spares for goods of the trade mark proprietor.[4] Each of these exclusions is subject to the requirement that the use 'is in accordance with honest practices in industrial or commercial matters'.[5] It will be interesting indeed to see what the courts make of this but it seems unlikely that the protection from a finding of infringement will be lost by conduct which would not be considered essentially dishonest by a reasonable person. The old law that activities which commenced before the date of first use or registration by the proprietor were not infringements has also been preserved, although in slightly different terms.[6] There is now an express provision that use of a mark on goods which have previously been marketed within the European Economic Area by the proprietor or with his consent does not infringe.[7] Whilst the provision is new it does not change the law.[8] Finally a mark may be registered subject to a disclaimer to exclusive rights in particular parts of the mark or to other limitations. Any use falling within the scope of such a disclaimer or limitation does not infringe the registration.[9]

1   S 11(1) of the 1994 Act.
2   S 11(2)(a) of the 1994 Act.
3   S 11(2)(b) excludes from infringement indications of the kind excluded from registration by s 3(1)(c): see para 9.04 above.
4   S 11(2)(c) of the 1994 Act.
5   S 11(2) of the 1994 Act.
6   S 11(3) of the 1994 Act.
7   S 12 of the 1994 Act.
8   See ch 10, para 10.07.
9   S 13 of the 1994 Act.

REMEDIES FOR INFRINGEMENT

9.09   The remedies for infringement by way of damages, injunctions and accounts are those available in respect of the infringement of any other property right.[1] In addition, the successful plaintiff is entitled to erasure or obliteration of the offending marks from any materials in the defendant's possession and, if this is not reasonably practicable, to the destruction of those materials.[2] The 1994 Act also provides that the proprietor may apply for delivery up of infringing goods or other material.[3] Anything which is delivered up pursuant to such an application must be held by the person to whom it is delivered until the court determines whether it shall be destroyed or forfeited.[4] There is a curious provision that in deciding whether to make such an order the court shall consider whether the other remedies available to the proprietor for the infringement would adequately compensate him.[5] This implies that the court may allow the proprietor to keep and dispose of the goods which seems odd as the purpose of any proceedings is to prevent them being sold under a mark to which they are not entitled. An interesting and potentially important remedy is the possibility of having goods bearing an infringing mark treated as 'prohibited goods'.[6] Under these provisions the proprietor of a registered trade mark may give notice to the Commissioners of Customs and Excise of the importation of infringing goods and have them seized. Use of a registered trade mark is also a criminal offence.[7] The criminal regime is enforced by the Trading Standards Departments of local councils and penalties may be severe.[8] Whilst this is not strictly a remedy for infringement, criminal proceedings are sometimes used as an alternative to civil proceedings.

1   S 14(2) of the 1994 Act. This provision is identical to the corresponding provision in relation to copyright: see para 9.19 below.
2   S 15 of the 1994 Act.
3   S 16 of the 1994 Act.
4   Ss 16(4) and 19 of the 1994 Act.
5   S 19(2) of the 1994 Act.
6   Ss 89–91 of the 1994 Act. These provisions are complex and interact with a corresponding EC

Council Regulation (no 3842/86) in an extremely elaborate way. An important feature of their operation is that the Commissioners of Customs and Excise require to be indemnified by the trade mark proprietor against the consequences of any seizure being held to have been wrongful.

7 Ss 92 to 98 of the 1994 Act. There are also less serious offences of falsifying the register of trade marks and falsely representing that a trade mark is registered. The criminal regime is not new. It was introduced in 1986.

8 Summary conviction carries a possible statutory maximum fine (presently £2,000) or six months' imprisonment. Conviction on indictment carries an unlimited fine or up to ten years' imprisonment.

DEALINGS IN REGISTERED TRADE MARKS

9.10 Under the old law, licensing and assignment of trade marks was closely controlled, at least in theory. The 1994 Act greatly relaxes the regime governing dealings in trade marks, bringing it largely into line with the regimes for other forms of statutory intellectual property rights. A registered trade mark is personal property[1] and devolves upon assignment or operation of law in the same way as other personal property.[2] Such transmission may be either in connection with the goodwill of a business or separately[2] and of the whole registration or only part of the specification or geographical area covered by the registration.[3] Any assignment must be in writing and signed by or on behalf of the assignor.[4] A trade mark registration may be charged by way of security.[5] It may also be licensed either in whole or in part.[6] An exclusive licensee may be granted the right to bring proceedings for infringement in his own name.[7] Otherwise, and always in the case of non-exclusive licensees, the licensee may call upon the proprietor to bring proceedings and, if he does not, the statute gives the licensee the right to do so himself.[8] Transactions in registered trade marks must be entered on the register in order to be effective against those subsequently acquiring a competing interest and failure to register an assignment within six months of its occurrence will normally debar any pecuniary claim under the trade mark until registration has been effected.[9]

1 S 23(1) of the 1994 Act.
2 S 24(1) of the 1994 Act.
3 S 24(2) of the 1994 Act.
4 S 24(3) of the 1994 Act.
5 Ss 24(4) and (5) of the 1994 Act. It has long been assumed that a trade mark may be made the subject of an assignment or charge by way of security. The express provisions permitting this are, however, new. S 23(6) expressly excludes unregistered marks from these provisions. Thus, it remains the case that the goodwill of a business carried on under unregistered distinctive indicia may only be transmitted as part of the business itself.
6 S 28 of the 1994 Act.
7 S 31(1) of the 1994 Act.
8 S 30 of the 1994 Act.
9 S 25 of the 1994 Act.

REMEDY FOR UNJUSTIFIED THREATS

9.11 The 1994 Act has also introduced into registered trade mark law the right to bring proceedings against someone who threatens to bring proceedings for infringement of a registered trade mark unless the threatened proceedings are justified.[1] Under this provision the only defence is to show that the conduct complained of is in fact an infringement of the registered trade mark in question. A threats action will succeed if the activities complained of are outside the scope of protection conferred by the registration or if the registration is invalid. A threat of proceedings for applying the mark to goods, importing goods with the offending mark on or supplying services under the mark is not actionable. Nor is the mere notification that a mark is registered or that an application to register it has been made. These provisions are in substance identical to those found in the Patents Act 1977.[2]

---

1   S 21 of the 1994 Act.
2   S 71.

COMPARISON OF THE ACTION FOR PASSING OFF WITH THAT FOR INFRINGEMENT OF REGISTERED TRADE MARK

9.12   In principle an action for infringement of registered trade mark is simpler and cheaper than one for passing off. There is no need to prove reputation or damage. The former advantage that infringement was easier to determine has been largely eliminated by the infringement provisions of the new law. Only in the limiting case where the registered mark and the alleged infringement are identical does that advantage remain. The broadening of the infringement provisions to include use on goods or services similar to but outside the scope of the registration makes the action for infringement much more similar in scope to that for passing off and it has been suggested that as a result the action for passing off will in time be subsumed into that for infringement of registered trade mark. In reality this is unlikely to happen, at least for some time. Only those who bother to register will be able to bring proceedings for infringement and passing off is a very flexible and adaptable tool which can be used in many circumstances where it is difficult to say that any trade mark is being used. There also remains the possibility of bringing a single action for both passing off and infringement. Under the old law it was not infrequently the case that one claim succeeded whilst the other failed. Whilst this is less likely under the new scheme of registration, it may enable the plaintiff to obtain protection even where his registration is invalid.

Copyright

SUBSISTENCE

9.13   Copyright is a property right which subsists in a variety of works including original[1] literary and artistic works, films and sound recordings.[2] For present purposes it is necessary to consider only literary and artistic works. In conformity with the Berne Convention, there are no formal requirements for a copyright to come into existence: it arises automatically upon the creation of the work provided that the qualifying conditions laid down in the statute are met. Both literary and artistic works are very broadly defined. There is no requirement for literary or artistic merit, the authorities making it clear that all that is required is the expenditure of sufficient effort in making the work to make its content more than de minimis.[3] Thus, where the artistic work relied upon is a photograph, the required effort is minimal. Artistic works include any form of drawing, plan, diagram or photograph.[4] Literary work means anything which is written, spoken or sung and includes tables, compilations and computer programs.[5] It includes material which has not been written down but there is no copyright in an unwritten work until it is recorded.[6] The qualifying conditions for subsistence of copyright are extremely broad. The United Kingdom is a signatory to both the Berne and Universal Copyright Conventions which require subscribing countries to grant reciprocal protection to works made in other convention countries. Almost every industrialised country is a signatory to at least one of these with the result that works made almost anywhere qualify.

---

1 'Original' means originating with the author, ie not a copy: see *University of London Press v University Tutorial Press Limited* [1916] 2 Ch 601.
2 Copyright, Designs and Patents Act 1988 (CDPA), s 1.
3 See eg *British Northrop Limited v Texteam (Blackburn) Limited* [1974] RPC 68.
4 CDPA, s 4.
5 CDPA, s 3. Dramatic and musical works are excluded from literary works but they are protected separately.
6 CDPA, s 3(2). For present purposes only works which are written, that is only those which result in some kind of sign, are relevant.

LITERARY WORKS

9.14 As noted above a literary work is anything which is written spoken or sung. The adjective literary does not impose any minimum standard of literary quality or style.[1] It is sufficient that the work is in written form, either words or some other intelligible form of notation.[2] The requirement of originality merely prevents works which are copies of previous works from being the subject of copyright protection.[3] For present purposes, however, what is of interest is whether short phrases or slogans or even single words are capable of being literary works. Whether a single word qualifies was considered by the Court of Appeal in *Exxon Corporation v Exxon Insurance Consultants*.[4] Many earlier authorities are considered in the judgments which are accordingly a helpful summary of the development of the law. It is clear from the decision in that case that the expenditure of even extensive skill and labour will not necessarily result in the creation of a literary work if the result does not either convey information, provide instruction or give pleasure.[5] In the result it was held that a single word does not qualify because, although the plaintiff had expended considerable effort to find a word suitable to be used in any language, the result of the effort was, in literary terms, negligible.

1   *University of London Press v University Tutorial Press Limited* [1916] 2 Ch 601 at 608 cited with approval in *Exxon Corporation v Exxon Insurance Consultants* [1982] RPC 69 (CA).
2   *D P Anderson and Co v Lieber Code Company* [1917] 2 KB 469; *Pitman v Hine* (1884) 1 TLR 39; *Fournet v Pearson Limited* (1897) 14 TLR 82 (CA).
3   See *University of London Press v University Tutorial Press Limited* (above). Examples of works which were too closely derivative from earlier material to qualify as original are dog racing cards (*Greyhound Racing v Shallis* [1922–28] Mac CC 330) and a pocket diary containing standard information (*Cramp & Sons Limited v Smythson* [1944] 2 All ER 92). There are others but they are rare.
4   See n 1 above.
5   Following *Hollinrake v Trusswell* [1894] 3 Ch 420, 63 LJ Ch 719.

9.15   Titles as copyright works have been considered on a number of occasions. In *Ladbroke (Football) Limited v William Hill (Football) Limited*[1] Lord Hodson rejected the proposition that copyright could not as a matter of law subsist in a title but added that:

> 'No doubt they will not as a rule be protected since alone they would not be regarded as a sufficiently substantial part of the book or other copyright document to justify preventing their copying by others.'

The question of copyright in a title as being in itself a literary work was discussed in *Francis Day & Hunter Limited v Twentieth Century Fox Limited*[2] in which Lord Wright said:

> 'As a rule a title does not involve literary composition and is not sufficiently substantial to justify a claim to protection. That statement does not mean that in particular cases a title may not be on so extensive a scale, and of so important a character, as to be a proper subject of protection against being copied.'[3]

Advertising slogans[4] and two sentences in an advertisement[5] have also been held to be too insubstantial to qualify as literary works. In *Lamb v Evans*,[6] a combination of headings in a trade directory, each given in English, French, German and Spanish was held to constitute a literary work. This case is probably the exception. In general, protection for titles must be sought by way of an action for passing off. The right to claim passing off by misuse of a title[7] is entirely separate from the copyright in the work to which it is applied and the two causes of action may belong to different people.[8]

1   [1964] 1 WLR 273 at 276, 1 All ER 465 at 476.
2   [1940] AC 112. See also the following cases in which claims to copyright in titles were rejected: *Maxwell v Hogg* (1867) LR 2 Ch App 307 ('Belgravia'); *Broemel v Meyer* (1912) 29 TLR 291 ('Where there's a will there's a way'); *Dick v Yates* (1881) 18 Ch D 76 ('Splendid Misery').
3   Ibid at 123.
4   *Sinanide v La Maison Kosmeo* (1928) 139 LT 365 (CA).
5   *Kirk v J & R Fleming Limited* [1928–35] Mac CC 44.
6   [1893] 1 Ch 218 (CA).
7   Discussed fully at ch 3, paras 3.35–3.39 above.
8   As was the case in *Archbold v Sweet* (1832) 1 Mood & R 162.

TERM

9.16 Copyright in a literary or artistic work normally subsists until the end of the year which is 50 years after the death of its author.[1] In the case of a computer generated work, the period is limited to 50 years after the end of the year in which it was made.[2] For works of joint authorship[3] the period of copyright expires at the end of the year which is 50 years after the death of the last of the authors to die.[4] The period of copyright protection will be extended to 70 years after the death of the author when the UK enacts legislation to comply with EC Council Directive number 93/98. This should be no later than 1 July 1995.[5] Where a copyright work has been exploited industrially by the owner of the copyright or with his licence by making and marketing articles which are copies of the work the period of copyright is curtailed to 25 years from the end of the year in which such articles are first marketed.[6]

1 CDPA, s 12(1).
2 CDPA, s 12(3).
3 'A work produced by the collaboration of two or more authors in which the contribution of each author is not distinct from that of the other author or authors': CDPA, s 10(1). This does not apply to a compilation of individual works, as the contributions of the individual authors are separate.
4 CDPA, s 12(4).
5 Art 13(1). The Directive contemplates that it may be enacted earlier but history suggests that the UK government is never early in complying with EC Directives. On the contrary, it is usually late, viz. the recent enactment of the Trade Marks Act 1994 more than a year after it should have been done.
6 CDPA, s 52.

OWNERSHIP

9.17 The first owner of the copyright in a copyright work is usually its author.[1] However, this does not apply to works made in the course of the author's employment, the copyright in which vests directly in the author's employer.[2] It is also possible by contract to vest the title to copyright works which have not been made in someone other than the author[3] but it should be noted that, unless this is done, even someone who commissions and pays for the making of a copyright work will not acquire the copyright in the work, merely the article.

1 CDPA section 11(1).
2 CDPA, s 11(2).
3 CDPA, s 91 and see para 9.20 below.

INFRINGEMENT

9.18 The owner of the copyright has the exclusive right to copy the work,[1] issue copies of the work to the public[2] and, in the case of a literary work, make an adaptation of the work.[3] Copying means reproducing the work in a material form[4] and includes copying the whole or a substantial part of the work either directly or indirectly.[5] A substantial part of a work may be taken either by copying some of it exactly or all of it inexactly and what is sufficient to amount to a substantial part is a question of fact and degree in each case.[6] It is no defence to the claim that the plaintiff's work has been altered or added to if there is reproduction of a substantial part.[7] For there to be infringement there must be a sufficient degree of objective similarity between the work and the alleged infringement.[8] It is impossible to define with precision what constitutes such a degree of similarity. It has been suggested that the test is whether 'the defendant has taken a substantial part of the plaintiff's skill and labour'[9] or whether 'the defendant's work is so close the original work as to suggest that original to the mind of every person seeing it',[10] but these suggestions are only dicta and are not conclusive. It is also an infringement of the copyright in a work to import infringing copies[11] of the work into the United Kingdom otherwise than for private and domestic use,[12] to possess such copies in the course of business or sell or offer them for sale or hire or to exhibit or distribute them in the course of trade[13] as well as to make, import, sell or offer to sell articles specifically adapted for making infringing copies[14] knowing or having reason to believe[15] that the copies are infringing.

---

1 CDPA, s 17.
2 CDPA, s 18.
3 CDPA, s 21.
4 CDPA, s 17(1).
5 CDPA, s 16(3).
6 This topic is extremely complex and the reader is referred to the texts noted in n 3 to paragraph 9.01 for a discussion of it.
7 *L B Plastics Limited v Swish Products* [1979] RPC 551 at 661 (HL).
8 *Francis Day & Hunter v Bron* [1963] Ch 587.
9 *MacMillan v Cooper* (1923) 40 TLR 186 at 190.
10 *Hanfstaengl v W H Smith & Co* [1905] 1 Ch 519.
11 Essentially an article which was made in infringement of copyright or would have been so made if it had been made in the United Kingdom: CDPA, s 27.
12 CDPA, s 22.
13 CDPA, s 23.
14 CDPA, s 24.
15 That is having knowledge of such facts as would lead a reasonable man to have such a belief: per Morritt J in *L A Gear Inc v Hi-Tech Sports plc* [1992] FSR 121 at 129, a finding not challenged on appeal.

REMEDIES FOR INFRINGEMENT

9.19 The remedies for infringement of copyright by way of damages, injunctions, accounts and otherwise are those available in respect of the infringement of any other property right.[1] Damages for copyright infringement may also include 'such additional damages as the justice of the case may require' having regard to all the circumstances and in particular to the flagrancy of the infringement and any benefit accruing to the defendant.[2] To justify an award of additional damages requires more than mere deliberate infringement. The purpose of the provision is to enable the courts to award damages going beyond those which are merely compensatory where the defendant has acted in a manner which is morally repugnant or otherwise reprehensible.[3] It is a defence to a claim for damages for infringement that the defendant did not know and had no reason to believe that copyright subsisted in the work the subject of the action.[4] The length of copyright protection means that this is a very limited defence indeed as it is reasonable to assume that any design which is not obviously antique is likely to be the subject of copyright. It has never succeeded. The copyright owner is also entitled to have infringing copies of his work delivered up to him.[5] The court then decides whether such copies should be forfeited to the copyright owner, destroyed or otherwise dealt with as the court thinks fit.[6] The Act also contains provisions enabling infringing goods to be treated as prohibited[7] and their importation thereby prevented. Copyright infringement is also a criminal offence for which there are now potentially severe penalties.[8]

---

1   CDPA, s 96(2).
2   CDPA, s 97(2).
3   *Ravenscroft v Herbert* [1980] RPC 193; *Nichols Advanced Vehicle Systems v Rees* [1979] RPC 127 at 141.
4   CDPA, s 97(1).
5   CDPA, s 99.
6   CDPA, s 114. These provisions are identical to those found in the Trade Marks Act 1994: see para 9.09 above.
7   CDPA, ss 111–112. These provisions are subject to the same caveats as the corresponding provisions in the Trade Marks Act 1994: see para 9.09 above, n 6 and the text thereto.
8   CDPA, ss 107–110.

DEALINGS IN COPYRIGHTS

9.20   Copyrights are transmissible by assignment or otherwise as personal property.[1] They may also be licensed. Both assignments and licences may be of the whole of the copyright or any part of it both in relation to the activities covered and the period of copyright.[2] An assignment is ineffective unless in writing and signed by or on behalf of the assignor,[3] and an exclusive licence is only such within the meaning of the act if so made.[4] It is also possible to enter into a contract which provides that the copyright in works yet to be made is assigned.[5] The effect of such a contract is to vest the copyright in such works when they are made directly in the 'assignee'.[5] This provision is of particular importance to any business contemplating having literary or artistic material created for use in its business by outside contractors. If the business wishes to be in a position to bring proceedings for copyright infringement in the event that such material is copied, it is essential to obtain an assignment of the copyright. The easiest way to do this is to provide in the commission that the copyright shall belong to the commissioner.

---

1   CDPA, s 90(1).
2   CDPA, s 90(2).
3   CDPA, s 90(3).
4   CDPA, s 92(1).
5   CDPA, s 91.

OVERLAPPING RIGHTS

9.21 Many forms of written advertising such as brochures, catalogues and leaflets may contain material which gives rise to passing off, infringes registered trade marks and infringes copyright. The plaintiff for each claim may be the same or different. In *Masson Seeley & Co v Embossotype Manufacturing Company*[1] the plaintiff complained of the defendant's price list and catalogues. The court held that the defendant had engaged in a deliberate and concerted attempt to find a market for its inferior machinery by means of conduct calculated to induce people to believe that they were the same as the plaintiff's. Claims for infringement of copyright and passing off succeeded in relation to the contents of the brochure. In other cases claims of copyright infringement have succeeded on headings in a trade directory,[2] the contents of a chemist's catalogue,[3] a label and leaflet incorporating instructions for use of a herbicide[4] and illustrations in a catalogue.[5] Equally, an original artistic work which is used as a 'device' trade mark or logo will be protected both by copyright and either passing off or as a registered trade mark. In *Tavener Rutledge v Specters Limited*[6] the plaintiff succeeded in a claim for infringement of copyright and registered trade mark and passing off arising from the use by the defendant of a representation of boiled sweets on the outside of tins of such sweets. For example, a complaint of copyright infringement may succeed where the defendant is operating in a field very far removed from that of the plaintiff so that confusion is impossible to prove. On the other hand, copyright prevents only copying. Complaints of trade mark infringement and passing off may succeed even where the defendant is entirely ignorant of the existence of the plaintiff. All these cases demonstrate that a plaintiff may bolster his position by relying upon a raft of separate but overlapping rights so that if the claim in relation to one fails for any reason there will still be a potentially valid claim left. The opposite problem may arise where the rights to trade marks and copyright are in different hands. In *Karo Step TM*[7] it was held that a simple design used as a trade mark was an artistic work entitled to copyright. The fact that the copyright was owned by a person other than the proprietor of the registration of the mark meant that such use was contrary to law and the mark was removed from the register.[8]

---

1 (1924) 41 RPC 160. See also the similar case of *Purefoy Engineering Co Limited v Sykes Boxall & Co Limited* (1955) 72 RPC 89 (CA).
2 *Lamb v Evans* [1893] 1 Ch 218 (CA), an exceptional case: see para 9.15 above.
3 *Collis v Cater Stoffell & Fortt Limited* (1898) 78 LT 613.
4 *Elanco Products Limited v Mandops (Agrochemicals Specialists) Limited* [1979] FSR 46.
5 *Maple & Co v Junior Army & Navy Stores* (1882) 21 Ch D 369, 52 LJ Ch 67.
6 [1959] RPC 355 (CA).
7 [1977] RPC 255.
8 Under s 11 of the Trade Marks Act 1938. The same result would follow now under s 3(4) of the 1994 Act.

Registered designs

WHAT MAY BE REGISTERED

9.22 The design registration system is governed by the Registered Designs Act 1949[1] which was substantially amended by the Copyright, Designs and Patents Act 1988. Under the RDA a design which is new may be registered in respect of any article.[2] A design is not new if it is the same as a design which has previously been registered or published in the UK or differs from such a design only in immaterial details or features which are variants common in the trade.[3] A design may not be registered for an article if aesthetic considerations do not normally play a part in the acquisition of articles of that type.[4] Interestingly, this apparently allows designs for the treads of tyres to be registered. Design is defined by a complex definition in section 1(1) of the RDA:

> 'In this Act "design" means features of shape, configuration, pattern or ornament applied to an article by any industrial process, being features which in the finished article appeal to and are judged by the eye, but does not include—
> (a)   a method or principle of construction, or
> (b)   features of shape or configuration of an article which—
>   (i)   are dictated solely by the function which the article has to perform, or
>   (ii) are dependent upon the appearance of another article of which the article is intended by the author of the design to form an integral part.'

The terms shape and configuration have much the same meaning, as do pattern and ornament. This definition has been the subject of extensive judicial debate. There is little difficulty in understanding that the basic intention of the definition is to allow design registration for features of design which are aesthetic or have 'eye appeal' rather than those which are simply functional. However, the exclusion by subsection (1)(b)(i) of features of shape and configuration which are 'dictated solely by the function which the article has to perform' has caused considerable difficulty.[5] It is generally accepted that features are dictated by function when their designer created them with functional considerations in mind and that it is not necessary for them to be excluded that no other shape could perform the function.[6] The latest consideration of its meaning by the Privy Council in *Interlego AG v Tyco International Limited*[7] (the *Lego* case) resulted in the conclusion that:

> 'The incorporation into the shape as a whole of *some* (perhaps a majority of) features dictated only by functional requirements will not bring the exclusion into operation so as to deprive it of protection, if there are also some features of the shape which are not attributable to function.'[8]

This is both clear and sensible. The Privy Council, however, also held that in considering whether a design is registrable for such an article the whole shape of the article must be considered. This latter finding is the cause of considerable difficulty and resulted in Parliament adding a further provision to the infringement section of the Act during the passage of the CDPA in an attempt to mitigate its consequences.[9] The result is that it is possible to register a design for an article which has no new features with eye appeal provided that it has some new functional features. It is submitted that this is not what was intended by the legislature.[10] The exclusion of subsection (1)(b)(ii) is new and corresponds to the exclusion of such features from unregistered design protection.[11] The effect of this exclusion has been considered by the Registered Designs Appeal Tribunal and the Divisional Court in *Ford's Registered Design Applications*.[12] It was held in this case that design registration is not excluded merely because an article is intended to be used as part of a larger article. However, it is not possible to register the design of an article forming part of a larger article where it contributes to the overall form of the larger article, even where the designer has some freedom over the precise shape of some of the features of the article. Thus, specifically, designs for car wheels were allowed whilst designs for car body panels were refused. It should also be noted that, in common with patents, a successful defence of an invalidity attack entitles the proprietor of a design registration to a certificate of contested validity. The effect of such a certificate is to entitle the proprietor to indemnity costs in any subsequent infringement or validity proceedings.[13]

---

1   Referred to in this section as the RDA.
2   RDA, s 1(2).
3   RDA, s 1(4). To be a variant common in the trade it must be available from more than one trade source: *Amp v Utilux* [1970] RPC 397 at 429 per Graham J sitting in the Court of Appeal.
4   RDA, s 1(3).
5   Before the RDA the exclusion was of 'a mere mechanical device'. Luxmoore J in *Kestos Limited v Kempat Limited* (1936) 53 RPC 139 interpreted this as meaning 'a shape in which all the features are dictated solely by the function or functions which the article has to perform' and it appears that these words were simply later enacted.
6   *Amp Inc v Utilix Pty Limited* [1972] RPC 103 (HL); and see *Stenor Limited v Whitesides (Clitheroe) Limited* (1948) 65 RPC 1 (HL).
7   [1988] RPC 343.
8   Ibid at 356.
9   S 7(6), see para 9.23 below.
10   In the appeal to the House of Lords in *Ford's Registered Design Applications* (reported in the Registered Designs Appeal Tribunal at [1993] RPC 399 and in the Divisional Court at [1994] RPC 545), the court was asked to reconsider the result in *Lego*.
11   See para 9.28 below.
12   See n 10 above. The appeal to the House of Lords has been heard and a decision is awaited at the time of writing.
13   RDA, s 25.

RIGHTS OBTAINED BY REGISTRATION

9.23   Registration of a design gives the registered proprietor from the date of the grant of the certificate of registration of the design the exclusive right to make or import for sale, hire or use in trade and to sell, hire or offer or expose for sale or hire articles made to the design or to a design 'not substantially different therefrom'.[1] This is a true monopoly: it is unnecessary to establish derivation or copying. As well as being an infringement to do any of these acts it is also an infringement to make anything for enabling an article made to the design to be made or to do such acts in relation to a kit[2] which would be an infringement if done in relation to the complete article.[3] There is as a result of the *Lego* decision a new exclusion from the infringement provisions for reproduction solely of features which are left out of account under section 1(1)(b) of the RDA in determining whether the design is registrable.[4] The scope of the exclusive right given by a registered design depends upon how close it is to prior art designs and the nature of the statement of novelty filed with the application for registration. All registrations must have a statement of novelty.[5] This often says no more than 'the features of shape and configuration [or pattern and ornament] as shown in the accompanying representations'. The effect of such a statement of novelty is to require all the features of the article's shape [or pattern] to be taken into account both when assessing validity and infringement. This may result in a design which is valid — because it has some feature not found in previous designs — but which is of very narrow scope because it can be avoided by not adopting that, or indeed any other, feature of it.[6] In judging whether a defendant's article is the same as or not substantially different from a registered design the court has regard to the extent to which the design represents a departure from the prior art. If the degree of novelty is small, the extent of protection from infringement is correspondingly small. Conversely, if there is a substantial degree of departure from the prior art, the extent of protection is correspondingly increased.[7] Thus, where a design is validly registered, the test for infringement is most simply expressed by asking whether the infringement is closer to the design than to the prior art. If so, there is infringement. If not, there is not. A registered design is granted initially for a period of five years. It may be renewed for further periods of five years up to a maximum of twenty-five years.[8]

---

1 RDA, ss 7(1) and (5).
2 A kit is a complete or substantially complete set of components intended to be assembled into the completed article: RDA, s 7(4).
3 RDA, ss 7(3) and 7(4).
4 RDA, s 7(6). The problem with this is that the *Lego* decision says that you take all features of the article into account in determining registrability so that this subsection does not have the intended effect: see para 9.22 above. This neatly illustrates the difficulties caused by the *Lego* approach.
5 Registered Designs Rules 1990, r 15.
6 See, for example, the result in *Sommer Allibert (UK) Limited v Flair Plastics Limited* [1987] RPC 599 (CA).
7 See *Hecla Foundry Co v Walker Hunter & Co* (1889) 6 RPC 554 (HL).
8 RDA, s 8.

REMEDIES FOR INFRINGEMENT

9.24 A design registration is a proprietary right and all the usual rights and remedies for infringement of such a right are available. Thus the proprietor will be entitled to an injunction, damages or an account of profits and delivery up or destruction of infringing goods and anything for enabling infringing goods to be made. An innocent infringer will not be liable for damages and an innocent infringer is one who was not aware and had no reasonable ground for supposing that the design was registered.[1] This exemption corresponds to that found in the patent legislation before 1977 and does not extend to an account of profits.[2]

---

1   RDA, s 9(1).
2   See Patents Act 1949, s 59; compare Patents Act 1977, s 62(1) which specifically includes an account of profits. The RDA was not altered in this respect when the 1988 amendments were made.

OWNERSHIP OF AND DEALINGS IN REGISTERED DESIGNS

9.25   Where a design is created in pursuance of a commission for money or money's worth or in the course of employment the commissioner or employer is the first owner of the design. In any other case, the author is the first owner.[1] The author of a design which is computer generated is the person who makes the arrangements necessary for the creation of the design.[2] The Act follows the traditional approach of simply treating a design as personal property[3] and providing only for the mechanics of recording a new proprietor of an application or registration.[4] The person whose name appears on the register has power to licence and otherwise deal with the design subject to any vested rights of which there is notice on the register but this does not prevent equities (which do not appear on the register) being enforced as they would be for any other personal property.[5] An assignment of a registered design will carry with it the corresponding unregistered design right and vice versa,[6] and the registrar shall not record an interest in a registered design on the register unless satisfied that the person to be registered is entitled to a corresponding interest in the unregistered design right.[7]

---

1   RDA, s 2.
2   RDA, s 2(4).
3   Modern statutes say so expressly and probably unnecessarily.
4   RDA, s 19(1).
5   RDA, s 19(4).
6   RDA, s 19(3B) and CDPA, s 224.
7   RDA, s 19(3A).

REMEDY FOR UNJUSTIFIED THREATS

9.26   There is a right to bring proceedings against someone who threatens to bring proceedings for infringement of a registered design unless the threatened proceedings are justified.[1] Under this provision the only defence is to show that the conduct complained of is in fact an infringement of the registered design mark in question. A threats action will succeed if the activities complained of are outside the scope of the registration or if the registration is invalid. A threat of proceedings for making or importing goods is not actionable.[2] Thus, the action is limited to threats against those who merely deal in articles made to the design within the UK. Mere notification that a design is registered is also not actionable.[3] These provisions are in substance identical to those found in the Patents Act 1977.[4] Under both sets of provisions a threat is actionable by any person aggrieved by the threat. The person aggrieved need not be the person threatened. It is common for an action for threats to be brought by a manufacturer whose customer is being threatened. The action is often accompanied by an application for an interlocutory injunction for this is the real remedy against threats. As the balance of convenience will almost inevitably favour the grant of the injunction (the threatener can simply sue if he really believes in his case) it is usually granted.

1   RDA, s 26.
2   RDA, s 26(2A), introduced in 1988.
3   RDA, s 26(3).
4   See s 71.

Unregistered designs

9.27   The declared purpose of the unregistered design right is 'to provide protection on copyright principles but without the more objectionable features of full copyright protection.'[1] It is intended to sweep away the anomalies inherent in the application of artistic copyright to industrial designs. Whilst it succeeds in this, it provides only limited protection and, thus far, does not appear to have provided an effective remedy for the copying of industrial designs. The right is entirely statutory and is contained in Part III of the Copyright, Designs and Patents Act 1988. All references to section numbers in this part of this chapter are to that act unless otherwise stated.

1   White Paper on intellectual property and innovation, Cmnd 9712, para 3.28.

SUBSISTENCE

9.28   Design right subsists in 'original designs' falling within the definition set out in s 213. Subject to certain exceptions this is 'the design of any aspect of the shape or configuration (whether internal or external) of the whole or part of an article'. The exceptions are for a method or principle of construction,[1] features which must fit or must match parts of another article[2] and surface decoration.[3] The meaning of original in this context is partially negatively defined by section 213(4) which provides that 'a design is not "original" for the purposes of this Part if it is commonplace in the design field in question at the time of its creation.' There is no authority on the meaning of commonplace.[4] All one can say at present is that the mere fact that someone else has previously made the same design probably does not deprive a design of originality. It probably has to be shown that articles made to the design have been available from more than one source, even though a single source may have supplied the market with many thousands of articles made to the design. Design right 'does not subsist unless and until the design has been recorded in a design document or an article has been made to the design'.[5] This presumably covers recording in a computer on a CAD system or the like in line with the approach taken to the meaning of document in discovery.[6] It also finally removes the anomaly under which industrial designs only obtained protection other than registered design protection if they were first recorded in a drawing rather than a model or prototype unless this could be said to be a sculpture.

---

1   This mirrors the exception for registered designs: see para 9.22 above.
2   These too largely mirror the exceptions from registered designs for functional features and matching features: see para 9.22 above. Although there are some significant differences between the two, they do not merit further discussion in this context.
3   This consigns all forms of surface appearance to copyright protection: see the discussion of the interrelationship between the two at para 9.36 below.
4   The best guide is the meaning attributed to 'variants commonly used in the trade' found in the Registered Designs Act: see para 9.22 above.
5   S 213(6).
6   See for example *Grant v Southwestern and County Properties Limited* [1975] Ch 185 (tape recordings); *Barker v Wilson* [1980] 1 WLR 884 (microfilms are documents for the purposes of the Bankers Books Evidence Act 1879).

Qualifying conditions

9.29   Design right only subsists in designs made after the coming into force of the Copyright, Designs and Patents Act 1988 on 1 August 1989.[1] Earlier designs are covered by artistic copyright modified by the transitional provisions.[2] All pre-1988 Act designs are now subject to licences of right.[2] It is an essential requirement for the subsistence of design right that the design meets the qualifying conditions set out in the Act. Designs not made in pursuance of a commission or in the course of employment qualify if the designer is a qualifying individual.[3] The designer is 'the person who creates' the design except in cases of computer-generated designs when it means 'the person by whom the arrangements necessary for the creation of the design are made'.[4] The latter reflects the definition of the author of a film in the copyright provisions[5] and means that a corporation can be the author of a computer generated design. Commissioned designs and those made in the course of employment qualify if the commissioner or employer is a qualifying person.[6] The definitions[7] of qualifying individuals and persons are complex. Briefly, a qualifying individual is a citizen or subject of or habitually resident in a qualifying country. A qualifying person is either a qualifying individual or a body having legal personality formed under or having a place of business at which 'substantial business activity' is carried on in a qualifying country. Qualifying countries are the UK and other EEC countries.[8] This may be extended by Order in Council.[9] A design which does not qualify by virtue either of having been made by a qualifying individual or under a commission or employment by a qualifying person may nevertheless qualify by virtue of first marketing in the UK, another EEC country or another country to which

the provisions have been extended.[10] This method of qualification is limited
to designs which are so marketed by a person who is exclusively authorised
to put articles made to the design on the market.[11]

---

1 S 213(7).
2 See para 9.35 below.
3 S 218.
4 S 214.
5 S 9(2)(a).
6 S 219.
7 All contained in s 217.
8 S 217(2).
9 To the Channel Islands, Isle of Man and colonies under s 255 and to other countries granting
   reciprocal protection under s 256. Orders have been made in relation to a number of former British
   territories: see SI 1989/1294.
10 S 220(1).
11 The definition of exclusive authorisation is complex: see s 220(4). It appears to have the effect of
    limiting it to a contractually enforceable exclusivity originally granted by the person who would
    have been the first owner of the design if he had been a qualifying person.

Term

9.30 Design right lasts for fifteen years from the end of the calendar year
in which the design right came into being or, if articles made to the design
are made available for sale or hire within the first five years of that period,
ten years from the end of the calendar year in which this occurred.[1] In any
case, licences of right are available under the right during the last five years
of the term.[2]

---

1 S 216.
2 S 237.

INFRINGEMENT

9.31 Like traditional copyright the design right is a right to prevent
reproduction by copying. It is not an absolute monopoly so independent
designs will not infringe even if identical. The owner of a design right
has 'the exclusive right to reproduce the design for commercial purposes'.[1]
Reproduction means 'copying the design so as to produce articles exactly
or substantially to that design'.[2] Reproduction may be direct or indirect.[3]
There has been little litigation on the scope of design right protection
but it is likely that the courts will take a similar approach to that taken
for registered designs[4] rather than copyright as the nature of the infringing
act does not include reproduction of a substantial part. Thus, the scope of
design right protection is likely to depend upon the degree of originality of
the design. There is, of course, an important difference between the two. For
registered designs there is a squeeze between infringement and validity. With
design right this is not obviously so. The court may simply take the approach

taken in copyright and say that the right subsists unless all its features are commonplace but that it is only infringed by taking those parts which are original.[5] The primary act of infringement is to do or authorise the doing of anything which is the exclusive right of the owner of the design.[6] The secondary infringement provisions relating to design right protection are in substance identical to those for copyright as is the definition of an infringing article.[7]

1   CDPA, s 226(1).
2   CDPA, s 226(2).
3   CDPA, s 226(4).
4   See para 9.23 above.
5   See per Lord Pearce in *Ladbroke v Hill* [1964] 1 WLR 273 at 293 for the approach to copyright infringement.
6   CDPA, s 226(3).
7   See para 9.18 above.

REMEDIES FOR INFRINGEMENT

9.32   The remedies for infringement of design right are similar to if rather more limited than those available for copyright infringement.[1] Thus the usual rights to an injunction to restrain further infringement, damages and an account of profits are available.[2] A claim may be made for additional damages in exactly the same way as in a copyright action if these are merited having regard to the circumstances, and in particular the flagrancy of the infringement and the benefit accruing to the infringer.[3] In addition an order may be made for the delivery up or disposal of infringing articles in the same way as for infringement of copyright.[4] There is a defence of innocence to an allegation of design right infringement but it is in a rather curious form. It provides that there is no entitlement to damages for primary infringement where the infringer did not know and had no reason to believe that design right subsisted.[5] It does not prevent any other claim so an account of profits is still available to the plaintiff. In contrast, the *only* remedy against secondary infringers who show that they or a predecessor in title of theirs acquired the infringing article innocently is 'damages not exceeding a reasonable royalty'.[5] The logic of this is difficult to discern.

1   There is no right of seizure as with copyright infringement (CDPA section 100). This is clearly deliberate although it is difficult to see why it was done.
2   CDPA, s 229(2).
3   CDPA, s 229(3) which is worded identically to s 97(2) dealing with copyright: see para 9.19 above.
4   CDPA, ss 230 and 231.
5   CDPA, s 233.b.

OWNERSHIP AND DEVOLUTION

9.33   First ownership rights in design right mirror the qualifying conditions for subsistence.[1] The first owner of the design right in a design created pursuant to a commission or in the course of employment is the commissioner[2] or the employer.[3] Otherwise the first owner is the designer.[4] These rules do not apply to designs which only qualify for protection by reason of first marketing in the UK or European Community in which case the first owner of the design right is the first marketer of articles made to the design.[5] As with copyright, design right is transmissible by assignment, testamentary disposition or operation of law as personal property[6] and all assignments (whether of the whole or any part of the right) must be in writing and signed by or on behalf of the assignor to be effective.[7] Future design rights may also be assigned in the same way and with the same effect as future copyrights.[8] Assignments of design right and registered designs carry the other right with them unless a contrary intention appears in the assignment.[9] As with copyright, an exclusive licence carries with it considerable benefits for the licensee but to qualify as an exclusive licence it must be in writing signed by or on behalf of the design right owner.[10]

---

1 See para 9.29 above.
2 CDPA, s 215(2).
3 CDPA, s 215(3).
4 CDPA, s 215(1).
5 CDPA, s 215(4).
6 CDPA, s 222(1).
7 CDPA, s 222(3).
8 CDPA, s 223.
9 CDPA, s 224 and RDA, s 19(3B).
10 CDPA, s 225.

REMEDY FOR UNJUSTIFIED THREATS

9.34 Unlike copyright there is a right to bring proceedings for groundless threats of proceedings.[1] This is important as it provides the possibility of a remedy against someone who wrongly claims to be entitled to a design right to the detriment of someone else's business. The action for threats has long been a feature of patent[2] and registered design[3] law. The comments made above on the registered design provisions[4] apply equally here. With the introduction of this right the legislature has taken the opportunity to extend this action. Artistic copyright now stands out as anomalous in this respect[5] and its continued exclusion is difficult to understand. Threats of proceedings for making or importing articles are not actionable.[6] Thus, the threats action brings a new combination of factors together in that the only infringement which can be the subject of threats proceedings are acts of secondary infringement requiring an element of knowledge.[7] It is not, therefore, safe to write a letter to a possible secondary infringer alleging infringement without first notifying him of the existence of the right claimed and giving him sufficient information to provide reason to believe that the articles complained of are infringing.[8]

1   CDPA, s 253.
2   Patents Act 1977, s 70.
3   RDA, s 26.
4   See para 9.26 above.
5   A threats action in relation to registered trade marks having been introduced by the Trade Marks Act 1994: see para 9.11 above.
6   CDPA, s 253(3).
7   See para 9.31 and the reference therein to para 9.18 above.
8   A person who does not have the requisite 'reason to believe' is not an infringer. Thus a threat against such a person must be groundless.

TRANSITIONAL PROVISIONS

9.35   As noted above design right is available only in relation to designs created after 1 August 1989. There is a complex set of transitional provisions giving similar rights to pre-existing artistic works. In relation to such existing works, the removal from infringement of artistic copyright of the making of three-dimensional copies of a two-dimensional work[1] does not apply for ten years.[2] The effect of this is that such designs continue to be protected by artistic copyright. Licences of right are available under this transitional protection for the last five years[3] so that all such designs have been subject to the grant of licences of right since 1 August 1994.

1   CDPA, s 51(1): see para 9.36 below.
2   CDPA, sch 1, para 19(1).
3   CDPA, sch 1, para 19(2).

INTERRELATIONSHIP BETWEEN COPYRIGHT AND DESIGN RIGHT

9.36   Copyright and design right are intended to provide a seamless body of protection against reproduction of industrial designs without ever providing dual protection. It is not an infringement of the copyright in an artistic work to make an article to the design it depicts.[1] Such conduct is of course infringement of design right. Correspondingly it is not an infringement of design right to do anything which is an infringement of the copyright in a work which includes a design.[2] As noted above. surface decoration is specifically excluded from design right,[3] but unauthorised reproduction of a surface decoration which is depicted in a drawing in which copyright subsists may be prevented by copyright. The consequence of this careful parcelling out of protection is that in any case of doubt[4] it is essential to plead the case in both copyright and unregistered design right to be sure that the court will find infringement. Both these rights and registered design can be used to restrict competition from articles of similar shape or decoration even where it is not possible to show that those features of appearance of the article have become distinctive of a particular trade source as is required to found a claim in passing off by get-up.

9.36 *Related causes of action*

They are therefore powerful alternatives where the real cause of complaint is copying rather than straightforward customer deception.

---

1   CDPA, s 51(1).
2   CDPA, s 236.
3   See para 9.28 above.
4   For example, the pattern woven into a piece of cloth or the pattern on the surface of embossed wallpaper.

CHAPTER 10

EC competition law

Introduction

10.01 In 1951 Belgium, France, Holland, Italy, Luxembourg and West Germany signed a treaty establishing the European Coal and Steel Community ('ECSC'). Its objective was to create an economic community amongst the peoples of those countries and thereby remove the possibility of further armed conflict between them. It was merely the first step in progressively closer European integration. In March 1957 the same six states concluded the Treaty of Rome, which founded the European Economic Community on 1 January 1958. Its objective was to create a single market for goods and services throughout the member states and to create a right of free movement and establishment for all citizens of the member states throughout the Community. At the same time the signatories also signed a further treaty establishing the European Atomic Energy Community ('Euratom'). This, as its name indicates, was to bring together the development of the use of nuclear energy in the member states and was intended to run in parallel with the EEC Treaty. Both the ECSC and Euratom continue to function. However, they are dominated by the EEC Treaty which has expanded both its scope and its geographical coverage as further states have joined the Community and additional treaties have been made extending its spheres of operation. The United Kingdom, Denmark and Ireland acceded to all three treaties in 1973, Greece in 1981 and Spain and Portugal in 1986. Now, therefore, there are 12 members of the EEC and 4 further states have negotiated to join.[1] The United Kingdom's accession to the treaty was given effect to by the passing of the European Communities Act 1972. The effect of this is to make the provisions of the EEC Treaty part of English domestic law with the result that they must be given effect to as if they were contained in domestic legislation.[2] The final arbiter of the correct interpretation of the Treaty of Rome is, however, the European Court of Justice[3] to which the national courts of the member states must refer any dispute of interpretation.[4]

---

1 They are Austria, Finland, Norway and Sweden who will join in January 1995, in the case of Norway still at the time of writing subject to a referendum approving the decision.
2 See *Applications des Gaz SA v Falks Veritas Limited* [1974] Ch 381, [1974] RPC 421.
3 Referred to in this chapter as 'the Court'.
4 Under Article 177 of the Treaty. See also Article 164.

10.02 The move towards ever closer European integration has continued since then. In 1986 the Single European Act, whose objective is a closer European union, was signed between the member states of the EEC. In February 1992 the EEC began its biggest ever step forward to complete European integration with the signing of the Maastricht Treaty.[1] This makes many sweeping changes to the Treaty of Rome, notably renaming it the European Community, reflecting the fact that its objectives now extend far beyond economic matters into areas of social policy, monetary union, defence and the environment. The content of the Maastricht Treaty was the subject of considerable public debate throughout the Community both before and after it was signed and its ratification by the signatory states has not been without its incidents and complications.[2] However, it was finally ratified and entered into force in November 1993.[3] It was given effect to in the domestic law of this country by the passing of the European Communities (Amendment) Act 1993. The economic effect of the EC was further enlarged in May 1992 when the member states of the Community and the European Free Trade Area ('EFTA') countries[4] signed a treaty creating the European Economic Area ('EEA') in which the treaty is intended to create free movement of goods, services and people.[5]

1 The official title of the treaty is the 'Treaty on European Union' (TEU).
2 There were constitutional challenges in Germany and the UK (see *R v Secretary of State for Foreign and Commonwealth Affairs ex parte Rees Mogg* [1993] 3 CMLR 101), and Denmark had two referendums on whether to ratify the treaty. The first referendum rejected the treaty and the second only accepted it after there had been a summit meeting of the heads of state in Edinburgh at which a special decision was passed clarifying the effect of certain of the treaty's provisions.
3 In accordance with the effect of the Maastricht Treaty the term European Community and the abbreviation EC are used hereafter in this chapter. All references to the Treaty of Rome are to the treaty as amended by the Maastricht Treaty.
4 These are Austria, Finland, Iceland, Liechtenstein, Norway, Sweden and Switzerland.
5 The effect of this treaty is to make the EC rules on free movement of goods apply throughout the EEA. Whilst the term EC is used in this chapter it must be remembered that the rules will now in fact apply to goods originating from or first marketed in any country within the EEA.

10.03 EC law is a large and complex subject.[1] The purpose of the present chapter is simply briefly to review the competition provisions of the EC Treaty in order to indicate how they operate and how they may affect claims for passing off in this country. We have seen in chapter 1 that all systems of law must seek to balance freedom to compete with fairness of competition. One of the primary objectives of the EC is to ensure free competition and trade throughout the community and it contains provisions intended to prevent restrictions on trade created either by agreements or concerted practices between traders or legislative or other governmental acts. Its competition provisions therefore provide one of the balances against excessive exercise of intellectual property rights, including for these purposes the right to make a claim of passing off. Those of direct relevance to owners of intellectual property are the provisions of Titles I and V of Part Three of the Treaty of Rome which set out amongst other things Community Policies on free movement of goods and competition. As the Court has interpreted the Treaty, the provisions of Chapter 2 of Title I containing Articles 30 to 37 concerned with the elimination of quantitative restrictions on trade between member states of the EC have turned out to be the most important in controlling the effects of intellectual property rights on inter-state trade. Chapter 1 of Title V contains the Treaty's rules on competition. These are divided into three parts, rules relating to undertakings, anti-dumping provisions and state aids. Only the rules relating to undertakings found in Articles 85 and 86 are of direct importance to intellectual property rights. Accordingly, in this chapter the effects of these two sets of provisions on the exercise of intellectual property rights are considered. The chapter concludes with a consideration of the specific application of the rules created by the Court under these provisions to claims for passing off. It should be noted at the outset that it is unusual for the competition provisions of EC law to have an impact on such claims. However, there are circumstances in which it can and the subject is therefore both relevant and important.

---

1   There are many works dealing with various aspects of EC law. The most comprehensive is *The Encyclopaedia of European Community Law*. An authoritative work devoted to the competition aspects of EC law is *Common Market Law of Competition*, Bellamy & Child (4th Edition Sweet & Maxwell 1993).

The principles of EC competition law

10.04   Before beginning an analysis of the relevant provisions, it is necessary first to consider the circumstances in which the requirement of free movement of goods in the EC and the prohibition on anti-competitive behaviour by undertakings may have an impact on a passing off action and to outline the principles which have been developed by the Court in determining the effect of these rules. The system of law created by the Treaty of Rome is supra national. Intellectual property rights are by their nature territorial in effect and of national scope.[1] For so long as this division exists there is a dichotomy between the way in which the owner of an intellectual property right may seek to exploit it separately in each of the individual states in which it exists, and the ability to deal freely in goods in all the member states of the Community once they have been put onto the market anywhere within it. For example, a patent holder may wish to prevent goods made under his patent in one member state from being exported from that state to another member state so as to maximise the price he can obtain for his goods in the two places. If he is able to do this, he prevents the free movement of those goods between the two states. Where this happens between two unrelated countries, the patent owner can indeed prevent the trade.[2] The Treaty of Rome, however, prevents this kind of division of the EC into separate markets by imposing restrictions on the use of intellectual property rights. This kind of trade is generally referred to as parallel importing and that term will be used here. There are three primary rules which the Court has developed to decide how and when the use of intellectual property rights should be restricted in cases of parallel importation. These are the distinction between the existence and the exercise of a right, the scope of its specific subject matter and the exhaustion of the right. The effect of each of these is now outlined.

---

1   They exist under the domestic legal systems of individual states. This will remain so until community wide rights such as the Community Patent and Community Trade Mark come into being.

2   As indeed can the owner of any other intellectual property right. See, eg, the same result in an action for trade mark infringement and passing off in *Colgate-Palmolive Limited v Markwell Finance Limited* [1988] RPC 497 (CA) and the further cases discussed in ch 4, para 4.26 above.

THE DISTINCTION BETWEEN EXISTENCE AND EXERCISE OF A RIGHT

10.05   By Article 222 of the Treaty of Rome the provisions of the treaty do not prejudice the rules governing ownership of property in the member states of the Community. Thus, the treaty cannot affect the existence of an intellectual property right in any individual member state. It might be thought that this would prevent the provisions of the Treaty from interfering with such rights because their nature and scope is simply an adjunct of their existence under national laws. To escape this consequence the Court has sought to distinguish between the existence of a right and its exercise and has held that, whilst the existence of rights is unaffected by the Treaty, the circumstances in which they may be exercised is not.[1] It has consequently imposed restrictions upon the circumstances in which rights may be exercised.

---

1   There are many examples of this, first in decisions under art 85 and subsequently in cases in which arts 30 and 36 have been the foundation of its jurisdiction. Typical cases are *Van Zuylen Frères v Hag AG* [1974] ECR 731 at 743–744, [1974] 2 CMLR 127 at 1434; *Merck v Stephar* [1981] ECR 2063 at 2080, [1981] 3 CMLR 463 at 480. There are many others including most of the cases cited later in this chapter.

THE SPECIFIC SUBJECT MATTER OF A RIGHT

10.06   The principal restriction the Court has imposed on the exercise of intellectual property rights is that they may only be used to protect the 'specific subject matter' of the right. This specific subject matter will differ from right to right. In relation to patents it is the right to use the invention by making goods under the protection of the patent and putting them onto the market for the first time witthin the EC.[1] For copyright it is to protect the moral rights in the work and provide a reward for the creative effort involved in making the work.[2] The specific subject matter of a trade mark, which is closely analogous to the right to make a claim of passing off, has been constantly refined and restated by the Court. The latest restatement is found in *Hag II*[3] and is in the following form:

'the specific subject matter of trade marks is in particular to guarantee to the proprietor of the trade mark that he has the right to use that trade mark for the purpose of putting a product into circulation for the first time and therefore to protect him against competitors wishing to take advantage of the status and reputation of the trade mark by selling products illegally bearing that mark. In order to determine the scope of this right exclusively conferred on the owner of the trade mark regard must be had to the essential function of the trade mark, which is to guarantee the identity of the origin of the marked product to the consumer or ultimate user by enabling him without any possibility of confusion to distinguish that product from products which have another origin.'

Thus, any attempt to prevent the remarketing of trademarked goods which have previously been put on the market in another member state of the EC will be legitimate only where the circumstances of the remarketing are such as to lead to the possibility of confusion.

---

1 *Centrafarm BV v Sterling Drug Co* [1974] ECR 1147, [1974] 2 CMLR 480.
2 *Radio Telefis Eireann v EC Commission* [1991] II ECR 485, [1991] 4 CMLR 586 at 71.
3 *Cnl-Sucal NV v Hag GF AG* [1990] I ECR 3711, [1990] 3 CMLR 571 at 14.

EXHAUSTION OF RIGHTS

10.07 The principle of exhaustion of rights is closely linked to the concept of the specific subject matter of a right. In accordance with this principle, once the specific subject matter of a right has been exercised the right is exhausted and cannot be exercised further. In particular, once goods have been marketed in the EC under an intellectual property right by the owner of that right or with his consent,[1] the right is exhausted and parallel rights in other EC member states cannot be invoked to prevent the subsequent remarketing of those goods elsewhere within the EC. The principle of exhaustion of rights does not, however, affect a right owner's ability to prevent the importation of goods from countries outside the EC (commonly called 'third countries').[2] Nor does it have any application where the goods were first marketed without the consent of the right owner.[3] It is, therefore, not sufficient for a defendant to invoke the doctrine merely to establish that the goods were purchased on the open market in another member state of the EC.[4] As will be seen below, exhaustion of rights is not a complete answer to a complaint of trade mark infringement if the goods have been altered since they were first put on the market, so the two concepts are not entirely interchangeable. In many circumstances, however, they are different ways of expressing the same essential idea that once you have put goods onto the market in the EC you have no further right to control what is done with them.

---

1 For the meaning of consent see para 10.08 below.
2 *EMI Records Limited v CBS United Kingdom Limited* [1976] ECR 811, [1986] 2 CMLR 235, [1976] FSR 457.
3 *Terrapin v Terranova* [1976] ECR 1039, [1976] 2 CMLR 482.
4 *Keurkoop v Nancy Kean Gifts* [1982] ECR 2853, [1983] 2 CMLR 47; see also *EMI Records Limited v*

The CD Specialists Limited [1992] FSR 70 where a defence advanced on this basis was struck out by the English court.

CONSENT

10.08   The question of what constitutes consent has been considered by the Court on many occasions. It is not always easy to resolve. It is clear that marketing by the right owner himself or by a subsidiary is with consent. Indeed, that much is obvious. Equally, the voluntary grant of a licence is consent. However, where a licence arises under domestic law requiring the grant of a compulsory licence, there is no consent.[1] Nor does it appear that there is consent where the scope of the parallel rights in the two member states is different and the goods were sold by the right owner in the state with the lesser right. In such circumstances he can object to the exercise of the greater right in the second member state.[2] It should be noted that the decision in which this approach was taken was a case concerning copyright protection and was apparently in conflict with an earlier decision in relation to patent rights in which it was held that a patentee was deemed to have consented to the marketing of products in a member state in which he could not obtain patent protection.[3] It may be the case that the two decisions are in fact reconciled by the difference between the nature of the specific subject matter of patent rights and copyright[4] although the position is not entirely clear. It had been held that there was consent to the marketing of goods under a trade mark where the mark was assigned to a different proprietor in one member state.[5] Recently, however, the Court has reconsidered this question in relation to the disposal of part of a business carried on in more than one member state under the same trade mark and held that after the disposal there is no longer consent.[6] The now rejected doctrine of 'common origin'[7] was also an aspect of deemed consent.

---

1   *Pharmon v Hoechst* [1985] ECR 2281, [1985] 3 CMLR 775.
2   *Warner Brothers v Christiansen* [1988] ECR 2605, [1990] 3 CMLR 684.
3   *Merck v Stephar* [1981] ECR 2063, [1981] 3 CMLR 463.
4   *Basset v SACEM* [1987] ECR 1747, [1987] 3 CMLR 173.
5   *Sirena Srl v Eda Srl* [1971] ECR 69, [1971] CMLR 260.
6   *IHT Internationale Heiztechnik GmbH v Ideal Standard GmbH* (Case C9/93, as yet unreported).
7   See para 10.12 below.

Free movement of goods

10.09   Articles 30 to 37 of the Treaty of Rome contain a set of provisions to eliminate restrictions on the movement of goods between member states of the Community. The substantive provisions are found in Articles 30, 34 and 36, the remaining Articles being concerned with transitional matters. Article 30 provides that:

'Quantitative restrictions on imports and measures having equivalent effect shall, without prejudice to the following provisions, be prohibited between member states.'

Article 34(1) contains an identically worded provision with the word 'exports' substituted for 'imports'. The purpose of these provisions is to ensure that goods may move freely and without inhibition between member states of the EC and thus to promote a common market in goods throughout the Community. It is these provisions which have been primarily relied upon by the Court in developing its jurisprudence in this area. The Court has held that the prohibition by the Articles of 'measures having equivalent effect' to quantitative restrictions on imports and exports prevents the exercise of rights under domestic national law to stop the importation of goods which have been previously marketed by the owner of the intellectual property right or with his consent elsewhere in the EC,[1] the national law being in those circumstances such a measure. The only escape from this result is provided by Article 36 which says that:

'The provisions of Articles 30 to 34 shall not preclude prohibitions or restrictions on imports, exports or goods in transit, justified on grounds of public morality, public policy or public security; the protection of health and life of humans, animals or plants; the protection of national treasures possessing artistic, historical or archaeological value; or the protection of industrial or commercial property. Such prohibitions or restrictions shall not, however, constitute a means of arbitrary discrimination or a disguised restriction on trade between member states.'

The Court has recognised that industrial property includes intellectual property rights and specifically patents,[1] registered trade marks,[2] registered designs[3] and copyrights.[4] Thus, the enforcement of intellectual property rights is permitted under EC law but only insofar as it is justified on the ground of protection of industrial property, or, in other words, necessary to protect the specific subject matter of the right, insofar as it does not constitute a means of arbitrary discrimination or a disguised restriction on trade between member states. In effect, therefore, the owner of an intellectual property right has the right to put the goods onto the market in the EC for the first time[5] and cannot thereafter control dealings in them unless they are altered or interfered with in such a way as to bring their remarketing within the protection required to enforce the specific subject matter of the right. Determining whether this is so in any particular case can be extremely difficult and the effect of the decisions in the most important cases will now be examined with particular attention to decisions in trade mark cases as these are generally closely analogous to passing off.

---

1 *Centrafarm BV v Sterling Drug Co* [1974] ECR 1147, [1974] 2 CMLR 480.
2 *Centrafarm BV v Winthrop BV* [1974] ECR 1183, [1974] CMLR 480.
3 *Keurkoop v Nancy Kean Gifts* [1982] ECR 2853, [1983] 2 CMLR 47.
4 *Deutsche Grammophon GmbH v Metro SB Grossmärkte GmbH* [1971] ECR 487, [1971] CMLR 631.
5 Commonly referred to as putting the goods into circulation within the EC.

GOODS MADE AND SOLD INDEPENDENTLY OR OUTSIDE THE EC

10.10 The principle of free movement of goods has no application to goods which were first made or marketed in the EC without the proprietor's consent. Thus, a trade mark or passing off right may be enforced against a third party's goods bearing the same or a confusingly similar mark emanating from another EC member state.[1] Indeed, it would be odd if they could not as such rights can be enforced against goods originating within the same state. Nor does it appear that there is any inhibition on the enforcement of rights against goods first marketed by the right owner or with his consent outside the EC and imported into the EC without his consent.[2]

---

1 *Terrapin v Terranova* [1976] ECR 1039, [1976] 2 CMLR 482.
2 *EMI Records Limited v CBS United Kingdom Limited* [1976] ECR 811, [1976] 2 CMLR 235, [1976] FSR 457. See also *Colgate-Palmolive Limited v Markwell Finance Limited* [1988] RPC 497 (CA).

REPACKAGED AND RE-MARKED GOODS

10.11 The principle of exhaustion of rights applies to goods bearing a registered trade mark[1] so that parallel importation of trade marked goods cannot be prevented by reliance on a registered trade mark,[2] or a right to prevent passing off if those goods have been first marketed elsewhere in the EC by or with the consent of the right owner. Often, however, goods are reworked, repackaged or remarked in some way before being imported and resold. It is therefore necessary to determine what changes to goods or their packaging will permit a right owner to say that his rights have ceased to be exhausted. This is essentially a question of fact and is largely determined by whether the alterations are such that the identity of the origin of the marked product is no longer guaranteed to the consumer.[3] This can often be tested by asking whether, particularly in the case of repackaging, the consumer can be sure that the goods are in the same condition as when they left their original manufacturer.[4] Many of the cases have concerned parallel importation of medicines as the differing regulatory controls in EC member states lead to large price differentials which make such a trade highly lucrative, and it is now established that leaving the goods in their original internal packaging guarantees that they have not been affected by any treatment they have received even if the importer has added new external packaging.[5] The position is different if the goods are originally marketed by the trade mark owner under different marks in the two member states. In these circumstances the trade mark owner is entitled to prevent the mark he uses in one country being applied to goods sold by him in the other unless the use of different marks is being done in order to partition the market in which case it constitutes a disguised restriction on trade between member states.[6]

---

1 *Centrafarm BV v Winthrop* [1974] ECR 1183, [1974] 2 CMLR 480.

2   It used to be the case that domestic registered trade mark law prevented the importation of goods bearing a registered mark. Under the Trade Marks Act 1994, there is now an express limitation on the scope of trade mark registrations which prevents them from being enforced against goods first marketed within the EEA so that it is in fact no longer necessary to invoke EC law for this purpose: see s 12, and ch 9, para 9.08 above.

3   See the explanation of the specific subject matter of a trade mark in para 10.06 above.

4   *Centrafarm BV v American Home Products Corporation* [1978] ECR 1723, [1979] 1 CMLR 326.

5   *Pfizer v Eurim-Pharm GmbH* [1981] ECR 2913, [1982] 1 CMLR 406. However, there is presently pending before the Court a series of cases against Eurim-Pharm for adding material to goods and cutting up the internal packaging to provide suitable sized packs for different markets in which the Court will have to consider again the extent to which a parallel importer can rework goods and remain protected by the doctrine of free movement.

6   *Centrafarm BV v American Home Products Corporation* [1978] ECR 1723, [1979] 1 CMLR 326, [1979] FSR 189. See also *Cheetah Trade Mark* [1993] FSR 263.

GOODS SOLD UNDER MARKS FORMERLY IN COMMON OWNERSHIP

10.12   It was long thought that it was not possible to enforce in one EC member state a trade mark registration against goods emanating from a manufacturer in another member state whose right to use the mark had a common origin with that of the proprietor of the registration in the first state. This was the doctrine of common origin laid down in the *Hag I* decision[1] which has its root in the concept that the division of trade mark rights within the Community gives implicit consent to the use of the mark throughout the Community by either subsequent owner of the right. The decision was a particularly harsh one in that it related to a division of trade mark rights which occurred before the Community had been created or even conceived and resulted from wartime expropriation in one of the states. In particular it was held that it prevented the enforcement of trade mark rights against goods made under a parallel registration which had been voluntarily disposed of before the Community was created.[2] The decision was the subject of extensive criticism over many years. Recently, however, the question has been completely reconsidered in what amounts to a rerun of the *Hag I* case, commonly known as *Hag II*.[3] In that case the doctrine of common origin was rejected as a true creature of Community law and it was held that there was no implied consent in such circumstances. Subsequently the Court has held that where a business formerly in common ownership under a single mark is split by the sale of that part of it carried on in one member state there is no implied consent by either proprietor to the use thereafter of the mark by the other in his territory.[4] This is sensible as otherwise it would not be possible to dispose of part of a business carried on in the Community with the right to continue to use its established trade marks. However, where the disposal is part of an attempt to partition the market, it will be treated as a disguised restriction on trade and the resulting rights will not be enforced.

---

1   *Van Zuylen v HAG* [1974] ECR 731.

2   *Sirena v Eda* [1971] ECR 69, [1971] CMLR 260, [1971] FSR 666.

3   *Cnl-Sucal NV v Hag GF AG* [1990] I ECR 3711, [1990] 3 CMLR 571.

4   *IHT Internationale Heiztechnik GmbH v Ideal Standard GmbH* (Case C9/93, as yet unreported).

PLAINTIFF'S SUBSTANDARD GOODS[1]

10.13 Where a trade mark owner allows substandard goods to be marketed in one member state he will not generally be able to prevent their subsequent importation into another member state and resale there. In *Dansk Supermarked A/S v Imerco A/S*[2] Imerco had china with a particular decorative pattern and trade mark on it made for it by Broadhurst, a UK manufacturer. Substandard items were rejected but Imerco permitted Broadhurst to sell those items in the UK subject to a requirement that they were not exported to Denmark. Dansk Supermarked purchased them in the UK and exported them to Denmark where it resold them without informing its customers that they were substandard. Imerco sought to prevent those sales by an action for infringement of copyright in the design and registered trade mark. The Court held that Imerco's agreement to the sale of the goods exhausted its copyright and trade mark rights and that it could not rely upon the agreement not to export the goods as this contravened Article 85(1) of the Treaty of Rome.[3] The Court did not preclude action under Danish laws of fair and proper market usage which suggests that an action might have been brought under those laws if the sale of substandard goods would have damaged Imerco's reputation. This has considerable potential impact on the enforcement of passing off rights in this country in the case of the plaintiff's own substandard goods.[4]

---

1   See ch 4, paras 4.19–4.27 for a full discussion of the actionability in passing off of misrepresentations relating to the plaintiff's own goods.
2   [1981] ECR 181, [1981] 3 CMLR 590.
3   See paras 10.15–10.16 below.
4   See para 10.18 below.

CONFUSING SIMILARITY

10.14 The question whether two marks are confusingly similar is primarily a matter for domestic law.[1] However, concepts of confusing similarity vary throughout the Community and it is possible that a domestic court may find confusingly similar two marks which are objectively so dissimilar that the finding is unreasonable. Thus, the decision in the German courts that the marks 'Terrapin' and 'Terranova' are confusingly similar is somewhat surprising to English trade mark practitioners. In *Hag II*[2] Advocate-General Jacobs cited in his opinion the example of the Bundespatentgericht in Germany finding that the marks 'Lucky Whip' and 'Schöller-Nucki' were confusing as an illustration of the possible variations in the test for confusing similarity between the courts of different member states. As he said the decision 'seems to postulate a body of consumers afflicted with an acute form of dyslexia'. He went on to comment that an unduly broad application of the concept of confusing similarity might be held not to be 'justified' or might constitute 'a disguised restriction on trade' within Article 36. In *Audi v Renault* the Court had to reconsider the impact of Community law on the question in relation to a finding, again of the German courts, that the marks 'Quattro' and 'Quadra' were confusingly similar.[3] The Court confirmed that the question is essentially one of domestic law but that an excessively broad approach may be rejected under the provisions of Article 36. The legal position nevertheless remains rather volatile. The coming into force of the Directive on harmonization of trade mark laws[4] has probably made the concept of confusing similarity a matter for Community law: the whole purpose of the Directive is to obtain a uniform approach throughout the Community and this cannot be achieved without a common standard of confusing similarity. It follows that the Court may well have to lay down standards for the assessment of the issue of confusing similarity by domestic courts. If it does so, then those standards will be part of English law and will presumably have direct application in domestic passing off actions.

1   *Terrapin v Terranova* [1976] ECR 1039, [1976] 2 CMLR 482.
2   *Cnl-Sucal NV v Hag GF AG* [1990] I ECR 3711, [1990] 3 CMLR 571.
3   Case 317/91, as yet unreported.
4   EC Council Directive number 89/104/EEC.

Anti-competitive practices

10.15   Anti-competitive practices of commercial organisations are governed by Articles 85 and 86 of the Treaty of Rome. Article 85 is concerned with agreements between different commercial undertakings or concerted practices of groups of undertakings whose object or effect is to distort or restrict competition between EC member states. Article 85(1) provides that:

> 'The following shall be prohibited as incompatible with the common market: all agreements between undertakings, decisions by associations of undertakings and concerted practices which may affect trade between member states and which has their object or effect the prevention, restriction or distortion of competition within the common market.'

The general prohibition is followed by a series of specific examples. Article 85(2) provides that all such agreements or decisions are automatically void. The terms of the prohibition are extremely wide-ranging and there are many aspects of it on which there is considerable jurisprudence. In the present context we can only outline those aspects of the operation of Article 85 which are directly relevant to the enforcement of passing off rights. Article 86 is concerned with abuse by individual undertakings of a dominant position in any particular market for goods or services within the EC. It provides that:

> 'Any abuse by one or more undertakings of a dominant position within the common market or in a substantial part of it shall be prohibited as incompatible with the common market in so far as it may affect trade between member states.'

Again, the general prohibition is followed by a list of specific examples falling within it. Before the Court began to use Article 30 to restrain the use of intellectual property, these provisions were seen as the ground for preventing anti-competitive exploitation of intellectual property. Thus, the basis for the decision in *Hag I*[1] was that the division of the Hag trade mark between Germany on the one hand and Belgium and Luxembourg on the other had its genesis in an agreement[2] which in the events which then occurred had the effect of restricting competition between EC member states contrary to Article 85(1). Similarly, in *Sirena v Eda*[3] the parties had both obtained their right to use the trade mark 'Prep' for toothpaste from an American company. Sirena had obtained the mark in Italy by an assignment and Eda was licensed to use it in Germany. When Sirena brought an action to restrain the sale of Eda's products under the Prep mark in Italy it was held that these arrangements, which had been entered into before the Community was created, were contrary to Article 85. Accordingly the parties were not entitled to enforce their rights under the arrangements against each other.

1 See para 10.12 above.
2 The agreement was the assignment before the 1939–45 war by Hag AG of its Belgian and Luxembourg trade marks to a Belgian subsidiary set up to carry on the business in those countries. After the war the Belgian government expropriated the Belgian subsidiary as enemy property after which the Belgian and Luxembourg registrations were in different hands from the German registration.
3 [1971] ECR 69, [1971] CMLR 260, [1971] FSR 666.

10.16 Both the decision in the *Hag I* case and the decision in *Sirena v Eda* have now been reversed on their particular facts by later decisions of the Court.[1] However, there is no doubt that trade mark licensing arrangements in which the parties continue to act together in order to divide the common market will be struck down under Article 85. If this occurs, any attempt to enforce the rights obtained under such an arrangement will fail. In *Etablissements Consten SARL and Grundig v EC Commission*[2] the parties entered into a licensing arrangement under which Grundig agreed to supply its goods for sale in France only to Consten and Consten agreed not to resell those goods elsewhere. To ensure that this arrangement could be enforced against third parties Grundig assigned the trade mark GINT in France to Consten and applied that mark to all its goods as well as the Grundig mark. Thus, Consten was in a position to sue any other importers of Grundig goods into France under the GINT registration. Grundig had similar agreements with distributors elsewhere, the purpose of which was to protect the distributors (including Consten) from competition from supplies emanating from other distributors. This arrangement was struck down. Similarly, agreements between owners of similar marks under which they agree to divide the market will be struck down on the same basis.[3] This possibility exists even where the agreement is entered into in settlement of litigation, unless the parties can show that they have adopted the least restrictive solution available in the circumstances.[4] It follows that if settlement of litigation on the basis of market sharing or cessation to use a trade mark is contemplated in circumstances where trade between EC member states may be affected, careful consideration should be given to the possibility of infringement of Article 85 and, if necessary, clearance sought from the EC Commission under Article 85(3).

---

1 See para 10.12 above.
2 [1966] ECR 299, [1966] CMLR 419.
3 *Advocaat Zwarte Zip* [1974] 2 CMLR D79; *Sirdar/Phildar* [1975] 1 CMLR D93.
4 *Re Penney's Trade Marks* [1978] 2 CMLR 100, [1978] FSR 385.

10.17 The mere ownership of a trade mark right, or a right to prevent others from marketing particular goods under a particular trade mark in the territory of an EC member state, does not constitute a dominant position for the purposes of Article 86.[1] However, there are circumstances in which a right to prevent others applying a mark to particular goods may give rise to the right owner having a dominant position in a particular market. An area in which this has often been alleged is the supply of spare parts for trade marked goods. The Court has held that the market for spare parts is generally a separate market from that for the goods of which they form part for the purchaser of the spare part is in practice constrained to buy a part which is a copy of the part originally fitted.[2] Attempts to restrict the sale of spare parts by the use of trade mark and passing off rights are, therefore, liable to be attacked under Article 86.[3] The English Court of Appeal has, however, said in such a case that 'it cannot be an abuse of a dominant position to stop someone from passing off your goods'[4] and the line between merely preventing passing off and abusing a dominant position in spare parts for your goods may be difficult to draw.

---

1 *Sirena v Eda* [1971] ECR 69, [1971] CMLR 260, [1971] FSR 666.
2 *Volvo v Veng* [1988] ECR 6211, [1989] 4 CMLR 122.
3 See, eg, *British Leyland v T I Silencers Limited* [1981] FSR 213, [1981] 2 CMLR 75.
4 *Lansing Bagnall Limited v Buccaneer Lift Parts Limited* [1984] FSR 241, [1984] CMLR 224.

Application of EC law to passing off actions

10.18 Although the right to prevent passing off is very similar in its effect to the right to enforce a trade mark registration, it is not clear whether it is 'industrial or commercial property' within the meaning of Article 36.[1] EC rules on free movement of goods do not, however, prevent a claim to restrain a misrepresentation of the kind that is at the heart of a passing off action. Thus, in *Dansk Supermarked v Imerco*[2] the Court left open the possibility of such an action, notwithstanding the fact that the plaintiff's rights under its copyright and trade marks were exhausted. Equally, in *Industrie Diensten Groep v Beele*[3] the Court held that a right under Dutch law to prevent confusing imitation of the plaintiff's product was enforceable against another's products imported from

Germany. This is hardly surprising. A similar attempt to invoke Article 30 on the basis that the term 'Löwenbrau', which was distinctive of the plaintiff in this country, was used by a number of traders in beer in Germany so that its monopolisation here was a restriction of free movement and was rejected by the English High Court without a reference under Article 177.[4] Thus, a passing off action can be maintained in this country against goods emanating from another member state and may even be maintainable against goods of inferior quality which have been marketed in another member state with the plaintiff's consent. It also seems likely that the Court would, if asked, apply the same approach to enforcement of passing off rights as it has done to trade mark rights in the cases of parallel importation and market division. Although there is no direct authority for this, it is difficult to find a logical distinction between the two claims, particularly for these purposes. In the English courts no defendant has yet successfully raised a defence under the Treaty of Rome to a passing off claim.[5] Actions against goods which have been brought into this country by parallel importation from outside the EEA are unaffected by EC rules.[6] Rather more controversially, Graham J relied upon the provisions of Articles 36 and 59[7] of the Treaty of Rome to provide a plaintiff who had a reputation in the use of the name 'Maxim's' for a restaurant in Paris with a cause of action in passing off against a restaurant of that name in this country.[8] In doing so he refused to follow an earlier decision which he was unable to distinguish on the facts[9] but he concluded that not to give the plaintiff a cause of action in such circumstances would be a disguised restriction on trade between member states. It is extremely doubtful whether the decision is correct and the conventional approach of domestic English law is to be preferred.[10]

---

1 See Bellamy and Child *Common Market Law of Competition*, 4th edn, paras 8-042–8-045.
2 [1981] ECR 181, [1981] 3 CMLR 590. See para 10.13 above.
3 [1982] ECR 707, [1982] 3 CMLR 102.
4 *Löwenbrau München v Grunhalle Lager International Limited* [1974] RPC 492, [1974] 1 CMLR 1.
5 There are many reported and unreported attempts to do so. *ICI Limited v Berk Pharmaceuticals Limited* ([1981] FSR 1, [1981] 2 CMLR 91) and *Lansing Bagnall Limited v Buccaneer Lift Parts Limited* ([1984] FSR 241, [1984] CMLR 224) are typical examples.
6 *Colgate-Palmolive Limited v Markwell Finance Limited* [1988] RPC 497 (CA). See also *EMI Records Limited v CBS United Kingdom Limited* [1976] 2 CMLR 235, [1976] FSR 457.
7 The effective equivalent of arts 30 and 34 in relation to services.
8 *Maxim's v Dye* [1977] 1 WLR 1155, [1978] 2 All ER 55.
9 *Alain Bernadin et Compagnie v Pavilion Properties Limited* [1967] RPC 581, [1967] FSR 341.
10 For a full discussion see ch 3, paras 3.11–3.12 above.

APPENDIX A

Forms of injunction

1. 'EASTMAN KODAK' FORM[1]

'An injunction to restrain the defendant companies, or either of them, from

(i)   Carrying on business under the name "Kodak Cycle Company Ltd" or under any name comprising the word "Kodak" likely to mislead or deceive the public into the belief that the defendant company is the same company as or is connected with either of the plaintiff companies or that the business of the said companies or either of them is the same as or is in any way connected with the business of the plaintiffs, The Eastman Photographic Materials Company Ltd

(ii)   Selling or offering to sell any of their cycles or goods as "Kodak".'

2. 'SLAZENGER' FORM[2]

'An injunction to restrain the defendants from stamping the word "Demotic" on their lawn tennis bats so as to represent that their lawn tennis bats are manufactured by the plaintiffs, or in any other way from passing off their lawn tennis bats as the goods of the plaintiffs.'

3. 'LEGO' FORM[3]

'An injunction to restrain the defendants, whether acting by their directors, officers, servants or otherwise howsoever from passing off or enabling others to pass off irrigation equipment not of the plaintiffs' merchandise as or for the same or as merchandise connected or associated with the plaintiffs by advertising, offering for sale or selling the same under or by reference to the trade mark "LEGO".'

4. 'SEIXO' FORM[4]

'An injunction to restrain the defendants from affixing or causing to be affixed, to any casks of wine shipped to his orders, the brand or marks of a crown and the word "Seixo" or any other combination of marks or words so contrived, as by colourable imitation, or otherwise, to represent the marks or brands of the plaintiff, and from employing any marks or words which would be so contrived as to represent or induce the belief that such were Crown Seixo or the produce of the quinta do Seixo or in any wise using the word "Seixo" without clearly distinguishing the wine from the wine produced by the quinta do Seixo.'

5. 'CHARTREUSE' FORM[5]

'The defendants and each of them, their and each of their servants and agents, be perpetually restrained from using the word "Chartreuse" in connection with the sale of liqueurs other than liqueurs manufactured by the plaintiffs, as the name of or as descriptive of the liqueurs or without clearly distinguishing the liqueurs so sold from the liqueurs manufactured by the plaintiffs and this court doth also order that the defendants Henri Lecouturier, George Idle Chapman & Co Ltd, William Henry Garrett and La Compagnie Fermiére de la Grande

Chartreuse, and each of them, their and each of their servants and agents, be perpetually restrained from selling or offering for sale in England any liqueur or other liquors not manufactured by the plaintiffs, in such a manner as to represent or lead to the belief that the liqueur or other liquors manufactured or imported or sold by the defendants are the manufacture of the plaintiffs.'

6. 'MAGNOLIA METAL' FORM[6]

'The defendants and each of them be and they are hereby restrained from casting, packing, describing, advertising, offering for sale, selling or dealing with any anti-friction metal made up in such a way as not to be readily and clearly distinguishable from the "Magnolia Metal" manufactured by the plaintiffs. And further be and they are hereby restrained from using the word "Magnolia" as descriptive of or in connection with any anti-friction metal manufactured by them or either of them, without clearly distinguishing such anti-friction metal from the anti-friction metal of the plaintiffs.'

7. 'IRON OX' FORM[7]

'An injunction to restrain the defendants, their servants and agents, from offering for sale, selling, or otherwise dealing with, any medicinal compounds or tablets under the description of "Iron Oxide" or any description of which the words "Iron Oxide" formed part, without better distinguishing such medicinal compounds or tablets from the "Iron Ox Tablets" of the plaintiffs.'

8. 'STONE ALES' FORM[8]

'A perpetual injunction restraining the defendant from carrying on the business of a brewer at Stone, under the title "Stone Brewery" or "Montgomery's Stone Brewery", or under any other title so as to represent that the defendant's brewery is the brewery of the plaintiff, and from selling or causing to be sold any ale or beer not of the plaintiff's manufacture, under the term "Stone Ales" or "Stone Ale", or in any way so as to induce the belief that such ale or beer is of the plaintiff's manufacture, and from infringing the plaintiff's registered trade marks, or any of them.'

9. 'REDDAWAY' FORM[9]

'An injunction to restrain the defendants and each of them from continuing to use the words "Camel Hair" in such a manner as to deceive purchasers into the belief that they were purchasing belting of the plaintiff's manufacture, and from thereby passing off their goods as and for goods of the plaintiff's manufacture.'

10. 'BAUME' FORM[10]

'The defendant be restrained (whether by their directors, servants or agents or any of them or otherwise howsoever) from advertising, offering for sale or selling watches or other horological instruments not being goods of the plaintiffs under any name or mark containing the word "Baume" and calculated to pass off or to enable others to pass off such watches as and for the plaintiffs' goods.'

11. 'STURTEVANT' FORM[11]

'An injunction restraining the defendant company from commencing or carrying on business under the style or title of "Sturtevant Mill Co of USA Ltd" or under any similar or colourable style or title of which the word "Sturtevant" formed part or under any such other style or title as to lead to the belief that the defendant company was or was in any way connected with the plaintiff company [or that the goods of the defendant company were or were in any way connected with the goods of the plaintiff company].'

12. 'ADREMA' FORM[12]

'1   An injunction restraining the defendant companies and each of them (whether by themselves, their servants and agents or otherwise) from selling or advertising or offering for sale in the United Kingdom any addressing or listing machines or equipment therefor under any name or mark comprising the word "Adrema" or any other name or mark so closely resembling the name or mark "Adrema" as to be calculated to pass off or to enable others to pass off such machines or equipment as and for the plaintiff's machines or equipment.

2   An injunction restraining the defendant companies (whether by themselves, their servants and agents or otherwise) from carrying on in the United Kingdom any business of making or selling or advertising or offering for sale or servicing addressing or listing machines or equipment therefor under any style or title comprising the word "Adrema" or any other style or title calculated to induce the belief that such business is the same as or connected with or carried on in succession to the business of the plaintiffs or otherwise to lead to confusion between the business of the first defendants and the business of the plaintiffs.'

13. 'MANUS' FORM[13]

'The defendants be restrained from applying themselves, or by their servants or agents, to milking machines or parts therefor not of the plaintiffs' manufacture the name "Manus" or in any other way representing that the business of the defendants is in any way connected with the business of the plaintiffs.'

14. 'SAVILLE V JUNE PERFECT' FORM[14]

'An injunction restraining the defendants and each of them, their servants and agents from passing off or enabling others to pass off perfumery or toilet articles not being the goods of the plaintiffs as and for the plaintiffs' goods and from selling or offering for sale any perfumery or toilet articles under or in connection with the word "June" or any other word calculated to deceive without clearly distinguishing such perfumery or toilet articles from those of the plaintiffs.'

15. 'RODGERS V RODGERS' FORM[15]

'The defendant Joseph Rodgers Simpson, his servants and agents be perpetually restrained from passing off table knives and other cutlery not being the goods of the plaintiff company as and for such goods, and from carrying on the business of a manufacturer or seller of knives or cutlery under the name of Rodgers, or under any style in which the name of Rodgers appears, without taking reasonable precautions to clearly distinguish the business carried on and the knives or cutlery manufactured or sold by the defendant from the business carried on and the knives and cutlery manufactured by the plaintiffs, and from carrying on any such business under any name or in any manner so as to mislead or deceive the public into the belief that the business of the defendant or the knives or cutlery manufactured or sold by him is the business or are the goods manufactured by the plaintiff company.'

16. 'PARKER KNOLL' FORM[16]

'The defendants are restrained from selling, offering for sale or advertising for sale furniture under the mark "Knoll" or "Knoll International" or any other mark which by reason of its similarity to the trade mark of the plaintiffs Parker Knoll Limited that is to say "Parker Knoll" is likely to cause confusion or deception and to lead to goods of the defendants Knoll International Limited being passed off as the goods of the plaintiffs Parker Knoll Limited without clearly distinguishing their goods from the goods of the plaintiffs.'

17. 'ANGOSTURA BITTERS' FORM[17]

'An injunction to restrain the defendants, their servants and agents, from using the words "Angostura Bitters" or the word "Angostura" on any bitters or other fluids contained in bottles, not made by the plaintiffs, so as to induce the belief that such bitters or fluids are made by the plaintiffs, and further, from selling or offering for sale any bitters or other fluids in the bottles, in the wrappers, and in the general form in which the defendants were selling the bitters called by them "Angostura Bitters" at the commencement of this action, or in any other wrappers or form contrived or designed to represent and induce the belief that the bitters or fluids sold by the defendants, and not made by the plaintiffs, are the goods of the plaintiffs.'

18. 'HAVANA' FORM[18]

'An injunction restraining the defendant, his servants and agents, from selling or supplying, in response to any order for "some cigars – Coronas" or "Corona cigars" or "a Corona cigar" or "Coronas" or "a Corona", cigars or a cigar not of the Corona brand, unless it be first clearly ascertained that the customer giving the order does not require cigars or a cigar of the Corona brand and no other brand.'

19. 'CHAMPAGNE' FORM[19]

'An injunction to restrain the defendants from passing off by their servants or agents or otherwise howsoever as and for wine produced in the district of France known as the Champagne district wine not so produced by advertising offering for sale or selling the same as Spanish Champagne or under any other name or description that includes the name "Champagne".'

20. 'SHERRY' FORM[20]

'The plaintiffs and each of them be restrained (whether by their respective directors, officers, servants or agents or any of them or otherwise howsoever) from using in the course of trade the word "sherry" in connection with any wine not being wine coming from the Jerez district of Spain otherwise than as part of one or more of the phrases "British Sherry", "English Sherry", "South African Sherry", "Cyprus Sherry', "Australian Sherry" and "Empire Sherry".'

This form of injunction was accompanied by two forms of declaration for the benefit of the plaintiffs who were held entitled to use various combinations of "sherry' with qualifying words but not the word "sherry" simpliciter:

'THIS COURT DOTH DECLARE that each of the plaintiffs is entitled to continue to sell, advertise and offer for sale any wine heretofore sold by any of them respectively under any of the descriptions "British Sherry", "English Sherry", "South African Sherry", "Cyprus Sherry", "Australian Sherry" or "Empire Sherry" and is entitled to sell, advertise or offer for sale any similar wine under such descriptions without infringing any right of any of the defendants.

AND THIS COURT DOTH DECLARE that none of the defendants has any such rights as would entitle them either severally or in conjunction with all other shippers of sherry wine from Spain and England to restrain any of the plaintiffs from selling, advertising or offering for sale any such wines as aforesaid or similar wine under the respective descriptions "British Sherry", "South African Sherry", "Cyprus Sherry", "Australian Sherry" or "Empire Sherry".'

21.   'SCOTCH WHISKY' FORM[21]

'1   That the defendants and each of them be restrained from doing within the jurisdiction of this court (whether by their servants or agents or any of them or otherwise howsoever) the following acts or any of them that is to say doing anything calculated or intended to lead to the passing off in any country as and for Scotch Whisky of a product that consists of or includes spirits that were not obtained by distillation in Scotland from a mash of cereal grain saccharified by the diastase of malt, and

2   That the defendants Henry Ost and Company Limited be restrained from doing (whether by their servants or agents or any of them or otherwise howsoever) the following acts or any of them that is to say supplying to the defendants Vinalco SA Productora Ecuatoriana de Licores or any other person any Scotch Whisky or bottles or labels or other things or documents and from permitting and/or licensing the use of any trade mark or label for the purpose of enabling and/or which are calculated to enable spirits that consist of or include spirits that were not obtained by distillation in Scotland from a mash of cereal grain saccharified by the diastase of malt to be passed off in any country as and for Scotch Whisky.

PROVIDED that nothing contained in either of the foregoing injunctions shall prohibit the supply by the defendants Henry Ost and Company Limited of Scotch Whisky or any of the above mentioned articles for admixture purposes (meaning thereby the production of a mixture consisting of Scotch Whisky and a spirit or spirits other than Scotch Whisky) if the defendants Henry Ost and Company Limited have reasonable grounds for believing and do in fact believe that such admixture will not be passed off as and for Scotch Whisky, and

3   That the defendants Vinalco SA Productora Ecuatoriana de Licores be restrained from doing the following acts or any of them that is to say ordering from the defendants Henry Ost and Company Limited or from any other person, firm or company carrying on business within the jurisdiction of this court any Scotch Whisky or bottles or labels or other things or documents or from doing any other thing within the jurisdiction of this Court for the purpose of enabling spirits that consist of or include spirits that were not obtained by distillation in Scotland from a mash of cereal grain saccharified by the diastase of malt to be passed off in Ecuador as and for Scotch Whisky.'

22.   'ADVOCAAT' FORM[22]

'An injunction to restrain the first defendants, their directors, servants and agents and the second defendants, their partners, servants and agents from advertising, offering for sale, selling or distributing any product under or bearing the name or description "Advocaat", or any word so nearly resembling "Advocaat" as to be likely to be confused therewith, unless such product basically consists of spirit and eggs and does not include wine and further from representing that a mixture of wine and eggs is Advocaat.'

23.   'JIF' FORM

An injunction to restrain the defendants from marketing preserved lemon juice in any container so nearly resembling the plaintiffs' Jif lemon-shaped container as to be likely to deceive without making it clear to the ultimate purchaser that it is not the goods of the plaintiff.

Declaration in lieu of an injunction

24. 'TREASURE COT' FORM[23]

A declaration that 'The defendants are not entitled to sell as "treasure cots" any toy cots not supplied by or through the plaintiffs without making it clear to the customer that they are not connected with the plaintiffs' with liberty to apply for an injunction in corresponding form.

---

1 *Eastman Photographic Material Co Ltd v Griffiths Cycle Corpn Ltd* (1898) 15 RPC 105.
2 *Slazenger & Sons v Feltham & Co* (1889) 5 TLR 365, 6 RPC 531.
3 *Lego Systems AS v Lego M Lemstrich Ltd* [1983] FSR 155.
4 *Seixo v Provenzende* [1865] Ch App 192, 14 LT 314.
5 *Rey v Lecouturier* [1910] AC 262, 79 LJ Ch 394.
6 *Magnolia Metal Co v The Atlas Metal Co* (1897) 14 RPC 389; *Magnolia Metal Co v Tanden Smelting Syndicate Ltd* (1898) 15 RPC 701.
7 *Iron-Ox Remedy Co Ltd v Co-Operative Wholesale Society Ltd* (1907) 24 RPC 425.
8 *Montgomery v Thompson* [1891] AC 217; affg (1889) 41 Ch D 35.
9 *Frank Reddaway & Co Ltd v George Banham & Co Ltd* [1896] AC 199, 65 LJ QB 381.
10 *Baume & Co Ltd v A H Moore Ltd* [1958] Ch 907, [1958] 2 All ER 113.
11 *Sturtevant Engineering Co Ltd v Sturtevant Mill Co of USA Ltd* [1936] 3 All ER 137, 53 RPC 430. The words in square brackets were ordered to be omitted from the injunction asked for.
12 *Adrema Ltd v Adrema-Werke GmbH* (1958) RPC 323.
13 *A/B Manus v RJ Fullwood & Bland Ltd* [1949] Ch 209, [1949] 1 All ER 205.
14 *Saville Perfumery Ltd v June Perfect Ltd* (1941) 58 RPC 147, HL.
15 *Rodgers v Rodgers* (1924) 41 RPC 277.
16 *Parker-Knoll Ltd v Knoll International Ltd* [1962] RPC 265, HL.
17 *Siegert v Findlater* (1878) 7 Ch D 801, 47 LJ Ch 233.
18 *Havana Cigar and Tobacco Factories Ltd v Oddenino* [1924] 1 Ch 179, 93 LJ Ch 81.
19 *Bollinger v Costa Brava Wine Co* [1960] RPC 16, [1961] RPC 116.
20 *Vine Products Ltd v Mackenzie* [1969] RPC 1.
21 *John Walker & Sons Ltd v Henry Ost & Co Ltd* [1970] 2 All ER 106, [1970] RPC 489.
22 *Erven Warnink BV v J Townend & Sons (Hull) Ltd* [1979] AC 731, [1980] RPC 31, HL.
23 *Reckitt & Colman Products Limited v Borden Inc* [1990] RPC 341.
24 *Treasure Cot Co Ltd v Hamley Bros Ltd* (1950) 67 RPC 89.

Index

275

Index

Index